STILL RENOVATING

MCGILL-QUEEN'S STUDIES IN URBAN GOVERNANCE
Series editors: Kristin Good and Martin Horak

In recent years there has been an explosion of interest in local politics and the governance of cities – both in Canada and around the world. Globally, the city has become a consequential site where instances of social conflict and of cooperation play out. Urban centres are increasingly understood as vital engines of innovation and prosperity and a growing body of interdisciplinary research on urban issues suggests that high-performing cities have become crucial to the success of nations, even in the global era. Yet at the same time, local and regional governments continue to struggle for political recognition and for the policy resources needed to manage cities, to effectively govern, and to achieve sustainable growth.

The purpose of the McGill-Queen's Studies in Urban Governance series is to highlight the growing importance of municipal issues, local governance, and the need for policy reform in urban spaces. The series aims to answer the question "why do cities matter?" while exploring relationships between levels of government and examining the changing dynamics of metropolitan and community development. By taking a four-pronged approach to the study of urban governance, the series encourages debate and discussion of: (1) actors, institutions, and how cities are governed; (2) policy issues and policy reform; (3) the city as case study; and (4) urban politics and policy through a comparative framework.

With a strong focus on governance, policy, and the role of the city, this series welcomes manuscripts from a broad range of disciplines and viewpoints.

1 Local Self-Government and the Right to the City
Warren Magnusson

2 City-Regions in Prospect? Exploring Points between Place and Practice
Edited by Kevin Edson Jones, Alex Lord, and Rob Shields

3 On Their Own Women, Organization, and the Right to the City in South Africa
Allison Goebel

4 The Boundary Bargain Growth, Development, and the Future of City–County Separation
Zachary Spicer

5 Welcome to Greater Edendale Histories of Environment, Health, and Gender in an African City
Marc Epprecht

6 Still Renovating A History of Canadian Social Housing Policy
Greg Suttor

Still Renovating

A History of
Canadian Social Housing Policy

GREG SUTTOR

McGill-Queen's University Press
Montreal & Kingston · London · Chicago

© McGill-Queen's University Press 2016

ISBN 978-0-7735-4814-5 (cloth)
ISBN 978-0-7735-4815-2 (paper)
ISBN 978-0-7735-4857-2 (ePDF)
ISBN 978-0-7735-4858-9 (ePUB)

Legal deposit fourth quarter 2016
Bibliothèque nationale du Québec

Printed in Canada on acid-free paper that is 100% ancient forest free (100% post-consumer recycled), processed chlorine free

This book has been published with the help of a grant from the Canadian Federation for the Humanities and Social Sciences, through the Awards to Scholarly Publications Program, using funds provided by the Social Sciences and Humanities Research Council of Canada. Funding was also provided by the Wellesley Institute.

McGill-Queen's University Press acknowledges the support of the Canada Council for the Arts for our publishing program. We also acknowledge the financial support of the Government of Canada through the Canada Book Fund for our publishing activities.

Library and Archives Canada Cataloguing in Publication

Suttor, Gregory F. L., 1957–, author
   Still renovating : a history of Canadian social housing
policy / Greg Suttor.

(McGill-Queen's studies in urban governance ; 6)
Includes bibliographical references and index.
Issued in print and electronic formats.
ISBN 978-0-7735-4814-5 (cloth). – ISBN 978-0-7735-4815-2 (paper). –
ISBN 978-0-7735-4857-2 (ePDF). – ISBN 978-0-7735-4858-9 (ePUB)

   1. Housing policy – Canada – History – 20th century.
2. Canada – Social policy – History – 20th century. I. Title.
II. Series: McGill-Queen's studies in urban governance ; 6

HD7305.A3S88 2016   363.5'5610971   C2016-904794-6
                                              C2016-904795-4

This book was set by True to Type in 10.5/13 Sabon

Contents

Tables and Figures   vii

Acknowledgments   ix

1 Introduction   3

2 Early Postwar Foundations   25

3 The 1960s: Urban Development and Social Agendas   45

4 The 1970s: Baby-Boomers and Neighbourhoods   76

5 The 1980s: Shifting Down   111

6 The 1990s: Devolution and Retrenchment   125

7 The 2000s: Modest Re-engagement   151

8 Conclusions   171

Appendix A – List of Abbreviations   207

Appendix B – List of Persons Interviewed   210

Notes   213

Bibliography   263

Index   293

Tables and Figures

TABLES

1.1 Main turning points and periods in Canadian social housing
     policy 9
8.1 Canadian social housing, 1949–1996: Key features of major
     programs 196
8.2 Turning points in Canadian social housing: Summary of the
     social policy and housing/urban factors 198
8.3 Social housing commitments, Canada, 1951–2001 200
8.4 Social housing commitments: Details, 1951–2001 202
8.5 New affordable rental housing in post-1996 programs 204
8.6 Social housing and net change in Canadian occupied housing
     stock, 1961–2001 205

FIGURES

1.1 Annual social housing commitments, Canada, 1954–2011 4
1.2 Social housing production: Units per 1,000 population 7
1.3 Social housing and low-income renters: Estimated net change
     in Canada, 1961–2011 24
3.1 Postwar increase in larger urban centres: Canada and peer
     nations 52
3.2 Increase in owner and renter households, Canada: Average
     annual change by five-year period 62
3.3 Annual social housing commitments: Ontario and other
     provinces, 1951–78 73
4.1 Growth rate of real GDP per capita, 1950–2000 79

4.2   Home-buyer affordability: Carrying cost of 25-year mortgage (5-year term, 10% down) for average Toronto resale home   81

4.3   Federal housing expenditure, 1970–93 (inflation-adjusted 2015 dollars)   107

7.1   New affordable housing commitments (non-profit & co-op & municipal): Estimates for 1996–2013   167

8.1   Average annual social housing commitments, Canada, by program period, 1950–2013   173

Acknowledgments

My largest thanks go to the persons interviewed, who contributed their time, knowledge, and reflections. This book rests on the foundation of earlier scholarship, noted in chapter 1 and a source of important evidence and ideas.

Chapters 3 to 6 started as the core of my PhD research at the University of Toronto. I appreciate that opportunity, the year or so of university and SSHRC funding, and the great resources of its library. I was also helped by staff at the Ontario Archives and the Queen's University Archives. It was my good fortune that my early career fell within the final period of Canada's *ancien* social housing regime, followed by interesting years of helping make the best of the post-devolution era – bringing direct knowledge that informs this book.

Thanks to the people who made it possible for this research to become a book. Jacqueline Mason at McGill-Queen's University Press took an early interest, and the anonymous academic reviewers of the manuscript were favourable. For financial support to the publisher for the production costs, I am grateful to the Awards to Scholarly Publications Program, and to the Wellesley Institute and its CEO, Kwame McKenzie.

This book is dedicated to the many smart and committed people I have worked with and for in Canada's social housing sector, including its public agencies. And it is dedicated to my parents, who valued history.

STILL RENOVATING

1

Introduction

WHY THIS BOOK

This book is a policy history of Canadian social housing – subsidized public or non-profit/co-op rental housing for people with low and moderate incomes. This study does not deal with public assistance for private rental or home-ownership, nor rehabilitation programs.[1]

It tells the story of how and why social housing came to be a policy priority in the postwar years, of the shifts over time, and how activity faded by the end of the twentieth century. "Policy" here means what governments and their agencies do – the priorities they implement – more than what they say. This is a story of broad forces, evolving contexts, and specific people and decisions which brought about change in the priorities and activities of Canadian governments, and – in turn – of public and community-based agencies. As conditions and priorities shifted, policy was repeatedly recast – the renovating to which the book's title refers. The long perspective enables this book to offer some reassessment of the history. It is written for scholars in policy studies, social policy, and comparative welfare state research, and for the interested general reader, student, or policy-maker who seeks to explore this subject in some depth.

The focus is the almost seventy years since social housing arrived in Canada as an element of social policy, with greatest attention to a thirty-year prime period from the mid-1960s to the mid-1990s. At the turning points that opened and closed that heyday, social housing waxed and waned dramatically as a policy priority. Annual production of social housing expanded tenfold in the mid-1960s to a level sustained fairly steadily for three decades, and then in most provinces reverted to the per-capita levels of the 1950s, where they remain. The Canadian approach

Figure 1.1   Annual social housing commitments, Canada, 1954–2011. In the 1960s, production rose tenfold to levels sustained for thirty years. The rise and fall reflected social policy shifts.

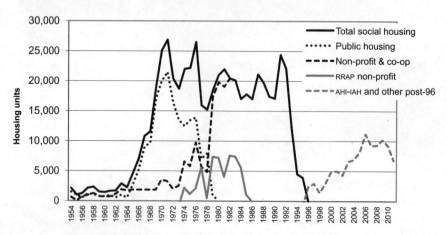

Sources: CMHC, Canadian Housing Statistics, various years and tables; Ontario unilateral, total attributed by year as per data for GTA projects; post-1996 as per figure 8.1 in this book.

in the 1970s and 1980s was well-regarded internationally, and yet the policy framework on which it rested collapsed quickly in the 1990s. Social housing policy in its prime period was led by the federal government and was fairly consistent across Canada, but today its importance varies greatly among the provinces and territories. This book examines the factors, cascading from broad to specific, that brought about the rise and fall of social housing in Canada.

We can learn much that is relevant to today's policy choices by understanding how the social housing era came and went, and what it meant. Advocates who seek more affordable housing need to know how their agendas have always depended on social policy turns and housing market conditions. Policy-makers need to understand the minor scale of today's programs for new affordable housing compared to those of the social housing prime. Scholars need to drop the received notion that the largest policy change was the 1970s shift from all-low-income "public housing" to mixed-income non-profit housing, and the notion that those two models were poles apart. In fact, production across the 30-year heyday did not come in spurts but was fairly consistent over time. There was constant flux and interplay between locally rooted initiatives and well-resourced federal or provincial agencies, and between low-income targeting and social mix.

It is important to know our own history, and a reassessment of Canadian social housing policy in its heyday is overdue. Much was written about it from the 1970s to the early 1990s when it was on the political agenda, but very little since then. This book is the first in Canada to cover all six turning points from the early postwar period to the turn of the millennium. It is the first to examine each of those critical junctures using a consistent analytical framework, and it provides the first detailed account of the why-and-how of policy change at the two largest turning points, the mid-1960s and the mid-1990s. It is informed by ideas that have evolved greatly in recent years, in scholarly work on comparative welfare state evolution, and on the interplay between institutional continuity and political forces of change.

The Urban Housing Problem

Canadians doubtless have varied views about social housing. For many, the image of the "public housing ghetto" comes to mind – a US image imported into Canada and Western Europe where a majority of social housing is far more income-mixed, racially mixed, and intermingled with other housing than in the stereotype. Others may think of the co-op or seniors apartment building down the street, which are more typical Canadian examples. Many who work or volunteer in this sector may think of the shift in the 1970s from "public housing" to a more successful approach of income-mixed, community-based non-profit and co-op housing. Some may think of affordable rental housing as part of Canada's "caring society"; others may wish for a larger system like those of Northwestern Europe; others may consider it a poor use of public money.

How low-income renters get by in urban housing markets is an enduring question. Although Canada's social housing prime period ended in the 1990s, urban stresses keep nudging housing issues onto the policy agenda. The market realities for low-income renters are high costs for poor housing, the need to use food banks to afford the rent, down-market buildings in disrepair, neighbourhoods that other people avoid, and renting a room or a basement when that's all one can afford. The legacy of social housing stock built a quarter- to a half-century ago is in the news media, including its deepening funding pressures and huge waiting lists. Although there is rising concern about declining quality and unfunded repair needs, older social housing still provides better quality than most down-market rental units, at less than half the rent.

The challenges of managing urban development, urban housing markets, and neighbourhood decline are prominent in our city-regions, and social housing policy is relevant to each of these. And so this book fits in the publisher's series on urban governance. The big challenges in Canada today include widening disparities in urban labour markets, urban housing markets, and urban space; but these are not beyond the capacity of policy to manage and to mitigate. Yet while housing is an urban issue, it is not primarily a local issue: the demographic, social, and economic forces that shape it are regional, provincial, and national in scale. Social housing exemplifies the fundamental concept that urban does not mean only municipal. The big fiscal resources and state powers in this sphere, just as in labour markets or infrastructure, are federal and provincial, as is the main story this book tells.

In the postwar era, social rental housing was understood in most affluent Western nations as the answer to the "low-income housing problem." Today it is often seen as part of the problem. Production of this housing was high in most such countries in that period, and declined sharply in the neoliberal era since the 1980s.[2] The prominence of social housing in the postwar period resulted from a unique conjuncture and departed from the long-run tendencies of welfare capitalism. That period had a reconstruction imperative, rapid growth and urbanization, and a political consensus resting on a particular economic and class structure, labour politics, and fresh memories of the 1920s to 1940s crises.[3] Canada follows this international pattern. But each country is affected, in Peter Gourevitch's phrase, by "the force of epochs" and the "force of national trajectories."[4] Canada followed international trends with a lag at the beginning, a lag at the end, and among the sharpest, most abrupt curtailment seen in any affluent country.

In international comparisons, Canada clearly fits the liberal-welfare regime type with low social spending.[5] In such regimes, it is said that social housing is residual and that "housing is provided almost exclusively through the market and access is directly determined by income."[6] Yet no case quite conforms to this. Among the predominantly Anglo countries, social and subsidized housing accounts for 4 to 5 percent of households in the United States, Canada, and Australia, a little more in Ireland or New Zealand, and 18 percent in Britain[7] – sufficient in each case to house somewhere between one-third of low-income renters and almost all of them. Moreover, these countries' private-rental sectors are deeply structured by public policy.[8] The axiom

Figure 1.2   Social housing production: Units per 1,000 population. Canadian production per capita was higher than in the US by 1970, and similar to Europe or Australia by 1980.

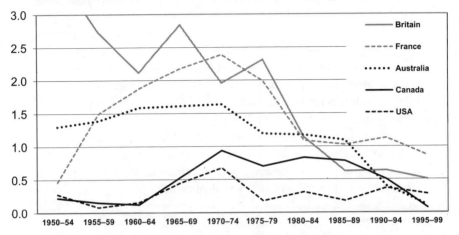

Average annual production by five-year period, using population at base year for each period.
Units per 1,000 fairly compares countries of varying size. For sources, see Suttor, *Rental Paths*.
US includes publicy assisted income-targeted private rental from 1960.

begs the question: just how residual is social housing in each country, and how did policy evolve?

Canada's social housing regime in its prime reflected the "mid-Atlantic" character of Canadian social policy in the 1970s and 1980s[9] – intermediate between those of Northwestern Europe and the more residual US model. Despite its open labour and housing markets, by the 1980s Canada reached high relative public expenditure for civilian consumption; our welfare state had high social transfer payments by international standards, and our social spending reached levels associated with social-democratic, not liberal-welfare regimes.[10] The stronger social programs were contentious at the time and have not endured except in health care and education. But they substantially offset the widening inequality in the labour market; they meant less income inequality and less extreme poverty in Canada during the 1970s and 1980s than in the US or UK, although more than in most of Western Europe.[11] The ongoing expansion in social housing achieved somewhat the same in the housing market. It was part of the "small differences that matter" between the United States and Canada.[12]

In its three-decade prime, social housing was significant in the building of our cities and suburbs.[13] It accounted for almost 10 percent of all housing built, and thereby accommodated half the increase in low-income renters that is an integral part of ongoing rapid growth. It created an "in kind" income transfer program as large as Unemployment Insurance or the Guaranteed Income Supplement (GIS – the income-targeted add-on to Old Age Security). It offered middle-class apartment housing for poor people, in the same neighbourhoods most other people lived in. It provided rents at less than half of market levels to more than one in every three low-income renters. Social housing prolonged the distinctive house-and-apartment mix of Canadian suburbs for two decades beyond the collapse in the 1970s of the postwar private-sector rental development system.

Absorbing half of net low-income renter demand did not solve the low-income housing problem, as critics pointed out, or prevent visible extremes of poverty in some neighbourhoods. But building new homes for people with lower incomes, first through the private-sector rental apartment boom of 1955–75, which housed a wide social spectrum, and then through strong social housing production in 1965–95 – and doing this in neighbourhoods where most other housing was being built – meant far less low-income demand to be met in the market. And that meant far less of the inevitable market response: fewer low-quality older rental units and far fewer households sacrificing other needs to pay the rent. It was one reason that neighbourhood decline and concentrated poverty in our cities occurred in pockets at the time, rather than being widespread as they increasingly are today.[14] Most experts looking at the contrasting central-city trends of Canada and the United States from the 1960s to the 1980s would point to the US racial divide, earlier deindustrialization, slightly weaker social programs, and municipal fragmentation. But the systemic impacts of social housing were also significant in the contrasting urban trends.

THE TURNING POINTS AND PERIODS

The heyday of Canadian social housing lasted about thirty years, from the mid-1960s to the mid-1990s, with three main periods, each lasting about a decade. Bracketing the heyday were a 1949–64 period, and two distinct ones in the 1990s to 2010s. Accordingly, we have six periods from 1949 to the present day, marked by six turning points or critical junctures, summarized in table 1.1.[15] Each turning point responded to shifting conditions and political forces, and each put in place revised policy approaches and institutional arrangements that endured in a relatively stable way for a decade or so. At several of these points, the full policy shift played out over some four or five years.

Table 1.1
Main turning points and periods in Canadian social housing policy

		Key events and characteristics
	EARLY POSTWAR TURNING POINT	Sell-off of wartime housing; creation of CMHC; National Housing Act; first income-targeted social housing program.
	Early public housing (1949–1964)	• *Modest volumes, about 1–2 percent of total housing production, no systemic significance.*
	MID-1960S TURNING POINT	1964 NHA amendments and creation of provincial housing corporations, leading to a ten-fold increase in production.
	Public housing heyday (1965–1973)	• *Much larger volumes, about 10 percent of total housing production, all-low-income projects.*
SOCIAL HOUSING PRIME PERIOD	EARLY 1970S TURNING POINT	Shift to mixed-income non-profit and co-op housing, amid an expanding government role in all housing sectors.
	First non-profit decade (1974–1985)	• *Production volumes sustained, somewhat peaking* • *New mixed-income non-profit/co-op model operating initially in tandem with "public housing'"model.*
	MID-1980S TURNING POINT	Management of programs devolved to provinces, but with a continued federal lead in policy and funding, happening amid a broadly contracting government role in housing.
	Second non-profit decade (1985–1993)	• *Production volumes at first sustained, then declining.* • *No more all-low-income "public housing"; but non-profit/co-op housing become more income-targeted.*
	MID-1990S TURNING POINT	End of active federal policy, including no more funding for new social housing, devolution of program management to the provinces, multiyear phase-out of federal subsidies.
	Devolution era (1994–2001)	• *Diverse approaches by province; greatest retrenchment and devolution in Ontario; least in BC and Quebec.*
	EARLY 2000S TURNING POINT	Re-starting "affordable rental" production, volumes one-fifth of pre-1996 levels (higher in Quebec, BC).
	Modest re-engagement (since 2002)	• *Modest volumes, little systemic significance.* • *Federal-provincial capital grants, no operating subsidies, few geared-to-income rents (except Quebec, BC).* • *Great variation by province; more in Quebec BC, Alberta.*

The turning point of 1964 was fundamental – a ten-fold increase in program activity as part of a large welfare state expansion. The early 1970s shift was quite significant, as its invention of a better targeting and delivery model sustained the priority for social housing in Canada for two decades while it waned around the world. The mid-1980s saw a major change from a federal to a provincial lead in running the programs, and an end to the expansive 1970s state role in housing. The mid-1990s' turning point was again fundamental, bringing extreme social housing retrenchment and devolution, as an element in a broader downsizing of social programs. The turning point at the millennium was smaller, but it softened devolution and created the programs active today. The Canadian social housing system of the early twenty-first century is the product of three things: the legacy of the prime period in terms of housing stock, funding flows, and legacy institutions; devolution and retrenchment in the 1990s; and the modest post-millennium programs.

Social housing policy was never driven mostly by the issues that low-income people face in the rental market. The shifts in priority and in program approaches were propelled above all by two sets of factors. First, they reflected the main turning points in broader social policy and associated federal-provincial relations; and second, they reflected issues in housing and urban development. Before we turn to these ideas, let us consider the existing research on Canadian social housing policy.

BUILDING ON EARLIER STUDIES

This book builds on earlier studies of Canadian social housing policy, most dating from the 1970s to early 1990s. They are essential sources, articulating themes and evidence, but they are unavoidably incomplete accounts today. Most are imbued with the social welfare premises of mid- to late twentieth-century Canada, or critiques of them.[16] None of them has examined the pivotal mid-1960s turning point in detail, and most predated 1990s retrenchment and devolution. This study follows Keith Banting[17] in its central argument about the relation of social housing policy to broader social policy turning points and federal-provincial relations. His analysis of the 1964–85 program regimes in those terms is extended in this book over a longer period. This book builds fundamentally on Banting's framing, but pays more specific attention to critical junctures, economic conditions, and issues in housing and urban development, and it bears international comparisons more in mind.

John Bacher's *Keeping to the Marketplace*,[18] written a quarter century ago, is the last book-length analysis of Canadian housing policy evolution including social housing. His thesis was that pro-market politics of the early postwar years set the mould of a residual social housing sector avoiding competition with the capitalist real estate industry. He wrote a richly documented and well-argued account of the struggles of the 1930s and 1940s that ultimately set the course of early postwar policy. His emphasis, however, was on actors and decisions rather than systemic factors, with limited attention to welfare state evolution and housing market conditions. Bacher's view that the National Housing Act of 1949 set the parameters of federal policy for the next three decades misses the transformative character of the expansionary turning points in the 1960s and early 1970s. His chapter on the 1960s to 1980s, characterizing policy as "drift within close confines" of the early postwar approach,[19] falls far short as an account of the prime period of Canadian social housing and underplays its significance. He viewed public housing, co-operatives, and European models through the eyes of a 1970s social democrat, and perhaps the prime period can be seen as policy drift if the premise is that Canada could have been a Scandinavian welfare state. This book focuses on the thirty-year prime period which was an epilogue for Bacher, and covers the generation since his book.

George Fallis[20] has provided careful accounts of social housing programs and analysed their relation to broader changes in the welfare state and political ideas, and to evolving housing and urban issues. He applied a strong interest in the relation of housing policy to redistributive social programs and the shift from expansion to retrenchment. Key themes included the evolving priorities from private-rental to social housing, and from public housing to non-profit, with declining output and deeper targeting over time. He expressed increasing scepticism about social housing as a form of ill-targeted resource allocation, a twentieth-century phenomenon that came and went.[21] This book picks up some of these themes in a more optimistic interpretation of the thirty-year heyday.

David Hulchanski[22] has emphasized social housing as a sphere embedded in a "housing system," which reflects the broader political economy and political culture. He noted the central importance of federal-provincial relations, a policy dualism treating the rental and owner sectors very unequally, and the 1990s agenda of social policy devolution shaping the same in social housing.[23] His own and joint-authored work[24] includes overviews of the postwar years through the

1980s in this vein, with identification of main turning points and periods. All these are main foundations for this book.

Barbara Carroll[25] has provided good short overviews of the policy history, and Carroll and Ruth Jones[26] offer one of the few general accounts of devolution. But the periodization taken from the overview of housing policy broadly[27] underplays the significance of the transformative mid-1960s turning point. Roberto Leone and Carroll's account of the post-1999 programs[28] is rounded out in this book with a fuller picture.

The books by Michael Dennis and Susan Fish[29] and by Albert Rose[30] were policy analysis (written to directly inform policy-making) as much as policy studies. Dennis and Fish's *Programs in Search of a Policy* was written in 1971 as a policy review for Central Mortgage and Housing Corporation (CMHC)[31] and helped propel the shift from public to non-profit housing, expressing the vision of mixed-income non-profit housing which became received truth for a generation. Rose's book *Canadian Housing Policies* was the concluding work by this leader in postwar Toronto housing advocacy and policy-making. With broad scope and incisive interpretations, these books offer details on program history and structure from the 1950s to the 1970s, the housing market context, federal-provincial relations, political forces, and (in Rose's case) postwar urbanization, welfare state evolution, and the political constraints on policy possibilities. They are essential sources for social housing policy of that period, but are now historical documents of their long-ago time.

On the 1990s devolution period and since then the research literature is patchy. Fran Klodawsky and Aron Spector[32] were incisive on the shifting discourse and the relation of housing policy shifts and broader retrenchment. Michael Prince[33] too articulated social housing devolution as part of major social policy restructuring. Jeanne Wolfe[34] and Tom Carter[35] provided good overviews of the changes in that period. Jason Hackworth[36] captured important aspects of institutional change at devolution, applying neo-Marxian concepts of "roll-back" and "roll-out" neoliberalism. Sean Purdy and others have applied post-modernist and Foucault-influenced "critical" ideas to Canadian social housing.[37] Numerous recent studies have examined specific cases and local situations of the present and the past – reflecting in the research world the long littleness of local initiatives in Canada's post-devolution era. Steve Pomeroy and Nick Falvo[38] have provided an important account of housing policy under the Harper Conservative government. But no source provides a comprehensive account of the mid-1990s turning point or the one at the millennium, or the program regimes of the two decades that followed.

These sources and others[39] are drawn on extensively in various chapters of this book, their evidence and arguments reinterpreted for today. For the two largest turning points, however, the mid-1960s and the mid-1990s, there exists no comprehensive account and we must look to primary sources. For the mid-1960s, this book draws on public documents and newly mined archival material. For the 1990s, key informant interviews are the main source, as essential government documents are still restricted, and people who shaped policy are alive and well.

LINKING SOCIAL HOUSING TO SOCIAL AND URBAN POLICY

Evolving Canadian Social Policy

"The evolution of federal/provincial relations in social housing has broadly paralleled that in the Canadian welfare state as a whole and has been driven by the same underlying political forces."[40] This was Banting's thesis in his analysis of Canadian policy from the 1970s to the mid-1980s. The two major turning points in social housing in the 1960s and 1990s, and the smaller ones before, during, and after the three-decade prime all reflected broader welfare state trends and turns.

The Canadian welfare state lagged in its development in the early industrial period – circa 1890–1930 – in comparison with the UK, most of Northwestern Europe, Australia, or the United States. Public health and workers' compensation plans emerged as urbanization and industrialization arrived, but there was only embryonic unemployment insurance and limited pension coverage.[41] Compared to most of those peer nations, Canada felt only a faint impact from the new labour politics arising from industrialization. Social housing was only slightly on the agenda in Canada,[42] whereas in Britain and elsewhere in Northwestern Europe it became significant in the Edwardian years, and a large government program by the 1920s; and in the United States and Australia it became significant by the 1940s.[43]

The key planks of a welfare state were put in place in Canada in the 1940s and early 1950s: family allowances, Unemployment Insurance, Old Age Security pensions. This occurred in a context of strong federal political and fiscal dominance, and was supported by constitutional amendments. A small public housing program was initiated by the federal government in 1949, in partnership with interested provinces. But from 1945–65 Canada had much less social housing per capita than the UK, United States, or Australia:[44] in those terms production was fifteen times higher in Australia than in Canada, and far larger in San Francisco or Philadelphia than in Montreal or Toronto.[45]

Canada branched away from the US welfare state model in the 1960s.[46] Quebec politics, which had held back welfare state development until the 1950s, now embraced an active state role in the Quiet Revolution. Key changes federally included widely subsidized post-secondary education, the Canada Pension Plan, public health insurance, generous unemployment insurance, the income-tested supplement to Old Age Security, and federal cost-sharing of provincial social programs through the Canada Assistance Plan (CAP). In social housing, the mid-1960s brought a related transformation, including formation of provincial housing corporations, greatly augmented funding, and ten-fold increase in production. These housing policy changes were directly linked to the Canadian government's policy agenda of welfare state expansion.

Growth of social programs continued in the early and mid-1970s, but the politics of social policy moved beyond a focus on large government programs. The range of advocacy groups and the political claims became greater and more complex. Nationalist politics in Quebec now opposed federal welfare state expansion and focused on the provincial level. Western Canada, affluent and populous in the resource boom, joined the demands for decentralization. By the late 1970s, the federal government increasingly accommodated these demands as fiscal pressures arrived.[47] This period also saw a shift from large state-delivered programs, to a "mixed economy of welfare," with more delivery by state-funded community-based agencies.[48] In social housing, all this was reflected in contested federal and provincial roles, ongoing expansion, and a shift from public housing delivered exclusively by provincial and municipal agencies, to delivery by community agencies too.

In 1980s Canada, neoliberalism affected policy more slowly than in the United States, Britain, Australia, or (after mid-decade) France. In the Mulroney Conservative government there was a tension between neoliberal voices and "regional brokerage" politics – the role of public spending in ensuring support from regional political bases. Social spending kept rising but there were large debates about the desirable role of the state and about income-targeted versus universal programs. There was the start of cutbacks from the generous levels of the 1970s,[49] and incremental devolution to the provinces. In social housing, this was reflected in mostly sustained production volumes but also a transfer of program management from the federal to provincial levels, and a return to tighter income targeting.

Canadian social policy in the 1990s was dominated by severe retrenchment and devolution to the provinces. The proposals for constitutional devolution in the Meech Lake Accord (1987) and Charlottetown Agreement (1992) had collapsed. But now in the mid-1990s, devolution became a means to restructure and reduce the fiscal and social policy obligations of the federal government for the long term. Smaller transfers and major changes to social programs were pushed through with little public debate, and declining federal transfers encouraged cuts in provincial social spending.[50] This brought about a corresponding change in social housing. The federal government ended funding of new units, which ended production in most provinces; it withdrew from long-term funding responsibility and devolved virtually all program management to the provinces and territories.

The years at the turn of the millennium brought reinstated federal health and social transfers to the provinces, and new social policy initiatives such as the National Child Benefit. David Cameron and Richard Simeon called this "collaborative federalism," with frameworks jointly negotiated by the federal and provincial governments rather than federally led.[51] These changes softened but did not reverse the narrower scope of the post-1990s social programs and the institutional restructuring. Canada in the early twenty-first century has a more targeted "post welfare state," flat-lined more than reduced, but no longer offsetting rising inequality in the labour market. Benefits are less universalist, and policy is shaped by concerns about work disincentives and spending control.[52] This shift is echoed in social housing policy, with loose federal-provincial frameworks for modest volumes of new affordable rental, inconsistent income targeting, uneven provincial engagement, avoidance of long-term fiscal commitments, and no restoration of pre-1990s goals, mandates, or capacity.

Factors in Social Policy Change

The large expansion of the Canadian welfare state and of social housing from the 1940s to the 1970s rested on a convergence of powerful historical factors: surging industrialization and urbanization, three-fold growth of GDP per capita, and a unique political tilt arising in Quebec and labour politics, all occurring amid an international Keynesian welfare state consensus. (The latter refers to the postwar political compromise of a capitalist economy with a large government role in public services, non-market transfers, and macroeconomic management). Here let us introduce some main explanatory theories that appear in various ways in the chapters that follow.

Federalism greatly affects social policy evolution in any federal state.[53] On one hand, federalism can impede welfare state development or lead to weaker social policy, as the multiple governments mean more veto points, as regionalism fragments interest groups or trumps class politics, or as responsibilities are sloughed off to another level of government.[54] On the other hand, federalism can mean "competitive state-building" at the national and subnational levels, and sometimes can mean more policy innovation among the subnational jurisdictions. Each of these patterns appears at various points in this history of Canadian social housing.

Structural factors were emphasized in early theories of welfare state development,[55] including fundamental economic and social change, and the "logic of industrialism." As industrialized society emerged it achieved much higher economic output, while well-being now relied less on ᵢly and kin and mostly on the labour and housing markets. Together ᵢ other changes such as rising skill requirements, mass literacy, and ᵢger old age, this created new types of political demands and led to an expanding state role.[56] Structural explanations have come to the fore again in today's globalization era.[57] The welfare state that sought to manage employment, growth, and capital flows, and mitigate inequalities with public spending, is being supplanted by a market dominated by transnational corporations, international wage competition, and global capital markets. This tends to undermine the forces that created the welfare state, make the national state weaker, and reduce the role of public goods and transfer income.[58]

Such structural factors explain a lot about Canadian welfare state development. Canada lagged its peer nations in affluence and industrialization, the best predictors of welfare state expansion in broad long-run comparisons. In 1870–1900, when labour and welfare state politics were born, this nation's GDP per capita was similar to the West European average and well short of the United States, United Kingdom or Australia.[59] Canada caught up in the great booms of the Edwardian years, the 1920s, and World War II, and our social structure and politics changed accordingly. GDP almost doubled every 15 years from the 1940s to the 1970s,[60] and this paid for the period of greatest welfare state expansion. Our social policy was not simply a matter of political forces but of surging GDP and its societal ramifications. Canadians, by the 1970s and 1980s, had urban housing issues much different from their grandparents and could also afford to spend $2 billion a year on social housing.

One structural reality in Canadian economic history and welfare state evolution is the strong influence of the United States. Both countries retained a large farmer vote into the mid-twentieth century, reflecting the fertile continent they share. Canada's watered-down postwar Keynesianism reflected the politics of US trade and investment, and the leakiness of demand management in a trade-dependent economy.[61] Although most boom periods rested on exports to the United States, postwar growth was also fuelled partly by a "Fordist" economy of high wages supporting strong domestic demand.[62] Canada's departure from the US welfare model in the 1960s and 1970s reflected these new structural realities. The period of softer US influence on our trade, labour market, and political discourse was the heyday of a distinctive Canadian social policy and a distinctive social housing policy.

Economic ups and downs also matter. Oil self-sufficiency helped Canada sustain higher growth in the 1970s than the United States, Britain, or Australia. This helped delay neoliberalism because with less deindustrialization and a better fiscal situation, there was less voter dissatisfaction, and less push by elites to end the postwar social compact. But oil was a source of federal-provincial conflicts both in the 1970s boom and in the early-1980s downturn. Lagging 1980s growth and a severe early-1990s recession underlay 1990s retrenchment. The social policy initiatives of 2000 onward were made possible when the federal deficit was overcome, due not only to spending cuts but also to lower global interest rates and strong export-led growth.[63] Each of these ups and downs echoed not only in social policy broadly but in social housing policy specifically.

Labour-based political movements in many countries propelled a rising state role. They waged a "democratic class struggle"[64] to claim a larger share of resources and of power, culminating in the postwar social contract between capital, labour, and the state. The decline of labour/left politics in the post-industrial era is a significant factor in welfare state retrenchment. In Canada, labour politics were weaker than in Britain, Western Europe, or Australia – influenced by apolitical currents from US unionism, undermined by open labour migration across the US border,[65] and trumped by regional and cultural divides.[66] Our welfare state is interpreted less as a social contract than as a way for political elites to use rising affluence to assuage regional inequalities and the French-English divide with a "discourse of nation-building."[67] Yet labour/left politics were significant in Canada. The early postwar social policy agenda responded to the surging 1940s labour vote; the 1960s social policy agenda responded partly to the formation of the New Democratic Party (NDP); and the NDP supported program expansion in the 1963–68 and 1972–74 minority governments. Although social housing was never central in Canadian labour political platforms, it was carried by the agenda of welfare state expansion that labour supported strongly.

Ideas are central in policy change, shaping our understandings of what is and what should be. No one looking at social housing policy can escape the deeply contested ideas about what the state and the market should do. Policy issues are not primarily facts or givens, but are matters of framing and interpretation,[68] of how a matter is understood and constructed. Ideas create a public discourse with a particular character and content in any given time and place. Socialist ideas, norms of fairness, labour attitudes of solidarity, religious ideas of social reform, Fabian and Progressive-era ideas about the state, and beliefs about the prerequisites for social stability or economic growth have all supported social welfare politics at various points. Ideas and discourse are central in agenda formation[69] – in whether an issue gets on the policy agenda and is considered worthy of political attention.

Shifting ideas and borrowed ideas have been big globally in welfare state development.[70] In Canada, influences came mostly from the United States and United Kingdom as the centres of international Anglo culture. Until the 1950s those countries produced the majority of Canadian immigrants, educated many of our elite, and drew off a huge brain drain of talented, educated Canadians. The cultural and demographic roots of English-speaking Canada in the northeastern United States run very deep,[71] and the divergences of recent years do not negate the enduring cultural affinities. London, New York, and Paris publishers still fill the bookshelves of Canada, and their journalism and cultural production permeate our news and entertainment. British welfare state thinking strongly influenced interwar advocacy for social reform,[72] reconstruction and social welfare planning during World War II,[73] the postwar platform of the Co-operative Commonwealth Federation (CCF) and the NDP,[74] and 1960s Liberal social reformers.[75] The social program expansion in 1940s Canada followed upon the sea change of the US New Deal. In Canada, borrowed ideas are everywhere in social housing too. In recent years, international market-oriented ideas have profoundly influenced Canadian policy.

Urban Development, Housing, and the Welfare State

In any policy study, we must pay attention to how policy interacts with the larger sphere of the market. Studies of income security are rooted in analysis of conditions and change in the labour market. Studies of health care consider the interests of doctors, HMOs, drug companies, and so on. And studies of housing policy must consider conditions and trends in the housing market. Along with broad social policy, issues in housing and urban development shaped Canadian social housing policy.

Urban development and housing have an ambiguous relation to the welfare state. Housing is very important in social welfare, and urbanization is large among the structural changes noted earlier. Yet for housing scholars, housing is famously the shaky or "wobbly pillar"[76] of the welfare state in that it is only slightly decommodified. Housing existed as a market sector before the welfare state, far more than health care or pensions or education. Millions who never saw a doctor, or lived to be old, or paid a schoolmaster, lived in cottages or shacks as tenant farmers, or rented homes in pre-industrial London or Istanbul or Beijing. Housing is mostly a commodity and a market sector in all nations, and increasingly so.

Social or non-market housing became a main plank of social policy in Europe within a decade or two of the early Bismarckian and Edwardian social security initiatives.[77] The political program of twentieth-century socialists, social-democrats, and social-welfare reformers included creation of a large decommodified, non-market housing sector. Prices were to be set based on construction costs, without profits to landowners, builders, developers, or rental landlords. A monthly rent would not exceed a week's pay, about a quarter of income. For labour political movements, housing was almost as important as wage levels, job security, pensions, or unemployment benefits. It was not about helping people pay market rents, but about building new forms of community as well as housing assets for the long term.[78]

Urban politics tend to put consumption and distribution issues in the foreground, even if production issues and market logic dominate at senior levels of government.[79] As urban population exploded in the nineteenth century, public health and water and sewer systems led to an expanding local state. By circa 1900–20, municipal control of power companies and urban transit was mainstream thinking.[80] New York City and London in that period had a role in providing collective goods and social welfare that exceeded the equivalent role at the national level,[81] in the form of hospitals, factory inspections, tertiary education, and by the interwar years, public housing.[82]

Yet national housing systems map erratically onto welfare regimes.[83] For example, the United Kingdom, a centre of global capitalism for three centuries, has one of the world's largest social housing sectors. Differences arise from the timing of urbanization, political particulars, or a separateness of housing from welfare state politics. Things were different in the affluent new-world settler societies of the United States, Canada, and Australia: wages were higher than in Europe and urban land cheaper, and rapid growth meant less economic power for existing owners of capital and land.[84] The resource export economy, absence of peasants and gentry, cash-crop farming norms, and hugely successful capitalist economies, made markets the norm and the ideology.

The timing and trajectory of urbanization is important. Early twentieth-century Canada was less urbanized than its closest Anglo and Franco peers.[85] Britain and Belgium were the world's most urban industrial countries. Although the United States and France had large farmer populations like Canada, France had the world's third largest city while the United States had three of the global top ten, plus half a dozen cities the size of Montreal. Those cities dominated economic, political and cultural life, and so urban issues were larger in national politics. Australia had the world's largest relative share of population in big cities, and urban issues and labour movements were prominent in its politics since the 1890s. Canada had a larger farmer vote than urban vote until the 1920s, and a larger farmer vote than labour vote until World War II. The modest and late-arriving labour/left politics in that period are rooted in this later trajectory of urbanization.

This later timing affected Canada's housing politics. Most working-class residents in early twentieth-century Canada, except Montreal, rented an attached or single house at a reasonably affordable price.[86] For the truly poor in Montreal or Toronto, conditions were dire.[87] But Canada then lacked the urban voting base and big-city urban poverty[88] that put housing on the social agenda in other countries. Big cities present a "metropolitan housing problem," in Fallis's term.[89] Their issues differ in quality and scale from those of smaller centres – not just poor renters stretching to pay the rent, but an enormous gulf between big-city housing prices and low wages, and not just a shabby "wrong side of the tracks," but entire districts of low housing quality and social distress, and increases of tens of thousands of poor renters in a decade. Although urban reformers of the 1970s or 2010s have celebrated the early initiatives in Toronto in the 1910s as the roots of later social housing,[90] this is historical symbolism more than history.

The situation changed in mid-twentieth century Canada. A rapid catch-up in urbanization and a set of related market pressures and middle-class concerns about housing affordability put housing on the political agenda in a big way. Social housing was part of the response to these concerns in the 1960s and 1970s, and rode these coattails politically. When interest rates and prices plummeted in the 1990s and rental demand shrank, housing affordability evaporated as a mainstream political concern, and one bit of collateral damage was that social housing fell off the policy agenda.

POLITICS AND INSTITUTIONAL CHANGE

When political forces create a significant change in policy, this leads to new institutional arrangements which entrench the political settlement of the issue, at least for a time. These institutions may be formal laws and regulations, or state institutions with particular mandates which become a hub of particular expertise and resources. Institutions also include the informal "procedures, routines, norms and conventions embedded in the organizational structure of the polity or political economy."[91] Institutions shape and entrench certain ways of framing and understanding social and political issues, create interests and rights and relationships, normalize specific policy practices and approaches, and set in place flows of resources. For example, we take for granted parliamentary elections and federalism and medicare, and we pursue advocacy or careers through existing networks and parties. By setting norms and practices and ongoing resource flows, institutions define the bounds of pragmatic policy-making in a given context.

Policy frameworks can be viewed as institutions: they are backed by law and state power, are very often durable, and they shape incentives and resources in their sphere.[92] This historical institutionalist[93] view of policy change is central in the approach taken in this book. The entrenching of political settlements into institutional arrangements happens differently in different countries, reflecting specific politics but also deep-rooted and enduring elements of national political culture – the central concern of welfare regime theory.[94]

This approach creates a tension between institutional continuity and the social-economic or political forces of change. Two concepts are most important in approaching this tension. The first is path dependency. Small events or decisions at an early stage can have a larger effect on institutional arrangements than larger later events may have.[95] The institutional arrangements set in place by early decisions can create positive feedback effects, may constrain subsequent choices, and are not easily altered by small challenges. Once a system of resource-allocation exists with a political constituency or beneficiary group, it is politically more difficult to dismantle it than it would have been to resist its creation in the first place.[96]

The second concept and line of explanation is about political, economic, or other shocks coming from outside the system.[97] For example, the 1930s Depression produced social distress and political challenges to capitalism that favoured welfare state development. Often resulting is a pattern of punctuated equilibrium, "periods of continuity punctuated by 'critical junctures,' i.e., moments when substantial institutional change takes place thereby creating a 'branching point' from which historical development moves onto a new path."[98] At these junctures, the shocks weaken institutional power and constraints and widen the range of possibilities. Other explanations look to smaller changes over time, including non-adaptation of policy as circumstances shift,[99] or "endogenous" changes that occur within the framework of institutions, without shocks.[100] The interplay between institutions that create continuity and political or other forces that create change may be rather different in periods of expansion and of retrenchment.[101] Canadian social housing history fits strongly within this model of political decisions creating institutional arrangements which have momentum for some years, but which are unsettled at critical junctures by political forces, leading to further policy and institutional change.

THIS BOOK'S APPROACH

A robust explanation of policy change must pay attention to factors ranging from the broad to the specific. This includes the structural socio-economic context, political forces, prevailing ideas, specific actors and events, and how all of these shift, evolve, and interact.[102] It must examine how changes at key junctures create or alter institutional arrangements. This approach constructs a "funnel of causation," in the classic metaphor of Simeon.[103] The emphasis on institutional change is highly compatible with the funnel of causation.[104]

In this book the main middle ground of explanation about social housing includes two spheres: broad social policy change and issues in housing and urban development. This is balanced out with one eye upward to the broader socio-economic and political context and shifting ideas, and another downward to specific people and events. Each chapter except the first and last focuses on one of the main turning points, and moves across the full range of factors in policy change, from broad to particular.

The provinces are part of the national story and so are regional or local urban issues. This is Canada, probably the world's most decentralized federation,[105] and federal social housing policy has always interacted with and flowed through provincial programs. Urban issues and housing market conditions must be discussed in terms of local realities, not abstract national averages. But not all readers will find their province or territory adequately represented. This book pays greatest attention to Ontario, Quebec, British Columbia, and in recent years Alberta; in urban issues it pays most attention to Toronto, Montreal, and Vancouver. There are reasons for this impolitic imbalance. The four largest provinces are where 86 percent of Canadians live and so their policy is most important to the lives of more people. Ontario played a catalytic role at the largest expansionary turning point of the 1960s, and since the 1990s Ontario, on the one hand, and British Columbia and Quebec on the other, are the extremes of policy divergence. The three largest urban areas are home to 35 percent of Canadians and their housing demand. Their urban issues above all erupted into federal housing policy at the turning points of the 1970s and at the millennium. There would be great value in a comparative policy history across the various provinces and territories, but that would be a different book.

Also given less attention in this book is social housing as it relates to First Nations and urban Aboriginal people, as well as Canada's North. The rising needs and populations especially from the 1970s onwards made these issues a rising focus of federal policy, even while many needs went unmet. The Rural and Native Housing Program and the Urban Aboriginal housing program were significant priorities in the 1980s and 1990s, and housing on First Nations reserves remains an area of federal activity in the devolution era.

Each chapter also summarizes the program model the particular turning point gave rise to, and its output. These frameworks may seem at first glance to be all about production. This book does not deal with the management of social housing projects, or their social issues, or the large debates and misconceptions and shifting approaches in their architecture and design. But the program funding frameworks, besides being the main focus of policy-making at the time, were of enduring importance. They not only funded production but also determined who was served and what sort of organizations owned and operated the housing, and brought those bodies into being. This created an array of interests and attitudes and debates that influenced later policy. The programs created a significant non-market sector and a large transfer program of subsidized rent, sustained under legal agreements for many

Figure 1.3   Social housing and low-income renters: Estimated net change in Canada, 1961–2011. In 1966–96, social housing accommodated over half the increase in low-income renters that was part of ongoing population growth.

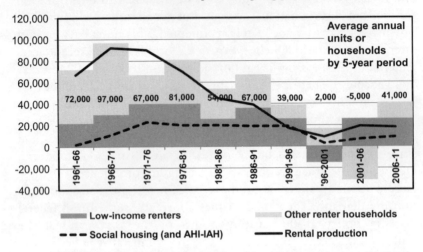

Source: Census; CMHC, starts and completions data; social housing from CHS (CMHC) and supplementary data for 2001–11 (figure 11 in this book). Low-income renters is the count in the first quintile calculated from census microdata. Horizontal numbers are totals.

years. Those frameworks set thirty to sixty-five years ago are now rapidly expiring, and do not address today's issues of good repair or regeneration, or how Canada might sustain a significant non-market housing sector in the twenty-first century. But they set the main parameters of social housing policy for almost three generations.

2

Early Postwar Foundations

The era of ongoing Canadian government involvement in social housing arose in the 1940s. The pivotal events were amendments to the National Housing Act (NHA) in 1949, associated new federal and other funding, and the start of Canada's first three public housing projects in Toronto, Halifax, and St John's. This event closed a decade of big housing and urban pressures, rapid social change, and a great expansion in the role and capacity of the Canadian state. To meet the intense pressures of wartime and then demobilization, the federal agency Wartime Housing Limited (WHL) built 46,000 rental homes during the 1940s. This precedent, the transition to peacetime, and the invention of the basic Canadian welfare state in that decade, put clearly in question what the postwar policy in social housing would be.

World War II had changed things. In Europe and East Asia it was a story of destroyed cities and infrastructure, hunger and disease, massacres and bombing, and 50 to 80 million dead. In Canada, although over 45,000 died from the war, it was mostly a story of other things. Munitions production for six years – weapons and ammunition, uniforms and supplies, vehicles and aircraft, shipped out to bases in Britain and battlefields in Europe and East Asia – brought astounding growth of manufacturing employment. This led to a rapid increase in urban population, which created a housing crisis in almost every urban centre across the country.

The exigencies of war also led the Canadian federal government, as in other countries, to take a strong role in managing the economy, to orchestrate flows of money, materials, and workers in a society fully mobilized to carry out the war. The government and especially the minister of munitions and supply, C.D. Howe, used their connections to get numerous Canadian business executives, still on their company's payroll, to work as "dollar a year men" for the government, to manage and over-see these wartime state functions. This warfare state showed the capac-ity of the modern state to orchestrate resources. For progressive thinkers, it could now become the welfare state, mobilizing the resources of an affluent industrial society to ensure social well-being.

But the war hadn't changed everything. For much of society and for dominant elites, return to normalcy meant return to an economy and a housing system shaped by corporate investment and governed by market forces. The 1949 NHA settled this dynamic, fluid period of the 1940s into a social housing policy regime that lasted for fifteen years, through half the postwar period.

POLITICAL AND ECONOMIC CONTEXT: AFFLUENCE AND CAPACITY

The decisions of the late 1940s had their back story in the 1930s and wartime. The Depression and the war were very different, but each saw a struggle between intense advocacy for a stronger government role in social policy, including housing, and strong resistance to it.

Throughout the 1930s, Canada's governments – Conservative until 1935 and Liberal after that – were centrist fiscal conservatives.[1] US president Roosevelt announced the New Deal in the 1932 election cam-paign and rapidly implemented social welfare and job creation pro-grams. Canada's Conservative prime minister R.B. Bennett followed suit and announced his New Deal in his closing months in office, as he faced defeat in the 1935 election. Mackenzie King's new Liberal gov-ernment then referred the pending legislation for judicial review, which was still at that point a responsibility of the United Kingdom's Judicial Committee of the Privy Council. It ruled most of the proposals to be *ultra vires*: beyond the powers of the federal government under Cana-da's constitution. So Canada awaited gradual US economic recovery and the war.

The war transformed Canada into a more affluent society. GDP per capita rose by two-thirds between 1939 and 1944.[2] The war greatly ex-panded the functions and capacities of the Canadian federal govern-ment. Drawing on the larger economy, its tax revenues expanded more than four-fold, from $0.5 to $2.2 billion (fiscal 1939–40 to 1945–46),[3] and total expenditures by all levels of government rose by a similar pro-portion. The government took on new roles, not only in wartime pro-duction and the related coordination of resources, but in labour issues and social security programs. Wartime manufacturing employment almost doubled from 0.7 to 1.2 million,[4] a plateau that held until the growth of the 1960s and 1970s. The aggregate wages and salaries of production workers rose more than 200 percent during those five years.[5] It is reported that employment in Montreal rose from 170,000 to 290,0000, that Hamilton steelworker jobs doubled from 6,000 to 11,000, and that Windsor autoworker jobs tripled from 8,000 to 23,000.[6] Canada during the war had 12 to 13 million people – one-third of today's population – so an equivalent change in Canada today would be about 350,000 added full-time jobs in Montreal, 15,000 in Hamilton, and 45,000 in Windsor.

Coming on the heels of the great social and economic crisis of the 1930s, the new strength of labour led to big wartime strikes and a surging vote for the social-democratic Co-operative Commonwealth Foundation (CCF). Formed in 1935 in the Depression, the CCF defeated the Conservative leader in the 1942 York South by-election, became the official opposition in Ontario in 1943, took power in Saskatchewan in 1944, and took 16 percent of the vote in the 1945 federal election. The centrist Liberal and Conservative parties both had large internal debates about how to respond to and co-opt the new politics.

This context of a changing society and politics led to the early planks of the Canadian welfare state. Like Britain and Australia, Canada established a special government commission during the war to set out a postwar social and urban policy strategy, the Advisory Committee on Reconstruction.[7] This body produced the 1943 Marsh report (Report on Social Security for Canada). Unemployment insurance was introduced in 1940, family allowances in 1945, and Old Age Security pensions in 1952. The political sea change was powerful enough that constitutional amendments were passed to enable these. Thus Canada overcame the political struggles, business-led opposition, and impasses of social policy of the interwar years, and caught up with reforms introduced up to a generation earlier in the United States, United Kingdom, and Australia. But whereas in the latter two countries the official reconstruction report became a blueprint for the postwar welfare state, in Canada it set the stage for thirty years of gradualism.

Canada's rapid economic and urban growth in the 1940s and 1950s altered political expectations and fiscal capacity, propelling steady welfare state expansion. There was a wide 1950s political consensus on two things: first, growth led by private investment and "free enterprise," but second, a role for government in creating the right conditions through macroeconomic management and using a share of the rising output to expand public services and programs. The moderately reformist, moderately Keynesian Liberal governments of the 1940s through the mid-1950s had staying power in the strong economy.

Not only was the pie growing quickly but it was sliced more equitably amid "wage compression" and narrowing disparities.[8] At the 1951 census, for the first time ever, the poor were a minority thanks to growth, unionized manufacturing jobs, steady employment, family benefits, unemployment insurance, and people leaving their farms. Before the 1940s, secure jobs, regular vacations, a family car, urban home-ownership, and high school education had been privileges of an urban middle class that was a modest percentage of Canadian society. But now, ordinary families "with steady incomes and a little to spare could now break out of slum housing, find a home in the suburbs, buy a second-hand car, live healthier lives, and see their children continue a few years further in school."[9]

HOUSING AND URBAN CONTEXT: GROWTH PRESSURES AND RENTAL

In the 1940s and 1950s, Canada became a predominantly urban nation. During the 1940s, this brought acute housing pressures and distress, but these steadily alleviated as the 1950s progressed.

The huge increases in manufacturing and port employment brought larger increases in population in Canadian cities. In the 1940s Montreal and Toronto grew by 35 and 40 percent, adding over 750,000 to their combined 2 million at the start of the decade. Edmonton doubled; Hamilton and Vancouver grew by 60 and 67 percent; Windsor, Ottawa, Quebec, and Halifax by 45 to 50 percent; and Winnipeg by one-quarter, adding a combined 800,000 to the 1.5 million in these eight cities.[10] Job trends suggest that the larger share of growth happened in the first half of the decade, during the war, in an economy that had almost no housing construction as resources were directed to war production.

Housing distress was already much higher at the end of the Depression than a decade earlier. Wartime growth brought extreme shortages of housing, overcrowding, sharp rent increases until controls were introduced in 1941, evictions, and homelessness. With production virtually ceased, middle-class families were not moving out to new homes and not freeing up dwellings for new arrivals or those with lower incomes. The pressures were only modestly reduced by federal incentives to subdivide dwellings into duplexes, exhortation to rent out rooms, and production for war workers by the federal WHL. Families doubled up in shared dwellings. Most single people rented just a room, and many shared with several beds to a room; others lived in basements (next to a huge coal furnace in those days) or other low-quality spaces. In such circumstances, the imbalance of market power was huge, and renters with little money were at the mercy of property-owners. Municipalities or local bodies set up housing registries, but they were overburdened. Local social agencies could provide housing help only to the literally homeless. These conditions were a large concern to many city governments.[11]

The issues increased steadily during the war as urban population boomed. They might look like the problems of privilege from wartime European or Asian eyes, but it was a crisis in most Canadian cities. And then in 1945–46, hundreds of thousands of demobilized servicemen and women arrived home. Although wartime rent controls were still in place, there were constant issues of rent gouging and there was a crisis of evictions in 1944–45.[12] Toronto established an emergency housing program, sheltering large numbers of people in recently decommissioned munitions plants.[13] Canada consequently had large housing backlogs at the end of the World War II.[14] At six years, the duration of wartime urban growth but constricted housing production had been more than half again as long in this country as in the United States. In 1951, 23 percent of urban dwellings lacked their own bath or shower and in 1956 some 285,000 families were still doubled up.[15] This became the impetus for a federal policy whose concern was to ensure that market housing financing and market housing production worked well for the broad middle of society.

Very rapid urban growth continued after 1945, and Canada had about the most rapid postwar urbanization among the large affluent countries.[16] From 1945 to 1975, the population living in urban areas with over 100,000 people more than doubled from 5.6 to 12.8 million.[17] Between 1941 and 1961 the populations in the urban areas of Montreal, Toronto, and Vancouver approximately doubled in each case, and the same was true in several mid-sized cities.[18] The rapid expansion of suburbs was a way to accommodate this great rise of the urban population and of the material standard of living.

Housing starts recovered nicely in the latter 1940s then rose from 59,000 in 1951 to an annual average of 139,000 in 1955–59.[19] In the home-owner sector and the middle-class mainstream, the 1950s were benign years in housing, despite policy-makers' concerns about financing and capacity. Production of single and semi-detached houses met net demand, with average annual production of 88,000 nationwide (1951–63). In the key Toronto market from 1953 to 1963, average resale prices rose only from $14,400 to $16,500, or not at all in real-dollar terms, and there were mild real-dollar year-to-year decreases in 1956, 1958, 1960–61, and 1963.[20]

Half of Canada's postwar growth was in the rental sector. It rose steadily, sustained by high immigration and rapid growth, and weaker policy support to home-ownership than in other similar nations. Measuring households by tenure, postwar growth was 47 percent rental in Canada (1951–71) versus 20 percent in the United States and 15 percent in Australia.[21] Rental was supported by federal policy in the 1950s. It was an integral element in CMHC financing of private-sector housing production,[22] and postwar tax law was favourable to rental. By 1959, CMHC introduced NHA mortgage insurance for new rental apartments, to facilitate private financing of booming production in that sector.[23] This helped foster a development sector of large corporations and large capacity, with rental apartment production fully integrated into their business model. In the mid-1950s a rental apartment development boom started that would last for two decades and bequeath a distinctive built form and income mix to this nation's postwar suburbs. In 1951–60, 23 percent of housing units built in Canada were rental apartments, rising from 14 percent at first to 29 percent by 1958. In the booming big cities, rental apartments comprised much more than a quarter of activity: by 1957, this sector accounted for half of housing production in the Toronto urban area.[24] This corporate private-rental sector housed much the same lower-middle income segment of net growth which, in the first two postwar decades, Western Europe and Australia accommodated in new social housing.

IDEAS: PRAGMATISM AND THE MARKET

Throughout the 1930s and 1940s there was very strong advocacy on low-income housing issues. Local committees in almost every mid-sized or large city across the country carried out surveys of the bleak housing conditions that resulted from protracted high unemployment in the Depression. They put forward proposals, and they pointed to the active programs operating in Britain and starting up in the United States. These voices increasingly gained allies in housing-related bodies in the political mainstream. The National Construction Council adopted a position in favour of social housing in 1934, as did the Royal Architectural Institute of Canada.[25] The National Employment Commission, a high-profile strategic advisory body appointed by the new Liberal government, focused on economic stimulus but in 1937 it also recommended a low-rent federal housing program with 50/50 cost-sharing of rent subsidies by the federal and other levels of governments.[26]

In his history of Canadian housing policy in that period, Bacher painted the struggle between conservative-minded governments and progressive reformers as one – symbolically and literally – between the two Clarks.[27] On one side was W. Harold Clark, a Canada Trust executive who understood housing finance, but a Red Tory who dissented from his social world's social views and was a leader in Toronto and national housing advocacy. On the other side was W. Clifford Clark, a Canadian who had made his early career as an investment and real estate executive in Chicago, and brought those perspectives to his new job as custodian of Canadian economic policy as deputy minister of finance for two pivotal decades, from 1933 to 1952.

The interwar years in Canada were a time of a profound transition to a predominantly urban, industrial society.[28] Intense advocacy on social housing was part of the political consequences of that transition, as well as of the Depression. In Toronto, this led to a City commission headed by the provincial lieutenant governor, which produced the Bruce Report that recommended a social housing program of slum redevelopment.[29] Other struggles took place in Vancouver.[30] One can imagine a scenario in which swirling 1930s housing advocacy in Canada led to a significant public housing program, as in the United States, or in which the growth pressures and housing shortages of wartime and demobilization led to large-scale production by state agencies, as in Australia.[31]

To understand why Canada adopted a weak social housing policy in the 1940s, it is instructive to look at those two countries. The United States and Australia were similar societies to English-speaking Canada, and while our 1930s struggles of progressive advocates and reformers against conservative elected officials and newspaper opinion appear less intense than theirs,[32] they were not different in character. But Canada had weaker labour and social-welfare politics, and less weight of urban issues in national affairs. The Roosevelt administration, New Deal Democrats, and Australia's Labor governments all championed homeownership, yet social housing was an integral part of their welfare state agendas. Housing commissions were created in South Australia (1937) and Victoria (1938) by centrist governments supported by or dependent on the Labor Party, and in New South Wales in 1942 by a Labor government;[33] the large postwar public housing program[34] was initiated by a federal Labor government. The 1937 Act that created US public housing was sponsored by Senator Robert Wagner from New York – the same who had co-sponsored the National Labor Relations Act – and he worked in close concert with experts and advocates in the Labor Housing Conference in drafting the housing bill.[35] New York City, the epicentre of US social housing, was dominated in the La Guardia era by a social-democratic politics[36] which had little equivalent in Canada. Their governments were not held back by constitutional caution about federal powers or by their large electoral base in conservative Quebec. So while Canada had strong, intelligent research and advocacy on housing, it lacked a fertile political climate to adopt a more active policy.

Open markets were the strategy of the Canadian corporate and government elites. Postwar economic growth was strongly fuelled by US investment, and the same applied in housing. The dominant theme in housing policy was "keeping to the market."[37] An expert and meritocratic public service had been constructed by the federal government by the interwar years, and in the long Liberal rule from 1935 to 1957 it came to have strong links to that political establishment. It was imbued with a "free enterprise" mentality and was well attuned to the realities of Canada's dependence on US and global trade.[38] Canada's federal financial elite would experiment with floating exchange rates in the 1950s when this was quite unorthodox, and deregulate mortgage rates in the 1960s, years before the United States or Britain.[39]

Bacher portrays W.C. Clark as outmaneuvering the housing advocates through his authority in the public service and his advice to cabinet; the housing acts during his tenure "appeared to accept the principle of subsidized rental housing but made it impossible to deliver."[40] More dispassionately, his policy in housing can be seen as most concerned with resuscitating the real estate lending sector and construction sector in the context of a grave economic crisis. Those sectors, besides being inside the paradigm as social housing wasn't, were economically weighty sectors that policy-making must necessarily concern itself with.[41]

The main barriers to social housing were political. The negative views of senior public servants were in sync with the lukewarm attitudes of federal politicians and the market-oriented, home-owning mainstream of Canadian political life.[42] The real estate lending sector and construction sector were also politically weighty, and connected with local governments, provincial governments, senior public servants, MPs and cabinet ministers.[43] These sectors lobbied extensively on federal housing bills and on proposals for social housing, and on the fate of WHL.[44] It was even worse at other levels: reliance on federal policy "was fostered by outright and fairly strong hostility to public housing programs, a hostility far more evident within the councils of local government and the legislatures of provincial governments than anywhere else in Canada."[45] Although some municipalities greeted enthusiastically the contribution of WHL there was widespread and strong local opposition to public housing.[46]

During the war, as policy thinkers turned their minds to what would happen afterwards, "reconstruction" became a major theme. Housing was a front-and-centre concern in the ideas about social security, and strongly informed the federal Curtis report on housing and community development. The continuing role of WHL in 1945–48, when half its production happened, reflects the agenda of reconstruction after five years of booming wartime growth but severe housing shortages. The "yes" vote in the plebiscite by which Toronto voters in 1947 approved funding of $6 million for the Regent Park redevelopment ($75 million in 2015 dollars)[47] was something of a happy surprise,[48] but reflected the powerful climate of housing advocacy in the city and the strong reconstruction mindset which had also led to adoption of a master plan in 1944.[49]

By the 1950s, attitudes about state versus private production were pragmatic within the market-oriented political bounds – more so than today, in the early twenty-first century. The ethos of reconstruction and the mixed economy saw a role for government in fostering housing production through financing, serviced suburban land, and counter-cyclical stimulus. The role of government in financing housing was far larger than today. Ontario's 1950s Frost government, a mix of elite and small-town Conservatives, undertook public land assemblies[50] on a scale unthinkable today. Metropolitan Toronto Council, mostly centrist Conservatives, oversaw production of new low-income housing at higher per-capita volumes than in Greater Toronto today, and favoured public- rather than private-sector development of seniors rental because it would achieve lower rents.[51]

A mix of housing type and price was not only taken for granted in the lived reality of mid-century cities, but was strong in urban planning ideas of the period. The roots of this are in the Garden City movement with its models of public land ownership and income mix, New York regional plan thinkers of the 1920s,[52] and the British planning tradition. The Community Planning Association of Canada, an advocacy coalition fostered by CMHC in the 1940s, had a mandate that included social housing as well as urban planning, reflecting the integral place of housing in the newly emerging planning profession and policy sphere.[53] By the 1950s, the means of ensuring price mix were the construction of bungalows affordable by the lower middle class, and rental apartments.

Canadian social housing ideas were strongly shaped by the United States and Great Britain, the centres of an international Anglo culture. From them came most of Canada's leading postwar planning and housing professionals and their ideas,[54] prominent in Canadian social housing right through the century.[55] The institutional models for Canadian social housing came from British philanthropic housing (the Limited Dividend company – LD) and the United States (the housing authority). Canada's federal housing statutes, discussed below, were significantly influenced by US housing legislation.

Canada was anomalous in that the primate city, Montreal,[56] was not the focus of social housing advocacy and activity. The biggest city dominated in our peer nations: London was the leading locale of early philanthropic and council housing; Paris had a disproportionate share of French social housing; and New York had far more public housing per capita than other US cities. In 1940s and 1950s Canada, the focus was Toronto, the number two city, a place with far fewer low-quality dwellings in slum neighbourhoods than Montreal. Quebec had not yet embraced the new mid-century ideas of active state roles in social policy, and Duplessis's politics held back the political effects of the rapid social modernization occurring. Quebec was less influenced by the Anglo-sphere discourse of reconstruction and the example of the US and UK policy; many bourgeois Montréalais were small landlords as owners of a "plex." Public housing was far more controversial in Montreal than in Toronto or even Vancouver in the 1940s and 1950s.

The limited federal role was also rooted in the understanding that, constitutionally, housing is part of the provincial sphere of "property and civil rights."[57] This has always been a fiction: the paramount policy levers in housing are monetary policy, regulation of lending, direct mortgage financing by government, tax law and policy, fiscal stimulus, and mortgage insurance. All of these are solely or primarily federal, and through Canada's decades of devolution this has scarcely been challenged. It is land tenure law and associated real property matters that are clearly provincial, and non-market housing programs that are shared or contested. But the received understanding mattered. Speaking in Parliament on the 1949 legislative amendment that would frame social housing policy for the next 15 years, Prime Minister St Laurent invoked the constitutional division of powers: "In most of its aspects, housing is a function of property and civil rights [and these] fall within the jurisdiction of the provincial and municipal governments ... Both constitutionally and practically, low rental housing policy must be initiated either by the provinces or by municipalities empowered to do so by the provinces."[58] The decisions in the latter 1940s to sell off WHL, get out of federal wartime rent controls, and do public housing only in partnership with the provinces were informed by the received understanding that "housing" is a provincial sphere.

EVENTS AND DECISIONS: THE EARLY POSTWAR

The Canadian federal government passed a Dominion Housing Act (DHA) in 1935 and a National Housing Act (NHA) in 1938, partly modelled on the US housing legislation of 1934 to 1937[59] and partly worked out in concert with the institutional lender sector of insurance firms and trust companies.[60] The DHA was part of the Bennett Conservatives' abortive New Deal, just as the US Act was part of the Roosevelt Democrats' very active New Deal. The focus of the housing legislation in both countries was to support the residential mortgage market and thereby stimulate job-creating construction. The US legislation also sought to resolve a crisis of families losing their homes and farms as lenders foreclosed for non-payment, and it initiated a large US social housing program. The United States built 25,000 units in the mid-1930s as part of the stimulus program and then had average production of 42,400 public housing units annually in 1939 through 1941,[61] before that nation entered the war.

But just as Bennett's New Deal was hollow, its housing statute lacked any provision for social housing. The purpose of the DHA was to stimulate private-sector lending and construction while having the appearance of responding to the advocacy for social housing.[62] The King Liberal government replaced the largely ineffectual DHA[63] with the NHA in 1938, and although it had a new Part II that enabled funding of public housing, this was subject to restrictive rules and never budgeted for or implemented in the short time before the war arrived.[64] These Acts set up a National Housing Administration within the federal Department of Finance, to facilitate private-sector institutional lending and thereby private residential construction, as important economic sectors.

Social housing on a significant scale was initiated in Canada by the federal agency, WHL, which built 46,000 rental homes for working-class munitions employees and returned veterans, from 1941 to 1948. [65] This output in less than eight years was substantial: about 6,000 units annually, a level of per-capita production equivalent to 60 percent of that in the social housing heyday of the 1970s and 1980s.[66] This crown corporation was created by Order-in-Council in February 1941 as munitions jobs surged in urban communities experiencing great housing market stresses.[67] The federal government spent $50 million[68] ($700 million in 2015 dollars) on such war-worker housing between 1941 and 1944. This was not housing for families with low incomes; it was cost-recovery housing for those earning steady lower-middle incomes in manufacturing and other jobs.[69] WHL faced great antagonism from Department of Finance officials. Unlike the National Housing Administration, it was under a different department; it was building permanent rather than temporary housing; and it was building for rental rather than home-ownership.[70] Most significantly, it was carrying out direct state provision rather than enabling market forces and market actors. None of this was very acceptable, even in wartime, to Finance Minister James Ilsley or his deputy minister W.C. Clark. The approach was supported by C.D. Howe (the minister of munitions and supply, and later minister of reconstruction and supply) but as a wartime expedient, and he envisaged its winding-down at the end of the war.[71]

The war brought step-by-step additions to the institutional mandates and capacity of the federal government in housing: administration of wartime rent controls from September 1940 onwards, WHL, a much expanded NHA in 1944, and the Central Mortgage and Housing Corporation in 1946.[72] These bodies became organizations in which thinking and speaking about social housing was normalized, and where important roles were taken by people sympathetic to the social housing agenda. Frank W. Nicolls, head of the National Housing Administration, was somewhat sympathetic. The Curtis committee on housing and community planning included several experts who were advocates of social housing.[73] The board of WHL included several local social housing advocates and was chaired by one such man, Hamilton construction businessman Joseph M. Pigott.[74] WHL collaborated with the City of Halifax on the first rent-subsidized project, and with the City of Hamilton on the first to be subsidized by way of a 30-year mortgage at a below-market 3 percent interest. There was strong finance department criticism of these as the thin edge of the wedge of a model of direct state provision such as existed in "socialist" upside-down New Zealand, and as an activity competing with the private sector.[75]

These new wartime bodies became internal government locales of expertise on housing, new thinking, and new practices in policy research. WHL carried out systematic surveys of housing needs in various urban communities – not something the federal government had ever done.[76] In due course WHL commissioned a comprehensive report by the associate economic advisor in the Department of Munitions and Supply on housing issues. This included a strong articulation of the need for low-rent housing and of the need for federal policy to stabilize the very cyclical housing sector on a long-term ongoing basis; it also gave considerable information on the social housing systems of other countries.[77] This new policy research reached its peak in the Report on Housing and Community Planning (Curtis report), prepared by a subcommittee of the Advisory Committee on Reconstruction noted above. The Curtis report proposed a mix of measures to support home-ownership, subsidized housing rehabilitation, and low-rent housing production. For the latter it proposed 100 percent federal subsidy, municipal administration, and production of 92,000 units in the immediate postwar years. The Curtis report was the largest report produced by the reconstruction committee and got wide public attention.[78]

As the end of the war approached, the government had to set a framework to meet housing backlogs and support postwar growth. There was little question about the general thrust of policy, which would be to support market financing and market production, and especially home-ownership, along the lines of the 1938 NHA but in a more effective way. This was the purpose of a new 1944 NHA, which had no provisions for low-rent housing.[79]

This mainline policy direction did not resolve the place, if any, of social housing or other direct state provision in the postwar regime. This included the future of WHL as an organization, property owner, landlord, and repository of expertise reporting to the reconstruction ministry, as well as its relation to the housing-finance and market-supporting functions of the NHA that had existed in the Department of Finance since 1935. The resolution between the two ministries could have gone in various directions, and more than one approach was put on the table. The decision was taken to consolidate the divided federal housing functions in one agency, and to this end the Central Mortgage and Housing Corporation Act was passed in 1945[80] and implemented the following year. Although CMHC was a crown corporation like WHL and accountable like it to C.D. Howe as minister of reconstruction and supply, the main CMHC purpose was "to stimulate private enterprise to serve as large an area as possible of the housing field, thus reducing the demand for publicly assisted housing."[81] It assumed the market-enabling mandate of the NHA, and the Finance Department appointed a majority of its board which at that time had a public policy role. David Mansur – a protégé and ally of W.C. Clark, like him a finance and real estate professional, and head of the NHA under Clark during the war – became CMHC's first president, serving until 1954.

WHL was handed over to become part of CMHC. In the short term, the WHL approach of direct provision of break-even worker housing got a new a new lease on life as CMHC initiated a large veterans' housing program with a target of 10,000 new units, to meet the end-of-war housing crisis. The pragmatic C.D. Howe supported this as an expedient in the circumstances, as he had done during the war, and favoured the idea of WHL moving into the low-rent housing field.[82] These bungalows or storey-and-a-half homes, often in contemporary subdivision layouts, were quite popular and set a new standard of lower-middle income neighbourhood design in Canada, and still grace the older postwar neighbourhoods in almost every city.

The cabinet as well as the CMHC and finance department leadership were concerned about getting drawn into an ongoing role in direct state provision of housing, and were "horrified" when the National Welfare Council proposed that the WHL homes be transferred to municipalities.[83] Some municipalities were keen to see the WHL subdivisions become "normal" home-owner housing, and many residents were keen to purchase. CMHC was keen to get out of the direct production and landlord business, and in October 1948 decided to sell most of the homes to the residents. It sold 29,452 between 1949 and 1952,[84] retaining some of the veterans' rental apartment buildings until the much deeper federal withdrawal in the 1990s.

The June 1949 NHA amendments that created the 1949–64 policy regime were a way to assuage local expectations and social housing advocates, while ending the federal role in direct housing provision.

> The continuing demand for wartime housing by municipalities increased the federal government's suspicion of these bodies as highly susceptible to political demands for more social housing. Consequently, Mansur would frame the National Housing Act amendments of 1949 with the goal of increasing provincial political responsibilities and municipal costs for public rental housing. This accomplished the desired result: a transfer of political pressure for housing away from the federal government, and a rapid decrease in the level of social-housing construction.[85]

Although the prime minister had invoked provincial jurisdiction in regard to the 1949 legislation, it appears that these other concerns weighed more in the decision. This was not, after all, an era where the federal spending power was much constrained. CMHC's president Mansur told its board that the requirement for 25 percent provincial or municipal cost-sharing would limit the production volumes, while joint federal-provincial ownership would decrease the municipal interest and momentum on social housing; the board concurred in this strategy.[86] The provincial positions at the time would ensure only modest take-up. Quebec, Manitoba, and Alberta were all led by conservative governments that opposed social housing ideologically. The British Columbia and Ontario governments were somewhat negative although as growing urban provinces they were willing to facilitate federal-municipal initia-tives. CCF-led Saskatchewan was interested and so was Newfoundland with its dire urban housing conditions and its desire as a new province to access federal funds. The Maritime provinces were either willing to fa-cilitate or indifferent.[87]

In this series of events that framed social housing in the 1940s and 1950s, the proponents and their opponents were a small circle of ac-tivists, politicians, and public service policy-makers who mostly all knew each other. For example, a key 1944 meeting hosting US housing officials was attended by the Toronto planning commissioner and the chairman of the new advocacy organization, the Citizens' Housing and Planning Association. When the Community Planning Association of Canada was formed, the inaugural meeting was attended by the vice-president of CMHC and by federal minister of reconstruction, C.D. Howe.[88]

The federal-local connections grew as policy evolved incrementally in the 1950s. Humphrey Carver, a prominent social housing advocate in 1940s Toronto, became chair (1955–67) of the Advisory Group that was a policy resource group for the CMHC president. That committee in 1955 organized policy borrowing sessions that were attended by Albert Rose, scholar-activist and now board member of the Metropolitan Toronto Housing Authority (MTHA) as well as the Vancouver and Toron-to municipal planning directors.[89] When CMHC president Mansur re-tired in 1955 he took a voluntary role as chair of MTHA, the most high-profile local agency implementing public housing under the 1949 NHA amendment he had created.

As the federal public housing program got going, the Duplessis Union Nationale government in Quebec had no interest in participat-ing, and Montreal's Mayor Drapeau labelled the urban renewal plan of 1957 as communist. Things softened somewhat at the provincial level once Paul Dozois became minister of municipal affairs in 1956–60. His term as minister coincided with the 1957–60 hiatus in Drapeau's long reign, enabling the start of Jeanne Mance, Montreal's first public hous-ing project. But that project was a federal-municipal partnership large-ly without provincial involvement.[90]

When Stewart Bates became CMHC president in 1955, he brought a major shift in the CMHC climate on social housing.[91] He fostered interest in the dimensions of housing relating to social welfare, neighbourhoods, and urban development strategy, as distinct from the dominant focus on market-making, financing, and sheer production. Bates created the new Advisory Group just noted, and US experts were brought in for sessions whose express purpose was – to use today's term – policy borrowing.[92]

Local activists' and CMHC officials' ideas on larger-scale social housing activity were held back during the 1950s by the market-minded Liberal and Conservative governments and their appointees to the CMHC
board. In the closing months of the St Laurent government, the board
reminded Bates that public housing should provide only "a bare mini-
mum of housing for the occupants" and should primarily serve economic development or local redevelopment objectives; it should not
compete with "private enterprise."[93] This worsened under the Diefenbaker Conservative government (1957–63), as Bates came into conflict
with the board and federal ministers on social housing.[94] "Repeated
pressure by CMHC for an expanded social housing program ... was re-
sisted by the federal cabinet and its senior policy advisors. During that
period the Corporation [CMHC] advocated an increase in the volume of
low income housing produced, increasing the share of subsidies borne
by the federal government, the establishment of a substantial non-profit
housing sector."[95]

SOCIAL HOUSING PROGRAMS IN THE 1949–64 PERIOD

The emphasis in early postwar housing policy was to enable an effective market housing production and financing system, to serve the
broad middle class of Canadian society. Its policy instruments were direct CMHC financing of builder/developers, stimulus in recessions, and
home-buyer mortgages. The latter included direct CMHC mortgages,
and joint CMHC/private lender loans.[96] In 1954 the federal government
responded to the pressures by providing CMHC mortgage insurance
based on the US model, which greatly diminished lender risk, and by
permitting banks – no longer only just trust and insurance companies
– to do mortgage lending. CMHC moved in steps toward lower down-
payments and longer amortization terms.[97]

Social housing was a minor add-on to this market-enabling policy
regime. The 1949–64 period had two funding and delivery models of
social housing: public housing and charitable or municipal limited dividend (LD). Public housing projects were ultimately owned by CMHC,
and their capital costs fully were debt-financed 75 percent by CMHC
using public funds, and 25 percent by the province or municipality. LD
units were owned by the sponsor corporation, and financed 90 percent
by CMHC. Public housing received a small operating subsidy that was
75 percent federally funded and 25 percent provincially or municipal-
ly funded; LD was not eligible for operating subsidy. The NHA required
direct provincial involvement in public housing, but none in LD. Pub-

lic housing included some projects for families and some for seniors; most charitable and municipal LD housing was for seniors.[98]

Charitable LD was very important in British Columbia, and encouraged by the Social Credit government as a non-government way to provide affordable rental units.[99] From the mid-1950s the NHA specifically distinguished "municipal" LD from "charitable" and "entrepreneurial" (private sector) LD. In Ontario, municipalities including Metro Toronto, the City of Toronto, Ottawa, Windsor, and Oshawa created LD corporations to build seniors apartments that would operate at break-even. Using the LD provisions of the NHA enabled municipalities to achieve more production than was possible with the limited public housing allocations, and to avoid the multi-party approval loops that applied to public housing. Lacking operating subsidies, most LD projects received small municipal capital grants and property tax reductions.[100]

Institutional roles were dominated by CMHC. It did the main project financing. Its staff or consultants designed the housing and they oversaw the construction contractors. It interacted with and oversaw the local housing authorities that would sponsor and manage the projects. The provinces played a role in co-funding and collaborating with CMHC, or enabling municipalities to do so. Provinces did not develop or administer their own programs. Land acquisition, site servicing, and related legal agreements were sometimes handled locally. But CMHC was the central reservoir of expertise on which local people relied.

The first public housing projects were initiated rapidly within a year of the passing of the 1949 amendment. These were Ebsary Estate and Churchill Park in St John's, Regent Park in Toronto, and Bayers Road in Halifax. The 1947 City of Toronto budget for the Regent Park development depended on a mix of municipal funds and a $1.15 million federal grant under the 1944 NHA ($14 million in 2015 dollars). But the 1949 NHA quickly became the source of money to build Regent Park. Ontario, like Nova Scotia and Newfoundland, shortly passed legislation in 1950 to enable it to finance its 25 percent share and to meet the other NHA requirements.[101]

The majority of production in 1949–64 was in Ontario, where roles and institutions were different from other provinces. Unlike most provinces, where municipalities were left to pay half or all the 25 percent provincial share the NHA required, Ontario set the municipal share at 7½ percent of costs, itself paying 17½ percent. The Housing Branch of the Ontario Department of Planning and Development (later Economics and Development) played a large collaborating role with CMHC,[102] handling several elements of program and project delivery.

These included assessing need and prioritizing which communities would get new public housing; arranging the provincial-municipal 25 percent of financing; co-ordinating the non-CMHC development functions such as land acquisition, local servicing, and related legal agreements; and overseeing local housing authorities in their administration of completed projects.[103] The Housing Branch acted as a resource for the emerging sector, with an annual conference for Ontario housing authorities and a monthly newsletter. For public housing, Ontario also provided grants for half the cost of land and servicing, to a maximum of $500/unit;[104] and for LD, grants of up to $500/unit ($4,000 to $5,000 in 2015 dollars) or 50 percent of the cost beyond the LD mortgage loan, whichever was less. Ontario, with about the same 1950s population as Quebec, used twice as much 1950s and 1960s urban renewal funding and eight times as much pre-1964 public housing capital, and housed a far higher share of low-income renters in subsidized housing.[105]

Public housing in this period was a mix of break-even "full-recovery" housing for moderate-income earners, and "low-rent" or "low-rental" housing for the poor. Full recovery meant that rents covered operating costs and amortization of the dwelling – a financial model quite similar to UK, European or Australian public housing of the early to mid-twentieth century. Low rental meant that rents were set below this break-even market level, but not usually calibrated in a ratio to tenant income. Overall, 57 percent of Ontario public housing up to 1962 was full recovery, 35 percent low-rent, and 8 percent rent-geared-to-income (RGI).[106] Such a mix was somewhat contentious: Mansur as chair of MTHA argued against it to ensure no competition with private landlords.[107] In 1960 RGI was introduced in Ontario, based on the US model. Only at the 1964 turning point did "public housing" rather than "low rental" housing become the clearly preferred term.

The 1949–64 policy regime produced 14,314 public housing units and 11,641 municipal and charitable LD units across Canada – 26,000 units or an average of 1,700 annually over fifteen years.[108] This was 1.4 percent of total nationwide housing production in the period, a level not systemically significant. It was enough to absorb about 1 in 10 of the low-income renters added each year as part of the spectrum of ongoing rapid growth. Social housing in 1964 was 0.5 percent of Canada's total housing stock of 5.0 million dwellings. It housed a tiny share of the nation's low-income renters, and was essentially irrelevant in the housing options open to that population.

Just over half the 1949–64 social housing was in Ontario, reflecting its urban character and the housing politics in Toronto. The Ontario total by the latter date was 7,549 public housing units and 6,976 municipal and charitable LD units, averaging just over 900 units annually. Nova Scotia had by far the highest public housing stock per capita at 2,100 units; this reflected its explosive wartime growth and the severity of its housing crisis in the 1940s and early 1950s. British Columbia, with a 1950s population twice Nova Scotia's and one-quarter of Ontario's, was a distant number three with 1,400 public housing units by 1964. Manitoba and British Columbia were the only provinces besides Ontario that exceeded 1,000 LD units.[109] Social housing was more significant in Toronto than elsewhere: the 6,000 units existing in 1964 comprised 1½ percent of total housing stock in the urban area. At 6,000 units, Toronto was approaching the scale of public housing stock in then-comparable US cities including Cleveland, Boston, Washington, DC, and San Francisco-Oakland – ultimately 9,000 to 12,000 units each and all built by 1964.[110]

Canada's 1949–63 social housing policy was not significant by the international standards of the day, and our weak institutional arrangements were a main reason. Because by 1937–42 most US big cities had housing authorities, and the larger Australian states had housing commissions, the flow of 90 or 100 percent federal money right after the war led to strong production and reinforced these housing agencies as federal partners and stakeholders. In Canada, local social housing institutions had to be invented in the 1950s, and provinces or municipalities had to put up one-quarter of the funding. The United States had 170,000 public housing units by 1949 when Canada passed its NHA amendments,[111] and 570,000 by the 1964 turning point – more than twice the Canadian stock per capita. Australia had 137,000 by the latter date, over ten times the Canadian level relative to population, even after selling 43 percent of its production.[112] Production of *habitations à loyer modéré* (HLM) in France, which had three times Canada's 1950s population, rose from average of 19,000 annually in 1950–54 to 65,000 in the second half of the decade, and 85,000 a year by the early 1960s.[113]

Canada's welfare state of the 1940s and 1950s was about social security for the social mainstream, including the lower-middle and working class; it was not about low-income targeted programs. Housing policy was influenced by the new discourse of the welfare state, found then mostly at the federal and not provincial level.[114] But housing policy was a matter of market welfare, not decommodified provision. Moreover, the CMHC institutional model established an ambiguous relationship of housing to the mainstream of federal policy-making and the welfare state. CMHC was not a department to deliver programs but a crown corporation with a market-making mandate. It stood symbolically removed from the downtown Ottawa power centre and quartered in a neo-Georgian office building befitting an insurance company[115] – and mortgage insurance soon became its main business.

Despite the minor place of social housing in the 1949–64 housing policy regime, having a permanent federal housing agency would prove very significant. WHL had set an institutional mould and culture that carried over into parts of CMHC. It set a pattern of federal dominance in social housing, in framing Canadian thinking, in direct federal relationships to municipalities, and in linking housing production and new norms of neighbourhood design. It established federal capacity which was not matched provincially for a generation.[116] CMHC became a repository of expertise and experience in social housing, a place where from the mid-1950s onwards new top management and policy advisors could work toward a higher priority for social housing.

Canadian social housing policy was rather similar in the 1949–64 period and the first fifteen years of the current century. Each period had strong economic growth (despite one significant downturn each time), surging home-owner demand and supply, and a successful market housing system. The political mainstream supported home-ownership and celebrated the dynamism of the market. The net housing demand of low-income renters was met mostly by the filtering of housing from half a century before: in the 1950s this was in neighbourhoods built in the Laurier boom; in the 2000s it was in apartments of the postwar suburbs. Opinion was mostly indifferent to the dysfunctional market dynamics involved and the residents' housing problems. A small social housing production program served to assuage the advocates and deal with some worst-case needs. Certainly there were various differences in the program models in the two periods,[117] and the legacy stock of decent low-rent housing was in the market in the 1950s but is in the non-market sector today. But national production volumes per capita were about the same in each, and activity varied greatly among the provinces. The housing produced was a mix of low-end market units along with low-income units that mostly lacked geared-to-income rents.

The difference between the 1950s and the early twenty-first century was the trajectory. The decisions of the early postwar years had set basic directions in social housing policy at the federal, provincial, and municipal levels. Canada had broken with the past and created institutional roles, funding, practices, and policy discourse different from the US and UK models. On these early postwar foundations was built a ten-fold increase in activity at the next turning point in the mid-1960s. The scale of social housing in Canada was about to be transformed.

3

The 1960s:
Urban Development and Social Agendas

The mid-1960s was the pivotal expansionary turning point in Canadian social housing. The early, iconic projects of the 1950s, such as Toronto's Regent Park or Montreal's Jeanne Mance, turned out to be merely prelude. This chapter provides the first general account of that policy juncture, drawing partly on new archival research, and setting it in the context of Canada's social policy and urban growth in that centennial decade. The mid-1960s brought about a ten-fold expansion of production in social housing, and opened three decades of active policy. Canadian social housing production surged to per-capita levels notably higher than those in the United States, although still well short of Australian or West European levels. This was done through a large increase in federal funding, and by taking development out of the hands of municipal agencies and putting it into the hands of well-resourced provincial government agencies.

In the dominant Canadian social housing literature from the 1970s and 1980s, "public housing projects" run by the state were the negative exemplar, a recipe that disrupted neighbourhoods and ghettoized poor people. Little distinction was drawn between pre- and post-1964 except that the 1960s produced more projects. Those writers advocated mixed-income non-profit housing operated by community-based agencies – indeed a more socially successful model. But what is most significant in the 1960s policy turn looks quite different in historical perspective than it appeared to critics a decade or so later. In the 1970s the question was why governments in the preceding decade had embraced an inferior social and design model of social housing. In the long view, the question is why they put in place a systemically significant non-market sector. What led Canadian governments in the 1960s to devote resources to higher social housing production levels that would continue for a generation?

The 1960s policy involved a significant element of urban social integration, beyond the micro scale of the project or neighbourhood which was the focus of its 1970s critics. Low-income social housing piggy-backed on the private-rental apartment boom, in large part as a purposeful agenda of provincial housing agencies. This created a new geography: social housing was no longer just a response of central-city municipalities to slum issues as in the United States, but instead became an integral element in broader urban development, as it was then in much of Western Europe or Australia. Private-rental and social housing development together dispersed low-income renters from the central city to the postwar suburbs where most other people were living. Had the 1949–64 policy regime endured, Canadian social housing would consist of a few stigmatized inner-city slum redevelopment projects housing a tiny fraction of low-income renters. Most of that population, and of that slice of rapid ongoing growth, would have been housed in low-quality private rental units concentrated in declining older neighbourhoods – not unlike the situation in US cities then or Canadian cities today. But the success story of urban Canada in the 1960s to 1980s was manifestly different, and one part of it was that social housing came to accommodate half of the low-income renter segment of rapid urban growth, and in most larger cities this housing was spread well beyond declining older areas.

The mid-1960s turning point was propelled by broad political agendas. Social housing and urban renewal were an integral part of the Pearson government's purposeful and large expansion of social programs. Ontario invented the provincial housing corporation model as part of its active housing and urban development agenda, and this model also suited Quebec's nationalist approach. The resulting policy regime soon carried across the country. As the 1965–75 decade progressed, policy shifted in response to rapid changes in economic, political, and housing market conditions. Strong controversies arose about shortcomings in housing market performance, public housing development, and urban change. But the institutional capacity and normalized higher funding levels established in the mid-1960s became a platform on which governments could address the mushrooming political claims amid the turbulent politics and careening housing markets of the 1970s (chapter 4).

POLITICAL AND ECONOMIC CONTEXT:
PEAK OF THE LONG BOOM

The 1960s expansion of social programs was directly the context for the 1964 policy and funding changes which transformed Canadian public housing. The small scale of 1950s social housing programs had reflected the tone of early postwar social policy – mostly not redistribution to the poor, but policies for the mainstream. But now Canada moved ahead with more universalist programs and more ample targeted ones, including subsidized post-secondary education, the Canada Pension Plan, public health insurance, much augmented unemployment insurance, and federal cost-sharing of provincial social programs through the Canada Assistance Plan (CAP).[1]

The early 1960s brought economic recovery after a recession. It had been a severe downturn by postwar standards, with high unemployment for the majority of the Diefenbaker term.[2] When the 1963 election brought to power the Pearson Liberal government with its social agenda, strong economic growth meant ample tax revenues to fund that. From 1961 until the mid-1970s, Canada's average growth in real (inflation-adjusted) GDP would be 5½ percent annually, thereby doubling in fifteen years – not as strong as France or Japan in that period but far above long-run norms.[3]

Change was also happening in Canada's position in the continental North American economy, which affected the politics of welfare state evolution. Open markets remained the strategy of the Canadian economic elite, and the main exports remained commodities and forest products to the United States, but a more autonomous Canadian economy was also emerging. Postwar household incomes were rising strongly, and growth was now propelled partly by a domestic "Fordist" economy[4] where a virtuous cycle of domestic industrial production supported fairly high wages and large consumer demand. Continental labour market integration faded with US immigration reform in 1965. Until then there had usually been unrestricted migration across the US border, but now Canada had a US immigration quota just like other nations and Canadians needed a visa to move to the United States or to work there.[5] All this created a less continentally integrated Canadian labour market and consumer economy, and this helped shape a less US-dominated flavour in 1960s and 1970s social policy.

Prosperity and other factors made the mid- to late 1960s a very optimistic time. A great self-awareness developed of Canada as a modern, urban nation, reflecting the reality of Canada's economic maturation and rapid urban growth. It was expressed in official documents such as the 1967 CMHC annual report and the 1968 review of the Economic Council of Canada. A more confident national identity emerged. French Canada was modern and assertive; English-speaking Canada was no longer just a social and economic fringe of the Empire and the United States. For the first time ever, Canadians were not poor cousins to Americans; indeed, some felt superior in their newly urban, bicultural society as they watched US protests and central-city riots on TV.[6] The mood of national self-confidence was expressed exuberantly in the 1967 Centennial celebration of confederation, and in Expo 67, the world's fair held in Montreal that year.[7]

In opposition, the new Liberal leader Lester Pearson faced the populist Diefenbaker Conservatives with their huge 1958–62 majority, and the challenge of the NDP. The latter was created in 1961 as a labour-based recasting of the CCF, and was a significant impetus to the Liberal Party's welfare state expansion platform.[8] Pearson in opposition had revised the party's social policy stance, to the surprise and some dismay of the party's old guard. Famous as a diplomat but with little background in social policy, he gathered around him a circle of left-leaning Liberals, relative outsiders to the Ottawa Liberal establishment.[9] Prominent among them were the Winnipeg journalist Tom Kent, who would remain Pearson's social policy advisor, and Toronto businessman Walter Gordon, who would be his first minister of finance. Pearson's circle organized a party-sponsored Study Conference on National Problems in 1960 in Kingston. Attended by a wide range of elected officials, active citizens, and prominent business people, its purpose was to put on the table, and gain traction for, a purposeful agenda of expanding social welfare programs.[10]

The Pearson Liberals were in office as a minority government from 1963–68, and NDP support was important in their new social policy initiatives. The government was extraordinary in its cabinet talent and agenda.[11] Fully eight of the ministers had been public servants with all the knowledge that brought, and the cabinet shared a consensus on the expansion of social welfare programs. The Pearson social policy platform included action on pensions and medicare, and along with Quebec-federal relations, these dominated politics during his government's time in office. Along with these large initiatives that benefited the middle-class mainstream were ones targeted to low incomes: the Guaranteed Income Supplement to Old Age Security; CAP; and social housing.[12]

The political moment was also favourable in the two provinces that comprised two-thirds of Canada's population. In Ontario, Premier Robarts's Progressive Conservative government was different in tone from the federal Liberals but in a similar space politically. Private-sector growth should be fostered by a government active in creating suitable conditions for it,[13] and some of the rising public revenues should be used to expand social programs. Housing was part of economic development, and social housing was situated in the Department of Economics and Development created in 1961 at the start of Robarts's tenure.[14] Ontario's welfare state expansion, besides post-secondary education, included an announcement in 1962 of an Ontario medical insurance plan and supplements to the federal pension system.[15] Such a platform, left of centre by today's standards, was middle-of-the-road in its day.

The Quiet Revolution in 1960s Quebec rejected the traditional, Catholic, rural definition of Quebec's character and embraced its new reality as a modern urban society. The state – the provincial government or ultimately a sovereign national government – was the tool by which Quebec society would take control of its own destiny and ensure that it fully caught up economically and otherwise with other provinces and countries.[16] "Quebec sought to establish a comprehensive *provincial* welfare state that would be fully controlled and integrated at the regional [Quebec] level and would reflect what nationalists saw as a distinctive cultural approach to the social needs of a modern society."[17] While this Quebec social and political agenda soon led to federal-Quebec conflicts, it also supported the general climate of welfare state expansion. The Pearson Liberal government accommodated various Quebec demands: acceding to a separate Quebec Pension Plan parallel to the Canada Pension Plan; and agreeing to opt-out provisions in various social programs so that Quebec could run its own separate program without loss of federal funds. In the 1960s, these conflicts modified the shape of social program expansion but did not hinder it.

HOUSING AND URBAN CONTEXT: APARTMENTS IN THE DOUBLING CITIES

Rapid urban growth and resulting housing market pressures were important context for Canada's expanded social housing priority in the 1960s. Some readers may think, "Ah, the baby boom," but this rapid urban growth and surging rental demand from the 1950s to the 1970s arose from other powerful forces, too. These included large increases in real earnings, high immigration, high rural-urban migration in the early postwar years, longer lifespans, more separation and divorce, "lifestyle" preference for delayed child-rearing and living alone, and the social consequences of affluent urban living. Together these meant more purchasing power, fewer people living in farmhouses, more living in smaller households, and more in the under-thirty and over-sixty age groups – together boosting greatly the number of urban homes required in proportion to any given population.[18]

Postwar Canada had far more people moving from the farm to the city than in Australia, and relatively far more disembarking from the immigrant ship than in the United States. These people initially lacked down-payments and secure jobs. Average incomes were lower than in the United States and the average unemployment rate was much higher than in Australia. Although home-ownership was the main thrust of Canadian housing policy, this nation lacked the intensity of those nations' policy support for it. Unlike the United States, Canada had no savings-and-loan institutions and no income tax write-off of mortgage interest. Unlike Australia, Canada had no building societies, no allocation of low-interest mortgages by state banks, and no discounted sales of thousands of public housing bungalows.[19] Policy discouraged self-build houses on the sewerless urban fringe. And so, though middle-class Canadians became home-owners in vast numbers, more people rented longer in postwar Canada than in those two nations, and they mostly rented in apartment buildings.[20]

As Canada approached the mid-1960s, housing market conditions were benign. A strong economic expansion was under way, but the rising prices and real estate boom of the late 1960s were in the future. The uncertainties of the immediate postwar decade and the severe late-1950s recession were now well in the past. Canada had a thriving market development sector, a successful state role in orchestrating financing, and a cost-revenue equation favourable to rental production. By the latter 1960s the housing market became far more turbulent, with price escalation in a real estate boom along with rising interest rates[21] propelling mainstream concern about housing, which reinforced political support for a state role in housing (chapter 4). Affordability concerns of the social mainstream were not a concern yet in the mid-1960s.

In Toronto, Vancouver, and Montreal, and increasingly in Ottawa, Hamilton, and other mid-sized centres, private-sector developers were producing large volumes of apartments and townhouses. Canada's private sector was building 100,000 rental apartment units a year in the

1960s – a scale of per-capita rental production not remotely matched in the private sector in peer nations such as the United States, Britain, Australia, or France. In market reality as well as in plannerly thinking, there was a mix of "product" to suit a mix of household types and budgets. Metro Toronto in the 1960s had four added renter households for each one added home-owner household.[22] The extent to which high-rise rental living was normalized in middle-class choices and lifecycles is strongly evident in William Michelson's classic work[23] on residential preferences. Apartment development was an integral part of land use and development planning, of the business model of the large development firms, and of actual suburban development.[24]

And so mixed-tenure, mixed-income suburban development became a normal thing. Although the postwar suburbs were disparaged by later reformers of a Jane Jacobs mindset,[25] those built from the 1950s to the 1970s differed notably from the low-density home-owner tracts that dominated US or Australian suburbs at the time, or Canada since then. Most suburbs in Toronto, Montreal, and Vancouver in that period had a significant mix of rental tenure, multiple dwellings, and income levels, and this was also evident in Ottawa, Edmonton, Kitchener-Waterloo, and other mid-sized centres. In larger Canadian cities, apartment units comprise over 30 percent of dwellings in neighbourhoods built primarily in the 1950s, and over 40 percent in neighbourhoods built in the 1960s; rented dwellings were and are over 40 percent of the total in each of these rings of urban growth.[26] The negative exemplar cited by the critics was Toronto's Don Mills, but this suburb had middling densities overall, apartment sites designated in its planning, and a cluster of rental apartments integral in its development.

IDEAS: SOCIAL WELFARE AND THE GOLDEN GOOSE OF GROWTH

Across most affluent Western nations, the greatest expansion of social welfare programs occurred from the late 1950s to the mid-1970s, the peak years of postwar economic expansion.[27] There was a widespread attitude that society was now affluent enough, and government systems sophisticated enough, that long-standing problems of poverty and social insecurity could largely be solved. Social welfare moved beyond concerns of general social security – pensions, health care, and unemployment insurance – toward ensuring that the poor received a better slice of the pie in the affluent society. In Ramesh Mishra's concepts,[28] there was a shift and extension beyond the "Keynesian" system-management dimensions of the welfare state toward stronger "Beveridg-

Figure 3.1   Postwar increase in larger urban centres: Canada and peer nations. Canada's postwar urban growth rate was high; the resulting pressures helped foster an active government role in housing.

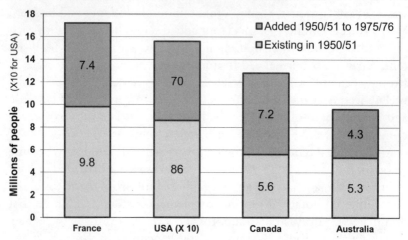

Population in urban centres of 100,000 population or more.
Source: See Suttor, *Rental Paths*, 2009.

ian" social equity dimensions. Canada's welfare state expansion of the 1960s, carried out by centrist governments federally and provincially, reflected this international climate;[29] it also raised Canada to international norms for its level of affluence. Social program expansion was supported across most parts of the political spectrum.

In the United States, this was the period of President Johnson's "Great Society" expansion of social programs, including Medicaid for the elderly and programs to address racial inequality and inner-city issues.[30] In Britain it was the peak of postwar prosperity and of welfare state expansion under the Wilson Labour government. In both those countries in the 1960s, housing issues were central in the anti-poverty agenda, and social housing was an integral and prominent part of social program expansion. France in the 1960s under De Gaulle's centrist government carried out a similar, large expansion of social programs including social housing. Canada's housing policy discourse was informed explicitly by international ideas about urban policy, welfare state expansion, and comparative welfare state models. British and international thinking shaped the CCF-NDP postwar platform, crafted by thinkers such as David Lewis who had studied at Oxford and been active in its 1930s political debates,[31] and it became integral in the ideas of Liberal 1960s social reformers.[32]

The 1960s were the heyday of public housing globally, and it was entrenched and normalized as part of social programs and urban development in Anglo liberal-welfare societies. Public housing production peaked then in the United States and Britain, rising fairly steadily in the former case from fewer than 30,000 units annually in the early 1960s to 77,000 in 1970, and averaging 164,000 units annually in Britain in 1965–70.[33] Likewise, this was the peak of public housing production in Australia, Sweden, and France.[34] Across the Western world, what 1960s welfare state expansion meant in social housing was higher priority for low-income households. These had not been the main target group of early postwar European social rental production, with its break-even rents for working class tenants (the lower-middle of the period), while most of the poor still lived in old central-city private rental. But there was increasing contrast between the higher norms of this new mass affluence and the living conditions of the urban poor in affluent nations. Now low-income people became a social housing priority – through new income targeting in European and Australian social housing, and through augmented public housing production in the United States and Canada.[35]

In Ontario there was concern about how to ensure enough housing supply at moderate costs in the big cities. In the 1967 provincial election, important Robarts speeches were about housing.[36] Federal Finance Minister Walter Gordon shared this worry,[37] reflecting the climate in Toronto where his seat was. The government of Ontario wanted to ensure enough rental housing production to nourish the golden goose of urban growth. By this point, Ontario was taking an active role in managing urban development, especially in the Toronto region. This was implemented through the Ontario Municipal Board's oversight of municipal land use decisions, the Metropolitan Toronto government which the province had created in 1953, the Ontario Water Resources Commission which built water and sewer infrastructure, and large land assemblies. Ontario pursued a vigorous policy of municipal restructuring to ensure suitable fiscal capacity and boundaries to foster competent local growth management, especially in the Toronto region.[38] Its Department of Economics and Development took a strong role in growth strategy for the region. By 1967, Government of Ontario (GO) Transit was operating a new regional commuter rail service.

Ontario saw housing as a bigger policy concern than medicare, which was the federal priority.[39] Ontario-based financial firms could handle medical insurance under the pre-Medicare framework, and the feds could keep their noses out, but housing supply was viewed as a more urgent concern which certainly required federal capital.

In Montreal by the 1960s, an urban renewal agenda propelled a new interest in public housing that had not existed in the preceeding decade. Montreal had been almost twice as large as Toronto in the early industrial era of circa 1880 to 1930, a city of many low-wage manufacturing and port and warehouse jobs, and a city of renters. In the postwar era, much of the working class moved up to better jobs and out to the suburbs, and demand softened for rental units in plexes in older neighbourhoods. Some were slums with housing in very poor repair. Public housing and urban renewal were a way to do away with "blight" through slum clearance, and to provide affordable housing of decent quality to the residents while revitalizing the area. For the City of Montreal, public housing was also a way to relocate people displaced by the massive demolition it was carrying out to make room for commercial development and new downtown expressways. Displacement became a major concern of community-based groups in the 1960s.[40] Given Montreal's abundant older rental housing, there was not the same political concern as in Toronto about the adequacy of rental housing production to meet the scale and pace of growth.

Across Canada, building a mix of tenure and income, as part of managed urban expansion, was strongly present not only in actual urban development but in the thinking about it. Today, urban planners' ideas about mixed-density suburban development with transit-oriented shopping and apartment nodes are focused environmental objectives, transit-supportive density, and creating walkable, high-amenity spaces. Similar ideas were current in the 1960s but they were explicitly about a mix of prices, tenures, social classes, and stages of the life cycle; the case for this new model of suburb was articulated by a leading federal housing policy-maker, Humphrey Carver.[41] The premise, in the context of rapid growth, was that the housing of people in Canada's cities was a matter of what was to be built. The corollary, expressed in the high-profile 1964 Murray report (see below) was that "filtering" as a means to meet low-income need was neither socially acceptable nor practically adequate in volume. In other words, the housing of the lower-income households that would be added as part of rapid growth could not simply be left to the market to accommodate by way of price and quality decline in older neighbourhoods. This is not to say that everyone shared these ideas; a presumption that "private enterprise" or "the market" would just take care of things was as commonplace then as now. But these ideas were clearly articulated in this high-profile report co-sponsored by the federal CMHC and the Ontario government.

Public housing in 1960s Canada was little stigmatized by the standards of the United States then or Canada today. The negative example of US public housing – already ghettoized and residualized – was much in the minds of those advocating more Canadian production and those opposing it.[42] Advocates of social housing knew other models, particularly West European ones, and public housing was not seen primarily as a matter of slum replacement for the central-city poor as in the United States. The Murray report articulated the progressive vision of that period, with active social housing policy as part of mixed urban development. Once provincial housing corporations got going, their official reports presented many images of gleaming modernist new buildings.

And, of course, close to half of social housing was for the elderly. The elderly public housing tenants of the 1960s had spent their working years in the early to middle decades of the century. It had been a much poorer Canada with wider wage disparities, many poor farmers, no Canada Pension Plan, little coverage by employer pensions, and lower urban home-ownership. This was their slice of postwar prosperity in old age.

EVENTS AND DECISIONS: THE MID-1960S

The key events occurred federally and in Ontario and Quebec. The 1963 federal election brought to power the Pearson Liberals: a centrist government with a clear and ambitious social agenda including social housing, and a minority government dependent on the support of the social-democratic NDP. Ontario invented the provincial housing corporation model that same year, through accidents of politics, on a parallel welfare state agenda, and on the foundation of its active and distinctive 1949–64 role in social housing. In nationalist Quebec, although social housing was not a priority, it could not be left in the hands of a federal agency, and so Quebec also moved to set up a provincial housing corporation. The 1964 National Housing Act (NHA) amendments enabled funding of either municipal or provincial corporations, but with Canada's two largest provinces embracing the latter, provincial delivery was soon promoted by a collaborative federal government as the vehicle for the new policy. Within five years this approach was adopted, province by province, in the other one-third of Canada too. For social housing advocates and officials, this approach ended decisively the great shortcomings of the 1949–64 program model.

Within the circles of advocates and public officials involved in social housing, the early 1960s saw a ferment of disgruntlement and ideas for change. There was a search for better options than the under-performing 1949–64 program model, its residual character and small output, its dysfunctional tri-level relations in project development, its lukewarm fiscal resources, and its mismatch to social welfare norms by this time in history. In the words of Albert Rose, "By 1961 it was clear to all interested parties that the federal-provincial partnership had collapsed."[43] Yet the dominant note of the period was ferment and hopefulness, and how to have a less cumbersome development process and simpler government roles. In any period from about 1970 onwards, the delays arising from community opposition would be viewed as legitimate accommodation of neighbourhood interests – but not so then. Toronto was the focus of the Ontario government's concerns in regard to such "red tape." In this ferment, there were strong links between activists and key public servants, and between CMHC and Toronto actors. There was also broader advocacy from the labour movement – a more accepted mainstream voice in that day – and from churches.[44]

The leading streamlining idea was a stronger municipal housing authority, possibly with a more direct federal-municipal relationship, based on the US model.[45] Instead of local housing authorities with joint federal-provincial-municipal governance and tri-level project approval processes, it would be local bodies developing housing on the strength of mostly federal funding.[46] Financial ideas in play by 1962 included 50/50 federal-provincial subsidy[47] and the US model of 90 percent federal capital financing for public housing – both to become key elements in the 1964 NHA amendments. The 1964 policy changes were directly a reaction to the inadequacies and small production of the public housing regime of the preceding fifteen years,[48] once a new government created a receptive climate for these new proposals.

The Federal Social Agenda and 1964 NHA

The Pearson Liberals' social agenda was directly the context for the 1964 policy and funding changes which transformed Canadian public housing. Action on the latter was part of a clearly articulated social program, even if a minor part fiscally and politically. The government's social policy priorities were pensions, medicare, student loans, and broad new federal-provincial cost-sharing. More generally, its political priorities were federal-Quebec relations, federal-provincial fiscal arrangements, and the intensely controversial new national flag. Unsurprisingly, public housing is absent from memoirs and biographies of key ministers and advisors of the period.[49] In urban affairs, the platform and throne speech put far more emphasis on a new Municipal Development and Loan Board for low-interest infrastructure financing than on housing. Housing was not on the agenda of the November 1963 federal-provincial conference early in the term of the new government. It had no great prominence in intergovernmental relations with Ontario,[50] the key partner in the new social policy agenda.

But social housing and urban renewal were always integrally part of the Pearson agenda. They were among the half-dozen main agenda items at the 1960 policy conference held while Pearson was in opposition. When his social policy strategist, Tom Kent, in March 1962 prepared a confidential provisional legislative agenda and financing plan for a future Liberal government, the capital plan included $50 million annually ($400 million in 2015 dollars) for "CMHC urban renewal and low rental housing," with a slot in the year-two legislative program.[51]

Once the Pearson government took office in spring 1963, the ideas for an expanded program, coming from CMHC officials such as Bates and Carver and percolating in Ontario, now matched a similar cabinet agenda.[52] Public housing and urban renewal were in the new government's first throne speech in May 1963 and the February 1964 throne speech for the second parliamentary session – the same timing Tom Kent had sketched out.[53] When the government organized a November 1965 Federal-Provincial Conference on Poverty and Opportunity to stir up interest in its priorities, social housing was among the half-dozen agenda items. For the conference, Kent's 1962 paper was adapted,[54] with public housing and urban renewal two of the dozen items on the list of needed social policy measures; and an ample CMHC housing background paper[55] was commissioned.

The NHA amendments were passed in June 1964. The main new provisions were in the delivery vehicles, funding formula, and volume of funding. CMHC was now empowered to fund not only municipal corporations as in the 1949–64 program model, but also provincial housing corporations. This meant an enormous potential increase in institutional capacity. The change in funding formula was the second key element. Instead of project capital costs and operating "deficits" being shared 75/25 percent federal/provincial, as in the 1949–63 formula, the federal government would now cover 90 percent of capital costs, with operating costs split 50/50.[56] But perhaps most significant of all were the "almost unlimited amounts of capital" made available by the federal government.[57]

To understand the significance of this funding shift we must consider the context. Today's governments can borrow extremely cheaply, but they avoid multi-year commitments for new social programs because large recurring costs of existing programs make the containment of future spending a major concern. In the mid-1960s the picture was reversed: revenue growth was good, housing operating subsidies were small, and capital was the big hurdle. This was not the post-1980s world, awash in a sea of capital; the systemic challenge was how to enable enough capital formation to finance Canada's rapid residential growth, from money flows in a much smaller economy and at higher interest rates than today. For most provinces, the new formula with the higher, 90 percent federal capital financing was far more attractive, despite the increased 50 percent provincial operating subsidy.

CMHC had played a large role in financing market housing since the 1940s through development and construction loans to firms, and mortgages for household purchases. The new public housing financing was a matter of increasing overall CMHC housing financing allocations, and shifting a small part from private-sector to public-sector production. Post-1964 CMHC capital commitments for public housing started at $100 million annually, with an associated rise in CMHC's draw on the federal Consolidated Revenue Fund from $2 to $2.5 billion annually (from $15 to $19 billion in 2015 dollars) to cover this along with rising private-sector producer and home-owner requirements.[58] Such funds for housing capital were financed by long-term public debt, part of overall federal borrowing to pay for infrastructure and other needs, and repaid by CMHC to the federal treasury over the decades that followed.

Ontario Events

Amid the ferment of the early 1960s, Ontario's Premier Robarts, one year into his term of office, announced in 1962 a Twelve Point Program for housing. This was high profile, with glossy publications and speeches by the premier and Bob Macaulay, the minister of economics and development.[59] The twelve points included accelerated land assembly and public housing production with streamlined procedures; purchase of rental buildings to augment this; a "rent certificate" program – an early cousin of rent supplement;[60] efforts toward housing conservation including mortgage guarantees for rehabilitation of home-owner dwellings; provincial grants and loan guarantees for non-profit and co-operative housing; and formation of a Housing Advisory Committee.[61]

There is continuity between the Twelve Point Program and later decisions. There are strong threads from there to the new Ontario minister's April 1963 speech in the legislature, and the provincial housing corporation model that emerged in 1964, including the objectives of meeting social needs at scale and the specific program features of expanded activity, purchasing apartments, and less cumbersome delivery arrangements. Moreover the Twelve Point Program established the Advisory Committee which led to the idea of creating an Ontario housing corporation.

Two government-sponsored advisory initiatives in this context fed the thinking that culminated in Ontario's 1964 decisions. The "Murray report"[62] arose from a proposal from housing authorities – in this period engaged local citizens more than patronage appointees – which found favour with CMHC and Ontario officials who co-funded it as a nationwide study. The links to postwar urban development ideas are exemplified in its chairman, James A. Murray, designer of Don Mills, founder of Canadian Architect magazine, leading presence at the University of Toronto's School of Architecture, and doyen of modernist postwar planning-and-housing thinking in Canada.[63]

The Murray committee sent subgroups to study social housing in the United States, Britain, Sweden, Denmark, West Germany, and the Netherlands, and commissioned background papers by Albert Rose and others. This was not a case of advocates speaking to political circles to whom they were outsiders; the advisory committee included the president of the Community Planning Association of Canada (Harold Clark), the president of CMHC, the managing director of Ontario's Housing Branch, the executive director of the Metropolitan Toronto Housing Authority (MTHA), and others. The report[64] articulated a position against relying on filtering, and included an analysis of projected household growth and households at different income levels. It saw a need for public policy to ensure development of the one million extra dwellings that would be needed for low- and moderate-income households over the two decades following, and recommended an expansive social housing program. But the committee's vision of European-style community housing was pushed aside, and its report was released in August 1964 one week after Ontario announced the creation of the Ontario Housing Corporation (OHC).[65]

The second initiative was the Ontario Advisory Committee, established as part of the Twelve Point Program. This body first proposed the institutional and delivery model which became realized as OHC.

The minister[66] and OHC's chairman[67] both credited the idea to the committee. By March 1963, its finance subcommittee had developed the idea and got authorization to flesh it out, including a draft corporate by-law and specification of the corporation's powers. This proposal was shaped with active involvement by the managing director of the Housing Branch, H.W. (Bob) Suters, and the minister Stanley Randall. Both were new to their positions in 1963, ambitious to do more, and ready to champion new approaches. Suters cleared with the Treasury Board whether there were any legal barriers to the proposed structure, and briefed the minister before the Advisory Committee's chairman formally presented the idea to him in December 1963.[68] As recounted by Rose, an insider to these events, the new managing director and minister knew each other and "between them, they hatched up the idea of Ontario Housing Corporation," a recipe that might never have come into being under their predecessors.[69]

As the federal and Ontario policy agendas converged, there was direct collaboration between these two governments in the lead-up to the NHA amendments and creation of OHC. The federal minister responsible for CMHC, Jack Garland, corresponded with Premier Robarts and the successive Ontario ministers Macaulay and Randall about the proposed NHA changes, with a tone of collaboration and common purpose. Ontario provided input to CMHC in formulating the NHA amendments[70] and thus helped shape the new regime. The idea of funding provincial housing corporations came to the fore. Garland's successor John R. Nicholson thanked Robarts for "the valued assistance provided by the provinces during the formative stages of the proposed legislation."[71] Ontario officials readily described this collaboration to interested MPs and MPPs.[72]

Randall, Ontario's minister of economics and development, played a driving role. Joining cabinet after the 1963 provincial election, he was responsible for OHC from the inception of the model in late 1963 through most of its production heyday until he retired in 1971. The style of Robarts's cabinet was of substantial ministerial autonomy: Robarts was the "captain of the good ship Ontario" but did not operate with the direct decision style of his predecessor Leslie Frost nor, until the very end of the decade, with the new central-agency apparatus. As recalled by Don Richmond, "Randall really was a driving force. He was a real entrepreneur in government clothes." He was the great "can-doer" in the cabinet and was also trying to out-do his predecessor in the portfolio, Bob Macaulay. In December 1963 he seized enthusiastically the OHC model proposed by the Advisory Committee, putting aside other ideas. It was a case where "truly the personality of politicians makes a big, big difference. You have to credit, in my view – or blame him – Stan Randall for being the catalyst and pusher."[73] Randall communicated almost daily with the managing director of the Housing Branch and then of OHC (assistant deputy minister and then deputy minister in today's terms) – on matters large and small, administrative and political.[74]

Randall was apparently persuaded, or at least sought to persuade others, that OHC would pay for itself in the long run. He wrote to Robarts articulating the matter,[75] and spelled this out at the inaugural OHC board meeting.[76] Once created, OHC commissioned a confidential study by consultant Lionel Feldman to analyse this.[77] It included projections whereby the prospective OHC portfolio was "self-liquidating," – that is the rents and moderate subsidies at 1965 levels would amortize the debt and carry the operating costs over three or so decades. For the minister, what made the 1964 program model far more attractive was that the province would own the property asset rather than sharing ownership with CMHC.

Although the scenario of self-liquidating social housing is absurd in retrospect, it was not an unreasonable expectation then. European and Australian social housing was then breaking even on a mix of low and moderate incomes, low-cost financing, and low pre-1960s development costs. The Feldman study noted that incomes of the poorest had been rising in recent years, propelled in part by expanding income transfer programs. OHC had not yet settled on an all-RGI model; Feldman's projections were premised on a mix of market-rent units and RGI, akin to the mix of break-even and low-rent units in the pre-1964 program.

In early 1964 Randall took the proposal for OHC to Robarts, and then in April to cabinet. As remembered by a key Robarts policy assistant present at the meeting, Don Richmond, "Robarts was slightly ambivalent, but worried very much about the fact that the subsidy split, instead of getting 75 percent [federal share of operating subsidy], was only going to be 50. Nevertheless he went along with it."[78] Cabinet reaction was cautious, with doubts about everything that would prove the downfall of OHC – getting into a program of substantial proportions; whether OHC real estate would truly be self-liquidating; the potential flood of municipal requests; and the prospect of the province becoming directly the target for community opposition. The answers were arguments about integration into overall apartment development, the momentum of collaboration with CMHC, ongoing municipal cost-sharing, and the need to respond to bubbling advocacy and get out ahead of the Murray report, anticipated shortly.[79] In the context of the times, the feder-

Figure 3.2   Increase in owner and seholds, Canada: Average annual change by five-year period. Rent nstream in the 1960s–80s, comprising 40 percent of growth. Social e these coattails politically.

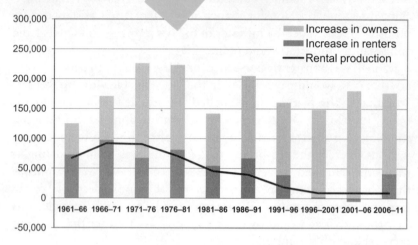

Source: Statistics Canada, census; CMHC production data (with estimates).

al policy shift under way, and ministerial autonomy, it would have taken more heated concern than this to slow down the minister's plans. The bill was introduced and An Act to Incorporate the Ontario Housing Corporation received third reading and royal assent in May 1964.

In August 1964 Robarts and Randall announced the start-up of OHC.[80] The stated goals were to achieve a larger, more effective program; make best use of the new federal framework and funding; deliver in municipalities that lacked interest; and realize streamlined development through an autonomous corporation using a flexible array of development and procurement methods in a simpler process.[81] Media coverage was quite favourable, emphasizing the government's messages of cutting red tape, being more effective within Metro Toronto, and meeting the needs of a modern society.[82] The *Toronto Star* and the *Telegram* newspapers both wrote favourable editorials.[83] A CBC TV special was arranged, with Randall to stand before a suburban greenfield patch and talk about building mixed housing.[84]

The shift in Ontario to delivery by a provincial agency was not only a departure from the emerging direction of program ideas, which was to improve delivery via enhanced local capacity. It was also a departure from any existing model of US, British, French or Canadian public housing, which all involved the federal or central government funding and financing local bodies that arranged project planning, production, ownership, and management. OHC, as a large subnational agency with a near-monopoly in social housing, was parallel to the Australian model – but entirely unwittingly. But two precedents for OHC are evident: first, CMHC itself, and second, the various Ontario government agencies dealing with urban and infrastructure matters. OHC was in effect a CMHC for Ontario. Robarts's Ontario saw itself as a subnational government somewhat parallel to the federal government, expanding its capacity and expertise, and such "province-building" was a large theme across Canada in that period.[85] In that vein, Ontario fought a long rear-guard battle to maintain its own medicare program, and instituted a supplementary seniors' pension stacked on the federal GIS. Secondly, OHC was one more vehicle to implement provincial policies in urban development. OHC joined the range of agencies (above) implementing a deep provincial involvement in this sphere.

Quebec and Other Provinces

In 1964, in the context of the Quiet Revolution, the Lesage Liberal government also moved toward the creation of a provincial housing corporation. Social housing was a minor priority within the nationalist agenda of social and urban policy and the building up of Quebec institutions. But with pressure from community groups and municipalities, and after several studies, an interdepartmental committee was formed in April 1964. Spring 1964 was precisely when the proposals for OHC were going to Ontario's cabinet and legislature and when the federal NHA amendments were passed. This committee recommended in April 1965 that a Quebec housing agency be created to enable the province to control the social housing relationships between municipalities or non-profit organizations and the federal government.[86]

The bill to create a Société d'habitation du Quebec was introduced in the 1965–66 session, but not passed before dissolution for the election of June 1966, which saw the Liberals defeated. But the momentum continued after the more conservative Union Nationale government took office; the same Paul Dozois who had championed public housing in 1950s Montreal was now the minister of municipal affairs. In 1967, a similar bill, although with less wide-ranging powers, was reintroduced and passed. The legislative debates at both dates were concerned less with the content of the Act than with the goal of ensuring that Quebec had the institutional capacity to operate in this sphere and to prevent direct relations between municipalities and the federal agency, CMHC. In-

forming this were the ideas of maximum Quebec autonomy and housing as a vehicle of social policy – the latter being necessarily a matter of
provincial jurisdiction. Lesage's minister of municipal affairs, Pierre La-
porte, stated that "it is essential that we retrieve our jurisdiction and that
we exercise this completely ... it is really a social field where we can normally have requirements that other provinces would not have."[87] The
Quebec agenda in social housing was not as much about low-income
housing or urban development needs as positioning this sphere as an element in the new Quebec social policy role, to steer the social future of
the Quebec nation.

Other provinces did not influence the federal decisions or the provincial housing corporation model that shaped the new policy regime.
None of them except Nova Scotia had a provincial housing corporation, and there is no evidence that in 1964 any of them were entertain-
ing the idea.

Public housing was not a priority for the conservative Social Credit
governments of Alberta or British Columbia. The latter was opposed in
principle to any large state role in housing, and strongly favoured leaving it to the market. At the provincial staff level, there was collaboration
with the City of Vancouver and CMHC in developing the few projects
initiated from the mid-1950s to the mid-1960s. But British Columbia
maintained a hands-off position, avoided any leadership, let municipalities take the initiative or not, and left half the 25 percent non-federal share of funding to municipal governments. Throughout the 1960s,
that province continued to use the pre-1964 public housing program,
with its lesser provincial role in funding and ownership. It did encourage seniors housing development by non-profit groups under the LD
program, providing a provincial capital grant for one-third of project
costs.[88] Likewise in Alberta, although the municipalities of Calgary and
Edmonton had initiated a few projects, the provincial role was one of
passive facilitation of federal-municipal initiatives.[89]

Among the smaller provinces only Saskatchewan, Manitoba, Nova
Scotia, and Newfoundland had any social housing activity to speak of,
and this arose mostly in federal-municipal initiatives. In Saskatchewan,
"The province has been extremely passive in housing matters, relying
heavily on CMHC and the results of direct federal-municipal negotiations,"[90] and this extended throughout the 1960s even after the 1964
amendments. "Manitoba ... built almost no public housing until the
close of the 1960s."[91] It had virtually no social housing staff and at the
same time discouraged federal-municipal collaboration. The Nova Sco-

tia Housing Commission dated from 1932, but its main focus had been assisted ownership,[92] and "The province maintained a low profile in public housing negotiations and continued instead to encourage direct federal-municipal planning."[93] The Halifax public housing projects of the 1949–64 period were undertaken by CMHC and the municipality, not the province. Newfoundland activity had quieted down since its active start in 1950, while New Brunswick, Prince Edward Island, and the territories were not in the picture.

Completing the Policy Turn: The Late 1960s

The lack of engagement outside Ontario and Quebec changed by the end of the decade. Ontario's program delivery model and rapid ramping-up of production became the template adopted across Canada over the five years that followed, entrenching the policy regime which the federal government with Ontario's help had invented at the mid-1960s turning point.

Once the 1964 NHA amendments were tabled, the federal minister responsible for CMHC, Nicholson, did a tour across Canada with a new deal on public housing to promote the idea and foster implementation. But Ontario was the main interested partner; Ontario's minister Randall thought the new federal funding proposal "was the greatest thing since sliced bread."[94] OHC became the model for implementing the new federal policy: "Mr Nicholson is depending upon Ontario to show the way for the rest of Canada ... CMHC are to use The Ontario Housing Corporation Act in their discussions with other Provincial governments as the ideal method of handling a progressive housing program."[95] Ontario's minister Randall addressed the inaugural OHC Board meeting: "the eyes of the Federal government are on Ontario which is the only province geared to implement the recent amendments to the National Housing Act."[96] CMHC seconded several staff for the OHC start-up in the fall of 1964.[97] CMHC and Ontario actively and jointly promoted the OHC model, notably at a February 1967 national housing conference in Toronto, hosted by Ontario.[98]

The latter 1960s and early 1970s saw a new, rising politics of housing in Canada. Ultimately this created an upheaval that burst apart the 1960s housing policy regime (chapter 4). But while these new politics were bubbling up in 1965 to 1968, they reinforced a provincial priority for public housing and urban renewal as the way to address housing issues that had moved from the political fringes into the political mainstream.

British Columbia and Alberta formed housing corporations in 1967, as did Manitoba, New Brunswick, and Newfoundland.[99] The imitation of the OHC model was quite direct. For centrist provincial governments, active federal exhortation, abundant federal funding, and the Ontario precedent made it an easy political and fiscal choice to create a housing corporation to develop new public housing and redevelop older areas through CMHC-funded urban renewal. It could serve a multi-prong agenda of replacing decrepit older neighbourhoods, meeting the needs of low-income renters including the elderly, helping meet rental demand amid phenomenal urban growth, and responding to municipal advocacy as well as real estate interests. Alberta Housing Corporation in 1967–70 became active in building housing, quickly embraced neighbourhood renewal, and carried out land-banking.[100] Its activity, under a conservative government, is emblematic of how public housing had become mainstream politics by the late 1960s.

Prevailing attitudes in Montreal and Quebec toward the state role in housing changed dramatically in the latter 1960s, as the Quiet Revolution gathered force and new managerialist attitude on urban issues took hold. The rising place of urban issues in the provincial Lesage Liberal government's agenda was reflected in the Commission Provincial d'Urbanisme it established in 1963 (La Haye report), along with other commissions on urban fiscal issues and Montreal inter-municipal issues.[101] In the 1960s, community groups advocating government action on urban issues came to have a strong nationalist outlook, and the union movement advocated sole provincial jurisdiction in housing.[102]

The City of Montreal moved into a more active role in housing in that period. Although Drapeau, a strong mayor with executive powers, opposed an active government role in housing, his political coalition included some strong supporters of such a role, notably Lucien Saulnier, president of city council's executive committee through that decade and later the first chairman of the Montreal Urban Community and a provincial official.[103] Increasing disrepair of housing in older neighbourhoods, and some abandonment of housing, prompted a push toward more active intervention. Montreal had lobbied in favour of creation of a provincial housing corporation. One price for Saulnier and others' political support for Drapeau's bid to hold Expo 67 was the mayor's support on the housing agenda.[104] In 1965, the city charter was amended to empower the municipality to adopt a housing standards code and to offer rehabilitation subsidies, leading to a purposeful carrot-and-stick approach to improving housing conditions.[105] In 1967, Montreal created a housing department (Service de l'habitation),[106] and in

1969 it created a municipal housing corporation, the Office municipal d'habitation de Montréal (OMHM).[107] From the outset of this new municipal housing role, rehabilitation of older housing and neighbourhoods was one of the three main priorities and activities. Although the other two priorities were public housing and urban renewal, there now started to emerge a policy practice against demolition, mega-projects, and displacement of residents.[108]

The 1960s also saw a top-down transformation of the Quebec co-op housing movement, effectively a takeover by provincial officials and activist professionals. The main purpose and priority of Quebec co-ops in the 1950s and 1960s had been producer co-ops for low-income home-ownership; people pooled resources to finance and build their own homes. Following this top-down transformation, and reflecting the rising prominence of urban issues and the social welfare agenda, the priority in the movement now shifted to social rental housing.[109]

Provincial political changes in Western Canada fed the new priority. In Manitoba, social housing was greatly boosted by the election of the Schreyer NDP government in 1969. Duff Roblin, the Red Tory premier of 1958–67, had replaced the former policy of leaving the non-federal 25 percent of costs entirely to municipalities, changing this to equal provincial and municipal 12.5 percent shares. The latter years of his term saw some public housing built and then the creation of Manitoba Housing Corporation in 1967. Schreyer now did away with the municipal share of costs.[110] His government brought "a deep concern for low-income housing that was translated into a sudden and rapid expansion in the public housing program."[111] It undertook major public land assemblies in the Winnipeg area, and by 1975 Manitoba Housing had 4,900 units for families and 5,700 for seniors.

British Columbia's Barrett NDP government of 1972–75 likewise gave social housing a new priority. Although its term of office coincides with the big national policy shifts to non-profit housing (chapter 4), this government relied mostly on the 1960s housing program. While it pushed non-profit and co-op production slightly above the prior 2,200 annual level, its big thrust was the production of 4,300 public housing units in 1974–76, doubling that portfolio. It even purchased a construction company to help it rapidly establish expertise and scale.[112] It initiated a major study to prepare a framework for British Columbia policy, just as Ontario and Quebec were doing. When the Social Credit party returned to power in 1975, this policy priority and the related production activity were sharply curtailed.

SOCIAL HOUSING IN THE PUBLIC HOUSING ERA, 1965-73

Public housing in the 1965–73 period was developed with its capital costs fully debt-financed – 90 percent by CMHC using public funds, and 10 percent by the province or its housing corporation, the latter typically through debentures issued for the purpose.[113] Operating subsidies covered the difference between the sum of amortization and approved operating costs, less rent revenues, and were shared 50/50 by CMHC and the provincial housing corporation (or other sponsor). In some cases, notably Saskatchewan and briefly British Columbia, the province continued using the 1949–64 program. Virtually all rents were geared to income (RGI). Charitable and municipal LD projects also continued to be developed in small numbers, with essentially the same CMHC mortgage financing arrangements as in 1949–63.

Institutional Capacity

Central in the 1964–73 program model was institutional capacity in the form of CMHC financing and autonomous, well-resourced provincial crown corporations. It is virtually impossible to imagine municipal entities in Canada undertaking programs of such scale in the face of competing budgetary priorities, and soon in the face of neighbourhood opposition. Within CMHC and its local branch offices across the country, the loan and project approvals for public housing production became a significant part of program activity, even though a distant second to home-owner mortgage insurance. Provincially, OHC was the model. It started with a $60 million capital program in 1965, of which the provincial cost share was $6 million ($450 and $45 million in 2015 dollars). It envisaged a three-year program of $150 million and 12,000 units, two-thirds family units and one-third seniors units[114] – enough to double the province's social housing sector. OHC was launched rapidly on the platform of the two main institutions of the 1949–64 regime, absorbing the staff of the MTHA and the provincial government's Housing Branch. OHC also absorbed corporately and in its portfolio the former local housing authorities across the province.[115]

OHC ostensibly acted only at the request of municipalities. Without delay, OHC and CMHC conducted a roadshow for municipalities in fall-winter 1964–65, with glossy pamphlets and speeches by the federal and provincial ministers, the CMHC president, and others.[116] Municipal response was rapid and large, with 100 municipal requests for 7,315 units by February 1965.[117] Once such requests were made, OHC did its planning in-house and then brought forward specific proposals to the municipal council, at a fairly advanced stage of planning.[118] Ontario also made the model financially more attractive to municipalities. Although it soon decided to maintain the 7½ percent municipal share of operating subsidy, there was no capital requirement,[119] so municipalities could pursue their housing and urban renewal goals at minimal cost. The burdens of project coordination and neighbourhood opposition were taken out of local hands. Public housing was now a more attractive property tax proposition than before, and not a tax-exempt category as was common in the United States.[120] Most provinces in 1965–70 followed Ontario down the path of reducing the share of costs borne by municipalities.

Piggy-Backing on Private-Rental Development

The peak years of Canadian public housing production from 1965 to 1974 converged precisely with the peak of the much larger development boom in private-rental apartments, and the public housing strategy was to piggy-back on this. In Ontario, the initial discussions at the OHC board were of four modes of development: "builder proposals,"[121] purchase of recently built housing, direct construction by OHC, and purchase and rehabilitation of older housing.[122] The first two modes quickly took over. Initially, from early 1965 through mid-1966 OHC purchased a great deal of existing housing, often new apartments and townhouse complexes not yet fully rented. Secondly it ramped up a large production program by way of builder proposals. These served the objectives of rapid development as well as social integration. CMHC was concerned about spending part of its capital in ways that created no new housing, but reluctantly acceded to the purchase program.[123]

The mid-1960s proved to be a sweet market context for this development program. Not only was it near the peak of the postwar apartment boom, it was also a favourable transitional moment in the Canadian housing financing regime. Rising housing production required huge volumes of capital, but this was constrained by the NHA's limits on interest rates and prohibition on banks doing mortgage lending other than for NHA-insured loans. In 1966 this was resolved by deregulating interest rates and permitting non-NHA bank lending, and by large developers' ability to tap the new global corporate bond market that was emerging.[124] But meanwhile, in 1965–66, the OHC turnkeys were a large source of cash flow for developers, reducing their financing needs.[125] Moreover, by 1968–69, developers knew that the boom was peaking, so sales to OHC were a way to "move" some sites.[126] Builder proposals were used in urban areas with active private-sector apartment development – above all in Metro Toronto, but in cities across the country where rental developers were active: Hamilton, Ottawa, Calgary, and elsewhere.[127] OHC was careful to pursue good relations and collaboration with the private sector. Its managing director met with officials of the Homebuilders Association in the summer of 1964 and found a positive response to the acquisition plans. The Toronto Real Estate Board seconded an appraiser to OHC in its start-up period. A highly favourable article appeared in the December 1965 issue of the sector magazine, *Canadian Builder*. This collaboration soon faded but it got the heyday of Canadian public housing off to a good start. [128]

The Social Integration Agenda

Piggy-backing social housing on the private-rental boom also served a social integration agenda. From the outset, the explicit strategy was to scatter and integrate public housing as part of private-rental production.[129] In the context of 1960s Canada where rental apartment buildings were one-third of all housing production, and one-half in the big cities, this was not as strange as it sounds today. It was not a case of putting up rental buildings whose denser built form immediately labelled them as low-income housing, as in the United States; the closer parallel for Toronto or Montreal (which accounted for one-third of Canada's postwar growth) was Northwestern Europe in that period. In Toronto's postwar suburbs, the typical public housing tower sits in a cluster of such buildings, two-thirds of them being private rental. OHC articulated the integration objective at the 1965 federal-provincial Poverty and Opportunity Conference, promoting its approach while also citing the latest US thinking:

> A dispersal of public housing units into an integrated community is a conscious attempt at avoiding the "ghetto" complex which has plagued large scale projects in the past. By the builder proposal technique and purchase scheme now employed by Ontario Housing Corporation there is the very real possibility that "low-priced housing and heterogeneous scattering (of inhabitants) can be fully achieved" ... By purchasing and developing on scattered locations ... tenants would enjoy a high degree of anonymity and would not have to bear the stigma normally associated with public housing ... It is now widely believed that large public housing projects should

be abandoned and that most future ones should be of small enough size to fit easily into the existing structure of neighbour-hoods in order to reduce the differentiation which exists between public housing projects and contiguous private residential develop-ments [this] should also help the families which occupy them to become accepted by the surrounding community more quickly.[130]

This rationale was partly truth, partly rationalization, and partly expe-dience in development. Builder proposals were also a way to avoid community opposition, since such projects would already have mu-nicipal planning approvals. "Public housing units will no longer be readily identifiable as they will be scattered throughout the Munici-pality."[131] This regime did indeed achieve integration into private-rental apartment development, and thereby achieved integration into the overall geography of Canada's big-city postwar suburbs – unlike the US case. All through this period there was concern, study, and de-bate about the desirability of high-rises for families,[132] but that form of social housing was propelled by cost-savings and the momentum of the apartment boom.

Several things caused long-term failure in this integration agenda. Public housing agencies soon shifted to the US model where 100 per-cent of public housing units were low-income targeted with RGI. They did away with the pre-1964 mix of cost-recovery units at fixed below-market rent[133] redolent of UK or French or Australian social housing of that era. But broader historical forces more profoundly undermined social integration. After the private-rental production regime collapsed in the 1970s, very little rental was built in the newer suburbs, the hous-ing system offered few options for low-income renters outside these postwar apartment neighbourhoods, and by 1990s far fewer middle-income people rented. And so by the closing years of the century, low and moderate-income renters crowded into these neighbourhoods which thereby became places of deepening poverty and stigmatiza-tion, their social housing and private rental little differentiated in the public mind.

Metropolitan Agendas

In the latter 1960s, metropolitan institutions and boundaries became significant in Canadian social housing: it was increasingly a matter for the whole urban area, not just the central city. Most provinces restruc-tured municipal governments. Toronto's Metro government dated from

1954 and had been the main municipal partner in public housing from then to 1964, and this "Metro" spatial frame of activity was transferred to OHC when the latter was formed. Edmonton and Calgary were unitary municipalities covering the whole urban area. In 1967, British Columbia created the Greater Vancouver Regional District and transferred to it the City of Vancouver role in co-ordinating and developing social housing;[134] by 1974 there was a Metro Vancouver Housing Corporation. In 1969, Quebec created the Communauté urbaine de Montréal (CUM) and the Communauté urbaine de Québec;[135] Ontario created the Regional Municipality of Ottawa-Carleton; and Manitoba initiated the "unicity" amalgamation of Winnipeg, implemented in 1972. Thus Canada's eight largest cities all now had either metropolitan or unitary governments. In Ontario, Quebec, British Columbia, and Manitoba, this was an integral part of a policy agenda of strategic provincial management of urban growth and systems thinking on urban issues,[136] in which provincial housing corporations played a part.

Although responsibility for social housing was now provincial, these urban boundaries became a significant spatial frame of reference. While much social housing continued to be built in central cities, social housing apartments adjacent to suburban middle-class streets became common in most of the larger cities.[137] This contrasts with the main public housing development model then in the United States, which was central-city slum redevelopment, and that in Australia, which was entire low-density neighbourhoods on the urban periphery. Thus Canada in 1965–70 departed not only from the federal dominance, municipal delivery, and small output of US public housing, it also departed the "central-city only" geography that, although inspired by social welfare goals, reinforced the concentrations of racialized poverty.[138]

Production Volumes

Pre-1964 social housing production[139] had averaged 900 dwelling units annually in Ontario and 800 annually in the rest of Canada. In 1965–68, Ontario production rose rapidly to over 7,000 units (averaging 4,900 in the period) while the rest of Canada had a fairly steady 3,000 to 4,000. Ontario then sustained about 10,000 units annually through 1969–71, while the rest of Canada matched that by 1969 and reached 15,000 by 1970. In Quebec, production rose from under 800 dwellings in 1969 to an annual average of 3,000 in 1970 through 1974.[140] From the viewpoint of alarmed federal officials at the end of the decade, Ontario had taken most of the funding[141] and escalating nationwide pro-

Figure 3.3   Annual social housing commitments: Ontario and other provinces, 1951–78. After 1964, production rose rapidly to over 20,000 a year. Other provinces exceeded Ontario by 1970.

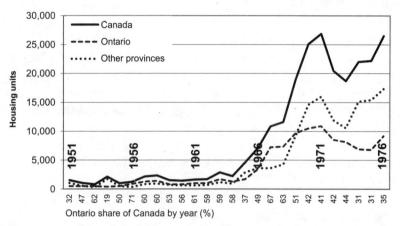

Ontario share of Canada by year (%)

Source: CMHC, *Canadian Housing Statistics*; *Housing in Canada*.

duction was out of control. In the historical long view, other provinces were following Ontario with three to five years' lag, in a nationwide shift to construction volumes at the low end of the normal range for an affluent society. The production levels reached in Ontario in 1967–68 and elsewhere in 1969–70 would be sustained, with a few ups and downs, for the two decades from 1972 to 1992.

Production averaged 12,000 to 13,000 units a year whether measured over 1965–73 or 1965–78. Including the small volumes of non-profit and co-op housing, total 1964–73 social housing production averaged 16,000 units annually. Ultimately, 115,000 public housing dwellings were built from 1965 to 1973, and another 56,000 to 1979. Ontario accounts for about 80,000 of these, including the 45,000 units in Greater Toronto that comprise over one-fifth of the national total. These large shares reflect Ontario's policy priorities then, but also mirror Toronto's share of national population and postwar growth. In the five short years ending in 1970, Toronto virtually caught up with Sydney or New York in public housing per capita – far higher than any other North American urban area. With the pre-1964 units and a few related programs, Canada's all-low-income "public-housing" stock totals 205,000 dwellings.[142] The product of this decade or so of intensive and little-loved development still provides today, half a century later, close to half of all RGI units nationally and in most provinces.

Opposition and Momentum

Large-scale public housing development and lack of community consultation caused great controversy by 1967–69. There were big and recurring protests in Toronto, and some in Montreal, notably about the
Milton Park redevelopment proposal.[143] Opposition exploded into a national discourse through coverage in the Toronto-based national English-
language media, and through the federal 1969 Task Force on Housing
and Urban Development, leading ultimately to the early 1970s turning
point discussed in chapter 4. But through the 1960s the dominant note
is the sheer momentum of the provincial housing corporation model.
No province ever directed a stop to public housing development, despite
the emerging storm of controversy, and neither did the Metro Toronto
government, which was at the centre of such controversies. The reasons
lie in institutional momentum, attitudes about social housing as social
welfare, a paternalist view of local opposition, and the place of public
housing in a broader housing agenda.

Local opposition inevitably arises to development of family social
housing. In the 1960s in Toronto, it took a couple of years for this to in-
tensify and to crystallize into political pressure, and meanwhile OHC
continued with production. Although the controversy in the press must
surely have concerned the Ontario cabinet, there were few direct com-
plaints to them from interest groups or constituents.[144] The Ontario
and Metro Toronto governments tried to ignore the protests, to ride
them out.[145] For the minister, Randall, and senior housing officials at
OHC and Metro Toronto, local opposition to social housing development was simply to be expected, and was no reason to pull back. They
had a strong a system-manager culture, and a paternalist attitude toward
local opinion. Randall, a conservative championing and overseeing
Canada's largest-ever government housing development program, considered himself to be under attack by "agitators," including "socialists."[146]

The welfare state consensus was fairly strong, and public housing was
how low-income housing needs were being met. As controversy escalated, Metro Toronto Council, dominated by moderate suburban conservatives, never rescinded or even reduced its request to OHC to build
4,500 units a year – more new units than federal-provincial programs
fund across Canada today. When later asked why he did not withdraw
support from OHC in this period, Ontario's Premier Robarts said, "Well,
sometimes you have to do what's right."[147] It was also recognized that
one subtext of suburban anti-OHC sentiment was class prejudice and

the emerging presence of tenants of non-European ethno-racial background following the immigration reforms of the late 1960s.[148]

Public housing was part of a broader housing agenda including student housing, seniors housing, and affordable ownership. Cabinet support in Ontario was sustained partly by OHC's role delivering assisted home-ownership programs. The centrepiece of this was the Home Ownership Made Easy (HOME) program of 1967 onward which assisted 24,500 buyer households with favourable terms.[149] OHC also supported affordable ownership via the embryonic condominium sector, providing mortgages at a time when mainstream lending institutions lacked confidence in this newfangled tenure. In 1969 through 1971, OHC financed an annual average of 16,400 housing starts: 35 percent family public housing, 18 percent seniors, 10 percent student housing, 24 percent condominiums, and 13 percent HOME lots.[150] The annual reports of the period convey a message of an active government meeting lower-income needs with public housing, and middle-class buyer needs with HOME lots and condominiums, in a context of shortages and escalating prices. Public housing construction contracts also sustained activity in the 1970–71 downturn for firms that were important donors to the governing party.[151] Such multi-prong activity serving a range of constituencies helped maintain support for public housing development serving the poor.[152]

The technocratic, centralized regime was the means to high output of public housing, but soon became the reason for its downfall. Embedded in well-resourced provincial corporations, this machine took several years to halt. Meanwhile, events federally would provide a channel for local opposition to public housing – a route not opening provincially – and create the early 1970s turning point.

4

The 1970s:
Baby-Boomers and Neighbourhoods

When "The Sixties" happened in the latter 1960s and early 1970s, it reverberated all across society and political life.[1] Globally and in Canada, housing and urban issues were one of the main flashpoints in youth protests, new activism, and political upheaval.[2] In Canada, social housing became part of intense, mainstream political concerns and debates about housing production, housing costs, and urban change. Opposition to public housing development converged with a new type of urban politics to create a fluid and uncertain policy direction.

But unlike the US case, protests against public housing did not undermine the priority for social housing in Canada. The issue was how – not whether – to foster a substantial social housing sector and active government role. Where the mid-1960s policy shift had transformed the scale of activity, the early 1970s policy shift transformed the program model. This sustained Canada's priority for social housing – ultimately for two decades – despite large changes in the economy and political life.

The five years from 1968 to 1973 saw a high-profile federal political task force, an experimental program, a major policy review, and amendments to the National Housing Act (NHA). The approach shifted away from government agencies developing, owning, and operating large public housing projects entirely for low-income families or seniors. In the new approach, community-based organizations owned and operated non-profit or co-operative housing projects that had a mix of regular tenants paying market rent, and low-income tenants with RGI. Accompanying this was a new priority for housing repair and neighbourhood renewal. Through the mid-1970s, the old and new models expanded in tandem. Then at the end of the decade "public housing" projects virtually ceased to be built, and non-profit and co-op became the standard Canadian approach to social housing.

This shift of the early 1970s was led by federal policy, interrupting the strong trend toward a stronger provincial role. But this became a period of expanding social housing activity at both the federal and provincial levels. And it was a period of expanding government roles in all housing sectors, including land development, assistance to home-ownership, and subsidies to private rental. Social housing was one element of this and rode on this tide.

This was enabled by unprecedented prosperity, ample fiscal resources, and high political expectations. Yet it was also propelled by economic strains in the postwar economic model, and a housing market that was experiencing strong pressures of growth and rising prices, and no longer working as well for the social mainstream. The range of political voices, claims, and interests had exploded. It was no longer a small circle of experts as in the early postwar years or the mid-1960s, but now a large constituency of local activists, tenant organizations, social advocacy groups, and local elected officials who were raising concerns. They pushed forward ideas that sympathetic public servants fed to a government looking for ways to respond to this tumult.

This early-1970s shift was a large one, creating a culture and a movement that endured for a generation among people involved in social housing, urban politics, and social advocacy. The decade between this 1970s turning point and that of the mid-1980s was the central, peak decade of Canadian social housing expansion. It remains for many people the best model, the quintessentially Canadian success story in social housing.

POLITICAL AND ECONOMIC CONTEXT: STRAINS AND CLAIMS

Two economic realities of the 1970s underlay the Canadian housing policy shifts in that decade. The first was positive: Canada continued to have high economic growth through the early and middle years of the decade. Its good fortune as an oil producer contrasted with the severe impact the 1973–74 oil crisis and the ensuing recession had on the economic performance of its oil-importing peers, the United States, Australia, and Western Europe. Canada in the 1970s had continuing modest growth in manufacturing jobs and output, with little of the deindustrialization starting then across much of the affluent West.

Secondly there was great economic turbulence and slowing growth as the 1970s progressed. It was the end of the historically extraordinary postwar growth, the *trente glorieuses* or "long boom." Inflation now rose steadily, propelling ever-higher mortgage interest rates: 9½ percent (for five-year terms) by 1973, and 14 percent by 1980.[3] The stock market crash and bond market collapse, and a long slide in real estate prices after the 1973 peak, meant a "lost decade" for investors. The end of fixed exchange rates and the new Eurodollar bond market moved finance into a less regulated global space. Then came the oil price hike by OPEC in 1973, and the ensuing 1974–75 recession. The latter 1970s were a period of "stagflation" with high inflation but slow growth. In 1979 came the Iranian revolution, the second oil price shock, the resultant inflation spike, and then the US decision to hike interest rates to unprecedented levels to counter inflation, bringing on the sharp recession of 1981–82. Canadian mortgage rates peaked at over 18 percent through sixteen months in 1981–82.[4] All this undermined what had once seemed certainties of postwar macroeconomic management.

This turbulent economy affected everything. The fiscal consequences in slower revenue growth and much higher debt service costs were soon felt in all policy spheres. The postwar political consensus about the welfare state broke apart, with criticism from both the Left and the Right. Expenditure constraint and limits to public borrowing were soon not just pragmatic responses, but central in the new neoliberal ideas that challenged the postwar Keynesian consensus and sought to end the expansion of the state. Prime Minister Trudeau's 1972–74 Liberal minority government "increased spending for eighteen months under the influence of the NDP, while his Department of Finance was rejecting Keynes."[5] The economic changes came on the heels of the large expansion of welfare state programs in the 1960s and early 1970s, a combination propelling chronic fiscal deficits in Canada and in most Western nations. Trudeau arrived back from a 1978 summit in Europe with a new agenda of "restraint" of public spending and public borrowing. As in other nations, this now became a large policy theme.

The 1968–73 period which transformed social housing policy preceded most of this turbulent decade. Despite a mild economic downturn in 1970, there were strong growth and rising fiscal resources. This was a time of rising expectations. The liberal social attitudes and demands of the baby-boomers challenged established norms, while popular movements and the New Left challenged the values, consensus, and power structure of the postwar order.

There was rising concern about poverty, a concern which in retrospect rested on the contrast between the new general affluence and the same old conditions of life for the poor. This was a common theme in political discourse and was reflected in reports such as that of a 1968 Senate Special Committee on Poverty, the 1968 annual report of the Economic

Figure 4.1   Growth rate of real GDP per capita, 1950–2000. Strong growth in the 1960s–70s supported rising social spending, and the early 1990s recession helped reverse that.

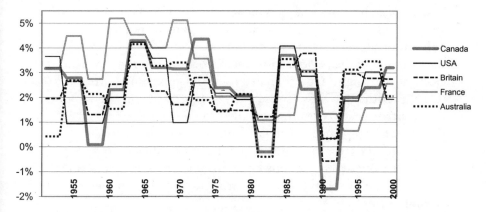

Source: Maddison GDP data series, constant 1990 dollars.
Average annual growth rate by three-year period calculated from that source.

Council of Canada, and in political speeches. Inflation pushed toward a stronger state role in the economy, culminating in wage and price controls in 1974. The state role was reinforced by new ideas about the need to manage the complex systems of modern society.[6]

Canada experienced fundamental federal-provincial conflicts, driven on the provincial side by three factors: expanding social programs and the rising provincial role in these; Quebec nationalism, with the Parti Québécois in power from 1976 to 1985; and "Western Alienation." The latter reflected partly the rising western share of national population and the Liberal government's weak western vote, and it involved the conflicting interests of oil-producing and oil-consuming regions. This manifested first amid rising oil prices and surging Alberta royalties in the 1970s, and then amid the global oil-sector downturn (and National Energy Program) of the early 1980s. The 1970s saw a growing consensus on decentralization of Canadian federalism. Although the Trudeau Liberal government was a champion of federal authority, from about 1977 onwards it accommodated demands for greater provincial power. Block funding for social programs under the Established Programs Financing Act institutionalized this, with recognition of mature provincial capacity in policy spheres such as health and education.[7]

Politics in key provinces supported the expanding 1970s government role and the priority for social housing. The neoliberal critique of the postwar welfare state and the politics of fiscal constraint did not have much impact provincially in this decade. There was a political consensus on the need for a managed housing system and a government role in social housing, with a sympathetic attitude toward non-profit and co-op groups. In Ontario, the overall tone of politics changed only moderately from the 1960s, but the politics of rental housing were intense in the period, and a major focus in the 1975 provincial election campaign.[8] Ontario had a minority government from 1975 to 1981, with the Davis Conservatives dependent on the NDP, so that centrist pragmatism outweighed the few neoliberal voices in the government caucus. NDP governments were in office in Manitoba from 1969 to 1977 and in British Columbia in 1972–1975. The Parti Québécois, in power from 1976 to 1985, was social-democratic in its social policy and strongly supportive of public and co-op housing.

HOUSING AND URBAN CONTEXT: TURBULENCE, PRICES, AND RENTERS

In housing and urban development, the 1970s sits in a "long decade" extending from the end of the 1960s to the very early 1980s, a more complex and volatile time than any other in the past 70 years. As many households were added each year as are added annually to a much larger existing base in Canada in the 2010s, and this rapid growth created housing market pressures and neighbourhood change that erupted into political life. There were four distinct sub-periods, including a great real estate boom in the late 1960s and early 1970s; a downturn in the mid-1970s; stagflation in the late 1970s along with volatile prices and production issues; and a real estate crash in the severe 1981–82 recession. The general themes were rising inflation and interest rates; strong household income growth and rising consumption; and very strong rental demand. Three new realities in the housing market were gentrification, the arrival in Canada of condominium tenure and condo production, and the collapse of Canada's distinctive postwar private-rental production regime. All this fuelled an expanding government role, and directly shaped housing policy decisions.

The 1968–73 global property boom was one culmination of the postwar economic expansion,[9] and it manifested in Canada in escalating house prices and peaking apartment production. The distinctive Canadian rental development regime went into overdrive, building an average of 104,000 new units annually from 1966 through 1974. But net

Figure 4.2   Home-buyer affordability: Carrying cost of average 25-year mortgage (5-year term, 10% down) for average Toronto resale home. The government role in housing was strong when affordability was a mainstream issue – both fading away in the 1990s.

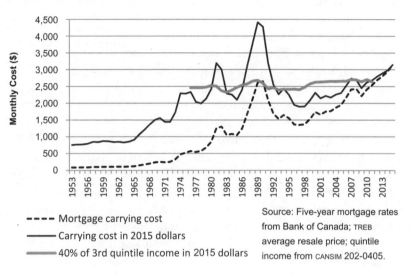

- - - - Mortgage carrying cost

——— Carrying cost in 2015 dollars

▬▬▬ 40% of 3rd quintile income in 2015 dollars

Source: Five-year mortgage rates from Bank of Canada; TREB average resale price; quintile income from CANSIM 202-0405.

demand – the number of renter households added each year – was almost as strong.[10]

In the owner sector, sharp price increases propelled strong mainstream political concern about affordability in the latter 1960s and early 1970s. For example, in the Toronto market which comprised one-fifth of Canadian housing production and households, resale prices in real (inflation-adjusted) dollars rose 90 percent in ten years.[11] Mortgage interest rates were rising too, driven by rising inflation. The carrying cost (principal and interest in 2015 dollars) of an average Toronto resale house at five-year mortgage rates rose from $1,100 to $2,300 between 1966 and 1976, then peaked at $3,200 at the point of highest interest rates in 1981.[12] Similar trends were seen in Vancouver. By comparison, the boom of 2001 to 2015 raised carrying costs in Toronto from $2,100 to $3,100 (in 2015 dollars).

In the stagflation of the latter 1970s, house prices subsided in real-dollar (inflation-adjusted) terms but as nominal prices rose along with interest rates, the strong prevailing sense was that affordability was worsening.[13] A sharp 1980–81 price hike of about 50 percent preceded the recession. Prices crashed in 1981–82, but rising interest rates made home purchase more expensive than in living memory. The escalating costs and severe volatility fed a sense that the housing market was not working well, and that government should intervene.

Market rental production was undermined by converging factors. On the supply side were rising mortgage interest rates, along with rising land and labour costs. On the demand side, middle-income demand sagged as an ever-larger share of renters were small households with small incomes. Rents could no longer profitably cover the carrying costs of new production. For investors in rental development, the combination of high interest rates and general uncertainty made returns very uncertain. Tax reform in 1972 and rent control in 1974 served as further deterrents to investors.[14] The peak interest rates of 1981–82 made rental development entirely non-viable, let alone profitable. At the same time, high rental demand was sustained by the cost barrier to home-buying and the entry of the baby-boomers into the housing market. The peak of the Canadian baby boom was the late 1950s, with most baby-boomers entering the housing market in their early 20s between 1975 and 1985. Market rental had been one-third of housing production in rapidly growing Canada for two decades since the mid-1950s, and the collapse of that postwar regime was a crisis in the housing market. This was a very different time from today: condominiums were then a new thing and a very small sector, whereas rental development and rental prices were large mainstream concerns. In the 1970s, with high rental demand but collapsing viability of market production, the question of how to encourage rental production became a significant political concern and policy priority. The shifting economics of rental production also dictated new social housing funding models, as we will see.

By the early 1970s, low-rent supply tightened in central-city areas of Toronto and Vancouver. In the 1950s and 1960s, rapid suburban expansion had freed up much older housing stock in inner neighbourhoods for lower-income renters. Now gentrification started, as downtown employment surged in big cities around the world.[15] As Toronto overtook Montreal as Canada's main financial and head-office centre, provincial government jobs expanded, and commuting distances lengthened, more middle-class young professionals chose the lively central city over the suburbs. This new middle-income demand for central-city houses led to large losses of low-rent flats and rooms through "deconversion," with further losses arising from tighter regulations on rooming houses. The mid-1970s also saw loss of many rental units through conversion of apartment buildings to condominiums. By the early 1980s, concern about loss of low-rent stock became a dominant theme in social housing discourse in Toronto, nudging aside the former city-building discourse.[16] Vancouver experienced similar housing trends and housing politics as the urban area reached one million people by 1971, youth flocked to the Left Coast, and employment shifted from lumber mills, salmon canning, and varied manufacturing to office jobs. Intense controversies arose over apartment redevelopment in the West End.[17]

Housing emerged as a big urban and neighbourhood issue in Montreal in this period for different reasons. Its housing market softened as the Anglo elite moved head offices to Toronto under the separatist threat, and growth sagged. Chapter 3 noted the city's large stock of old 1880–1930 rental housing experiencing low demand amid the surrounding affluence and expanding suburbs, and by the 1970s the East End and Southwest/Lachine areas experienced high vacancies and much disrepair. The well-being of Montreal, centre of Quebec's culture and economy and the number-two city of global *francophonie*, was a large concern of the Quebec government. Moreover, the working-class residents of older big-city neighbourhoods were a core political constituency of the provincial governing party – rather different from the situation in declining US inner cities. The city and provincial governments promoted social housing, especially co-ops, as a way to reinvest in these older neighbourhoods, improve conditions of life for their residents, and sustain the city's physical and social health.

Winnipeg was a bastion of housing activism. Its growth declined in the 1970s as Calgary and Edmonton grew rapidly in the resource boom and passed it in population. Winnipeg had little to offset severe loss of jobs in manufacturing, especially in its large clothing sector. The era of large Aboriginal migration from the reserves was also arriving. With slack demand and declining low-end incomes on one side of the social spectrum, and expanding suburbia on the other, the old working class North End neighbourhoods declined in income and housing quality. Under the Red Tory government of Roblin (premier 1958–67) and the NDP government of Schreyer (1969–77), Manitoba took a strong interest in Winnipeg's well-being and the urban challenges it faced, and social housing became part of the policy response.

Social housing rode on the back of these broader Canadian politics of housing in which a stronger government role enjoyed mainstream political support through the 1970s.

IDEAS: THE GRASSROOTS AND THE SYSTEM

The late 1960s and early 1970s were a time of challenges and competing new ideas about housing that pushed policy in new directions. Interacting with housing market conditions, this fuelled a Canadian public discourse on housing issues policy unmatched in vigour and contentiousness before or since. As the decade progressed, however, there was increasing disillusionment about social housing, as there was about public affairs generally.

Housing discourse in 1968–73 was shaped by the expanding welfare state and rising expectations, preceding the economic turbulence. A national housing conference in October 1968 can serve as an emblem of the time. It was initiated by the Canadian Welfare Council, the leading advocacy body on social welfare issues, in a collaboration of the main federal and Ontario social housing agencies – Central Mortgage and Housing Corporation and Ontario Housing Corporation – and the broad-based Community Planning Association of Canada. Organized, politically mobilized low-income tenants participated. This was the moment in Canada when the idea of a right to housing came into the media and the mainstream. These sentiments were incorporated into Liberal Party resolutions at a 1970 policy conference.[18]

Housing policy discourse was informed explicitly by international ideas about urban policy and welfare state expansion. Ideas from comparative policy theory were familiar to key actors in the policy debates and advocacy. The landmark Dennis and Fish report that changed federal housing policy (see below) opened its chapter on "housing and the institutions of government" by citing the then influential housing policy theory of David Donnison of the London School of Economics in its social-welfarist heyday. He and they characterized Canada unfavourably as being of a regime type where the policy emphasis was to foster the market, a backward stage of policy evolution. Donnison wrote "Background Paper no. 1" for the 1968 Canadian Conference on Housing.[19] Social welfare advocacy bodies were very engaged in housing advocacy and research.

Canada's politics of urban and housing issues were also influenced by the urban crisis in the United States, characterized by white flight, the race riots of 1965–68, and inner-city decline which was then a new and alarming rather than a chronic thing. The spectre of the hollowed-out US big city loomed large, and – though it may be hard to imagine today – the priorities of the City of Toronto's reform councils of 1972 onward were informed by trends of population loss and fears of a downtown empty and dangerous after business hours.[20]

Gentrification involved a new set of ideas, not just a housing market trend. It was understood at the time as a back-to-the-city movement and as a cultural shift – an element of the reaction on the part of younger, alternative people to the conformist and culturally bland postwar suburbs. Along with London, New York, Sydney, and San Francisco, Toronto was among the Anglo-sphere cities where this new urban discourse about neighbourhood, housing, and community was most prominent.[21] Importantly, this discourse was not just among young radicals or community activists, exemplified by Toronto's John Sewell. It melded in significant degree with a more familiar Red Tory civic politics, exemplified by that city's Mayor Crombie or William Kilbourn, or the urban reform liberalism of Vancouver's Mayor Art Phillips. Housing issues became central in urban politics, and program decisions that today would go under the political radar were reported to municipal committees and were debated and scrutinized in the media.

Housing politics in this period were full of a "discourse of rental supply": concern about the need to develop enough apartments to meet rental needs including overall net (incremental) demand, low-income needs, and young baby-boomer households. This is evident, for example, in Toronto's Core Area Housing Study and Ontario advocacy more generally.[22] By comparison, such discourse was largely absent in this period in Australia and appears only weakly in the United States.[23] Its roots in Canada included the much higher net rental demand than in those peer countries, the large middle-class renter vote, and the long-standing premises of federal policy-makers that assisted ownership was not a good option for low-income households. It rested too on a recognition by middle-class voters and indeed policy-makers that renters were their neighbours and their children, and not a class apart.[24]

A new discourse on preservation of neighbourhoods replaced the postwar emphasis on growth and production. Apartment development and public housing development were interrelated flashpoints in this. The development industry became the focus of a considered critique, on a spectrum from reformist to radical. This included a discourse about urban land and about how development created profits and ultimately raised the price of housing. Such issues and the related development industry structure were a main focus of the Spurr report on Land and Urban Development,[25] commissioned by CMHC and then published against its wishes. All this was mirrored in academic Marxist work of the period, in which some Toronto scholars were prominent.[26] Land became an area of reformist housing policy for Ontario and the City of Toronto (below).

A new citizen activism challenged the top-down institutions of the postwar "manager-state" such as public housing corporations, and baby-boom youth challenged the established power structures. They asserted the democratic against the technocratic, local interests against the logic of impersonal big systems and state institutions, and they championed grassroots and neighbourhood initiatives. "There is a growing disillusionment in Canada with the way decisions are made. There is a lack of trust in government, a sterility in the debate of the experts, and a distinct feeling that too many people are left out of those decisions that affect them."[27] This created a divided, contentious climate, and it altered mainstream political life. Young people responded to Trudeau's call in 1968 for "participatory democracy" and to the readiness of his minister Hellyer (below) to hear from people directly and sideline housing experts. The shift to community-based housing in 1973 corresponded to this new climate.[28] Housing issues were positioned as local neighbourhood issues, and programs were positioned as resources for local communities to address their needs.

The critique of public housing and the shift to non-profit housing was carried by a younger generation challenging an older one.[29] The old guard had grown up in a much less affluent Canada before World War II, championed social housing in the early postwar, and were in their mature career years by the 1960s. The activists had grown up in postwar affluence. Many of those who created the co-op housing movement in this period had become involved first in campus housing, with a student energy and attitude that "we can take control of institutions and do things."[30] The Ontario Habitat Foundation was staffed by such young people, and several later became leading housing policy-makers and public servants in the 1970s to 1990s. At least two of this background staffed the Dennis and Fish task force.[31] "Long-time reformers like Humphrey Carver were understandably dismayed to find that, because of the failures of urban renewal, [the] profit-motivated real estate developers, supporters of public housing, and CMHC all came to be lumped together in the public's mind as related parts of a sinister, self-serving establishment."[32] For Albert Rose, the landmark 1972 Dennis and Fish report was "the most comprehensive analysis of the housing problem" since 1940s reconstruction ideas, and yet it ignored prior battles, policy conundrums, and nuance, and savaged all social scientists, politicians, and the public for market-minded neglect of low-income housing.[33]

Yet there was a political consensus about mixed urban development, with an active government role in managing market conditions and growth, and ample production of both social housing and market rental development as part of this. These entrenched, normalized premises come through strongly in the documents of the period. The influence of systems thinking in urban and housing issues is also strong in the prominent reports of Harvey Lithwick and Eli Comay (below). Mixed-income social housing was understood as integral in mixed neighbourhoods.[34] The ideas of management of urban systems, and of bottom-up, community-based control, were in considerable tension with each other as well as with longer-established norms of the liberal-welfare state. But in the early 1970s they carried the day in social housing policy.

This 1968–73 climate endured for a couple of decades within the social housing sector, but faded within five years as a dominant note in federal policy. The politics of constraint arose, along with neoliberal ideas of a reduced state role and reliance on markets. Social housing was part of expanding public spending now being challenged; the rising expenditure trend increasingly concerned finance departments and treasury boards.[35] Neoliberal ideas were reflected in the latter 1970s in a campaign of the Urban Development Institute of Ontario (the developer sector) against social housing, and in federal Conservative positions in the 1979 federal election campaign. By 1980 it was evident to clear-eyed advocates such as Rose that the "vast housing program will be under severe financial and philosophical examination in successive fiscal years ... The government in power clearly wishes to restrain all public spending; there will be no exception for the field of housing ... The general public believes that government has gone about as far as it should in its intervention in the housing market."[36]

Origins of the Community-Based Mixed-Income Model

Where did the idea of mixed-income community-based housing come from? In the United States and United Kingdom, whose social housing models Canada had borrowed, mid-century social housing was entirely a matter of local governments developing public housing with federal or central government funds. Community-based non-profits were big in France, but it had minimal influence on Canadian housing policy. How did this new model arise, that soon sidelined old-style "public housing," and sustained Canada's social housing priority for two decades while it waned around the world? Several roots are evident, though from this forty-year distance it is difficult to judge the weight of each.

European mixed-income non-profit housing was long of interest to Canadian housing policy-makers, as far back as the 1944 Curtis report. It had been present, but never dominant at the 1960s turning point. The 1964 Murray report had studied these countries and systems, and assistance to co-ops and charitable groups was included in the 1963 Ontario Advisory Group proposal. At the federally sponsored 1965 Conference on Poverty and Opportunity, the CMHC background report floated the option of assistance to non-profits. In the mid-1960s the CMHC Advisory Group conducted cross-country consultations and recommended more CMHC support for community-based housing. The federal low-income housing task force (see below) noted such continuities and concluded that that "The European experience demonstrates the viability of using private non-profit housing as an alternative to state-provided housing."[37] Moreover, having a mix of RGI and market rent units was quite a familiar model, as it had been prevalent in 1949–64 Canadian public housing.

The interest of policy-makers and advocates in repair and neighbourhood renewal as an alternative to neighbourhood-destroying redevelopment likewise predates the struggles of 1968–72. Rehabilitation was part of Ontario's 1962 Twelve Point Program (chapter 3) and was supported by CMHC officials.[38] It was included in the draft specification of powers for OHC presented to Ontario's minister Randall in December 1963, in his speech to the Legislature on the OHC Bill,[39] and in the announced purposes of OHC at its creation.[40] In 1966, the City of Toronto and CMHC commissioned a report by Albert Rose on the subject.[41]

Mixed-income housing offered the promise of addressing overall net rental demand – the main concern of the distinctive Canadian "discourse of rental supply" – and to subsume the low-income housing problem in this recipe that served more mainstream needs. Without the enormous increase in renter households, especially from young boomers, and the corresponding concern about rental supply, there would have been little impetus for mixed-income social housing.[42] Mixed-income social housing never gained much traction then as a policy idea in the United States or Australia, where added rental demand in the 1960s and 1970s was relatively far weaker than in Canada.

The Canadian community housing sector had quietly evolved a small track record in the 1960s. Once the 1964 policy changes provided more support for charitable LD, such projects sprouted.[43] There were 201 such projects in 1965–67, and a surge once CMHC expanded its LD financing in 1968, with production rising from 1,100 to 3,400 units annually from 1965 to 1970. CMHC officials liked such sponsors as an "administrative pleasure" without the political problems of public housing.[44] Background reports for the Dennis and Fish task force[45] reviewed the non-profit cases in the 1970–71 $200 million Special Initiative then under way.

The co-op housing sector was emerging. The 1969 NHA amendments opened financing explicitly to co-ops, which previously had fallen between the NHA rental and home-owner stools. The Co-operative Housing Foundation was formed in 1968 and the Ontario Habitat Foundation in 1971, both sponsored by smaller pre-existing co-op movements, the credit union sector, and the labour movement, in the context of the idealism and activism of the period.[46] The housing co-op operative movement became a very organized and effective political voice for social housing in general.

The community-based model was also informed by US policy in the 1960s, as it shifted away from large-scale public housing projects to more diverse and community-based approaches. The 1960s anti-poverty programs had strongly encouraged local initiatives, and Community Development Corporations (CDCs) emerged in that period – neighbourhood-based organizations that carried out programs for local job creation, improved services, and better housing, thereby enhancing the capacity of disadvantaged communities to alter their own circumstances. In 1973, the United States initiated Community Development Block Grants to states and municipalities; these were federal funds to be used flexibly for a range of local initiatives usually including affordable housing repair or production.[47] This is not to say that the United States offered a model of a large community-based or municipal non-profit sector.

The Quebec community housing sector and Montreal's housing-and-neighbourhoods politics became important during the 1968–73 transition. Quebec was a bastion of the nascent co-op sector, based in its church-affiliated social action movements and labour movement, with 1,400 units developed in 1968–70. Quebec had used half of CMHC's charitable LD financing from 1964 to 1970 and developed 4,000 units versus 2,100 in Ontario.[48] Housing rehabilitation with public assistance now became central in Montreal thinking about the state role in social housing and urban development. There was a strong desire to preserve the distinctive built form and fine-grained social mix that were part of the character of the city's older neighbourhoods. There was an emerging desire to avoid megaproject redevelopments that displaced residents and obliterated several Montreal neighbourhoods. To such ends an estimated $45 million in public funds was spent in Montreal in the 1970s on the rehabilitation of 8,000 units.[49] This equates to an average of $14 to $28 million annually in 2015 dollars, and a large share of it was municipal money.

The precedents and approaches established in Montreal by the end of the 1960s were monitored and analysed by the federal low-income housing task force (below). These approaches were supported by the Quebec government. Key members of the federal cabinet were from Montreal, politically connected to its local issues, and what Quebec wanted mattered in federal policy. From the viewpoint of Montreal's senior housing official, Guy Legault,[50] the federal policy changes of the early 1970s were a case of bottom-up influence on senior government policy.

The community-based non-profit approach fit with broader shifts in social policy. It reflected the climate of grassroots action and suspicion of government and private sector alike. It was congruent with related Trudeau government initiatives, notably the Company of Young Canadians and the Local Initiatives Program. More fundamentally, the shift to non-profit and co-op social housing was part of a broader institutional shift in Canada to a "mixed economy of welfare."[51] Where social programs had mostly been large directly run government programs, these now operated alongside an expanding array of publicly funded programs delivered and in some cases designed by community-based non-profit social agencies.

EVENTS AND DECISIONS: THE EARLY 1970S

The route from opposition to "public housing" to the new non-profit and co-op housing model was propelled by a remarkable series of actors and events, over a period of some five years. In the words of housing scholar Carroll, referring to a decade of which the early 1970s was the peak:

The 1968–1978 stage was an almost classic period of innovation. There was political activism which was marked by a willingness to spend resources on housing, and there was a lot of creative activity marked by new ideas about housing. It was the height of rational analysis in policy-making and there was a group of people within all levels of government and the broader community with strong values and a commitment to act upon them. Many of the Canadian programs were adapted from those in the United States and its "War on Poverty." This stage was also marked by the domi-

nance of advocacy coalitions which included powerful development and social advocacy interests that developed and crafted the
housing policies.[52]

Opposition to Public Housing

The policy shift of the early 1970s was propelled largely by local opposition to public housing development. We may wish to avoid undue
focus on Ontario and Toronto, but they were central in the forces that
shaped national policy. In 1971, over 60 percent of Canadian social
housing (47,000 of 77,000 homes) was in Ontario, with half of this
(23,000) in Toronto. The largest volume of public housing production
was in that city, and so was the largest controversy by far. The two federal ministers who ushered in the policy change were from Ontario,
those who invented and articulated the new policy were from Toronto,
and that city is where the policy was implemented earliest and on the
largest scale.

There were three main streams of opposition to new public housing
towers in the late 1960s.[53] The largest was suburban neighbourhood
opposition to new apartment towers in general and low-income housing in particular. The context was one where 20,000 rental apartment
units – a few dozen buildings – were being built each year in Toronto.
This was a similar volume to the post-2000 condo boom but in an
urban area half as large as today, and with the new buildings appearing
in most neighbourhoods, unlike today. The majority of these were on
main roads in 1950s and 1960s suburbs, adjacent to low-density residential neighbourhoods built in those decades. Opposition to public
housing was inextricably tangled with opposition to high-rise apartment development, the two reinforcing each other. Suburban opposition also responded to OHC's large-scale purchases of new apartment
buildings. Middle-class neighbours were concerned about residential
status and amenity, changing social mix, income and race, and high-
density development as a surrogate for these. Suburban municipal
councils responded to such resident voices, but were also concerned
about demands for local services such as recreation facilities.[54] They
started to deny planning approvals for apartment buildings that might
be suitable for purchase by OHC. The neighbourhood issues became
large controversies in urban politics.[55]

Among housing activists and in central-city urban reform politics,
the critique took a more articulated form. Central-city neighbourhood

conflicts, such as in Toronto's St James Town and Trefann Court, were mythologized in writings of the activists. High-rise opponents organized media-savvy protest events and litigation, and Alinsky-style confrontational activism.[56] In the mainstream, by 1970, Toronto's influential Confederation of Resident and Ratepayer Associations (CORRA) was carrying out a study of public housing and contacted the premier.[57] There was a perception that public housing was concentrating low-income residents in a new way, and tenant and social advocacy groups were concerned about lack of social services and transit for suburban public housing residents. But the redevelopment projects that were flashpoints for these politically connected, middle-class voters and activists were mostly private-rental towers, not social housing.[58]

The third current of opposition was alarmed about the destruction of the intimate scale, mixed social profile, and transit-oriented character of pre-war neighbourhoods – the new Jane Jacobs view of urban life. For urban writers, thinkers, and planners, this view was replacing the big-system, big-infrastructure approach of postwar top-down planning. Jacobs's antagonist in her first home, New York, was Robert Moses; his counterpart in her second home, Toronto, was the Metro Toronto government and its allied provincial and municipal housing corporations.[59] There was opposition to housing development by the big new development firms, which were large in physical scale, corporate profits, and power and influence at City Council.[60]

Although Toronto was the epicentre, there was opposition to public housing across Canada. The large federal funding and the new provincial housing corporations had brought a surge of urban renewal schemes. The City of Vancouver had built ten large public housing projects of over 200 units, concentrated in low-income neighbourhoods and displacing residents.[61] "By 1968, two thousand homes a year were being demolished by urban renewal in Montreal"[62] – both public and private. Hamilton's downtown was a large brown demolition zone as public and private redevelopment proceeded. "An undisguised zest for demolition was characteristic of most urban-renewal studies funded by CMHC."[63] Although most urban renewal across Canada was still at the proposal stage, by 1969 a concerned CMHC was doing a policy review.[64]

There is much irony in the outcry on urban renewal, public housing, and perceived ghettoization. In 1971 less than 10 percent of Canada's low-income renters were in social housing,[65] and outside Ontario, social housing activity at scale had barely started. The profound and distinctive trend in urban Canada was dispersion of low-income residents from the working-class inner city into mixed-income suburbs then being created. The spatial segregation of low-income renters was decreasing, not increasing, and in any event social housing was a modest part of that trend. By the latter 1960s, as even Dennis and Fish and later Bacher acknowledged, the "Earlier large-scale projects associated with urban renewal were no longer being duplicated by public housing authorities at the time the criticism of their alienating, high-rise, ghetto-like concentration of the poor peaked."[66] In Toronto, most 1960s public housing was suburban infill; the large sites of over about 300 units had been initiated in the pre-OHC period and stood in contrast to the main OHC model.[67] Much of the hated redevelopment was private-sector, not public, and the rhetoric of protecting neighbourhoods from government-led change ignored the postwar transformation of urban Canada through private-sector development. But sins of commission are clearer than those of omission, and shortcomings of policy draw more criticism than the market. All in all, opposition to public housing was less a thoughtful position on urban development or social mix, and more a flashpoint in the new politics of urban reform and the old politics of suburban exclusion.

Housing activists and opponents of public housing looked to the federal government for a solution, and soon enough those federal decisions came. Yet it was provincial housing corporations that were carrying out public housing development. Why the federal focus? One reason is that provincial programs still revolved around federal program parameters and capital financing. Another was a perception of the Trudeau government as bringing in a new era, despite its centrist social-welfare politics largely continuous with the 1963–68 Pearson years. Most significant was a Toronto-federal political axis which bypassed the unresponsive Ontario government, found allies in other cities, and seized an opportunity opening federally. This was the channel of least resistance for local opposition to achieve policy change. The road to this had three stages: the 1968 Hellyer task force, a 1970–71 Special Initiative, and the 1971 CMHC task force on low-income housing.

Hellyer's Task Force and Andras's Initiative

In 1968, the new Trudeau government initiated sweeping reviews of several policy spheres: foreign relations, "Indian affairs," the military, and housing.[68] Paul Hellyer, the new minister responsible for CMHC, carried this out through a Task Force on Housing and Urban Development with himself as chair. He was a builder/developer with an interest in housing, representing a Toronto riding. He had a forceful presence and a truly independent mind. And he was a "doer," an entrepreneur in political life – ironically in this way rather like Stanley Randall, the Ontario minister who invented and oversaw OHC through the 1960s. The task force produced its report in a prompt six months, by January 1969, on the basis of high-profile hearings across the country, much dialogue with local residents and officials, walking tours, and doorstep conversations, but with little input from research or experts.[69] Though opposition to public housing was heard everywhere, it was most intense in Toronto, and the report and ensuing media coverage amplified this into a national discourse.

To read the task force report today is to enter a past world where mainstream voices demand an active government role in a mixed economy, where land development should be municipal and real estate capital gains should be taxed, and where such a report is factual and articulate and not a communications document. The task force's recommendations ranged widely across mortgage finance, housing allowances, manufactured housing, northern housing, metropolitan planning, and other matters. But central in the recommendations were an end to public housing development, to be replaced with priority for neighbourhood renewal, and community-based non-profit and cooperative housing.[70]

"The inflammatory tone of the task force's commentary on public housing ... caused a firestorm of criticism."[71] Hellyer had compared urban renewal and public housing to an atom bomb. Much of the counter-criticism came from housing and social policy advocates who believed it would set back the recently established priority for social housing and what it meant in improved living conditions for low-income Canadians. But the recommendations had bigger political implications than mere social policy. Given the provinces' jurisdiction and accelerating role in developing public housing through their housing corporations, a ramping-down of public housing had ramifications for federal-provincial relations. "[T]here was major opposition to the recommendations from the general public, the provincial governments, the federal government and thus from within the Liberal Party."[72]

Minister Hellyer made recommendations to cabinet that corresponded to his task force report. But this set up an all-or-nothing proposition where the cabinet had to initiate big and contentious policy change or else undermine the minister himself. It was soon clear that the cabinet had rejected the recommendations, and Hellyer shortly resigned. For key federal housing officials, the task force process and the unstrategic approach to cabinet proposals were frustrating and amateurish.[73]

In the short run Hellyer had failed. But the Hellyer report opened up a political discourse that led to further political action and major policy change within five years. The federal government seized the political opportunity to respond to widespread concern over urban and housing issues, and occupy that political space. Robert Andras, the new minister responsible for CMHC, "sought out every possible appropriate public platform to speak about urban issues and about the need for federal leadership in solving Canada's urgent urban problems."[74] The federal government moved quickly with decisions in 1970–71. It limited public housing approvals, started a short-term unilateral federal housing program, created a Ministry of State for Urban Affairs, and appointed two high-profile task forces: one on urban issues,[75] and one on low-income housing.

CMHC continued funding new public housing, but things were changing. In 1968 it signed an agreement with Quebec, providing the new Société d'habitation du Québec (SHQ) with annual block capital funding of $150 million ($1.0 billion in 2015 dollars), enabling SHQ to carry out project planning and development quite autonomously. At the same time, CMHC placed limits and delays on project approvals by OHC.[76] For Ontario, all this and the Hellyer proposals were a disruption of established fruitful CMHC-OHC collaboration in a provincial sphere, for crass political reasons.[77] For the federal government, this was partly a matter of rebalancing funding to share it equitably among the provinces, unlike in 1965–69 when OHC had taken the lion's share. It was also a response to political needs.

In 1970, CMHC launched a Special Initiative of affordable housing development other than public housing, with $200 million in funding over two years ($1.25 billion in 2015 dollars). This had a dual character. It was partly a stimulus program in the first downturn in a dozen years, a mild one but an alarming first taste of 1970s stagflation. The Special Initiative was also an experiment with the largest direct federal role since the 1940s, helping fund the production of moderate-cost homeownership, private-rental, and non-profit housing. Although only about 10 percent of the units it supported were social housing,[78] it produced precedents for the policy changes that ensued, helped build capacity in the co-op sector, and was closely monitored in the next stage of change, the CMHC policy review by Dennis and Fish.

Dennis and Fish

CMHC under the new minister, Andras, undertook a major policy review carried out by a low income housing task force set up in early 1971. Its report was ultimately published as *Programs in Search of a Policy* (the Dennis and Fish report). Reflecting the government's favourable attitude to the new advocacy ideas, the task force was chaired by non-CMHC people, two talented Torontonians: Susan Fish of the Bureau of Municipal Research and establishment lawyer Michael Dennis. They reported to staff initially advising the minister and subsequently integrated into a new CMHC Policy Planning Division.[79] This was an unusually strong political intervention to reshape the role and orientation of the public service within CMHC. This established a policy capacity on social policy and urban issues that was broader than the existing CMHC expertise on housing financing, markets, and production, soon emulated in the four large, most affluent and urban provinces (below).

The Dennis and Fish task force articulated evidence-based policy ideas and analysis that pointed in directions similar to the Hellyer notions, and framed these in a manner that gained strong support rather than opposition from social policy and housing advocates.[80] It recommended abandonment of public housing production programs of the 1960s type. The report's animus against public housing was extreme. For example it saw mostly bad and no good in OHC; cited the low 10 percent annual tenant turnover as an indicator of dissatisfaction; described the locations as "clearly marginal" without analysis; and enthused about municipal sponsorship without considering the small volumes and spatial concentrations this had always produced in the United States, and the spatial concentrations evident in Britain by the 1960s.[81]

The task force recommended federal lending to municipal and non-profit groups at below-market interest rates for construction of break-even rental.[82] It recommended that such a system meet fully 45 percent of national production in the 1970s, about 100,000 units annually. This vision of creating a large non-market sector on the postwar Northwest European model was a non-starter in Canada – a market-dominated liberal-welfare system where home-ownership prevails and large private-sector firms dominate the rental sector. Dennis and Fish could not realize that 1960s conditions, when rental had comprised almost half of net increase in households each year and rental production was easily viable, were rapidly fading.

But these were official reports that social activists could embrace. For a young Lloyd Axworthy, the Hellyer task force was a fresh wind in content and approach, and the eccentricity of its chairman and its process was participatory democracy breaking into the circle of experts.[83] The Dennis and Fish report directly informed policy change, articulating a policy rationale for a stronger federal government role. This served the Trudeau Liberal cabinet's agenda of responding to the bubbling politics of housing, trumping the ever-present market-oriented ideas and fiscal caution of Department of Finance officials.[84] Beyond that, the Dennis and Fish report became a widely read articulation of a new vision shared in the new community housing sector, a sort of bible for the Canadian model of social housing that would shortly be born.

The Federal Policy Changes of 1973

Once the task force report was completed in November 1971, the government quickly introduced NHA amendments (by June 1972), in line with its recommendations. When the bill died at Parliament's dissolution for the October 1972 election, the swirling housing politics led to much controversy.[85] The fuss was not because the government or CMHC had any issues with the report's policy recommendations; these had already been drafted into the 1972 bill.[86] But the controversy, and then minority government from 1972–74, ensured priority for the social housing bill in the 1973 legislative queue, ample funding for the new model, and a few enhanced provisions for co-ops between the 1972 and 1973 versions of the bill.[87]

Several factors underlay the shift from public housing to non-profit housing. Although the model of mixed-income, community-based social housing at scale had little precedent in Canada, the United States or United Kingdom, its roots in this country were noted earlier. But an idea's adoption rests on more powerful factors than its policy merits. The new recipe promised to address concerns over housing subsidy trends, to serve all provinces equitably, and to meet federal political needs in Quebec. Achieving a better federal spending balance among the provinces was a significant impetus.[88] Ontario had used three-quarters of federal funding for public housing in the 1960s. Creation of public housing corporations in most provinces in 1967–70 looked set to soften but not reverse this Ontario dominance. It was not sustainable politically to devote the lion's share of federal social housing expenditure to affluent Ontario.

Rising public housing expenditures were a serious concern to CMHC and more particularly to the federal Department of Finance and Treasury Board.[89] By 1968, OHC capital commitments for public housing, HOME, and other programs were $500 million – $200 million over budget ($1.35 billion over, in 2015 dollars). CMHC was accommodating this by reducing its development loans to private firms – a feasible approach now that their needs could be bank-financed after the 1966 NHA amendments (chapter 3).[90] The federal government was thus tilting its large postwar volumes of housing finance away from market production toward state production and public-sector land development as a direct function of the ballooning public housing program.[91] Key officials in the federal government found this trajectory very disquieting. Once this expensive program also became unpopular it had a short life left.

The new direct federal housing role was one vehicle for the Trudeau Liberal government's resistance, in the early and mid-1970s, to demands for decentralization coming from Quebec and other provinces. Related to this was the issue of political "visibility" – that the federal government get credit and benefit in public opinion for its spending.[92] With rising demands for spending on housing on the one hand, and rising provincial demands for autonomy on the other hand, the political risk for the federal government was to be principal funder without receiving any political credit, especially in Quebec.

The housing politics in Toronto and other cities, the emerging community housing sectors in Montreal and Quebec, and the co-op movement in cities across Canada created not only policy advocacy, but also organizations that could potentially deliver social housing programs and projects, that is, build and operate the housing. Officials from each of Canada's three biggest cities had discussions with CMHC[93] on program design. Toronto's political links to the left and centre in Ottawa helped move this policy change. Donald S. Macdonald, representing Rosedale (east downtown Toronto), was a member of the inner cabinet and "played a very important role" in this.[94] Housing activists in the co-op sector and in Toronto had links to the NDP, although housing was not prominent in NDP conditions for political support in the 1972–74 minority parliament.[95] All this helped clinch the shift to community-based social housing policy. Advocacy also came from the emerging community housing sector in Montreal and the co-op movement across Canada. Montreal and Vancouver now joined the Toronto-federal axis in housing. There was an active network of mayors from the larger cities across Canada. In Toronto Mayor Crombie's recollection,[96] funding to develop new brownfield neighbourhoods in Toronto (St Lawrence) and Vancouver (the early, west end of False Creek) was partly a matter of sharing around the federal largesse that was paying for the 1976 Montreal Olympics facilities.

What is striking in this policy shift is the prominent attention to affordable housing in the media and political life, its politicized character, and the way forces outside federal housing institutions and expertise intruded forcefully into policy-making. From the viewpoint of young housing activists, this was a fresh exciting response to their concerns. From the federal government viewpoint it was a politically beneficial response to the political ferment and a rocky period in federalism. For the Ontario government it was an intrusion into a provincial sphere. But in retrospective historical view it was a detour from long-run trends in Canadian federalism and social policy.

The Provinces Dive In

Provincial policy in the early 1970s moved in directions consistent with federal policy, responding to many of the same public concerns. Despite the renewed federal lead, this was a time of expanding affordable housing roles in most provinces,[97] and the resulting program activity made the 1970s the peak years for social housing in Canada. The provinces took diverse approaches, creating something of a national patchwork in the 1974–78 period.

Ontario in 1973 acted on its high-profile Comay task force and adopted multi-prong active roles in housing, including supporting an effective market system, assisted affordable ownership, housing rehabilitation, land development, more Ontario spending, and ongoing expansion of social housing under the new program model.[98] This 1973 report and related decisions set the mould for Ontario policy in the 1970s and in many ways for two decades. Ontario set up a separate Ministry of Housing, established a Community Housing Branch, and allocated $20 million in new annual funding (about $100 million in 2015 dollars) to top up the federal non-profit/co-op spending.

In Quebec in the early and mid-1970s, social housing became a major element of social policy. The social housing activities of neighbourhood groups blossomed in Montreal and other cities. The top-down transformation of the Quebec co-op sector at the end of the 1960s (chapter 3) had had mixed success: capacity was low, tenant participation was weak, and many co-ops failed. Now came a more effective and enduring transformation of Quebec's co-op housing sector, involving not just officials and professionals but many community-based, bottom-up initiatives.[99] The emphasis of neighbourhood groups was acquisition and rehabilitation of older rental buildings, converting them to co-ops owned and run by their residents. The agenda was also about empowering working-class residents, building social cohesion and integration, achieving better housing quality, and enabling people to stay in the neighbourhood they called home despite rapid urban change and deindustrialization.[100] Quebec's Liberal government responded to this context. It appointed Lucien Saulnier, long-time supporter of social housing, as head of the SHQ. With the framework and resources enabled by the 1973 NHA amendments, SHQ now provided 50/50 cost-sharing for the City of Montreal's housing rehabilitation initiatives.[101]

In late 1974, Quebec's Liberal government appointed twin special task forces on urban development and on housing, which published reports early in 1976. In the *Rapport du groupe de travail sur l'urbanisation* (Castonguay report), housing was among the main topics. Claude Castonguay was prominent among the socially oriented technocrats who put in place the policies of the Quiet Revolution, including its pension plan and medicare, and had been minister responsible for such matters in 1970–73 under Robert Bourassa.[102] His report on urban affairs endorsed a progressive view that that a city should be judged by how well it responds to residents' needs, of housing as a right, and of the role of local government in fostering a good urban physical and social environment. The housing task force was chaired by Legault, Montreal's senior housing official from 1967 to 1987. Its report, *Habiter au Québec*, carried out a thorough evidence-based analysis of the trends and issues, and recommended an active provincial housing policy.[103] It put forward strong objectives pertaining to affordability, housing mix, preservation of neighbourhoods and older stock, a provincial system-management approach, and clear roles for each level of government and the non-profit and private sector.[104] The report included a fully costed program with funding for non-profit housing development, public land assembly, housing rehabilitation, and strategies for declining neighbourhoods.[105] The framework and ideas for support to non-profit and co-op housing development and to those sectors were parallel to Ontario policy, and borrowed from it.[106]

The housing task force report in effect provided a blueprint for the new Parti Québécois (PQ) government elected nine months later in November 1976. The PQ then was social-democratic, with strong roots in Montreal's social movements, neighbourhood organizations, housing co-operatives, and labour federations. Social housing – *logement populaire* or "Logipop" – was a priority for all of them.[107] The government embraced the *Habiter au Québec* report, repackaging it as *Loger au*

Québec. It initiated support to non-profit housing development and active collaboration with municipal and community-based social housing goals. Quebec provided a small capital grant to projects; start-up funds to pay for incorporation and the services of planners, lawyers, architects and others; and budgets for resource groups (*groupes de ressources techniques* – GRT).[108] The latter also emerged in most large Canadian cities in that period, and were partly funded from project budgets under CMHC rules; but, with Quebec support they became a higher-capacity and more enduring part of the system in that province. In the 1970s, however, public housing continued as the main Quebec government activity in social housing; this decade was the peak of such production, averaging 2,900 units annually.[109]

Other provinces also supported the federally managed expansion of the non-profit and co-op sectors. British Columbia's Barrett NDP government of 1972–1975 gave social housing a big boost, as noted in chapter 3. The 1970s federal policy turn reinforced the British Columbia government preference for community-based rather than public-sector housing, which endured throughout the long era of Social Credit government. British Columbia allocated large volumes of rent supplement to community housing – subsidies to bridge the gap between market rent and the levels affordable to low-income tenants, mostly co-funded 50/50 with the federal government. By 1982 British Columbia had the most rent supplement units per capita of any province – the only one with more of that than of public housing – and a majority of it was in non-profit and co-op projects.[110] In the resource boom of the mid and late 1970s, Alberta Housing Corporation was active in building social housing. Not unlike Ontario in the Robarts years, that province was flush with fiscal resources, governed by centrist Progressive Conservatives, and the provincial housing corporation was one tool in its agenda of managing rapid growth as a support to economic development.[111]

The four large, affluent provinces expanded not only program activity but also their policy scope. Quebec, British Columbia, and Alberta quickly followed Ontario's lead and established ministries with a policy role extending beyond their housing corporations' build-and-manage mandate.[112]

Completing the Policy Turn: The Late 1970s

Decentralization in Canadian federalism in the latter 1970s soon extended to social housing. By that time, the Trudeau government's politics of resisting provincial demands had given way to accommodation and decentralization. Demands for block funding in housing became prevalent, on the precedent of the Established Programs Financing (EPF) arrangement. By 1977, the coalition of Western Canadian premiers took such a position, as did Quebec in 1978. By 1980 the provinces took a unanimous position that they should be "totally responsible for the majority of policy, program development, program delivery and program administration" in housing.[113] In this context, the federal cabinet wanted "to keep the housing sector from adding more fuel to the constitutional fires."[114] It abolished the Ministry of State for Urban Affairs in 1978–79 and altered the social housing programs.

In 1978 the federal government adopted significant policy changes in social housing which built on and extended those of 1973, but were also a portent of the 1980s. It virtually ended public housing production and made non-profit and co-op the sole approach to expanding social housing.[115] This was implemented in a new funding program, NHA amendments, and a consistent set of new bilateral federal-provincial agreements under which funding allocations were now made.[116] For municipal non-profit housing specifically, there was a shift to block federal transfers and a lead provincial role. In some accounts 1978 is seen as a major turning point, but it was not of the same magnitude as 1973 or 1985. The federal government remained in the lead; the volume of activity was maintained. What this mini-turning point did was complete the 1973–74 policy shift from public housing to non-profit housing. The 1978 changes were also made possible by the experience of 1974–78 which showed that with careful federal and provincial support, non-profit and co-op housing could achieve sufficient capacity to replace public housing by sustaining comparable production volumes.

The 1978 changes were driven by far bigger agendas than anything within social housing. With a sharp spike in the federal deficit in 1978, there was a new imperative of restraining spending: the politics of constraint had arrived. The current in social policy was decentralization to the provinces, and there was a need to adapt to challenging housing and financial market conditions. Capital-intensive social housing was a significant element in federal borrowing requirements, and CMHC's contribution to reducing these was to replace CMHC mortgage financing with CMHC-insured private financing[117] – applying to social housing the approach used for home-owner mortgages since the mid-1950s. This created an immediate reduction of about $120 million annually ($400 million in 2015 dollars) in federal borrowing needs.[118] The end of direct CMHC lending went hand in hand with the end of funding for public housing. It also meant an end to the federal land-banking funding that had enabled creation of the iconic new 1970s neighbour-hoods in Toronto (St Lawrence) and Vancouver (the early, west end of False Creek). All this reflected the reduced state role, in sync with the market-oriented approach of the high-profile report of a 1979 task force on urban land.[119]

Under the brief Clark Conservative minority government of 1979–80, social housing dodged a neoliberal bullet. The government's election platform leaned to mortgage interest deductibility for home-owners and shelter allowances for renters. The government appointed a sweep-ing policy review team led by Larry B. Smith, a leading market-oriented academic critic of 1970s housing policy.[120] This review[121] was far more neoliberal in outlook and recommendations than the one later ap-pointed by the 1984 Mulroney government (chapter 5). It could have created an earlier and much sharper neoliberal turn in social housing than Canada in fact experienced in the 1980s. But the defeat of the Clark minority government turned it into a policy might-have-been. In the recession of the early 1980s, the Trudeau Liberal government used social housing production as economic stimulus, and the new so-cial housing model that had been created in 1973 and 1978 became well entrenched across Canada.

SOCIAL HOUSING PROGRAMS IN THE FIRST NON-PROFIT DECADE, 1974–85

Program Structures and Output

Social housing programs in the first non-profit decade had two distinct phases. The first half, 1974–78, had a hybrid program model. The new approach of non-profit and co-op production carried on alongside the older model of public housing production by provincial housing cor-porations. Nationwide in 1974–78, public housing production was larg-er than non-profit and co-op production. This changed after 1978, as public housing production virtually ended and almost all new social housing was now non-profit and co-op. Co-ops and non-profit groups were part of the same program funding regime from 1974 to 1985, al-though with slightly different targeting and rent-setting rules.

Social housing production averaged about 19,000 units annually in this extended 1974–85 decade – about 30 percent higher than in 1965–73 when provinces had still been ramping up public housing produc-tion. Faltering slightly in the late 1970s, volumes were boosted again by the use of social housing as stimulus in the sharp recession of the early 1980s.

The shift to non-profit and co-op production was strongest at first in Ontario: such units were 42 percent of its new social housing in 1974–78 compared to one-third elsewhere, and Ontario accounted for 46 percent of national non-profit and co-op production.[122] The City of Toronto, under a new urban reform council, re-entered social housing with an ambitious agenda. In 1973–74 it adopted bold strategies, established a non-profit housing corporation, and hired Michael Dennis – who had led the framing of the new federal policy – to be its senior housing official and implement the new model locally.[123] Only in Ontario did non-profit become the main vehicle for low-income family housing in 1974–78, but that province also increased its public housing stock by half in the 1970s, mostly for seniors. The shift to non-profit and co-op was quite strong in Quebec and British Columbia as well, and thereby nationwide in terms of overall volumes of housing production.

Non-profit housing in 1974–78 was financed through direct CMHC mortgage loans to non-profit sponsors, for 100 percent of project capital costs. One main element in the 1974 policy changes was to provide 100 percent rather than 90 percent loans; to fundraise 10 percent of capital costs had been an enormous barrier for most community-based groups. Another key element was to increase the scale of funding. This new model was known as the NHA section 15.1 (non-profit) and section 34.18 (co-op) programs (later renumbered). Ontario provided non-profit and co-op projects with a grant for 10 percent of capital costs, enabling rents 10 to 20 percent below median market levels and thereby ensuring viability and marketability. Most provinces also provided stacked rent supplement, usually cost-shared 50/50 with the federal government, to ensure RGI rents in a portion of units in each project. The "stacked" term refers to the fact that it was a separate program, layered on the main funding program that provided financing of project capital costs, and was the framework for allocations, broad program management, and accountability. Some accounts of rent supplement as part of Canadian housing policy, noting its large presence in Ontario,[124] miss the fact that a majority of this was stacked rent supplement integral in 1970s non-profit program design.

A new funding model introduced in 1978 reflected the shifting economics of rental production as interest rates and development costs escalated. The early-1970s idea that non-profit production would achieve lower rents or cross-subsidy from market revenues to RGI rents reflected the highly profitable rental development of the 1960s. By the time the non-profit model was implemented in the mid-1970s it took a capital grant to push rents below market, and rent supplement to achieve low rents. By the latter 1970s, break-even (economic) rents were well above market rents for apartments and it took a large subsidy to make a new project viable at all. The 1978 decisions meant that CMHC would no longer act as lender using federal capital. Private financial institutions would now finance 100 percent of project capital costs with thirty-five-year mortgages; they faced almost zero risk because of the twin pillars of CMHC's mortgage guarantees and its commitment of multi-year operating subsidies. The latter equalled the difference between mortgage interest rates in the market and a hypothetical 2 percent rate. The new program was known as 56.1 ("fifty-six one," referring to the new NHA section), or "2 percent write-down."

Also extending through the 1974–85 period was the non-profit and co-op component of the Residential Rehabilitation Assistance Program (RRAP). Although RRAP mostly funded repairs for low- and moderate-income home-owners and private rental, the non-profit stream accounted for 51,700 of the 349,000 RRAP units in the period. One-third or 17,200 of these were rooms/beds in the expanding sectors of high-support congregate housing (group homes), women's or emergency shelters, and retirement homes, along with some non-profit rooming houses. The 34,500 dwelling units funded by non-profit RRAP equate to an average 4,300 annually over the period.[125] This added over 20 percent to the volume of the main non-profit and co-op social housing programs of the period – although the recipient could also stack funding from those programs and RRAP on the same project. RRAP was used to rehabilitate many smallish lower-quality private-rental buildings while turning them into social housing that would remain affordable for the long term. It was a big resource to community groups and local governments in Montreal and other cities as they undertook large neighbourhood programs, as well as reserves and smaller communities. Non-profit RRAP was discontinued in 1985.

In this period Aboriginal housing programs emerged, including the Urban Native and the Rural and Native Housing (RNH) programs, extending in various forms from 1978 to 1993; RRAP Aboriginal targets and delivery; and section 56.1 On Reserve which continues to this day. These are remembered in Aboriginal communities for the mix of ownership, rental, and rent-to-own that they supported. The Urban Native program funded 3,469 units while the On Reserve program funded 4,964 up to 1985 and 9,666 in 1986–93[126] – together an average 1,200 units a year through the full period. Although much smaller than the mainline programs, there was a considerable political focus on them, and CMHC put a lot of resources into capacity-building in the communities involved and for the young professionals who came from them.[127]

Program delivery of non-profit and co-op housing was overseen by CMHC staff in regional and local offices. Their role included an annual process to solicit and choose applications, the oversight of a staged project approval process, and a great deal of informal advice and assistance to non-profit proponents and their consultants. Ontario's Community Housing Branch encouraged interested community groups to get involved in housing; offered advice and know-how to them; was an intermediary in CMHC project approvals; and administered the $20 million annual Ontario funding.[128]

After 1978, the provinces oversaw municipal non-profit housing somewhat autonomously from CMHC, and increasingly took a system-manager role in low-income housing.[129] Some provinces such as Ontario continued to provide extra subsidies to ensure projects were viable, and stacked rent supplement to ensure that about half of municipal units had RGI rents.[130] This enabled municipal non-profit housing to play the former role of public housing: meeting general low-income needs not served by non-profit or co-op groups serving particular communities, and achieving ample overall volumes of new RGI units.[131]

Government Housing Spending

The new 56.1 program model proved a fiscal disaster. Its funding formula ran headlong into mortgage interest rates peaking at over 18 percent in 1981–82. Any debt-financed production in that period would have been very expensive, but this program was maximally exposed to high rates. This program also had the least provincial cost-sharing of any period.[132] The high federal expenditure for 56.1 also arose for four other reasons later largely forgotten: It was stimulus in a very sharp 1980–81 recession and its aftermath; the interest-rate subsidies mirrored home-owner assistance programs of that period (below); and the program was a means of rental supply as the younger baby-boomers entered a housing market where private-rental production was generally no longer viable. As well, as Fallis noted, "The subsidies to middle-income people in income-mixed buildings were a way to sustain the political consensus supporting housing assistance."[133]

Annual federal expenditures on social housing escalated rapidly through the 1970s and early 1980s to reach $1.2 billion by 1985 (figure 4.3 – $2.3 billion in 2015 dollars).[134] There were several cost drivers. In

Figure 4.3   Federal housing expenditure, 1970–93 (inflation-adjusted 2015 dollars). Federal housing spending rose rapidly in the 1970s, mostly for market housing. Social housing spending plateaued by the mid-1980s.

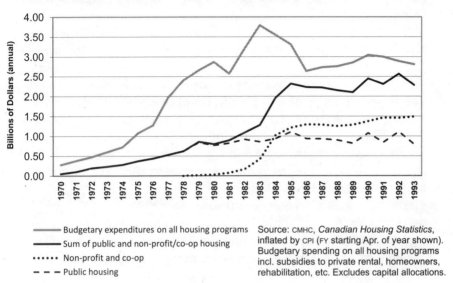

Billions of Dollars (annual)

Budgetary expenditures on all housing programs
Sum of public and non-profit/co-op housing
Non-profit and co-op
Public housing

Source: CMHC, *Canadian Housing Statistics*, inflated by CPI (FY starting Apr. of year shown). Budgetary spending on all housing programs incl. subsidies to private rental, homeowners, rehabilitation, etc. Excludes capital allocations.

public housing, the flat rents of RGI tenants contrasted with rising operating costs, and the difference was covered by subsidy. Non-profit and co-op housing was adding rapidly to the numbers of units each year, a significant share of tenants had RGI rents, and the amortization subsidies faced steeply rising market interest rates. Outside of CMHC operating funds, its large volume of mortgage loans in 1973–78 also contributed to rising total spending. By 1984, ongoing annual subsidies to non-profit and co-op housing exceeded those to public housing, for fewer low-income-targeted units.[135] The provinces' social housing spending also escalated, as they paid their 50 percent share of RGI subsidies and in some cases their top-up capital grants. For example, Ontario's annual social housing subsidies went from $11 million in 1970 to $51 million by 1975, and $150 million by 1985 (from $70 million to $220 million to $300 million in 2015 dollars).[136]

Social housing was one of five large areas of public spending on affordable housing from the mid-1970s to early 1980s. The other four were subsidies to private rental production[137] – helping sustain the apartment boom as investment conditions deteriorated – along with subsidies to home-ownership, a state role in land development, and government assistance to repair and renovate housing. This was the era of diverse programs in housing and urban development,[138] created in the early to mid-1970s as expansive welfare state politics responded to adverse housing market conditions. Non-profit housing rode on the back of this broader state involvement in housing, and on the agenda of rental supply.[139]

Although social housing was the largest element in direct government housing expenditures, through most of the 1970s it comprised less than half the total. It is informative to compare the dollars and unit counts in programs assisting private rental and home-ownership. The largest direct assistance programs to private rental, the Assisted Rental Program and the Canada Rental Supply Program, totalled over $450 million up to 1989 – about one-quarter the volume of social housing subsidies in the same mid-1970s to early 1980s period. Grants and loans to private rental, mostly repayable, totalled $1.2 billion.[140] Multiple Unit Residential Building (MURB) tax incentives to assist private-rental production cost an estimated $2.4 billion in tax expenditures.[141] The stock of about 350,000 private-rental units built from 1975 to 1982 with large public subsidies compares to 137,000 new social housing units approved in the same period. In assistance to homebuyers and home-owners, the $125 million cost of the Assisted Home Ownership Program (AHOP) for new buyers equalled about one-fifth of the $633 million cost of social housing subsidies in the same period.[142] The 19,000 households AHOP served annually just exceeded the 17,000 new social housing units annually in the same years. The Canada Home Ownership Stimulation Plan – interest-rate subsidies to home-owners facing 18 to 20 percent interest rates at renewal in the early 1980s – accounted for about one-third of federal housing expenditure in the years that it was running.[143] In this comparison and that for private rental, the balance would tilt further away from social housing if RRAP were included.

The late 1970s to early 1980s also saw the emergence of housing allowance programs (shelter allowances or housing benefits) in three provinces. This reflected a trend then in many affluent countries,[144] and in Canada they were part of the diverse program array created in this period of active policy. British Columbia was first in 1979, with its Shelter Aid for Elderly Renters (SAFER) program. Manitoba followed with a housing benefit program for seniors in 1981 and families in 1982, and Quebec introduced its Allocation-logement for seniors in 1983. Enduring to this day, these provide a monthly subsidy covering 65 to 75 percent of the gap between market rent (up to a ceiling) and an affordable rent at 30 percent of the recipient's household income.[145] The focus on seniors perhaps reflected implicitly ideas about the deserving poor but also (given the income floors provided by the federal GIS) reflected a more limited provincial fiscal exposure in assisting seniors. Although they were initially small programs in terms of coverage of the low-income renter population and the shallow depth of subsidy in Manitoba and Quebec, they were a significant policy departure.

Emergence of the Non-profit and Co-op Sector

Along with a large stock of community-based social housing, the most significant result of the 1974–85 program regime was the creation of an organized, significant, and politically active non-profit and co-op housing sector. "The sector," as it was sometimes called, had three distinct subsectors: co-operatives (operated collectively by the residents); private non-profit (community-based organizations); and municipal. All three had strong links to the other third-sector organizations that blossomed in that period. The main sponsor groups of private non-profit were social service agencies, neighbourhood and tenant groups, labour unions, church/faith organizations, service clubs (Lions, Rotary, etc.), and ethnic associations.

Public-sector housing providers remained important in the new non-profit and co-op program model. In Ontario almost 30 percent of total non-profit and co-op housing was municipal.[146] Municipal housing corporations were non-profit in terms of corporation law, program funding, income mix, scale of projects, and public perception; they were not viewed then as "public housing" akin to the big provincial agency. In Quebec, Saskatchewan, and Yukon the provincial or territorial housing corporation developed and operated housing directly under the 1978–85 non-profit program,[147] and provincial housing corporations later used the 1986–93 programs as well.

The housing programs directly supported capacity-building in the non-profit and co-op housing sectors. CMHC provided grants to the co-op sector organizations to that end.[148] Project budgets included amounts for sponsor groups to hire consulting project co-ordinators, planners, lawyers, architects, and others; there were interim grants and loans for the many expenses incurred to bring a project to the point of construction start. There was virtually no direct cost to sponsoring agencies or municipalities. All this resourced a small sector of non-profit "resource groups" and private "development consultant" firms that carried out these functions and the related liaison with government staff overseeing the process.

The co-op sector was well organized from early days, with a hierarchy of regional and national organizations. The Co-operative Housing Foundation soon became the Co-operative Housing Federation (CHF), actively negotiating with CMHC on program structures and resources. The Co-operative Housing Federation of Toronto (CHFT) was the earliest local/regional body, formed in 1973, and soon the Quebec co-ops were organized in set of regional federations. Provincial co-operative housing umbrella bodies were formed in 1982 in British Columbia and in 1987 in Ontario, the latter as the focus of activity shifted to the provincial level (chapter 5).[149] These co-op umbrella bodies provided advice and training to individual co-ops and their members on project development and management; vigorously represented the sector politically; and carried on liaison with CMHC and later Ontario, Quebec, and British Columbia on program implementation issues.

The diverse community-based non-profits moved more slowly toward an organized sector structure. The largest critical mass existed in Ontario, British Columbia, and Quebec. The Ontario Non-Profit Housing Association was founded in 1987, its municipal participants being always a big source of funding, board members, and volunteers. The BC Non-Profit Housing Association was founded in 1992.

Co-ops were the political face of the programs, and "co-op" soon became a term imprecisely but favourably connoting community-based mixed-income social housing in general.[150] This equating of co-ops and all non-profit housing was good for the image of the sector in the 1970s and 1980s, helping sequester the stigmatization of social housing within all-low-income public housing only, rather than across all social housing.

But the 1970s heyday and this new vision of social housing would be under increasing pressure as chillier political and fiscal winds came in. The subsidies to market rental and home-ownership were mostly curtailed by the mid-1980s, and mostly forgotten after that. This left social housing as the main tax-supported housing program, and the costs of this became increasingly controversial as the 1980s progressed.

5

The 1980s: Shifting Down

The 1980s in Canada were a time of conflict between the postwar social welfare model and the newly deregulated global market, between universalist programs and targeted ones, and between the federal lead and the trend of devolution. Election of the Mulroney Conservative government in September 1984 triggered again the pattern of big change once a decade in social housing. Housing policy reflected the larger tensions, but resolved them in a way that maintained a middle course and a significant priority for social housing through the decade.

This turning point was less fundamental than those of the mid-1960s or early 1970s, but it brought three main changes: in roles, program model, and the relation to broader housing policy. The federal government retained the lead in shaping policy and in being the larger funder, but devolved program management to the provinces. Selection of projects, flow of funds to public or non-profit/co-op agencies, and related oversight and accountability became provincial roles for housing developed after 1985. By partway through the period, the provinces were not just operating public housing, but were co-funding and overseeing the majority of social housing. Ontario, always the strongest partner of CMHC, responded to the federal pulling-back with a large unilateral (provincial-only) program. This opened an era of diverging provincial policy paths that would get reinforced in the 1990s onwards.

New social housing reverted to stricter low-income targeting, and the provinces were required to put in almost half the funds. Policy pulled back somewhat from the 1960s and 1970s agenda of mixed-income projects and neighbourhoods, rental supply, and mixed-tenure urban development. Social housing was no longer part of an expansive government role in housing that included assisted private rental, land development, and affordable ownership; besides the fiscally much smaller renovation programs, it was now the sole housing sector receiving large direct public funding. As social housing became detached from those broader agendas, it was increasingly targeted to populations with special needs, such as people with disabilities or homeless people.

The shifts in social housing policy under the 1984–93 Mulroney Conservative government were aligned with general trends in federalism, social policy, and fiscal policy. The federal government acceded to decentralization while retaining a lead in policy and funding. Social housing policy reflected the tension between neoliberal voices and "regional brokerage" – the role of public spending in sustaining regional political support for the governing party. Once the government won a second mandate in 1988, and as the early 1990s brought severe recession and a severe fiscal squeeze, the balance tilted toward restraining and then cutting social spending.

POLITICAL AND ECONOMIC CONTEXT: CONTENDING FORCES

By the mid-1980s Canada had put the 1981–82 recession well behind and entered a strong economic expansion. Real GDP growth averaged 4 percent annually in 1983–86.[1] Though tax revenues boomed, social spending pressures were large due to aging, health care costs, and labour force change. Social spending was maintained through the decade. Income security expenditure ratcheted up from about 8 to 10 percent of GDP in the 1981–82 recession, and then plateaued rather than decreased in the subsequent expansion.[2] But this was an accommodating incrementalism, not a social policy strategy.

The Mulroney Conservative government included significant neoliberal voices, contrasting with the 1980–84 Trudeau Liberal cabinet. The latter had maintained centrist social-welfare politics, implemented large housing stimulus in the recession, and "held the line" against conservative thinking and fierce attacks from business voices.[3] But now "Neo-conservatism had the governments of the United Kingdom and the United States in its grip and the Canadian business community in its thrall."[4] The same Donald S. Macdonald who had introduced wage and price controls in 1975 now championed US free trade as Canada's economic strategy,[5] and Bay Street's Michael Wilson was finance minister.

Neoliberal ideas were by then entrenched in federal central agencies, where globally they came to dominate[6] among a cadre educated in the Chicago School variant of neoclassical economics. By the 1990s, this ideology was strongly reinforced by fiscal concerns. The federal De-

partment of Finance and Treasury Board had ongoing concern over social housing programs' multi-year spending commitments that could
not readily be subjected to percentage cuts like most programs.[7] From
a CMHC vantage, "The retrenching was underway and demands for a
reduction in government spending were coming from everywhere. We
understood the necessity to tighten our belt."[8]

But the Mulroney government's decentralizing federalism and regional brokerage was more prominent than neoliberalism. With a large
Alberta and Quebec electoral base and cabinet presence, this government supported greater provincial power, culminating in attempted
constitutional reform in the Meech Lake Accord (1987) and Charlottetown Accord (1992). The language of the Mulroney government was of
private-sector reliance, spending restraints, and reduced public deficit
and debt. The actuality was an uneasy compromise between this and
the role of social spending in regional brokerage, and this limited the
extent of cutbacks.[9] Federal deficits, spiking amid slowing growth at
the end of the 1970s, and then recession-driven in the early 1980s, now
were large and chronic despite strong economic growth.

The second Mulroney term (1988–93) was more neoliberal than the
first.[10] The approach was no longer just spending restraint and tighter
targeting, but to cut back and sometimes cut out programs. There was
"a series of belt-tightening changes in eligibility requirements and the
amount and duration of benefits" and capping or de-indexing of transfers to provinces.[11] The 1990–93 recession, the worst since the 1930s except in Western Canada, would be the first since the 1940s not to see
housing programs used as economic stimulus.[12]

In Canada after the 1984 election, the federal lead in social housing
was out of alignment with trends in federal-provincial social policy relations. The federal role in direct delivery and detailed oversight was
greater in social housing than in much larger and more mainstream
social programs.[13] But as this direct CMHC role changed at the 1985
turning point, it made the federal role in social housing politically
vulnerable. The federal role now tended to be seen as back-door cost-
sharing of a provincial program, rather than a joint program provincially delivered.[14] Once social housing ceased to be a sphere where
federal cabinets and MPs could initiate things and receive political
credit, the emerging logic was to look to other ways to meet constituents' needs. CMHC officials warned their provincial counterparts
of this risk in the 1985 negotiations on the new policy framework,
and the program review report that year explicitly named this federal political risk.[15]

HOUSING AND URBAN CONTEXT: VOLATILE PRESSURED MARKETS

The housing market swung dramatically in the 1980s and early 1990s, creating a series of strong pressures and mainstream political concerns. Mortgage rates by 1983 had come off their early-1980s peak, but remained in the range of 10 to 13 percent (for five-year terms) through the decade. A house price boom took off in the latter 1980s across most large Canadian cities; Toronto in 1987–89 had the greatest recorded real estate bubble in the city's history. Real (inflation-adjusted) resale prices had bottomed out in Montreal in 1983, and in Toronto and Vancouver in 1985. By 1988 Montreal resale prices peaked at 51 percent above their 1983 low; the next year in Toronto at 92 percent above their low; and the following year in Vancouver at 70 percent above the low.[16] The price escalation meant mortgage carrying costs higher than at the interest-rate peak of the early 1980s (figure 4.2). In many cities the increases put home purchase out of reach for many young middle-income households and kept them in the rental market. The acute issues in Toronto and Vancouver kept housing affordability strongly on the political agenda in the mid- to late 1980s.[17]

Rental demand remained high – not as extreme as in the 1960s and 1970s but much higher than the years that followed in 1990–2015. The 1980s was the period when the younger half of the baby-boomers (born 1956–64) entered the housing market, most of them renting and very few of them able to purchase as young adults.[18] Then in 1985, the new federal government decided to increase immigration levels, and the numbers of people arriving doubled between 1985 and 1990 to a new plateau sustained for many years afterwards. These two demographic factors sustained high net (incremental) rental demand through-out the 1980s.

The 1980s also saw ever-lower private-rental production and severe losses of low-end private-rental units. Canada's postwar private-rental production regime was now over (except in Montreal), with the end of the large public assistance that had kept it alive in 1975–82. Social housing and second suites (basement apartments) came to be seen as the main vehicles of added rental supply. Demand pressures resulted in rising real rents, which meant great net loss of apartments in the lower rent ranges. On top of this was loss of low-rent rooms and flats in converted houses in Toronto, Vancouver, and other cities, as gentrification expanded from a trend affecting a few neighbourhoods to a wave across most of the central city. With fewer low-rent options and a tougher labour market, Toronto's homeless population doubled every five years in the 1980s and 1990s, reaching an average of 2,175 nightly in 1988–90.[19]

In the mid- to late 1980s, these interest rate and rental demand pressures, and these urban social stresses, propelled strong mainstream middle-class concern over housing affordability in general, rental affordability, and rental supply. This supported an active government role in housing, with emphasis on social housing[20] – but with the centre of the action now shifted to the provincial level.

IDEAS: MARKET LOGIC VERSUS SOCIAL RIGHTS

Beyond the strong arrival of neoliberalism, several currents of thinking shaped housing policy in the 1980s. Market-oriented attitudes on social housing revived strongly in Ottawa in the mid- and late 1980s. Remarks by two CMHC vice-presidents (one its future president) at a 1988 conference illustrate this. They were mindful of US and UK social housing as negative models, of social problems within social housing, and of a lack of income integration in social housing.[21] In their version of the 1960s history, "Provincial housing agencies and commissions sprouted nearly as fast as public housing projects ... Efforts to achieve subsidy reductions were forgotten. The idea of public housing being a stepping stone to homeownership slipped away when permanent housing for senior citizens was introduced."[22] Thus Canada's late postwar arrival to production levels at the low end of affluent-country norms becomes runaway expansion, and seniors social housing becomes a poverty trap. "The excesses from this frenetic pace of activity produced counter-reactions ... The creation of public housing ghettos became unacceptable ... They were perceived to limit people's ability to climb out of poverty."[23] Thus spatial dispersion of urban poverty and mitigation of its effects becomes its cause; and the mixed incomes of Canada's 1970s urban development and social housing morph into tabloid visions. Absent in this discourse were the 1960s and 1970s ideas of housing costs commensurate with incomes, housing as an integral part of social welfare, and the dysfunctions of filtering and down-market rental.

Social housing was increasingly characterized as expensive while also failing to "solve" the problem of low-income housing needs.[24] This framing ignored the modest scale of subsidy expenditures compared to rising GDP or aggregate market rents, and ignored the fact that a social housing system meeting half of incremental low-income rental demand leaves the remainder to be absorbed in market rental with all the inherent problems of affordability and quality. A critical CMHC evaluation of the 1979–85 program,[25] with its high subsidy requirements but weak low-income targeting, contributed to negative perceptions and was cited by opponents of subsidized rental.[26] Reasons for the high 1979–85 subsidies – stimulus, interest subsidies paralleled in home-owner programs, meeting rental needs as private-rental production collapsed, and the political price of income mix (see chapter 4) – were forgotten in mainstream discourse. Canadian social housing policy was torn in the 1980s between the fiscal logic and liberal-welfare idea of tighter targeting, and the political logic of broader targeting. In this it echoed the nation's social policy generally[27] in that period.

The resurgence of market-oriented economic ideas affected housing policy discourse. It was claimed that assisted rental merely substituted for market rental production,[28] that counter-cyclical stimulus magnified volatility. This analysis looked to neoclassical equilibrium theory, rather than to historical changes in economic conditions or the widening gap between tenant purchasing power and development costs. It categorized housing affordability as an income problem not a housing problem, rather than as inherently both. For solutions this analysis looked not to mixed-tenure urban development but to "filtering"[29] – the gradual relative price and quality decline of older housing, and the associated turnover of older neighbourhoods to poorer households. Government language spoke of private rental stimulus as disruptive, and of a need to facilitate the market and let it return to equilibrium. The declining legitimacy of counter-cyclical spending in orthodox public finance thinking helped undermine social housing policy, as job creation was always a large argument for social housing production.[30] The early 1990s recession was the first since the 1950s that did not see augmented social housing production funding as a significant form of federal stimulus.[31]

Market discourse easily appealed to centrist politicians. Although social housing had institutional momentum and many advocates, it was outside middle-class housing experiences and outside the liberal-welfare premises of Canadian political life. In 1980–82 the federal minister responsible for CMHC was Paul Cosgrove who had made his early career in Scarborough opposing public housing. Claude Bennett, the Ontario minister at the time, was quoted as favouring privatization and lauding non-profit housing at the same time.[32] Centrist elements in the Mulroney coalition held favourable views of social housing, exemplified in Bill McKnight and Alan Redway, ministers responsible for CMHC in 1984–89 and 1989–91 respectively.[33] Redway later recalled little change in attitudes – just a profound change in fiscal conditions.[34]

But in the 1980s context of chronic fiscal deficits, high social housing subsidies, and high housing development costs, advocates "had to make a bigger moral argument" than they had in the 1970s.[35] Increasingly, the moral arguments failed to clear the fiscal hurdle.

There was an increasing disjuncture between neoliberal thinking at the federal level and an ongoing centrist social welfare consensus locally and provincially. At the latter levels the prevalent discourse had few neoliberal elements in the 1980s, and ideas about meeting housing needs and a managed housing system remained strong. There was much news coverage in this vein,[36] and the language of housing as a social right was prominent. At the federal level, the cost gap – the need for large subsidies merely to make new rental housing viable at market rents – appalled the adherents of economic rationalism. At the local and provincial level, the cost gap made it obvious that market developers could not viably build rental housing, and therefore reinforced social housing as the supply strategy.

There was a disconnect between the social concerns of community sponsors and activists, and the economic facts and economic concerns of federal policy-makers. "Affordable housing" became the prevalent euphemism for social housing, avoiding the old plain-speaking "subsidized" or "low-rent" and evading the fiscal requirements. Cross-subsidy – dollars flowing within a project from market-rent revenues to help cover RGI subsidies – was long dead as a financial fact in new projects. But the notion remained alive in advocacy mythology, and also among MPs in the wake of co-op sector lobbying.[37] It endures even today in descriptions of co-ops as housing where projects achieve cost recovery while residents pay rents based on income.[38] In fact, by the 1980s, new projects required subsidies of about $500 monthly per unit simply to break even at market rents. As Fallis put it, "this created enormous confusion and controversy; ... tenants paying 'market' rents did not feel they were subsidized [yet the] limited government funds were not directed toward the neediest households."[39]

Social rights included housing for homeless people and "low-income singles," those who had formerly lived in rooming houses and survived on casual manual jobs, both now vanishing. The increasing homelessness and the tightening rental market fed these concerns. Subsidized housing for this population was pushed into policy discourse in the early 1980s by downtown agencies working with them in the big cities. New agencies with mandates to house this population were formed. Also feeding this was deinstitutionalization of people who had once lived in psychiatric hospitals, a policy change propelled by new psychotropic drugs, progressive ideas of recovery and integration into the community, and a new "consumer-survivor" movement – people who had survived institutionalization and now demanded their rights. The premise was that stable housing was the route to stable lives; that housing projects could be platforms for needed support services; and that housing was an opportunity for community development.[40] Toronto's central-city and metropolitan governments appointed special task forces on housing for homeless people and low-income singles.[41] Community agencies collaborated with all four levels of government on a pilot social housing project for this population.[42] This was "housing first" for people with a high prevalence of addictions or serious mental illness, three decades before US-style housing first program models arrived in Canada.

This advocacy received a great boost in 1987 as official United Nations "International Year of Shelter for the Homeless" (IYSH) conferences were held and governments initiated targeted programs. Ontario's minister appointed a special IYSH advisory task force, and it became a vehicle for advocacy for social housing.[43] Ontario decided to extend RGI eligibility to all legal residents including singles – no longer only seniors, families, and disabled people – and announced this in January 1988.[44] From 1987 onwards a large share of Ontario's new social housing was for consumer-survivors, homeless people, and low-income singles, the largest part of it funded in the first of Ontario's unilateral social housing programs, Project 3000.[45] Quebec likewise initiated a program stream targeted at homeless people,[46] within the overall federal-provincial program envelope.

Shelter allowances became a focus of policy debate from the mid-1970s onward, reaching a peak in the 1980s. The issue was the relative merits of "supply-side" programs to subsidize non-market production versus "demand-side" housing allowances to subsidize low-income households in the rental market. The debate reflected policy trends across most affluent countries with advanced welfare states: by the mid-1980s most West European nations and Australia had universal income-tested housing allowances. As the cost of non-profit housing programs accelerated and market-oriented ideas gained ground, the option of demand-side assistance was increasingly studied, advocated, and debated.[47] Mainstream economic opinion was that demand-side subsidies were preferable[48] because they would serve consumer choice and utility through efficient market mechanisms, at lower cost per unit than production subsidies. Housing advocates were more aware of the limited options open to low-income people in the rental market, and the severe compromises in housing quality required at low market rents.

The Canadian discourse about supply-side and demand-side strategies is distinctive internationally in the firm positions taken on the Left and the Right. Demand-side assistance was advocated by Canada's large corporate landlord-developer sector,[49] and opposed by the non-profit and co-op housing sector and social advocates; these positions were echoed in vague support for shelter allowances and in staunch opposition on the Right and Centre/Left respectively. This reflects competing 1980s ideas of social policy as decommodified non-market resources, versus social policy as residual benefits to mitigate the fallout of the market for those at the bottom. Although shelter allowances were the subject of a cabinet submission under the Clark government in 1979[50] and of interdepartmental discussions in later years,[51] how close these came to becoming federal policy has never been the subject of policy research.

Also intense in the latter 1970s and early 1980s was a debate on the merits of subsidies to private rental production versus social rental production. Mixed-income non-profit housing directly competed with the private sector for market share as well as public funds. Expansion of the non-profit sector contrasted starkly in the 1980s with a plateaued corporate rental sector. This debate highlighted ideological differences about incentivizing market actors versus creating a non-market sector, as well as genuine questions about the relative long-run cost-effectiveness of each.

The 1980s politics of rental housing became a matter of responding to a strong lobby from social activists, the non-profit and co-op housing sector, and municipalities. They had more votes than landlords or economists, and housing projects in concrete urban space had more political appeal than income transfers or "the more subtle, less identifiable achievements of the marketplace."[52] Important too was high net rental demand. Although allowances were a cheaper way to subsidize rents, there was little evidence that they would induce the additional supply needed to accommodate the 60,000 rental households added annually across Canada.[53] Shelter allowances might be good in theory, but in 1980s Canada, social housing had momentum and there was little political support for large new income-related transfers.

EVENTS AND DECISIONS: THE MID-1980S

The social housing policy framework that emerged at the end of 1985, some fifteen months after the election, was a compromise between three competing forces. These were the presence of neoliberal voices in the Mulroney Conservative cabinet; concerns of the Department of Finance and CMHC over the spending trajectory, lack of cost-sharing, and weak income targeting; and input from provincial and stakeholder interests. The established interests of the provinces and the community housing sector were now more important than the multitudinous voices that shaped policy change in the 1970s. In 1985, they also withstood the rising neoliberal influences.

Shortly after the Mulroney government was elected in 1984 it set in motion a sweeping Task Force on Program Review, known as the Neilson task force after its chairman. Among various "study teams" reporting to it on specific spheres, one dealt with social housing.[54] The report of the housing study team was distinctly less neoliberal than the overall thrust of the Neilson program review or the going-in position of the new government.[55] The latter included an agenda of devolving social housing, privatizing mortgage insurance, and transferring residual CMHC functions such as research to some other department. CMHC argued to get a representative on the study team from its program evaluation division. Its dispassionate, research-based approach, widely seen as unsympathetic to social housing in the critical 1983 evaluation, now furnished the needed evidence base in the study team's tight three-month mandate, and had large credibility with the central agencies and the chair[56] that dominated the deliberations.[57] The report, quickly made public, recommended an ongoing federal role in social housing with more stringent targeting, in a context of mixed market and non-market, supply-side and demand-side policy approaches.[58] As an official report it is of its time, too economic-rationalist to be a 1970s document but far too centrist (and too public) to be a 1990s document.

CMHC and the minister were simultaneously conducting a cross-country consultation on social housing.[59] The minister, Bill McKnight from Saskatchewan, was quite favourable to co-ops, and his approach was to seek input from all main quarters.[60] This enabled stakeholder voices to be heard from the provinces, and from the now large non-profit and co-op housing sector. Advocacy on social housing in the early to mid-1980s was strong in many Canadian cities. Tight networks existed between social advocacy bodies, tenant organizations, community housing groups, and some municipal staff and councillors, and this fed the climate in which federal consultations took place. "The Minister travelled across the country for meetings with each province; and negotiations continued at a conference of ministers of housing in Calgary."[61] This was one among several federal-provincial negotiations which the cabinet had initiated in various spheres. The consultations favoured an ongoing federal role, not at odds with the study team report.[62] Quebec, chairing negotiations in this sphere, and Ontario with its new reformist government, both favoured an ongoing federal funding role but no federal delivery role, and they worked to reach a viable new deal in the negotiations.[63]

For both Quebec and British Columbia, the devolution of program management at the mid-1980s turning point was a significant event. Quebec was now *maître chez soi* in social housing, unlike the 1974–85 period when CMHC was directly involved alongside SHQ. For the Bourassa Liberals, who had defeated the PQ in 1985, this was a species of the *fédéralisme rentable* they sought. Quebec also now had a program framework which enabled it to do non-profit and co-op projects that were predominantly low-income targeted, with RGI, filling the gap created by the end of public housing production in 1978 and the less targeted 1979–85 programs. In the City of Montreal, the urban reform government of Jean Doré and the Montreal Citizens' Movement /Rassemblement des citoyens et des citoyennes de Montréal (MCM) took power in 1986, with a strong agenda of social housing as a way to invest in the city, stabilize neighbourhoods, and improve social conditions.[64] The 1986 devolution agreements gave the City's provincial partner more resources and autonomy to assist it. Quebec funded small amounts of co-op housing over and above the federal programs, and so did Manitoba under the Pawley NDP government after 1985.[65] In British Columbia, the provincial government finally took a central and co-ordinating role in social housing. This became a major resource for community-based groups and the City of Vancouver as they struggled to meet affordable rental needs as prices escalated after Expo 86, amid high immigration and accelerating growth. In the 1986–93 programs, the three large provinces of Quebec, British Columbia, and Ontario allocated some of the funding to new co-operatives, a priority absent in most other provinces.[66]

Social housing became a much higher priority in Ontario in the mid-1980s. It was a significant issue in the 1985 provincial election, the advocates' focus shifting to this level amid a federal policy direction still unclear and a feeling that the feds were "beginning to withdraw."[67] The election brought to power the Petersen Liberals in a minority government, backed by the NDP in a formal parliamentary accord in which social housing was a significant plank. The social housing priority deepened once the Liberals gained a majority in the 1987 Ontario election, amid very high housing prices and very tight rental markets. Key members of the new cabinet were from Toronto, exposed to its housing politics.[68] In 1987 the province initiated its unilateral programs, namely Project 3000, to serve high-needs groups, and Homes Now, with a stated aim of building 20,000 units over a multi-year period. Large financial resources were marshalled to build social housing. Much political capital was spent in building up capacity, support, and active sponsorship in the non-profit/co-op sector, among municipalities, and in sectors including labour unions, social service organizations, and church denominational bodies.

When the Ontario NDP defeated the Peterson Liberals in the 1990 election, this reinforced the social housing agenda. It was a long-standing NDP priority, and people in the tenant movement, co-op movement, and social advocacy were active within the party. Initially, the main NDP government policy was slightly higher production, to differentiate themselves from the Liberals. The programs were largely continuous with those of 1987–90, and built on the large efforts then to develop capacity among community-based sponsors and municipalities. As the 1990–93 recession deepened, social housing production became the centrepiece of Ontario stimulus, as housing is labour-intensive and has large inputs of domestic concrete and lumber, and so has less leakage outside the regional economy than most sectors.[69] In "jobsOntario-Homes" (always thus italicized and concatenated), the social and stimulus agendas converged.[70]

SOCIAL HOUSING IN THE SECOND NON-PROFIT DECADE, 1986–93

The program that emerged from federal-provincial negotiations and CMHC and cabinet decisions at the end of 1985 was a more income-targeted program than in 1978–84, with predominantly federal funding but a provincial lead in delivery. The new Federal-Provincial program followed the 1978–85 precedent in financing 100 percent of project capital costs by way of a private lender mortgages insured by CMHC. The program provided unified operating subsidies to each project, covering the difference between rent revenues and amortization-and-operating costs – essentially the public housing subsidy model. This operating subsidy was shared 60 percent federal, and 40 percent provincial for units serving households in "core need," i.e. at incomes unable to afford average rents in the local market, approximately the lowest 20 to 30 percent of the income spectrum.[71]

Each province could opt to deliver the new program if they contributed 25 percent of funding; all but Prince Edward Island did so.

Each province could fund more than that and thereby increase its volume of new supply; the four large and affluent provinces of Ontario, Quebec, British Columbia, and Alberta did this.[72] Provinces such as Ontario also funded unilaterally the production of market-rent units in the same projects, thus delivering an income-mixed program built around the income-targeted federal core. The Ontario norm was 80 percent RGI per project – lower at 60 to 70 percent for co-ops and outer-suburban projects but higher, up to 100 percent, for small special-needs projects. This was more low-income-targeted than in the prior decade, but still in accord with the income mix idea that had animated social housing in Canada since 1974.

The program for co-ops was separated from this overall program. The co-operative sector knew that most provinces were hostile or indifferent and lobbied intensively.[73] It proposed a program model with a special financing mechanism, caught the interest of Bob McKnight, the sympathetic federal minister responsible, and negotiated the details with CMHC's staff. This Index-Linked Mortgage (ILM) program was created despite the strong reservations of CMHC,[74] but with political sponsorship it was approved on a five-year pilot basis.

The annual volumes of new units approved were initially maintained (1987–88) at about the same level as in the early 1980s: 20,000 to 21,000 annually. After that the volumes declined, and the federal programs averaged 16,000 annually in 1985–93 overall.[75] Ontario averaged an additional 3,000 unilaterally funded units annually across the decade 1986–95, and this maintained the nationwide production volumes at the established 1970s and 1980s levels through to 1995.

The new program model and federal-provincial agreements at the end of 1985 shifted activity to the provincial level. Numerous staff left CMHC to join the provincial ministries or housing corporations that now administered the active programs by selecting projects, overseeing sponsors in the development process, flowing subsidies, and setting operating policy. The focus of the community housing sector shifted to the provinces. Shedding the front-line delivery role removed CMHC from many direct interactions with municipal and community sponsor groups.

The 1986–93 programs were expensive, but the impacts on federal expenditure were contained. By the latter 1980s, the carrying costs of development – reflecting construction costs, condo land costs, and high interest rates – were well above prevailing rent levels. New market units typically required a subsidy of over $600 monthly just to break even, and RGI units typically needed over $1,200 monthly. Yet federal expenditures on social housing subsidies rose only from $1.2 billion in 1985 to $1.7 billion in 1993,[76] or barely at all in inflation-adjusted terms and in sharp contrast to the rapid rise in 1974–85. The main reasons for the flat trend were interest rates on a rolling plateau rather than escalating, declining production volumes, and reinstated provincial cost-sharing. The rise in provincial spending was especially marked in Ontario, with its large unilateral program. Its social housing spending rose from $150 million annually in 1985 to $1 billion by 1995. By then in Ontario, provincial housing subsidies exceeded federal ones, and the political reaction this engendered fed into the national retrenchment in the mid-1990s.

Thus the mid-1980s decisions in social housing and the program framework that ensued expressed the unstable social policy balance between conflicting tendencies – neoliberalism against regional brokerage, income targeting versus broader constituencies and agendas, and the established federal lead amid increasing decentralization. The premises that had underpinned Canada's social housing policy of the 1960s and 1970s – with its managed system, mixed economy, and expanding social benefits – were out of sync with neoliberalism and with actual fiscal pressures, and the federal lead was out of sync with decentralizing Canadian federalism. The federal pulling-back had led to a new divergence in provincial policy. A trajectory had been set of devolution to the provinces, program management at that level, and flattish federal subsidy trends, without which the next turning point in the mid-1990s could not so easily have happened.[77]

6

The 1990s:
Devolution and Retrenchment

The mid-1990s brought the end of the Canadian social housing prime period that had lasted for three decades. The critical decisions were made in 1993 to 1995 and were entrenched in new federal-provincial arrangements in the latter 1990s. This turning point involved fundamental long-run changes in federal institutional roles, capacity, and resource flows, and in the ways low-income housing issues were thought about, talked about, and addressed in policy.

Devolution is an international trend across affluent countries in the 1990s onwards. In Europe it reflects a loosening of the centralized state model into one with stronger regional identities and political power. It reflects the principle of subsidiarity, that democratic responsiveness is best served by locating responsibilities at the most local scale feasible. But devolution in social policy is also a means of retrenchment: it is an institutional scaling-back of the state, more permanent than spending cuts, a handing of responsibilities to smaller units even more mismatched than the nation-state to the continental and global scale of market power.[1]

The context for social housing policy change in Canada was the 1990–93 recession and its fiscal aftermath, setting the stage for big cuts in social programs. This converged with two other forces: the triumph of neoliberal attitudes and policy internationally, and a Canadian agenda of devolution. Each government now treated the next-lower level as a business adversary to whom costs might be offloaded, rather than a partner. The downturn caused revenues to drop sharply while social spending spiked. Policy change happened in the wake of this, in the sluggish mid-1990s recovery, as fiscal pressures converged with the constitutional momentum of devolution. While these broad factors affected all areas of social policy, housing market factors also undermined social housing. The recession brought a real estate crash, feeding a strong developer-landlord campaign against the non-profit programs. A simultaneous large drop in home prices and mortgage interest rates enormously improved home-buyer affordability, leading to large movement of renters into ownership, and the fading of rental issues from mainstream political concerns.

This is not to say that social housing ended, or that low-income housing issues disappeared from political view. The housing funded under the pre-1996 programs remains largely in place, and modest "new affordable" programs were initiated at the start of the next decade. But the system was fundamentally altered. The policy regime established in the 1990s ensures that the social housing share of the broader housing system is slowly but steadily declining, as is the federal funding that sustains it. The post-2000 re-engagement avoided any restoration of the capacity, scale of activity, and political priority that the decisions of the 1990s dismantled.

POLITICAL AND ECONOMIC CONTEXT:
RECESSION, FISCAL CRISIS, REFERENDUM

In 1990–93, Canada endured its most severe economic downturn since the Depression of the 1930s.[2] This intensified the loss of industrial jobs as manufacturing shifted to lower-wage Asian countries, and the adjustments ensuing from US and North American free trade. With many unemployed, income security spending rose to a new peak of 12 percent of GDP at the same time as public revenues sank with the economy.[3] Increasingly the main concern in federal politics became deficits and public debt.

The recession contributed to severe government electoral defeats federally in 1993, in Quebec in 1994, and in Ontario in 1995. The new federal government was a centrist one in a time when neoliberal ideas meant that severe spending cuts had become middle-of-the-road politics, never mind the social fallout. Federal public debt was 72 percent of GDP by 1993, the year that federal social housing expenditures reached $2.0 billion.[4] The prospect of a credit rating downgrade on Canadian debt threatened higher interest rates and thereby worsened deficits.

In Canada, the pocketbook logic of lower taxes took centre stage politically. The view from the middle class was one of stagnant incomes, essentially unchanged in the fifteen years since the end of the 1970s, but with taxes taking a rising bite. Average real incomes declined in the 1990–93 recession and were no higher in 1996 than in 1981.[5] Neoliberal politics identified government spending as a drag on economic performance and this drew voters dissatisfied with taxes and stagnating incomes. Within the Liberal and the Conservative parties, the welfare state consensus that had endured into the 1980s now yielded to the new market-oriented ideas, and the 1980s contestation of the Canadian welfare state became a neoliberal victory.

The new Chrétien Liberal government in its 1993–97 term faced a more severe deficit trend than its predecessor and was determined to address it, untempered by the regional brokerage of the Mulroney Conservatives. The federal spending strategy had been to limit the growth of program spending overall,[6] but this now changed to reductions. "Ministries of finance, as they went through the 'nineties' restructuring of the Canadian public finances, became deeply hostile to initiatives that had permanent expense streams attached to them."[7] A sweeping program review was undertaken in the year between the 1994 and 1995 budgets. All programs were assessed on six criteria: public interest; necessity of government involvement; appropriate federal and provincial roles; scope to increase private-sector or non-profit sector roles; scope for efficiencies; and fiscal affordability.[8] In this federal government environment, fiscal concerns overrode everything, even for centrist Liberals with a sympathy for social programs.[9] The priority was felt everywhere at the political level in the "tone from the top,"[10] i.e. the Prime Minister's Office and the Department of Finance. It was felt in all federal departments and agencies through deputy ministers' weekly group meetings with the Clerk of the Privy Council, and the carefully structured program review process.[11]

The 1995 budget, announcing the results of the program review, highlighted three-year savings of $29 billion, 45,000 fewer public servants, and related deficit reduction targets.[12] "Major changes to important social programs ... were implemented by stealth with no advance notice and little effective public debate."[13] The budget unilaterally eliminated the two pillars of 1960s and 1970s cost-sharing of social programs, the Canada Assistance Plan (CAP) and Established Programs Financing (EPF), substituting a new, lower Canada Health and Social Transfer (CHST). Major cuts were made in unemployment insurance, renamed Employment Insurance (EI). The overall result was a flatlined, more targeted "post welfare state," no longer offsetting rising labour market inequality as it had in the 1970s and 1980s.[14]

Federal cuts reinforced the agenda of restraint in many provinces. The EI cuts and the deep recession sent social assistance case loads surging, and federal cuts fed cuts in provincial social benefits. Federal-provincial transfers were reduced by 1½ percent of GDP during the 1980s and 1990s; they fell from $18 billion annually to $12.5 billion annually in the mid-1990s. For example, federal transfers covered 17 percent of Ontario revenues in 1980–86 but only 9 percent by 1996–2001.[15]

Conditions in Ontario were significant for the politics of social housing nationally. It had long had the strongest social housing priority and was the vanguard province at the turning points of 1949, 1964, and 1973. It had also been the most affluent and willing to spend on social housing. Now this reversed. The recession was very severe in Ontario, as its manufacturing sector became a weakness. By the mid-1990s, with unemployment still high, lagging the GDP trough, the majority of Ontario's unemployed were on provincial social assistance, ineligible for the newly reduced EI.[16] Ontario's unilateral social housing programs, and the associated annual spending that expanded from $150 million to $1 billion annually in 1987–95, were characterized as a "boondoggle" by the provincial Conservative opposition. That party adopted a US-style neoliberal platform and rhetoric, presenting itself as a clear alternative to the NDP government which slid ever lower in opinion polls as the 1990–93 recession ground on.

Devolution was large on the agenda in the early and mid-1990s, first with a constitutional impetus and then with a fiscal one. The 1992 Charlottetown Accord negotiated by the federal and provincial governments provided for significant constitutional restructuring. The associated federal proposals identified six spheres for devolution: tourism, forestry, mining, recreation, housing, and municipal/urban affairs.[17] "Housing" was always understood to mean housing programs, and never the paramount federal policy levers of monetary policy, tax policy, bank lending, and mortgage insurance that structure the housing market. The Charlottetown Accord failed at referendum in 1992, and the Liberal government elected in 1993 shared none of its predecessor's decentralizing agenda.[18] But devolution had become part of the established thinking in federal government circles;[19] and as the fiscal crisis worsened it became part of the recipe for fiscal restructuring.

The ground shifted fundamentally after the October 1995 Quebec referendum in which sovereignty lost by the slightest margin – a "near-death experience" in Ottawa.[20] The need to simultaneously resist and assuage Quebec nationalism converged with the hardening resolve to reduce federal spending structurally and for the long term. In winter 1995–96, the devolution agenda was resurrected,[21] and negotiations started with the provinces on various spheres. The closer link to fiscal concerns than to Charlottetown is indicated by the fact that the first sphere for negotiated devolution was labour market policy and another was immigrant settlement – neither having been on the Charlottetown list.

HOUSING AND URBAN CONTEXT: REAL ESTATE CRASH

The drop in house prices through the first half of the 1990s converged with declining interest rates to dramatically improve home-owner affordability and marginalize rental needs. The real estate crash was international, but very acute in Ontario where the big-city market was coming off a condo boom and its largest recorded price bubble. The property development sector experienced a downturn more severe than in living memory. Average annual market housing completions in Greater Toronto (net of social housing) declined from 37,000 in 1987–89, to 14,200 in 1993–95, and averaged fewer than 23,000 annually in each half of the 1990s – about half the volumes of 2000–15. House prices and overall production levels did not recover their pre-1990 levels until after 1996.

House price and interest rates declines, with easier down-payment rules, brought affordability for home-buyers to benign levels not seen since the 1960s. From 1989 to 1995, resale prices in Greater Toronto declined by 29 percent in nominal terms and 40 percent in real terms.[22] Montreal saw a more modest 27 percent real-dollar decline; Vancouver's prices (in real terms) rose until 1995 but were no higher in 2000 than in 1990, despite the hot condo market and immigrant buyer demand. CMHC reduced down-payment requirements to 5 percent, initially as an economic stimulus measure. Interest rates saw a historic drop from 12½ percent in 1989 (for five-year terms) to 7 percent in 1993 and 1995,[23] and were lower thereafter. They had come off the high plateau sustained for almost three decades by inflation and inflation-fighting monetary policy. Canadian banks, benefiting from global liquidity, now offered mortgages at low floating short-term rates. Although existing home-owners lost wealth as prices declined, most improved their disposable income when they renewed at lower rates. Improvements in home-purchase affordability continued in the latter 1990s, with slow price increases offset by subsiding interest rates.

In the rental sector, Ontario's social housing completions were peaking at over 10,000 units in 1993 at the same moment that Toronto vacancy rates spiked to over 2 percent in the recession, the same point when market development crashed. A rental developer-landlord sector in distress mounted a fierce campaign against social housing, which it saw as taking market share and having privileged access to public resources.[24]

The better affordability started a ten-year period, 1996 to 2006, when the share of Canadian households owning a home rose from 63.6 to 68.4 percent,[25] a large increase. The ownership rates of the second half of the baby boom, at depressed levels in their young adulthood in the 1980s, rose to match those of older cohorts, and many of the activists that had championed co-op housing in the 1970s and 1980s were now owners. Rental housing became increasingly the home of low-income ethno-racial minorities and new immigrants. Once federal policy doubled immigration volumes in 1986–90, that group replaced baby-boomers as the main source of net rental demand. Low-income housing issues now mostly affected groups outside the political mainstream, especially in the big cities which dominated the discourse on affordable housing. In 1996–2001 – in a nation which normally added over 20,000 low-income renters annually as part of ongoing growth across the income spectrum – Canada had big net losses of low-income renters. This extraordinary phenomenon arose as young adults and new immigrants adjusted to lower wages, less job security, and reduced social benefits. More of them now stayed with parents or relatives, shared an apartment, or rented a room.

Social housing could no longer ride the coattails of mainstream political concern about affordability, but stood alone as a costly public program in a market system that was performing well for most people.

IDEAS: TRIUMPHANT MARKET AND RENTAL SIDELINED

The 1990s was a time of triumphant neoliberalism around the world. Prevailing ideas celebrated the efficiency of the market, the creativity of capitalism, and globalization as a dynamic new force. This was the "Washington consensus" of the US government, International Monetary Fund (IMF), World Bank, Organization of Economic Co-operation and Development (OECD), and associated global elites. The collapse of the Soviet bloc was a three-fold victory for democracy, for the West and NATO in geopolitical terms, and for capitalism. Nations from Russia to the Czech Republic embraced extreme versions of neoliberalism, encouraged by international bodies. The far right entered the mainstream of US politics, dominating Congress and pulling centrist President Clinton to make severe cuts in social programs. As the European Union was born in 1993 and the Euro in 1995, the context was a discourse of market principles, expanding pan-Europe capitalism, and conservative governments in Germany, France, and Britain for most of the decade. Centrist "third way" government in Britain after 1997, and Germany after 1998, retained the market-oriented emphasis although with more investment in public services. This global pro-market climate was celebrated in Canada's business press, reverberated through the mainstream media, and affected the federal climate in Ottawa.

In the 1990s, excepting devolution itself, there was much less public discourse on social housing than in the 1960s to 1980s. "Outside the community of social housing providers, there has been very little notice of, or opposition to, devolution."[26] Social housing was absent from the federal discourse on social policy. This was linked to the changing housing market: "housing's near invisibility in current social policy debates is related to a situation in which housing need has become almost exclusively a problem of the poorest households."[27]

There was increasing discourse about social housing as expensive, but as ill-targeted and failing to solve low-income housing problems.[28] There was a common misapprehension that expensive social housing served many households that did not need it. "[T]he most damning criticism of social housing is that about one-half of social housing units are occupied by middle- and upper-income households."[29] The facts were at odds with this perception. In "public housing" all units were RGI and targeted to low incomes. In the non-profit programs of 1974–85, many units had stacked rent supplement to make them income-targeted, and in the end close to half were RGI. In the post-1985 stock, about 70 percent was RGI, about 80 percent RGI in Ontario. In the federal non-profit and co-op housing programs overall, "More than 90 percent of tenants have incomes below core need income thresholds (CNITs) in all programs except the 1978 [i.e. 1979–85] non-profit housing, where 78 percent of tenants were below CNITs."[30] Overall, Canadian social housing was about 70 percent low-income targeted with RGI. This was the sort of balance between social mix and low-income targeting toward which policy had strived and evolved, but it was the contrary perception that mattered politically.

There was rising stigmatization and negative sentiment about social housing. "The [co-op] sector was (and still is) seen by housing scholars and activists as a success story, but public sentiment generally did not differentiate co-operatives from traditional public housing complexes and the entire social housing sector became even more marginalized during the 1970s and 1980s as a result."[31] Reports on "ghettoization" in the Metro Toronto Housing Authority were congruent with this.[32] The narrower targeting of the post-1985 programs, serving the few and not the many, helped undermine broad public support.[33] But shifts in overall attitudes about social housing between the 1980s when the pro-

grams were sustained federally, and the 1990s when they were termi-
nated, was smaller than the profound shift in fiscal concerns.[34]

Changing international attitudes on social housing contributed to the
same in Canada. The idea that it could solve low-income housing problems was gone, even if it was still seen as having a role to play.[35] Social
housing was no longer a major plank of social welfare in Canada's peer
nations, although still much stronger in Europe. Shifting international attitudes perhaps had more impact in federal government circles than in
mainstream political life. In former CMHC president Rochon's recollection, when the UK Thatcher government sold off large amounts of UK
social housing in the 1980s onwards, Canada was watching "And I think
that influenced the thinking of senior politicians and public servants,
both at the federal and provincial level."[36] The entrenchment of neoliberal views among finance department officials was noted above, and the
declining legitimacy of counter-cyclical spending in orthodox public finance thinking helped undermine social housing, as job creation had always been a large impetus for its production in Canada.

In the early 1990s, coverage of social housing turned sharply negative
in the Toronto-based national English-language media. A full-on attack
in Ontario led by the landlord organization got media attention, trum-
peting shelter allowances as a more effective and cheaper policy.[37] By
this period any costly new income-related transfer was a non-starter on
the policy agenda, and so the valid policy option of shelter allowances
became mostly just grist in a campaign against social housing. For the
industry, this was rooted in its ideological bent, its interests in the real
estate crash, its sense of being frozen out by the provincial NDP government, and a reaction to the latter's policy bias. Then the high program
costs and the way in which administrative controls had lagged program
expansion were the focus of Ontario Provincial Auditor reports in 1992–
94, leading to grilling in the legislature,[38] in pursuit of alleged misfea-
sance by housing agencies.[39] This dominated news coverage and evolved
into a media campaign against social housing.[40] The campaign im-
planted in the public mind the phrase "social housing boondoggle"
which became a perceived truth[41] feeding a negative political climate; it
became an Ontario Conservative Party mantra in the 1995 election and
once in office. All this affected attitudes in federal government circles.[42]

Discourse changed in regard to social housing, community, and social well-being. In the early to mid-1990s, the long-standing positioning
that social housing was "community-based" with the state merely a fa-
cilitator[43] was turned around to the disadvantage of social housing.
Now the rhetoric implied that local communities could meet their own
needs as intrepid non-profit groups initiated projects – ignoring the

utter dependence of this sector on large public subsidies and capacity-building. Increasingly, there was an emphasis on social housing as an aspect of targeted social services, rather than as a dimension of mixed urban development or general social welfare.[44] As social housing shrank as a share of the housing system, there was an ever-stronger logic that it should be targeted especially to high-needs groups such as abused women, Aboriginal people, young single mothers, or homeless people.[45] Conservative ideas of tighter targeting converged oddly with social advocates' concerns about housing high-need groups.[46] The former era's recognition that most low-income households cannot afford adequate housing at market prices was yielding to an assumption that the market meets all needs except for people with disabilities or life-transition needs. In the 1990s context, where the federal government retained the more universal parts of income security such as pensions and EI, while it devolved the more targeted programs, a view of social housing as targeted social welfare pointed to the same logic of devolution as in other such programs.

The market-minded orthodoxy in Ottawa was extreme in the 1990s. CMHC housing market monitoring publications trumpeted improving ownership affordability, largely ignored rental affordability, ceased reporting on rental demand or completions, and omitted the unilaterally provincially funded units from most social housing data. This went hand in hand with increasing emphasis on land use rules and other "local regulatory barriers" as reasons for the lack of low-income housing – ignoring the fundamentals of market prices vis-à-vis low incomes.

Within federal central agencies, especially the Department of Finance, concern over multi-year funding commitments became ever more intense in the latter 1980s and early 1990s.[47] The fact that each year's new units bring another layer of multi-year funding commitments became a fixation of the department. From its vantage, social housing was neither a proper recurring income security program, nor a normal collective good such as health or education, nor a normal capital project "booked" within a fiscal a year or two. Once matched in 1994–95 by a government priority to restructure long-term fiscal obligations, these concerns played large in the decisions that sealed the fate of social housing federally.[48]

EVENTS AND DECISIONS: THE MID-1990S

Social housing retrenchment and devolution proceeded at the federal level through several steps. First came an ending of production, next a 1996 devolution decision, and then a process in 1996–99 to implement it. The new institutional arrangement was framed in devolution agreements between CMHC and each of various provinces and territories – known formally as "Social Housing Agreements" – which transferred CMHC's program management responsibility and long-term funding exposure to the provinces. Although reflecting the political and economic context, the specific decisions and institutional changes were by no means preordained.

The First Phase: Retrenchment

Throughout 1991 to 1995, the federal social housing agenda and policy processes were about expenditure reduction rather than devolution. There were several successive federal expenditure control and program review processes[49] extending across all spheres of activity. For example, in 1990/91, CMHC participated in an expenditure review mandated by cabinet, which identified some doable cost reductions; CMHC participated in a Treasury Board task force on overlap and duplication between the federal and provincial governments which found that the direct overlap in regard to coordination was small relative to their contribution to national consistency in programs.[50]

Spending was cut.[51] In the recollection of Alan Redway, minister responsible for CMHC in 1989–91, the dominant message from its officials was the need to respond to the Treasury Board imperative of expenditure cuts, more of them each year. The mayor of Vancouver was on the phone to him frequently, advocating for more social housing, but there was little he could offer.[52] Once Elmer McKay replaced him in the portfolio, there was no longer even an interested minister. The final, 1993 budget of the Mulroney Conservative government imposed a $2.0 billion flat-lined ceiling on social housing spending, and this was maintained in the 1993 budget of the new Chrétien-Martin Liberal government. In a nation growing in population by 11 percent across the 1990s, and with prices rising 23 percent, to flatline was to cut significantly.

Most of the $2 billion went to amortize mortgages and enable low rents in existing social housing, but CMHC pursued savings and efficiencies to make room within the reduced envelope. Its two largest steps were raising project revenues by changing the RGI rent scale from 25 to 30 percent of tenant income, and by shifting to CMHC rather than private mortgage financing.[53] The fifteen years since CMHC's shift to insured private financing in 1978 had brought new possibilities, as financial markets now enabled state-orchestrated financing without direct state debt. CMHC now returned to providing direct mortgage loans to housing agencies, sourced from mortgage-backed securities (MBS) which CMHC – not the federal treasury – issued on the capital markets.[54] Ontario in 1993 shifted to its own parallel state-orchestrated financing system:[55] individual housing agencies' mortgage renewals were bundled by the provincial ministry, which solicited bids for financing tranches on the capital markets from lenders which then financed each mortgage at the lower bulk rate.

The 1989 federal budget eliminated the Residential Rehabilitation Assistance Program (RRAP), including its rental stream which had funded rehabilitation of some 10,000 units annually since the mid-1970s, peaking at 18,000 in the early-1980s stimulus,[56] and been a major support to Montreal's program of neighbourhood reinvestment. Although RRAP was reinstated in 1994 by the new Liberal government, its rental program stream did not regain anything like its former scale, and the units funded under it averaged less than 2,000 annually from then until the end of the decade.[57]

New social housing production was ended. The 1990 budget cut commitments by 15 percent, and further in 1991 and 1992.[58] The 1986 co-op program, never viewed favourably by CMHC, was extended for one year, 1991, and then cancelled.[59] The 1993 budget announced the end of funding for new social housing, except on First Nation reserves. This meant an end of social housing production as an element in federal policy, after fifty-two years. This decision also meant the end of social housing production in most provinces, except Ontario until 1995 and Quebec and British Columbia after that. The February 1995 federal budget confirmed that funding for new social housing would end permanently, except on reserves.[60] Newly funded projects under construction were allowed to run their course to completion.

Cutting new production altered the political dynamic and altered the institutional and fiscal interests of the provinces and their housing agencies in relation to CMHC. Cutting co-op production first undermined the strongest advocacy voice, helping set the stage for further cuts.[61] For the provinces, the entangled dual federal and provincial roles in social housing were an acceptable price for 60 percent federal cost-sharing on new low-income targeted units. Once new production ended, the provincial interest tilted strongly toward simplifying the administrative relationship with CMHC on existing social housing.[62]

The pivotal 1994–95 program review had smaller consequences for CMHC and social housing than for many spheres. CMHC funding was reduced by 9 percent from $2.13 billion in 1994/95 to $1.94 billion in 1997/98.[63] Although the criteria in the program review included appropriate federal and provincial roles, the result in social housing did not include devolution. The budget papers noted that most federal funding for CMHC was for ongoing subsidy obligations to social housing for low-income residents.

In this context, CMHC created a committee that considered major changes to program structures, and it circulated five "think piece" papers in 1994, floating such potential reforms to achieve economies and perhaps free up funds for new initiatives. This was widely misunderstood in the housing sector and provincially as a nefarious federal agenda.[64] It led to a contentious federal-provincial-territorial (FPT) ministers meeting in June, and then a targeted CMHC consultation with the provinces and the housing sector that fall. In retrospect, CMHC perhaps did not go far enough in considering major restructuring options to help its social housing mandate and programs to survive in the new environment.[65] That 1994 meeting would be the last FPT housing ministers' meeting for six years, reflecting the contentious climate.

The Second Phase: Devolution

After the budget-cutting came a second phase, devolution in 1996–99. While there was some continuity between these phases[66] as elements of a restructuring agenda, there was a clear break point in the fall of 1995. The Quebec referendum was held in October. After that came a decision to devolve various policy/program spheres,[67] and it was then that restructuring by way of devolution became a government priority. But the fact that this soon played out in social housing, and the shape that it took, resulted from factors specific to this policy sphere and not simply the post-referendum climate.

CMHC's light losses in the 1994–95 program review soon decimated it in the larger struggle. Federal central agencies believed that under Eugene Flichel, CMHC president from 1990 to 1995, that agency had put up a fight and evaded a dutiful response to the government's budget targets and program review.[68] In the words of CMHC's next president and of its incoming chairman, "CMHC lived on another planet ... It was light years away from the government, not sensitive to the fiscal pickle we were in collectively";[69] it "was perceived to be this monstrous agency ... that didn't relate to the central agencies, that didn't take any direction from anybody."[70] In 1995 the Privy Council Office decided not to renew Flichel's term as CMHC president, and to appoint Marc Rochon. This was a major turning point, as Rochon was chosen to bring CMHC into line,[71] to "clean the place up." "My job, what I was told was go in there

... because we can no longer tolerate having these [CMHC] people out there making decisions that will impact on our fiscal framework without any sort of reins on them,"[72] "His marching orders from the [Clerk of the] Privy Council ... were to streamline the organization and to cut expenditures."[73] "Having Rochon there was essential to make sure that CMHC stayed on the government's path."[74]

Devolution to the provinces was a strategy developed in October to December 1995 by three CMHC senior staff working with Rochon.[75] Those involved at CMHC believed it was necessary in the circumstances, whether or not they thought it was desirable. The strategy conformed to the government's priority of fundamentally restructuring fiscal obligations for the long term. It conformed to the post-referendum agenda of devolution, and was directed by cabinet office "directly and indirectly."[76] It is unclear to what extent the shape of the proposal was directly mandated by the Privy Council Office (PCO). The minister responsible for CMHC, David Dingwall, and its new chairman, Peter Smith, were brought onside.[77] Smith's main concern on being nominated was to obtain assurances from the Prime Minister's Office (PMO) that CMHC would not be dissolved or privatized.[78] There was renewed talk at the time of privatizing CMHC's main function, mortgage insurance, and intense lobbying by GE Capital to expand its new private-sector role in that profitable business. "Some senior people in town were thinking of shutting the place down. It was full of cash, the government was broke, it was a very attractive target"[79] – "cash" referring to the surplus in CMHC's Mortgage Insurance Fund, a reserve against losses in a downturn. For Smith, the devolution agreements and CMHC mandate change were a means to preserve CMHC in the new environment, and to push privatization off the agenda by making CMHC better aligned with PMO and PCO priorities.[80] Dingwall was closely connected with the prime minister, and was lukewarm to federal agencies he saw as remote from local needs. Dingwall is remembered pitching the proposal strongly and effectively at the cabinet committee.[81]

Devolution was announced in the March 1996 federal budget. "CMHC will phase out its remaining role in social housing, except for housing on Indian reserves ... To further clarify jurisdiction in the social housing field, the federal government is now prepared to offer provincial and territorial governments the opportunity to take over the management of existing social housing resources."[82] This meant the devolution of all program management and long-run subsidy responsibilities.

There were five essential elements of the CMHC-provincial devolution deal, embodied in the Social Housing Agreements soon signed with most provinces. CMHC program management would be transferred to the provinces, building on their large existing role in operating pre-1970s public housing and their role administering the 1986–93 programs as well as rent supplements. Federal annual or monthly funding to individual properties and agencies under project-specific agreements would be replaced by a global annual transfer equal to the sum of such agreements. This federal funding would gradually reduce to nil over a period of about thirty years, reflecting the expiry of those agreements. There was an up-front transfer of CMHC risk reserve funds to the provinces. There would be broad targeting requirements, accountability and monitoring, and the program structures of 1949–93 were carried over into the new century, but provinces would have considerable scope to modify and harmonize programs as they wished.[83]

The devolution decision, framework, and agreements amounted to a change as pivotal as the turning points of 1964 or 1973, and were squarely identified as such in the social housing sector and the municipal sector.[84] As an administrative measure, devolution was sensible rationalization, but as an institutional strategy it was the end of a policy era. It put CMHC and the federal government at a distance from low-income housing needs, all but severing the connection from local housing issues to federal program responses. It removed from federal shoulders in the long run the ongoing income-related subsidies to the tenants – one of Canada's half-dozen main income-related social transfer programs. It removed CMHC from direct involvement in strategies to address aging stock, renewal, refinancing, and adaptation to evolving needs. The federal government was no longer on the political front line to re-start funding for affordable housing once fiscal conditions improved. Barring a scenario where provinces stepped up with large new funding, social housing was now on a course to be a steadily shrinking share of the housing system, and to experience long-run fiscal pressures at the provincial (and Ontario municipal) level. Moreover, the CMHC mandate was also changed in as part of this same policy re-engineering:[85] no longer was it to be an active shaper of policy in affordable housing, and its three priorities would now be the mortgage insurance business, housing research, and promotion of Canadian housing-sector exports.

The 1996 devolution proposal offered provinces three main advantages and CMHC, with Treasury Board approval, framed it with incentives for provinces to say "yes."[86] The first benefit was realizing provincial control and paramountcy, without detailed federal oversight. The second was the prospect of integrated program management, with rationalized funding and administrative rules between the program silos that had been created at each of the policy turning points. Third was a trio of fiscal sweeteners: the transfer of CMHC reserves noted above; an annual global transfer set at a level reflecting 1994–95 costs; and the very gradual phase-out of federal transfers. For Ontario, federal devolution offered a fourth advantage, of enabling provincial-municipal devolution. Each province or territory was also entitled, under its agreement, to any more favourable terms that a subsequent province might negotiate with CMHC.[87]

This framework was fiscally attractive to the provinces. The 1994–95 funding level for agreements to be signed in 1997 onwards meant surplus federal funding for the first few years, because declining 1990s interest rates meant lower mortgage costs for existing projects and therefore less subsidy needed. The pre-set multi-year federal transfer meant a shift from a framework where interest-rate subsidy savings were shared with CMHC, to one where the province realized all those savings. The gradual phase-out would kick the long-run fiscal issues into the next century. The devolution terms appealed to provincial housing agencies, as distinct from their governments. In a nationwide environment of spending cuts, the agreements provided targeted housing funds that could offset dollars the agencies were losing due to provincial constraint, and money earmarked federally for housing and little subject to provincial finance ministry hurdles.[88] For the first five years or so after 1997, the dominant trend was reduced net provincial housing spending,[89] enabled by surpluses within the federal transfers. The short- to medium-term logic mattered and the long-term pressures did not.

The federal devolution offer came at a favourable moment in political life. There was a "collapse of both the networks and the coalitions which drove earlier housing policies, and a splintering of the values and goals of the various stakeholders."[90] The political mainstream had lost interest. Social advocates were occupied with defending the welfare state in general. The federal Liberal caucus included many who were sympathetic to social housing, but the cabinet's and finance minister's agenda was a tide impossible to resist. Among the large provinces, Ontario and Alberta had neoliberal governments and Quebec a separatist one, none wishing to keep the federal government involved. Ontario's municipal and social housing sectors, potentially large players in national social housing politics, were preoccupied with provincial-municipal fiscal and program restructuring.[91] In the social housing sector, it was difficult to sustain a strong and unified position, with co-ops pursuing a separate strategy and provincial housing agencies mostly in favour of devolution.[92] The non-profit and co-operative housing sectors were largely excluded from federal-provincial processes leading to devolution.[93] For Rochon, the lack of any political challenge to the devolution proposals was notable in retrospect.[94]

The Co-operative Housing Federation (CHF), concerned about possible balkanization of the sector and alarmed at the prospect of administration by some unsympathetic provincial governments, pursued a strategy to have the federal co-op programs in English-speaking Canada detached from provincial devolution.[95] By 1997 Minister Gagliano was persuaded, and program management in Ontario, British Columbia, Alberta, and Prince Edward Island – the vast majority of English-speaking Canada in terms of population and co-op units – was transferred to a new autonomous co-op sector body, the Agency for Co-operative Housing. That agency, under an agreement with CMHC, administers these programs in a parallel way as the provinces do under their devolution agreements, with similar accountability to CMHC for federal funding.[96]

The devolution negotiations were entirely bilateral, reflecting the fractured and adversarial federal-provincial environment; there were no meetings at all of the FPT ministers between June 1994 and September 2000.[97] CMHC signed its first devolution agreement with Saskatchewan in March 1997, working out in those negotiations the detailed terms of what would become the standard agreement for all provinces.[98] Devolution agreements were signed with all six smaller provinces and the territories by 1999.[99]

Three of the four large provinces did not sign a devolution agreement in the 1990s, each for its own reasons. None of these three was against devolution, and only British Columbia cared about the fundamental change that devolution meant in federal political priority and capacity. Alberta's housing officials negotiated an agreement, but were overruled by a provincial cabinet that did not want the optics of more involvement in housing.[100] The devolution agreement was less important to British Columbia given its rising housing expenditure and active social housing policy outside the scope of cost-shared programs. So it held out for better terms, signing only in 2006 when strategic portfolio concerns made the agreement desirable.[101] The devolution agreement was also less important to Quebec, given its large existing autonomy, and would entail a politically unacceptable acknowledgement of the federal policy and funding role in this sphere. So Quebec has never signed, preferring to keep the provincial political credit for jointly funded programs unconstrained by a legal agreement, and with (in Rochon's words) "a small door down the road where they could come back and get more money."[102] The Ontario agreement was delayed until after the 1997 federal election by housing-sector and municipal lobbying, seeking to prevent devolution to municipalities;[103] but the federal government's agenda overrode its Liberal caucus concerns, and the Ontario agreement was signed in 1999.[104]

The period where institutional devolution topped the federal social policy agenda was brief, from 1996 to 1999. By 2000 there emerged a new politics of the "fiscal dividend" and urban agenda, new social program initiatives, and proposals for new affordable housing programs. But the devolution agreements were put through in most provinces and the territories before that millennial social policy turn, and the three years from 1996 to 1999 were long enough for fundamental change in the institutional arrangements of Canadian social housing. Many progressives and centrists in the 1990s Liberal policy establishment and caucus did not fully realize the fundamental character of the change the government pushed through.[105]

THE PROVINCES AT DEVOLUTION: DIVERSE PATHS

Across Canada the social housing sphere fragmented at devolution into three fairly equal chunks, if we measure by population. In the one-third of Canada that consists of eight small to mid-sized provinces and territories plus Alberta, federal withdrawal meant the end of subsidized rental production for virtually a decade. There were no federal commitments for new social housing from 1994 to 2002, excepting an average 1,100 annually on First Nation reserves and in the territories. Another one-third of the country, Ontario, saw the extreme case of municipal devolution. In another one-third of Canada, the Quebec and British Columbia governments maintained a modest ongoing priority for social housing.[106]

This section considers these distinct paths in Ontario, British Columbia, and Quebec. As well as being the places where three-quarters of Canadians live, their approaches since the 1990s occupy and illustrate the extremes of fragmenting policy in social housing. The federal policy story and that in other provinces picks up again in chapter 7 at the next policy turning point.

Ontario: Devolution to Municipalities

Ontario in the 1990s took devolution to a greater extreme than any affluent nation, devolving funding responsibility and program administration to municipalities.[107] This was part of a larger provincial-municipal fiscal trade which the Harris Conservative government, elected in June 1995, brought in. Ontario is important in the national story, not just because it is an extreme but because it has 42 percent of Canadian social housing.

The Harris Conservatives had campaigned on an explicit neoliberal platform, the "Common Sense Revolution," with a promise to get the government "out of the housing business." The new government's large budget-cutting focused on health care and education. Primary and secondary education were overseen provincially but managed and mostly funded by local boards, and so to achieve its fiscal goals the government in 1996 announced a major restructuring and trade of provincial and municipal spending and program responsibilities – "local service realignment" (LSR). This involved "uploading" education funding to the provincial level where it could be cut back, and "downloading" various social programs in exchange – including social housing.

There were five phases to social housing retrenchment and devolution in Ontario. The first, echoing the federal level, was a quick end to funding for new production. The second, agenda-setting phase extended almost a year and a half following the election and saw many different ideas and voices vying to influence decisions. In winter 1996–97 the plan for devolution took shape. The institutional and legal framework for the devolved regime was developed in 1998–99 and implemented in 2000–01. Only in the agenda-setting phase did the policy process in social housing align with the broader phases of Ontario's LSR.[108] This disconnect reflects the government's particular neoliberal agenda in housing.

The 1995 Ontario budget ended funding for new social housing – one among several big spending reductions, notably an immensely controversial 21 percent cut to social assistance rates. The end of social housing production was more abrupt in Ontario than elsewhere, as the 1980s volumes had been maintained until 1995. Existing social housing was little affected: efficiencies being implemented as a result of pre-1995 efforts, in tandem with dropping interest rates, were sufficient to meet the spending reductions required by cabinet and central agencies.[109]

The agenda-setting stage of the government's restructuring was marked by intense controversy over the "Omnibus" bill to give the cabinet new powers to drive the changes through. The government appointed a "Who Does What" (WDW) Panel[110] in an effort to obtain expert and politic input on how to sort out the fiscal trade, given its non-negotiable intention of transferring education costs to the province, and to reduce the likelihood of further controversies that might derail the agenda. The wDw Panel also co-opted local notables and experts, while keeping control in the Premier's Office; the government ignored its recommendation against uploading education and social services.[111] Social housing was nowhere in the mandate or activity or deliberations of the wDw Panel or its sub-panels,[112] and instead a parallel process unfolded to address social housing.

In "Megaweek" of early January 1997, the government announced the transfer of education costs to the province. In exchange, the municipalities would pay half the costs of large programs until then funded mostly 80 to 100 percent provincially, including social assistance, subsidized child care, nursing homes, and public health, as well as some smaller programs. And municipalities would pay all the subsidy costs for social housing. This led to intense municipal reaction, and debates pitching that sector's due diligence against provincial mantras of fiscal neutrality. Although municipalities are legally subordinate to the province, they could not be ignored politically. And so a phase of counter-proposals and provincial-municipal negotiation ultimately settled the shape of devolution by August 1997, when the municipal sector reluctantly acceded to a revised May 1997 government proposal as the best deal they could get.[113] But social housing was never part of these negotiations and the announcement that municipalities would pay all the subsidy was untouched by this process.

In one version of events, social housing was not part of the government's fiscal trade until it was added at the last minute to make it "fiscally neutral," as between the provincial and municipal levels. Given the uploading of education, "The problem was then approached as basic arithmetic: downloading other services until the gap left by education was filled, more or less. This largely explains why social housing – which was not part of the Crombie Panel's discussions – became part of the Megaweek equation."[114] Such an account had also been related by Minister Leach: "Anecdotally, there was a big cabinet meeting where they were looking over the devolution business plan and it was supposed to be revenue neutral ... and they were short $500 million. The premier said, 'Look, we're short $500 million, who's got a program worth around $500 million that we can move to the municipalities?' And Minister Leach said – laughingly when he told the story – that he put his hand up in the air. And that in the end sealed the fate of social housing."[115]

But the decision to devolve social housing was more purposeful than this, and was made firmly in December 1996. It reflected specific objectives in housing, separate from the negotiables of the provincial-municipal fiscal trade. First was the ideological reason: the government wanted to get out of the housing sphere, and devolution "was a convenient 'out'"[116] when privatization or sale to tenants quickly proved unfeasible. Secondly, the minister of municipal affairs, Al Leach, was the cabinet member leading overall Local Services Realignment and the related negotiations; he was perforce required to consider his own Ministry's program spending as one element in the fiscal trade,[117] and most of that spending was for social housing.

During the period from mid-1995 until late 1996, the government had to figure out what they meant by "getting out of the housing business,"[118] and many voices and interests attempted to influence this. The main ideas were privatization proposals from the private sector,[119] a "social housing reform" proposal from the non-profit and co-op housing sector,[120] and assorted voices of politically active local people in the Conservative caucus and cabinet. The option of privatizing or selling to tenants, with its political fallout, was quickly rejected by the government.[121] This was not mortgage-free UK council housing with lower-middle-class tenants, within the legal domain of a single sovereign government. To privatize, the same or larger subsidy flow would be required to maintain low rents for low-income tenants; alternatively Ontario would have to persuade CMHC to alter the NHA, let these units go to market rents, amend the related legal agreements, and economically evict the tenants. The cabinet soon learned that Ontario was constrained by its tangle of legal agreements with CMHC, and saw that privatization was not worth it if other possibilities could work. Red Tories weighed in with op-eds[122] and discussion papers explaining the system to the neocons and floating and assessing options for getting out of housing, such as shelter allowances, selling public housing, privatizing management, and devolving to municipalities.[123]

All main options had their advocates in caucus and cabinet.[124] It is unclear how fully the Ministry analysed the options during this agenda-setting period. The minister was occupied then with politically far larger matters – the lead-up to municipal amalgamation, rent de-control legislation, and the shape of overall restructuring and devolution.[125] But in due course documents went up for discussion in the minister's office and central agencies; and ultimately "three or four" options were put into a cabinet document.[126] Devolution was the preferred one because of its less severe political fallout.

During this period came the March 1996 federal offer to devolve, and this was soon recognized as giving Ontario the flexibility it needed to devolve program management responsibility and ownership of provincial public housing. In a quick process in the Premier's office and cabinet in

the closing weeks of 1996, the decision was taken to devolve social housing, throwing it into the fiscal trade. In early December, the social housing sector learned of a pending cabinet submission,[127] as did the WDW
Panel as it was wrapping up its work.[128] The dice were cast, and social
housing was excluded from the provincial-municipal negotiations of 1997.

In 1997 negotiations with the province, municipalities did not agitate
as much about social housing as about other spheres, for several reasons. They knew less about social housing than about the other programs involved: upper-tier municipalities were very involved in social
assistance, child care, nursing homes, and public health, but few understood much about overseeing or funding social housing and what
the changes would mean.[129] The primary municipal concern was fiscal
risk, and devolved social housing subsidy would be a fairly stable and
non-escalating cost for several years.[130] Moreover some municipalities
were of the view that as they were (since January 1998) paying the subsidies there was now a "say for pay" logic of moving quickly to municipal program management.[131]

The non-profit/co-op sector was a weak voice in these decisions and
outside the negotiations, and its idea of a grand bargain of debt exchange and autonomy had zero government support.[132] But the sector
"reform" proposal offered an opportunity for consultation by a government concerned about how social housing devolution would play
out politically[133] and about how to implement its complexities. It appointed an Advisory Council on Social Housing in June 1997[134] once
the overall restructuring and devolution deal was settled, and then a
Social Housing Committee.[135] The latter turned the sector reform ideas
into a proposed recipe for the funding and legal relationship between
municipalities and housing agencies, including simplified administrative arrangements and a structured subsidy formula. Above all, the government adopted "reform" as its new-speak communications messaging
for devolution.

The next phase was to develop the institutional and legal framework
for the devolved regime in 1998–99, set out in the Social Housing Reform Act (SHRA), 2000. The non-profit/co-op sector and the municipal
sector were largely outside players in this, too.[136] The SHRA was much
criticized as rigid and prescriptive,[137] but must be understood in context. The social housing system was complex, with some 200,000 community-based and municipal units, 84,000 OHC units, $1 billion in
non-federal subsidies, several hundred small housing agencies, a web
of legal agreements, ongoing accountability to CMHC, an array of rules
and practices on equitable intake, good repair, and funding accounta-

bility – all surrounded then by intense recent controversy. The SHRA was an endeavour of the provincial public service to ensure that the social housing system would be devolved in a viable form.[138] Much work and various cabinet submissions[139] codified administrative practices into a formal framework to be applied by the forty-seven municipal governments that would program-manage the devolved system. The goal was to ensure administrative capacity and expertise upon devolution and to protect against the risk that municipal decisions might lead to under-funding, inequitable intake or RGI rules, or failure to meet Ontario's legal obligations to CMHC. Cabinet and central agencies' control reflex and the cabinet's distrust of both the housing sector and municipal sector[140] contributed to rigidity. The goal was partly to limit the scope of municipal and housing-agency decisions and forestall controversy that might bite the Ontario government politically.[141]

In 2000–01, the new Ontario policy regime was implemented. Ownership of provincial public housing was transferred immediately to the forty-seven "service managers" – municipalities and municipal boards – designated for this purpose.[142] Program management was devolved to them in a staged way over a two-year period. Although they managed diligently and sometimes creatively the social housing system in the years that followed, the decision to place responsibility for a large income-related subsidy at the municipal level has succeeded well as a recipe for under-funding and much weaker policy priority than in the preceding half century.

British Columbia and Quebec: Continuing Priority and Capacity

As the federal government wound down its role in 1993–96, British Columbia stepped in with a unilateral provincial Homes BC program that sustained social housing production at about half the 1986–93 levels and maintained the institutional capacity.

The British Columbia economy had rebounded after Expo 86, and then became fuelled by a wave of middle- and upper-income Chinese newcomers as Canada doubled its immigration levels in 1986–90, and Hong Kong approached its 1997 handover to China. The early 1990s recession and its impacts were relatively light in British Columbia. While resale prices in Toronto plummeted by 40 percent in real-dollar terms from their 1989 peak to the 1996 trough, prices in Vancouver kept rising until a 1995 peak. In real terms they were 20 percent higher in 1995 than in 1990, and 89 percent higher than at the 1985 trough.[143] Housing starts for home-ownership were higher in Vancouver in 1991–96 than in the preceeding five years – almost matching the levels of the early 1970s – while they slumped by more than half in Toronto.[144] Vancouver's rental market continued to have low vacancies, and an estimated 26,000 rental units were demolished in British Columbia in 1987–95.[145] Vancouver had responded with controls on rental conversions to condominium from 1988 onwards, permitted by new provincial legislation.[146] Greater Vancouver, with its high home prices, remained a place with many middle-income renters, and strong mainstream concern about rental supply.[147]

In the 1991 British Columbia election the NDP took power, replacing the Social Credit governments in office since 1975. Affordable housing was a major priority of the party and the new government. The new premier was Michael Harcourt, previously mayor of Vancouver (1980–86), politically connected to urban community-based groups, a thinker, and a champion of affordable housing. His new government set up a Commission on Housing Options in 1992.[148] Its mandate was to determine what the provincial priorities and strategy should be in a context of constrained resources, high needs and pressures, and declining federal funds. Its work soon became a matter of responding to the federal announcement in 1993 that it would end funding for new social housing. The commission's main recommendations were that British Columbia maintain its annual level of funding for new units, give priority to low-income families and people at risk of homelessness, and pursue ways to encourage municipalities to contribute funding and land.

British Columbia launched its Homes BC program in 1994. The province had previously funded a small "Homeless/At-Risk" housing program in 1992–95, with production averaging about 150 units per year.[149] Homes BC was initially funded at a level equivalent to the provincial cost-share in the 1986–93 Federal-Provincial program, enough to develop 600 units a year. Its funding and targeting model was the same as the latter program, with 60 percent RGI and 40 percent market-rent units, but 100 percent RGI in projects for at-risk or homeless single people. Long-term operating subsidies covered RGI subsidies as well as mortgage payments.[150] In practice the program achieved higher volumes, as municipal land and other contributions were stacked on the provincial dollars. Almost all sites in the City of Vancouver were municipal land contributed at no cost to the project.[151] From 1997 onwards there were annual agreements between the City and BC Housing about municipal land, collaborative development priorities, and housing initiatives for the homeless and at-risk population.[152] Average Homes BC production province-wide in 1996–2001 was 916 units per year, compared to an average 1,500 annually in 1986–93 before federal retrenchment.[153]

As homelessness became a stronger concern, British Columbia established a Task Group on Lower Income Urban Singles in 1994. In Vancouver there was a particular concern about the 15,000 or so Single Room Occupancy (SRO) units. These residential hotels, concentrated in the Downtown Eastside, had once housed resource workers in the off-season and in disability and retirement, but now housed a population with prevalent mental health and addictions issues, who were dependent on social assistance. There ensued a decision to make non-senior single persons eligible for RGI assistance (as in Ontario in 1987); a new priority for homeless people and those at high risk; a singles/homeless component of Homes BC; and statutory powers for the City of Vancouver to require one-for-one replacement of SRO units in the event of redevelopment. In 1998, as the Canadian social housing sector wallowed in post-devolution doldrums, British Columbia announced that it was purchasing two SROs, to be operated by non-profit societies that would rehabilitate the buildings and receive provincial health funding for residents' needs.[154]

In 1996 British Columbia confirmed social housing production as a key element in a *Strategy for Affordable Housing.*[155] In a time of intensely market-oriented ideas and policy across Canada, it was a marked exception. British Columbia also adopted legislation to foster inclusionary housing, enabling municipalities to permit extra density in new development proposals in exchange for developer contributions to public amenities and affordable housing. From 1996, BC Housing also took an active role in orchestrating mortgage financing for new and existing social housing.[156]

In Quebec, a provincial election brought change that sustained some priority for social housing in the face of federal withdrawal. The PQ government that replaced the Liberals in 1994 adopted a more active social housing agenda, a softer reprise of what had happened when it first took power two decades earlier. The Bourassa Liberals had maintained some Quebec support for renovation programs in the 1990s as the feds withdrew. The PQ was nudged in social housing policy by its activist left wing, the City of Montreal, and the voices of its social sector partners in its tripartite corporatist social policy.

Both Premier Parizeau (1994–96) and Premier Bouchard (1996–2001) pursued a mix of neoliberal, market-oriented policy and socially progressive initiatives. This reflected the "big tent" coalition in terms of social and economic policy which the PQ represented by the 1990s.

Cost-cutting was less draconian than at the federal level. The government moved toward formalizing a relationship between the government and third-sector groups, including a dedicated secretariat.[157] It convened corporatist summit conferences of top officials from Quebec business, labour organizations, and the provincial government, "to iron out a societal consensus regarding the direction of public policy."[158] At two such events in 1996, community-based third-sector groups participated as full partners, leading to an emphasis on steps to "combat poverty and social exclusion."[159]

Social housing was integral in this rather European framing and discourse on poverty and social inclusion. Social housing had been a strong priority since the 1970s for the Quebec third sector, and this tripartite corporatism now integrated that sector and its agenda into a broader priority-setting process. In 1996 a working group on the social economy was created, and it brought to the second 1996 tripartite summit in October "a forty-page report containing a broad, inclusive definition of social economy (SE) and concrete proposals for launching twenty specific social economy projects ... The proposals prepared by the SE working committee were presented, discussed for hours and transformed into public policy decisions during the three-day socio-economic summit."[160] Along with Quebec's soon-to-be famous universal child care, these proposals included a social housing program.

The City of Montreal also lobbied the province.[161] Under Mayor Doré and the MCM, Montreal had adopted an ambitious housing strategy, Habiter Montréal. When the centrist Pierre Bourque took office in 1994, the severe decline in certain neighbourhoods kept housing on the mainstream agenda. And so the active municipal role and program capacity in housing and neighbourhood renewal that had been established under Drapeau and Doré was sustained through the unpropitious 1990s. Before the dual 1996 summits, Quebec had already implemented an experimental Programme d'achat rénovation pour coopératives et OSBL (PARCO / Acquisition-renovation program for co-ops and non-profits) with 1,100 units over the two years 1995–96, many of them in Montreal. By 1996 there were five small housing rehabilitation programs operating in the city, with a mix of provincial and municipal funds.

The larger Quebec social housing Plan d'action 1997–2001 was rolled out after the summits. The main element was AccèsLogis, launched in 1997 for a five-year period, to support new non-profit housing development with grants and operating subsidies.[162] Half the units were to be low-income targeted with RGI, and half at moderate market rents. Another element was a Fonds québécois d'habitation communautaire

(FQHC), a capital fund to recirculate mortgage payments for AccèsLogis projects into investments in further social housing. A third element was a Programme de revitalisation des quartiers centraux (PRQC / Revitalizing older neighbourhoods program) which offered interested municipalities 50/50 provincial-municipal funding and targeted rehabilitation dollars to high-need areas. All of these responded to City of Montreal issues and lobbying. AccèsLogis took its name and program recipe from a mini-program Montreal had run with its own resources since the early 1990s; PRQC too was based on a Montreal program.[163] In 1999, the province signed a three-year agreement with the City of Montreal for various collaborations in affordable housing.

AccèsLogis emphasized sponsorship by community-based groups, consistent with the prevailing ideas in Quebec's social housing sector. Production volumes were modest as the program ramped up, averaging 700 units annually in 1998–2001.[164] This was about half the volume per capita seen in British Columbia, but much higher than in the rest of Canada.

But British Columbia and Quebec, the one-third of Canada funding social housing production at about half the pre-1996 levels, were the exceptions to the national picture. Elsewhere, provinces administered and co-funded the pre-1996 programs and projects, but these were shrinking relatively as a part of the housing system and as an option for low-income Canadians. The federal government had withdrawn from active involvement. "The market" – more specifically the dynamics of down-market rental – thereby returned to a dominant position in the housing choices and conditions for low-income Canadians.

The end of the prime period of Canadian social housing was collateral damage[165] of the political economy of the 1990s with its economic stress, fiscal distress, neoliberal thinking, and adversarial approach to intergovernmental relations. Devolution to the provinces proceeded down a path started in the mid-1980s and earlier, and the CMHC lead had become an odd legacy given the momentum of social policy devolution and provincial administration of housing programs. Amid a housing market that was newly benign for the social mainstream, Canadian social housing had bumped up against the narrowing limits of the nation's welfare state consensus. The institutional momentum of social housing that had weathered various conflicts during thirty years could not withstand this convergence of factors. Neoliberal ideas now defined the bounds of pragmatism, and social housing was relegated into a legacy of a past welfare state era.

7

The 2000s: Modest Re-engagement

As the twenty-first century opened, programs for new affordable housing emerged, amounting to a modest re-engagement in affordable
rental by Canada's federal and provincial governments.[1] These included the federal-provincial Affordable Housing Initiative (AHI), related
federal funding, and somewhat larger programs in British Columbia,
Alberta, and Quebec. Across Canada in the first twelve years of the new
millennium, about 8,000 new affordable units were funded annually,
somewhat under half the average volume of the thirty-year prime but
less income-targeted. The production volumes dropped off after 2011.

The post-2000 initiatives softened but did not reverse the fundamental changes of 1990s retrenchment and devolution. The 1990s
institutional arrangements and roles remained in place. Program approaches and volumes vary widely among the provinces, and operating
subsidies are a matter left to them. There is no revival of the idea that
animated policy through the thirty-year prime, of sustaining a significant non-market housing sector. No government considers the approach then taken for granted, of subsidized rents on a scale large
enough to make housing affordable for one in three low-income
renters, and for half of ongoing growth in that segment of society.
Today's programs accommodate some worst-case needs and leave things
mostly to the market.

These programs emerged in a political and economic context which
was quite different at the end of the 1990s from most of that decade. A
strong economic recovery, along with cutbacks and lower interest rates,
put the federal budget into surplus by 1998. The deficit and the fiscal
concerns of the Department of Finance no longer trumped everything.
The new affordable housing programs fit a new form of "collaborative
federalism," where modest new programs arise from federal-provincial

negotiations. The programs also reflected a renewed concern for urban issues, with the well-being of Canada's cities increasingly seen as a key to national prosperity. Cities across the country were experiencing rising homelessness and more people living on the margins, in the wake of the profound labour market changes of the 1990s and of reduced social benefits.

AHI, initially a time-limited initiative, was sustained and boosted through two decades by a series of happy political accidents. It was never framed as a long-run program like those of the 1950s to the 1980s and was always funded in three- to five-year segments. This created recurring uncertainty, but the program and its siblings kept getting extended. Within two years the limited scope and budget of AHI broadened in a context of good fiscal times and a federal urban agenda. Minority governments in 2004–11 led to parliamentary deals to boost housing funding, and then came the Global Financial Crisis of 2008–10, leading to a brief international consensus on stimulus spending to rescue the economy.

POLITICAL AND ECONOMIC CONTEXT: STRONG GROWTH AND FISCAL DIVIDEND

In the latter 1990s, the federal government achieved fiscal recovery through warm luck and ice-hard decisions. A robust cyclical recovery led by exports to the United States greatly boosted federal revenues. Declining global and Canadian interest rates sharply reduced interest payments on the national debt. In this context, the severe 1990s reductions in social spending helped the federal government into surplus by 1998.[2] In 1996–2008 Canada experienced its strongest sustained economic growth since the 1970s, a dramatic change from the severe early 1990s recession. In the early years of the new century, Canada was carried on the global commodities boom, especially oil exports to the United States, enormous capital investment in the oil sands, and coal and other resource exports to booming China.

Economic and fiscal recovery led Canada and the governing Liberal Party to revert in 1998–2003 to more familiar centrist politics. There were debates in national politics about how to spend the "fiscal dividend." How much of it should go to paying down the national debt, to making further tax cuts, or to enhancing spending? If the latter, would priority go to restoring health or social transfers to the provinces, to renewed priorities such as public infrastructure and education, or to new social program initiatives? The government chose a little of all of these, in a climate of "relentless incrementalism."[3]

The context for new social program initiatives was set by the Social Union Framework Agreement (SUFA) signed in February 1998.[4] Under SUFA, any new social programs would be a matter of federal-provincial (and territorial) negotiations, giving shape to new programs that involved joint funding or joint tax credits. The provinces would play large roles in program design and carry out program delivery. Various federal-provincial-territorial (FPT) ministerial councils were created or resurrected in several spheres to discuss initiatives in each of them. This was not a formal constitutional arrangement, but a "fluid and ad hoc" umbrella agreement of the governments of the day, reflecting a new, post-devolution, post-referendum climate in Canadian federalism.[5] Initially this was seen by the affordable housing and municipal sectors as a limiting and inauspicious context for housing initiatives,[6] but it soon proved more fertile.

The largest early initiative was the National Child Benefit and Canada Child Tax Benefit, a federal-provincial collaboration starting in 1998. Federal health transfers were partly reinstated, and the CHST was split into a Canada Health Transfer and Canada Social Transfer, providing some safeguard for the mostly income-targeted non-health funds. Federal spending on tertiary education expanded. In 2004 the federal and provincial first ministers reached a multi-year federal-provincial agreement on health care funding.

There was talk of a broader urban agenda. In late 1999, the government announced a National Homelessness Initiative, a startling federal engagement in urban social issues and a foot in the door for new housing spending. The Federation of Canadian Municipalities lobbied hard for a tri-level urban infrastructure program, and the government responded in its 2000 budget, opening negotiations with the provinces. In May 2001 Judy Sgro, representing a Toronto riding, was appointed chair of a Prime Minister's Caucus Task Force on Urban Issues to do a cross-country consultation. Reporting in late 2002, it recommended three main funding and tax-based priorities: transit, other urban infrastructure, and affordable housing. Paul Martin, finally succeeding Jean Chrétien as Liberal prime minister in 2003, appeared interested in urban issues.

Minority governments in easy fiscal times gave a boost to social and urban initiatives. Paul Martin's 2004–06 Liberal government was the first minority in Ottawa since the 1970s. Dependent on NDP support, his cabinet tilted further toward new social spending. When Harper's Conservatives took office in 2006, it was again a minority. Harper surprised many with his pragmatism and willingness to use social spending to stay in power, eschewing the severe cutbacks that he had long advocated and that many now expected. This liberal attitude toward spending was dramatically reinforced as the Global Financial Crisis arrived in 2008–10.

HOUSING AND URBAN CONTEXT: SOCIAL STRESSES AMID THE BOOM

The decade from the latter 1990s until 2008 was the "best of times, worst of times" in housing and urban issues. For the middle-class mainstream and the affluent, it was a time of sustained income growth and job opportunities, and a housing market more benign than any time since the mid-1960s. But there were rising social stresses in cities, with more people living on the margin economically as labour market disparities widened. There was more social and physical distress in the rental housing sector. People saw that poverty had become racialized, in the context of ongoing high immigration and ongoing migration of Aboriginal people to cities. Strong political concerns about these issues emerged in cities across the country.

Canada in 1996–2006 experienced a home-ownership boom unmatched since the decade after World War II. In the decade straddling the turn of the millennium, the percent of households owning a home rose by 5 percentage points nationwide from 63 to 68 percent.[7] This had started in 1993–96 as interest rates and home prices plunged. After 1996 as the economy expanded, incomes grew and interest rates continued sliding, so far more people could afford to buy a home. This led to an absolute decrease in renters across Canada, most strongly in Ontario. Chapter 6 noted the net loss of low-income renters in 1996–2001. In 2001–2006, equally anomalously, there was an annual net loss of some 30,000 other, non-poor renters as a result of the ownership boom, felt strongly in the big cities of Vancouver, Montreal, and especially Toronto.[8]

The rental housing sector experienced new stresses. Prevailing rent-to-income ratios had ratcheted up to new plateaus in the economic crisis of the early to mid-1990s. In the years that followed, despite strong economic growth, these levels became the new normal. Rental housing had become permanently a lower-income sector. It was now home to many people in low-wage jobs who lived without savings, used food banks, and were often in arrears and on the brink of eviction. Rental apartments were being lost as buildings were converted to condominium – not so much in Toronto or Vancouver where laws and regulations prevented this, but in Calgary 3,500 rental units were converted in 1995–98,[9] and Winnipeg's more desirable older neighbourhoods saw many conversions. Rental housing had become the place where the fallout of labour force change and social policy retrenchment was manifest.

In urban Canada, housing and neighbourhood issues once again emerged as mainstream political concerns. In Vancouver, the Downtown Eastside was in a crisis of drugs and homelessness. Winnipeg's inner city was in long-term distress as a result of slow growth, deindustrialization, ongoing exodus to the suburban ring, and in-migration of low-income Aboriginal people from the First Nation reserves of northern Manitoba and northwestern Ontario. By the 1990s, the city's West Broadway and Spence neighbourhoods experienced generalized disinvestment, abandoned properties and severe disrepair.[10] In Montreal, loss of industrial and port jobs, and ongoing exodus of homebuyers to the suburban ring, led to a similar crisis in the inner east-end district of Hochelaga-Maisonneuve.[11] In Toronto, inner-suburban social issues were now in the news headlines. High immigration, labour force polarization, exodus of middle-class renters to home-ownership, and more reliance on filtering to house the low-income share of rapid growth, made many of Toronto's postwar apartment tower neighbourhoods enclaves of poverty, and a new concern about social polarization emerged.[12]

Homelessness surged in cities across Canada, reflecting these frayed edges of the labour market, housing market, and social safety net. Street-and-shelter homelessness doubled in Calgary in the mid-1990s, reaching 1,000 people a night.[13] In Toronto, emergency shelter usage had doubled every five years over two decades, reaching about 4,000 nightly by 2000. In Vancouver, demand for emergency shelters rose sharply, and people were turned away for lack of space.[14]

IDEAS: PRAGMATISM AND INCLUSION

In these years at the turn of the millennium, market-oriented assumptions about housing prevailed in Canada, as they did around the world. But there were counter-currents: concerns about rental supply; space for new social initiatives as the fiscal crisis passed; and a new discourse about poverty, opportunity, and social divides. Then in

2009–11, Keynesian ideas about counter-cyclical stimulus had a brief and dramatic reprise.

A large public-sector share of GDP, a regulated financial sector, redistributive policy, and fiscal stimulus as one element of macroeconomic management were anathema to the Chicago School, business school version of neoclassical economics. This paradigm had captured mainstream political thinking in the United States and England in the 1980s, and in Canada and most of Europe by the 1990s. The agenda of monetary and not fiscal policy as the main macroeconomic lever became strongly entrenched in Ottawa. Containing public spending and slaying the deficit remained the dominant notes in any discussion of taxes and the role of government. The order of the day was privatizing public enterprises and spinning off federal ports and airports, and provincial highways, power plants, and phone companies, to become self-sustaining enterprises.

But within the bounds of this climate of ideas, Canada's federal governments in the dozen or so years from 1998 to 2011 were quite pragmatic. This was true of the Chrétien-Martin Liberal government once the fiscal deficit was gone by 1998. The Harper Conservatives, while governing with two successive parliamentary minorities in 2006–11, were more focused on staying in power than in implementing a neoliberal agenda. There would be no return to the expanding government role and social programs of the 1940s to 1980s, but there was lots of political space for modest new spending initiatives to serve the interests of the national economy, local communities, or political gain. With the global commodities boom buoying the Canadian economy, there were ample federal revenues for these.

The fiscal orthodoxy changed dramatically as the Global Financial Crisis arrived in 2008. Governments and central banks around the world were worried about global economic collapse, and collaborated in bringing interest rates to their lowest levels ever, and in a large stimulus program. There was briefly an international consensus that what was needed was deficit budgets to support Keynesian-style counter-cyclical spending, and Canada's 2009–11 stimulus was part of a concerted action by the ten or so economically largest nations.[15] The biggest players in this were the United States and China, their demand helping to extend the global commodities boom and enabling Canada to float through the crisis with just a moderate recession. Housing was a significant part of Canada's stimulus program.

Counter-cyclical spending on housing meant a return to an open and purposeful federal policy lead. Federal policy dominance had never changed in the market sectors of the housing system, despite the devolution of non-market programs. Now this federal lead was made plain, as the levers of housing stimulus were federal, including sizable new spending, purchase of bank mortgage assets, tax incentives, and super-low short-term interest rates. And the pump-priming included use of the federal constitutional spending power in the ostensibly devolved non-market housing sectors.

There were also concerns about Canada's lack of new rental housing supply. Private-rental production, after the postwar boom collapsed in the 1970s, had declined further and further to a nadir in the 1990s. Canada had arrived at a place familiar in the United States or Australia, where most added rental supply occurred by way of renting out older houses in declining neighbourhoods, or renting condos. But Canada was a country where the happy postwar experience remained the entrenched expectation – that one-third or more of added households each year would be renters, and that their needs would be met by developing new rental apartment buildings. Metro Toronto set up a task force in 1997 on the lack of rental supply and what to do about it,[16] and the City of Vancouver produced periodic reports on the matter. Ontario's neoliberal government found that new rental supply did not magically spring to life when it de-regulated rents in 1998, so it set up a task force to commission research and study the factors at play.[17] Rental supply remained a concern of some policymakers at CMHC.

In those years at the turn of the millennium, European concepts of social inclusion and exclusion came to have some currency in Canadian social policy.[18] Dominant in EU social policy discourse by the 1990s, social exclusion had acquired a broad meaning encompassing widening income disparities, homelessness, racialization of poverty, and deepening poverty in social housing estates. It was a new way of framing unfashionable ideas of social equity; a way of describing disadvantage structured by a polarizing labour market and housing market and new class-race divides; and a language that probed the three-way relationship between the market economy, public policy, and civil society. In European social inclusion discourse, housing and related neighbourhood inequalities were very prominent, reflecting the many decades of housing as an integral part of decommodified public services.[19] Canada, with its market-dominated housing system and weak social housing priority, saw some efforts to integrate housing into the social inclusion discourse and the related hopes for a new post-neoliberal social policy.[20]

EVENTS AND DECISIONS: ENTERING THE 2000S

As homelessness and social distress rose in the low-end rental market, political concerns bubbled up locally. Community groups and municipalities carried out studies to document the scope of the problem, call political attention to it, and frame responses. In Calgary, a major homelessness study was carried out in 1996–97. The Calgary Homeless Foundation was created in 1998, spearheaded by business people working with social activists, approaching the matter as one that required leadership in the community, outside of government, and collaboration among business, government, and the non-profit sector. The Foundation and the municipality carried out research and documented the issues in detail. The Foundation got conservative politicians involved, sponsored housing projects and services, and put the issue effectively on the political agenda.[21]

The politics of homelessness was intense in Toronto all through the mid and late 1990s. Activists staged media events, and there was a flood of letters to the editor about homelessness. Subcommittees of Metro Toronto and City of Toronto councils became a forum for fractious confrontations, dialogue, and collaboration among activists, community agency staff, municipal staff, and elected officials.[22] The death of a homeless man on the street in January 1996 led to a coroners' inquest that became a forum for expert evidence and media attention to the systemic inadequacies in services and housing that underlay such personal tragedies.[23] This was not just a downtown issue, and in Toronto's western outer suburbs the Peel Coalition for Shelter was formed in 1996. The City of Toronto's Homelessness Task Force of 1998 became a fulcrum for politics of housing and homelessness. Mel Lastman, a populist conservative campaigning successfully in fall 1997 to be mayor of the new amalgamated City, stated that there were no homeless people in North York, his postwar suburban part of Toronto. When right afterwards a homeless woman was found dead in a North York gas station toilet, he was shaken, and promised to make homelessness a priority. Once elected he appointed Toronto's United Way CEO Anne Golden to head a task force, and with solid analysis and media savvy, the Golden Report captured the attention of the Toronto-based national English-language media.[24]

Local coalitions on homelessness and housing were formed in big cities across Canada and in mid-sized Ontario cities, including Vancouver, Edmonton, Calgary, Niagara, London, Hamilton, Ottawa, and others. In Peel Region, Durham Region (Oshawa and Toronto's eastern outer suburbs), Edmonton, and elsewhere, official task forces or advi-sory bodies were created. [25] For activists, homelessness is not only about housing, but always partly about housing. In March 1999, following the release of the Toronto's Homelessness Task Force report, the Federation of Canadian Municipalities (FCM) and the City of Toronto sponsored a National Symposium on Housing and Homelessness, attended by people from across Canada.

Homelessness was declared a national disaster, and housing was an in-tegral part of the solution. In the great ice storm of January 1998, Montreal and Ottawa were shut down without power, and tens of thousands across eastern Ontario and southern Quebec slept in schools and community halls; a national disaster was declared. Cathy Crowe, a nurse working in Toronto with homeless people, reframed this: if temporary homelessness of middle-class people was a calamity, why not the chronic homelessness of thousands on the streets and in shelters every day across Canada? The Toronto Disaster Relief Committee (TDRC) was formed[26] and its declara-tion of homelessness as a national disaster "was a call to action that swept the nation."[27] Declarations to that effect were adopted by Toronto City Council in mid-1998, by dozens of municipal councils across Canada, and in November by the Big City Mayors' caucus of FCM.[28] TDRC and allies formed the National Housing and Homelessness Network in early 1999, seeking media attention and lobbying directly.

FCM formed a National Housing Policy Options Team, led by Jack Layton. He was then a Toronto city councillor with a long involvement in housing and homelessness issues, the left-of-centre designate of con-servative Mayor Lastman on these issues, and an FCM vice-president. FCM at its convention in 1999 endorsed a National Housing Policy Op-tions Paper the team had prepared,[29] and the next year adopted a firmer set of proposals that put forth a national affordable housing policy framework.[30] Local elected officials and advocates lobbied MPs across the country, and these issues were hitting above their normal small in-fluence in federal politics.

Social policy advisors in the Prime Minister's Office (PMO) took an interest in all this. "The PMO in particular had kept a close watch on the [homelessness] issue, and was aware that the pressure points came not from one source, but from organizations, municipalities, members of Parliament, and the general public ... The PMO closely monitored the extensive work being done by Anne Golden in Toronto and knew in advance that her report would press for direct federal intervention."[31] Golden and her staff met with those PMO advisors and with Alfonso Gagliano, the minister responsible for CMHC.[32] But in 1998–99 it was early days in the emerging fiscal dividend politics, and it was unclear how much political appetite there was to re-engage in urban issues or devolved social housing. When FCM representatives met with Finance Minister Martin in late 1999, there was interest in infrastructure but little in affordable housing.[33] Would his department or cabinet's fiscal conservatism veto any new affordable housing initiatives?

In Ontario, provincial-to-municipal devolution was shifting the focus to the local level (chapter 6) and by 1999 the designated "service manager" municipalities were preparing frameworks for their new role. The main focus was to take on program administration of existing social housing, but the concerns extended to homeless services and new housing. Councils adopted policies providing municipal land, small capital grants, and property tax exemptions for new affordable rental, and exemptions from development charges and building permits; and in 1999–2001 the municipalities of Toronto, Ottawa, Hamilton, Peel, Waterloo Region, and Peterborough each launched small initiatives or pilot projects on this basis. Their new recipe was feasible in the environment of low mortgage interest rates and moderated late-1990s development costs: the local incentives could make a project financially viable at market rent, and production could happen on that basis without federal and provincial agencies needing to re-start the comprehensive pre-1996 programs. But the new program model was explicitly one on which the federal and provincial governments could be invited to stack contributions of land, capital grants, or tax breaks.

The National Homelessness Initiative was announced in 1999, a milestone in federal re-engagement in urban social issues. In March, responding to the advocacy, Prime Minister Chrétien appointed Minister of Labour Claudette Bradshaw to the new position of "federal coordinator on homelessness" with an unclear mandate. Bradshaw assembled a small secretariat and "toured more than twenty communities that summer, in every province and territory. She had long discussions with provincial and municipal politicians – but more particularly she visited shelters for the homeless and talked with police and social workers. She toured ... with front-line service workers. She listened to what the homeless had to say and she gave them hugs."[34] This culminated in a joint meeting with officials from local communities and federal ministries in August, and then a video presentation to cabinet in September, with "not a dry eye" at either meeting. Federal officials negotiated with provincial counterparts to arrange a program of direct federal funding to local organizations. The National Homelessness Initiative (NHI) was announced in December by Bradshaw and Gagliano, and

$753 million over three years was confirmed in the February 2000 federal budget.

The NHI was significant for affordable housing. The two centrepiece programs within it were the Supporting Communities Partnership Initiative (SCPI, pronounced "skippy") which funded homeless prevention and emergency services, and a $268 million three-year expansion of RRAP. Thus subsidized repair was part of the response to homelessness – far from a national housing program but a departure from the 1990s orthodoxy of devolution and reliance on the market. Within SCPI, one eligible project type was transitional housing. Toronto set the pace when its SCPI plan, the first in Canada, allocated 20 percent of funds to transitional housing.[35] Nationwide in the early SCPI years, transitional housing took 26 percent of funds in the main NHI programs (net of RRAP), and several projects were long-term supportive housing in practice.[36] The requirement that a local body be formed to administer SCPI galvanized collaboration among community agencies and local governments for whom housing was an integral part of the response to homelessness. NHI and SCPI, rebranded as the Homelessness Partnering Strategy by the Harper Conservative government in 2006, were extended several times through the two decades following.

But the extent of any federal re-engagement in housing remained quite unclear. FCM and housing advocacy groups kept up their campaigns. The National Housing and Homelessness Network called for restoration of pre-1996 spending[37] – an impossible ask in the circumstances, but part of a discourse that legitimized more limited proposals as a middle way forward. In October 1999 FCM proposed a detailed $13 billion annual urban infrastructure program, which included $2 billion capital each year for new affordable housing.[38] The government was heading toward a new infrastructure program, but would it include affordable housing? Mayors and FCM representatives met with Prime Minister Chrétien on this and with Gagliano.[39] Although the devolution agreements were signed while he was minister, Gagliano was a supporter of affordable housing and of new CMHC initiatives in the post-deficit context.[40] The February 2000 federal budget proposed a large new program for provincial highways and municipal infrastructure – but nothing on affordable housing.[41] FCM and the Canadian Housing and Renewal Association (CHRA) angled for what they thought was doable in the context of SUFA and soft federal interest: capital grants for new affordable rental that would be federally funded but administered by an autonomous foundation, and supplemented by provincial rent subsidies.[42]

In fall 2000, affordable housing issues bubbled into federal-provincial discussions and then federal electoral politics. The FPT ministers of housing met in Fredericton in September, for the first time since June 1994, and the possibility of a new affordable supply initiative was discussed in private.[43] FCM, housing-sector organizations, and homeless advocates were present uninvited, and set up camp outside the venue of the meeting to get media attention.[44] A federal election was called for November 2000 and, set to sweep Ontario and Quebec and win a strong majority, the governing Liberals included affordable rental in their platform, with annual capital funding of $170 million. The platform stated that "Canada's urban regions are experiencing a severe shortage of affordable rental housing. New construction of rental housing is at a near standstill ... A new Liberal government will work with our provincial partners to create ... a cost-shared capital grants program to help stimulate the creation of more affordable rental housing, both private and non-profit."[45]

The re-elected government announced in 2001 that it would make $680 million available nationally over five years for new affordable housing, in the Affordable Housing Initiative. FPT negotiations followed in the SUFA framework where the federal government needed provincial concurrence on the shape of the initiative. Intensive lobbying continued. At an FPT ministers' meeting in Quebec City in November 2001, an affordable housing framework agreement was reached.[46] The price of consensus was an exceedingly loose framework, a basis for bilateral federal-provincial (or federal-territorial) agreements that followed.[47] The model of a broad FPT framework, provincial autonomy in program design, and varied bilateral agreements fit the post-2000 shared-cost model of "collaborative federalism."[48]

Here was a return to federal leadership and federal-provincial funding for new affordable rental supply after nine years' absence. The federal positioning was that this was a program to meet a need for rental supply – implicitly a remedy for defects of market performance rather than a program targeted to low incomes. The FPT agreement referred to "declining vacancy rates and low production of rental housing" and the resulting "urgent requirement for short-term measures to increase the availability of affordable housing across Canada," while leaving more permanent measures for another day.[49]

Completing the 2000s Policy Turn

The initially short-term AHI became a program framework lasting the better part of two decades, extended and at times expanded in a series of political happy accidents.[50] These included a fuller blossoming of the urban agenda by 2003, a pragmatic approach and parliamentary deals under by the Harper Conservatives during their 2006–11 minority terms, and the stimulus responding to the 2008–10 economic downturn.

In 2003 in the closing months of Chrétien's term as prime minister, a second and larger round of AHI was announced, implemented under Paul Martin. This was part of the gathering momentum of the federal urban agenda, and responded to criticisms of AHI as inadequate in low-income targeting and funding. AHI had strong support from the ministers responsible for CMHC, Steve Mahoney (2003) and Joe Fontana (2004–05), both from urban Ontario ridings where the politics of affordable housing was boiling. This second round involved more money: a further $320 million, bringing the 2001–06 federal total to $1 billion.[51] This round of AHI was no longer positioned simply as a program to address rental supply shortfalls: it was explicitly low-income targeted.

Once the Harper Conservative minority government took office in February 2006, it renewed the AHI funding and associated federal-provincial agreements – initially for 2006–07 and subsequently for 2007–08 and 2008–09, at $135 million annually in federal funds with provincial matching. The Harper election platform had included a tax credit for development of low-income housing, looking to the US example. There was concern in the affordable housing and municipal sectors that this would spell the end of AHI's short life and of federal support for targeted local projects. But the government stuck with AHI and quietly nixed the tax credit idea. As Pomeroy and Falvo put it, "This government adopted a 'don't rock the boat' approach, abetted by ongoing fiscal surpluses such that, initially, there was no need to impose spending restraints in 'non-priority' areas, such as housing."[52] This spending also "may have been a strategic attempt of a minority government to assuage concerns of the urban voters – ridings that the Conservatives had failed to capture. Sustaining investment in cost-shared housing programs was also politically important to reinforce election gains in Quebec."[53]

Further funding came through a sister program created in 2006–07. In exchange for supporting the minority Liberals' 2005 budget, Jack Layton's NDP negotiated a set of lump sum federal transfers to the provinces for affordable housing, approved in legislation in summer 2005. This fit the pattern of allocating year-end surpluses to assorted government priorities in a politically advantageous way. When the new Harper Conservative minority was elected in 2006, "the commitment was honoured by the new government, largely because it had been approved by a vote in parliament."[54] It was implemented by way of trust funds totalling $1.4 billion paid out over three years. This included $800 million allocated per capita among the provinces, a $300 million Off-Reserve Aboriginal Housing Trust, and a $300 million Northern Housing Trust for the territories (two-thirds of it for Nunavut). Unlike AHI these trust funds did not require provincial or territorial matching funds.

When the economic downturn arrived in 2008, housing was given a large place in the stimulus program, Canada's Economic Action Plan (CEAP). "Housing was well positioned to assist the government's efforts, primarily because home construction and renovation have large economic multiplier effects. The profile of housing in contributing to the crisis in the United States also placed a spotlight on housing, stimulating efforts to reassure consumers, investors, and financial markets that Canada's housing system was not similarly vulnerable."[55] Just over $2 billion was allocated to federal spending on social/affordable housing over fiscal 2009–10 and 2010–11 – half for repair and retrofit of existing social housing and half for new supply. The latter included $475 million for seniors and disabled people – regular low-income renters not being "deserving poor" – plus $400 million for Aboriginal On-Reserve housing and $200 million for the territories, and an AHI extended through fiscal 2010–11.[56] After the 2009–11 stimulus, the Harper Conservatives again extended AHI in agreements for 2011–12 to 2013–14 and subsequently for 2014–15 to 2018–19. The 2011 decision gave provinces more flexibility in their use of funds, and rebranded the program Investment in Affordable Housing (IAH). It also merged into IAH the ever-popular RRAP existing since the 1970s, thereby requiring 50 percent provincial cost-sharing rather than the smaller provincial shares under the RRAP formulas.

The modest social policy initiatives of the early 2000s included housing allowances and rent subsidies in five provinces comprising 80 percent of the national population. Quebec had already in 1997 extended eligibility for its rather shallow housing allowance to cover families, not just seniors,[57] reflecting the same politics that created AccèsLogis. In 2005 British Columbia, in the lead-up to its new affordable housing strategy discussed below, announced a significant expansion, with a doubling of its SAFER program (see chapter 4) and a new Rental Assistance Program (RAP) for families. In 2005 Saskatchewan's centrist NDP government initiated a housing allowance, one of several modest new social programs funded from provincial savings arising from the National Child Benefit Supplement. This was sustained under the Wall Conservative government as the province, with strong revenues in the resource boom but facing escalating rents and loss of rental stock, issued a housing strategy and associated action plan in 2011. The latter affirmed the importance of affordable housing and endorsed a mix of subsidized supply, allowances, and other programs.[58] Manitoba, still governed by a centrist NDP, in 2009–11 issued a Poverty Reduction and Social Inclusion Strategy which identified affordable housing as one of various strategies to achieve related goals, and extended eligibility for the Manitoba Shelter Benefit (soon renamed RentAid) to include not only disabled people but also singles and families not on social assistance.[59] Ontario too initiated small programs, allocating a portion of the 2005 AHI round to housing allowances, allocating a large portion of the 2006–07 federal trust fund monies to it, and from 2008 onwards entrenching this in the menu of program choices that municipalities could use in allocating IAH funds.[60] Ontario also funded an average of more than 400 added rent supplement units annually as supportive housing for people with mental illness, addictions, or chronic homelessness.

These are not large housing allowance programs by international standards: the Ontario, British Columbia, and Saskatchewan programs, although providing a meaningful $200 to $300 monthly per household, benefit only about 6 to 12 percent of market renter households; in Quebec and Manitoba the benefit has been very shallow, only about $50 per household monthly. But they are an important extension of housing assistance beyond the largely plateaued RGI social housing system, in a society where more and more low-income renters must get by in the market. They were assisted by flexibility in use of federal funds from 2011 onwards.

THE POST-2000 NEW AFFORDABLE HOUSING PROGRAMS

The AHI program model involved a transfer of federal funds to each province and territory, each of them matching the federal dollars. Until 2005 the federal funds were for capital costs, with some exceptions; in 2005–09 some funds could be used for ongoing housing allowances or other rental subsidies if CMHC agreed; and after 2011 each province could allocate to affordable housing capital or rental subsidies as it saw fit. AHI/IAH has been not so much a program as a funding envelope enabling provinces and territories to design their own programs, subject to broad federal criteria. The program structure and the province- or territory-specific form and amount of matching funds is set out in each bilateral federal-provincial or federal-territorial agreement, with accountability to CMHC on the use of federal funds. Successor agreements have been signed with each wave of AHI/IAH.

The initial AHI framework of November 2001 was simple, loose, and sparsely funded. New affordable rental units were required to be at or below median market rents, with federal funding up to $25,000 per unit. There was wide scope for different priorities by province – new supply or repair, rental or ownership, rent supplement or supportive housing – and for diverse matching funding to be orchestrated by each province, be it from provincial, municipal, non-profit, or private sources.[61] The second round of AHI starting in 2003 provided more federal dollars and deeper funding, up to the lesser of $75,000 per unit or 50 percent of capital costs.[62]

Alberta exceeded other provinces in per-capita new affordable rental in the AHI/IAH period, with a strong peak in 2007–10. This relates to four influences. The first was the strong advocacy by the Calgary Homeless Foundation[63] and the Homeward Trust in Edmonton – coalitions of well-connected business people and community activists. "Housing first" ideas and therefore affordable housing have been central in their ideas and activity. The second factor was the positioning of new affordable housing as part of managing growth in the context of the resource boom and rapidly expanding populations in Calgary, Edmonton, and the Fort McMurray oil sands area. Both homelessness and growth concerns are reflected in the third influence, the 2007 Alberta Housing Task Force appointed by the provincial government with a dominant municipal and community-based membership.[64] Supporting all this was a gusher of public revenues and the generally pragmatic centrist politics of Alberta's Conservative government, together fostering a willingness to fund new affordable rental production.[65] The provincial government responded to the task force with a ten-year homelessness plan, in which new affordable rental had a significant role, and associated funding commitments.[66] Alberta's new affordable rental production dropped off after 2011 once the ten-year plan targets were met and the federal capital-only funding declined.

In Quebec, the arrival of federal AHI funds was used for a new Logement Abordable Québec (LAQ) program, which enabled low-rent market units to be developed by private firms and non-profit groups, averaging over 1,500 new units annually from 2004 until it ended in 2008. AHI soon also enabled Quebec to augment the scale of its Accès-Logis program.[67] Provincial priority for affordable housing was reinforced by the dramatically tightening Montreal rental housing market in 2002 which took most by surprise and created a crisis. AccèsLogis pro-

Figure 7.1   New affordable housing commitments (non-profit & co-op & municipal): Estimates for 1996–2013. Post-2000 affordable rental peaked at 10,000 a year in 2006–09 with the Trust Funds and stimulus, then declined.

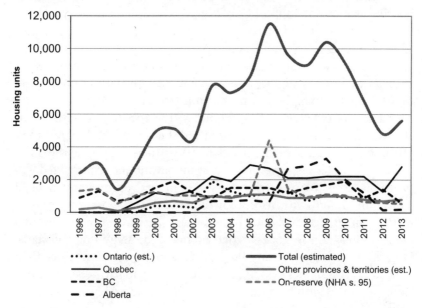

Source: Quebec, Alberta: data from annual reports; BC Housing data; Ontario: occasional provincial data and GTA municipal project reports; other provinces & territories estimated on prorated population (20% of combined Ontario + Quebec + BC); s. 95 on-reserve from CMHC, *Canadian Housing Statistics*. Excludes assisted private rental (1/3 of Ont total AHP-IAH, 1/2 of Quebec LAQ).

duction volumes rose from annual averages of 477 in 1996–2001 as the program ramped up, to over 1,600 in 2002–08 and 2,100 annually in 2009–13.[68] Most AccèsLogis projects have been 50 percent low-income targeted with RGI rents. All in all, Quebec more than matched federal AHI funds, and its new affordable production was at per-capita levels about the same as the national average.

In British Columbia, the advent of AHI in 2001 rescued the province's Homes BC program from a cost-cutting Liberal government that defeated the NDP in the election that year, and British Columbia quickly signed the first provincial AHI agreement with CMHC. The province's average commitments for added social housing rose from 945 units annually in 1996–2001, to 1,400 annually in 2002–13.[69] In 2002–04 supported independent living for seniors was a large, although not exclusive, priority. But soon the new government's cuts in social assistance, with the tightening rental housing market, were making homelessness and social distress in Vancouver's Downtown Eastside an even stronger political concern. The cabinet in 2004 formed a Premier's Task Force on

Homelessness, Mental Illness, and Addictions which recommended more supportive housing as one of four main priorities, and the post-2004 rounds of Homes BC were targeted accordingly.[70] The affordable housing agenda had support from Premier Gordon Campbell and Rich Coleman, minister for housing from 2006 onward. In 2006 the province adopted a revised affordable housing strategy which gave considerable emphasis to new supply.[71] Per-capita activity in British Columbia in the 2001–11 period was slightly above Quebec, mostly with RGI rents, and mostly targeted to high-need population groups.

Ontario started very reluctantly into AHI in 2002–03 under the Harris/Eves Conservative government,[72] and then, once the Liberals took office in late 2003, became an active AHI partner. But unlike the other three large provinces, Ontario never went beyond the required federal-provincial cost-sharing level in pursuit of higher volumes, and avoided a program design with strong low-income targeting or integral RGI. AHI/IAH in Ontario was known successively as the Community Rental Housing Program in 2002–03 (later rebranded "AHP Pilot"), Canada-Ontario Affordable Housing Program in 2004–11, and IAH since then – the latter two names evoking the federal-Ontario partnership, unlike some provinces with more active roles and distinctive brands. In 2002–03 it took assiduous lobbying by the Association of Municipalities of Ontario to get the Harris/Eves government to agree to a small program where the half-dozen most active municipalities would be permitted to match the federal $25,000 per unit,[73] and this round of the program funded only about 1,000 units.

After the 2003 Ontario election the program was redesigned with full provincial matching funds and equitable allocations across the province, and re-launched in May 2005. Delivery (project selection, funding the sponsor groups, stacking on additional municipal funding, agreements, and monitoring) was done by the forty-seven service manager municipalities under a provincial framework and fiscal accountability. AHI/IAH activity came in waves every two to three years as each new CMHC/Ontario agreement was signed. One-third of AHI/IAH in Ontario has been subsidized private rental,[74] providing rents at 80 percent of market averages under twenty- to twenty-five-year agreements. Two-thirds have been municipal and non-profit projects, partly at those 80 percent of average market rents and partly low-income targeted by way of stacked rent supplements, transfer of RGI funding from other projects, or deep capital subsidies.[75] After 2011 each of the service manager municipalities was given flexibility to allocate its share of funds among new supply, repairs, and ongoing rental subsidies, and the latter took an increasing share of AHI dollars. Ontario's per-capita production of new affordable rental in 2002–13 was slightly under half the British Columbia or Quebec level.

AHI/IAH averaged somewhat under 4,000 new affordable units annually or 2 percent of national production. The shared federal-provincial cost averaged about $400–$450 million annually out of the total AHI $535 million annually over 2002–11 (the larger figure also includes some repair funds and rental subsidies). But the nationwide picture is almost 9,000 new units annually in 2002–13,[76] double the cost-shared units counted in AHI data. (This includes an average 1,200 units on First Nation reserves.) Provinces such as British Columbia, Quebec, and Alberta have more than matched the federal funding, and added operating subsidies; their activity pushes the national totals much higher than AHI/IAH. A main feature of AHI/IAH is the great variability from province to province in program design and in volume of activity (figure 7.1). Viewed as a federal program framework, AHI has inconsistent income targeting, little long-term accountability, and no operating subsidies. But in several provinces it has supported programs that are more clearly low-income targeted, with RGI rents and operating subsidies. The variety in the four large provinces illustrates the fragmented yet dynamic national situation.

Production of new affordable rental in 2002–13 under AHI/IAH was slightly over one-third the volume in the 1965–95 prime period of social housing (figure 8.1; table 8.5), although with rents generally much less affordable to people with low incomes. Output peaked with the 2006–07 housing trust funds and the 2009–11 stimulus, and it appears that these AHI sister programs helped support the higher volumes in Quebec, British Columbia, and Alberta. As the early 2010s progressed, the volumes of new assisted rental declined, with federal funds dropping from that peak, and with several provinces directing more IAH dollars to rent subsidies rather than to capital for new housing. In some provinces, regeneration and replacement of older social housing was supplanting new affordable rental as the priority in housing development.

After the Justin Trudeau Liberal government was elected in 2015, its first budget announced the continuation of IAH for another two years, through fiscal 2017–18, budgeted at levels similar to 2007–11.[77] This was the available way to deliver on its promise of augmented funding without delay, and was positioned as an interim measure while the government developed a national housing strategy by 2018. A meaningful strategy would necessarily imply new program frameworks to replace IAH, address rental affordability, and sustain twentieth-century social housing projects. Meanwhile, the extension to 2018 made AHI/IAH the longest-lived production program of any since Canadian governments first entered the social housing field in the 1940s.

8

Conclusions

To draw together the threads of the policy history this book tells, this chapter first provides a summary of the six turning points and corresponding periods in Canadian social housing policy – a brief version of the preceding chapters – and then considers the broad themes that emerge in this policy history. Readers are referred to the preceding chapters for specific sources and citations.

POLICY HISTORY IN BRIEF: SIX TURNING POINTS AND PERIODS

The policy history of Canadian social housing falls into six periods, each lasting about a decade. Each was created by a turning point that echoed and responded to larger changes in the political and economic context, social policy, prevailing ideas, and conditions in the housing market and urban development. Each had a particular program framework for social housing production, which also determined what sort of agencies would own and operate the housing, how low-income targeted it would be, and how rent subsidies would flow for many years to come.

The first period ran from the National Housing Act (NHA) amendments of 1949 to those of 1964. Social housing was about 1½ percent of total annual production, slightly higher in Ontario. The second period was from 1964–73, the peak years of public housing production in all-low-income projects delivered mostly by provincial housing corporations and with the production volumes expanded ten-fold. Next was the first decade of the community-based non-profit regime, 1974–85, with emphasis on mixed-income social housing as part of a broadly expanding state role, subsidy to all housing sectors, and an urban agenda nationally, provincially and locally. Then came the second non-profit decade, 1985–93, with program management devolved to the provinces, a return to more stringent low-income targeting, and production declining toward the end. The years from 1993 to 2001 were a time of devolution and retrenchment, with almost no funding for new social housing and with program management and policy leadership transferred to the provinces. There was widening divergence among them. Ontario was the extreme case and devolved funding responsibility and program management to municipalities; Quebec and British Columbia maintained significant ongoing priority for social housing; Alberta, the six smaller provinces, and the territories mostly stood still for a decade. In 2001 to 2015 a modest re-engagement created new models of affordable housing funding, softening the severe retrenchment without reversing the fundamental 1990s downgrading of policy priority, program scope, and institutional capacity. There remained wide variation among the provinces.

Canada's social housing system in the early twenty-first century is essentially the product of three elements in the policy history: the legacy of the 1965–95 programs in terms funding, housing stock, and program structures; devolution and retrenchment in the 1990s; and the modest post-2001 re-engagement.

The Early Postwar Period, 1949–64

Federal decisions of the early postwar years opened a 1949–64 period in Canadian social housing policy that created a foundation in institutional roles, practices, and discourse that was different from US or UK models. The early postwar turning point marked a departure from the pre-war regime which lacked any purposeful state role in housing or almost any social housing production. It settled a policy direction after a turbulent 1930s and 1940s where on one hand the federal government rejected intense advocacy for social housing, and on the other hand delivered a large 46,000-unit program of break-even social housing to meet the intense pressures of wartime growth and demobilization.

The key event was a 1949 amendment to the NHA which created a small public housing program. This was one of a series of wartime and early postwar decisions which also included the creation of Central Mortgage and Housing Corporation (CMHC) in 1946. Several provinces quickly passed legislation to participate in the public housing program or enable municipalities to do so. The new NHA section 35 provided capital financing and operating subsidies, each shared 75/25 by the fed-

Figure 8.1   Average annual social housing commitments, Canada, by program period, 1950–2013. Strong production lasted thirty years, shifting from public to non-profit/co-op housing, and with non-federal programs by the 1990s.

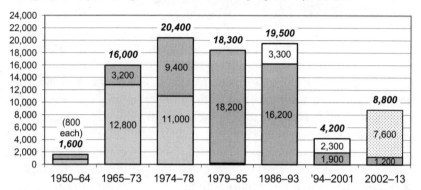

eral and provincial governments. That 25 percent funding requirement set a big hurdle to strong provincial or local take-up, but the first projects were soon built in several cities across the country.

The economic context was extremely rapid growth, with a doubling of Canada's manufacturing workforce in the 1940s and a doubling of GDP per capita. The interwar years had been dominated not only by 1920s growth and then 1930s Depression, but by the large transition to an urban, industrial society and the associated labour and urban social issues. The political consequences of these arrived with full force during the 1939–45 wartime boom. In the 1940s, with an economic pie that was growing and also more equitably shared, middle-class standards of living arrived for the majority of Canadian people. Growth and urbanization altered political expectations and transformed fiscal capacity, and together these propelled welfare state expansion. There was a wide 1950s political consensus on growth led by private investment and "free enterprise," but also on an essential role for government in macroeconomic management, and in spreading the rising output around through social welfare spending. From 1942 to 1952, Canada initiated Old Age Security, Unemployment Insurance, and Family Benefits. The small social housing program reflected international trends and ideas. But the new social programs were about security for the broad middle and lower-middle class, not income transfers to the poor, and the small scale of social housing activity reflected this.

Closely associated with economic growth was rapid urban growth. Canada in the 1940s and 1950s became a predominantly urban nation. In the postwar years (1945–75) the population living in urban areas of over 100,000 more than doubled. Housing starts doubled during the 1950s. The share of Canadians living in larger urban centres passed the US level and drew close to that of Australia. From 1941 to 1961, the Toronto and Vancouver urban areas doubled in population, with higher growth rates than counterparts such as Sydney or San Francisco, or even Brisbane or Seattle.

What most influenced social housing policy were market-oriented ideas – "keeping to the market." The CMHC priority was financing urban development – the house-building industry, municipal infrastructure, and mortgages for home-owners. CMHC absorbed Wartime Housing Limited, the federal agency that had built 46,000 homes in the economic boom of the 1940s, and sold off that housing. Yet attitudes about state versus private activity were pragmatic within these bounds – more so than today. An institutional mould was set involving an active state role in housing previously unknown; policy concern to ensure adequate housing production; federal leadership and capacity in these matters; and direct federal relationships with municipalities in housing. The 1949 social housing program was a minor add-on to this market-oriented policy. The provinces played a quite secondary role in co-funding and helping implement the federal program. Ontario took a far more active role than other provinces, leaving less to municipalities.

The 1949–64 period produced 14,000 public housing units and 11,000 municipal and charitable Limited Dividend units across Canada – an average of 1,600 annually over fifteen years. Over half of this, 900 units annually, was in Ontario. Public housing was a mix of break-even housing for people earning lower-middle incomes, and "low-rent" housing with subsidized rents for the poor. Social housing was a tiny 1.4 percent of total nationwide housing production – a much smaller per capita level than in peer nations such as the United States or Australia. It was enough to absorb about one in ten of the low-income renters added each year as part of the spectrum of ongoing rapid growth.

The Public Housing Heyday, 1965–73

The mid-1960s turning point brought about a ten-fold expansion of production in social housing, and opened three decades of active social housing policy. Canadian social housing production surged to per-capita volumes they would sustain for a generation, notably higher than the levels in the United States although well short of those in Australia or Western Europe.

The key events were in federal and Ontario policy. The 1964 amendments to the NHA enabled CMHC to finance 90 percent of project capital costs rather than 75 percent, and to fund provincial housing corporations rather than only municipal ones; accompanying this was a great increase in federal funding. Ontario that same year invented the provincial housing corporation, a high-capacity delivery model soon adopted by all provinces. The significance of the mid-1960s turning point is that it transformed the scale of Canadian social housing from trivial to systemically significant, and created one of the nation's half-dozen main income-related transfer programs in the form of rents geared to income (RGI). The broader public role, institutional capacity, and normalized higher funding levels became the platform on which governments could respond to the turbulent housing politics and careening housing markets that arrived in the decade that followed.

Canada in the 1960s branched away from the US welfare state model, with more universalist programs and more ample targeted ones, including widely subsidized post-secondary education, the Canada Pension Plan, public health insurance, and federal cost-sharing of provincial social programs through the Canada Assistance Plan. This was the period of peak welfare state expansion across most affluent Western nations, at the culmination of the postwar economic boom. In these countries, the climate of opinion was that governments could largely "solve" poverty, and that the welfare state should not only offer security against sickness and old age, but give the poor a better slice of the pie. Canada's housing policy was informed by international ideas about social policy and the place of social housing in it. Canada's 1960s welfare state expansion brought this nation up to international norms for the level of affluence we had reached. The 1960s to mid-1970s were one of the few periods when Canada's average annual growth in GDP exceeded 5 percent, thereby doubling every fifteen years, generating abundant fiscal resources to fund such programs.

The Pearson Liberal government was elected in 1963 with an explicit platform of social program expansion. The prime minster's social policy advisors were a sharp break from the 1950s Liberal old guard; they were concerned about the electoral challenge of the new social-democratic NDP; and his 1963–65 and 1965–68 governments were minorities dependent on the NDP. Ontario and Quebec, despite federal-provincial conflicts, were strong allies in social program expansion. The mid-1960s turning point in social housing was directly propelled by this federal agenda of welfare state expansion. Public housing and urban renewal were small parts of the Pearson welfare state agenda, but they were integral parts. They were among the half-dozen main elements in the Liberal 1960 social policy conference while in opposition, in the explicit thinking and writing of key social policy advisors, in the action plan prepared prior to the 1963 election, and in the legislative program that followed. This government, unlike any in Canada before it, was receptive to CMHC officials' and advocates' proposals for a more ambitious social housing program, and this is what led to the 1964 NHA amendments.

Urban Canada was growing at an astonishing pace, with surging rental demand. Toronto, Vancouver, and other urban areas were still doubling in population every twenty years. The number of Canadian households grew by over 35 percent per decade in the late 1960s and 1970s, compared to 15 percent today. The Ontario government, in particular, was concerned to ensure enough rental housing production to nourish the golden goose of urban growth. Social housing was one instrument in its growing involvement in managing urban development, especially in the Toronto region. The new Ontario role in low-income housing was part of a broad policy shift toward a significant role across a housing spectrum that included assisted private rental, land development, and assisted home-ownership.

The provincial housing corporation was a sudden departure from prevailing ideas, and from any existing model of US, British, French, or Canadian public housing. The new model arose from the priorities of Ontario and Quebec. The Ontario government had a province-building agenda to boost provincial government capacity; its new Ontario Housing Corporation (OHC) would be a provincial CMHC. Quebec had virtually no housing agenda in the mid-1960s, but the Quiet Revolution and associated Quebec state-building were at their peak, and Quebec wanted to ensure the province controlled the housing relationships between municipalities or local groups and the federal government. The NHA amendments responded to these agendas with provisions for funding provincial housing corporations. This model was soon promoted by CMHC as the standard delivery vehicle for the new policy regime, and within five years it was adopted in every province.

The peak years of Canadian all-low-income public housing production from 1965 to 1973 converged precisely with the peak of the much larger private-rental apartment development boom. Private firms were building 100,000 rental apartment units a year in the 1960s, and this shaped social housing policy. Ontario's explicit strategy was to piggy-back social housing production on that boom, and to integrate new low-income housing with these private-sector towers that comprised up to half of all housing production at the time, sprinkled across the new suburbs of the day. In most of Canada's larger cities, apartment blocks and townhouse complexes adjacent to suburban middle-class subdivisions became common forms of social housing.

Quebec attitudes toward the state role in housing changed rapidly in the latter 1960s, as the Quiet Revolution gathered force and new at-titudes toward urban issues – both managerialist and activist – took hold. For centrist governments in almost all provinces, abundant federal funding made it an easy political and fiscal choice to create a provincial housing corporation and pursue a public housing agenda to house the burgeoning population of seniors, meet surging rental demand, sup-port downtown megaproject ambitions, and undertake slum redevel-opment. The latter 1960s saw a new turbulent politics of housing in Canada, which would soon end the public housing program produc-tion regime. But initially these new politics reinforced the provincial priority for public housing as a way to address housing issues that had moved dramatically into mainstream political concerns.

In 1965–69, Ontario social housing production rose rapidly from less than 1,000 to more than 10,000 units annually. The rest of Canada fol-lowed with a three- to five-year lag, reaching 15,000 units in 1970. The social housing production levels reached in the latter 1960s would be sustained, with a few ups and downs, for twenty-five years, until 1992. Average public housing production nationwide in the heyday of 1965 to 1973 was 12,000 units annually, and it was about the same across the fuller period through to 1978, when that program ended. (Total pro-duction in the 1970s was higher than this, as noted below.) This was sufficient to accommodate about half the increase of low-income renters that is an integral part of the spectrum ongoing growth – half of the 300,000 or so low-income renters among the 2 million house-holds added in a decade. The 1964–78 period of intensive public hous-ing development still provides today, half a century later, almost half of all low-income-targeted units nationally and in most provinces.

The First Non-profit Decade, 1974–85

The early-1970s turning point brought a shift away from all-low-income "public housing" developed by provincial agencies, to social housing developed by a mix of community groups, co-ops, and municipalities, in projects that had a mix of regular tenants paying market rent, and subsidized low-income tenants. Accompanying this was a new priority for housing repair and neighbourhood renewal. The production volumes reached in the 1964–73 period were maintained, and reached a gentle peak in the years around 1980. The federal government led the policy shift and re-entered into direct program delivery. The decisive event was the amendment of the NHA in 1973, which enabled the new program model. It was the culmination of five years of turbulent policy change, including a high-profile federal task force, a large federal experimental program, and a major federal policy review led by outsiders to CMHC.

The significance of this turning point was that it sustained the social housing priority politically, by inventing a better social model and creating a larger interested constituency. The new model sequestered the inevitable stigmatization of low-income housing within the pre-1974 public housing sub-sector, and supported fairly steady social housing production in Canada for two more decades, in contrast to the sharply waning volumes in peer nations such as the United States, Australia, Britain, and France. Mixed-income social housing, along with subsidies to private rental, maintained rental apartments as a significant element in Canadian urban development well into the 1980s, and thereby mixed-tenure, mixed-income suburbs.

Mixed-income social housing was part of a widening state role in housing in the 1970s, which included large spending on programs of assisted home-ownership, subsidies to private-sector rental development, subsidies to private-rental tenants, and public land development. Social housing was one element of this and rode on the back of this broader shift. The mixed-income model hoped to subsume programs to meet low-income housing needs into a broader agenda of rental supply. Unlike the US case, protests against public housing did not dampen the priority for social housing in Canada. The contested issue was not whether to continue with substantial social housing production, but how to do so.

Despite federal re-entry, the 1970s were a time of strongly rising provincial roles in social housing. It was the peak of public housing production in most provinces. Ontario, following a 1973 housing task force, actively fostered the new model and funded add-ons to the federal programs; Quebec did the same starting in 1976. Provincial priority for social housing was boosted by minority government in Ontario from 1975 to 1981 and by the Parti Québécois government of 1976 to 1985; it was boosted by the election of NDP governments in Manitoba in 1969 and in British Columbia in 1972. Across Canada in the 1970s, the politics of fiscal constraint and the neoliberal critique of the post-war welfare state did not have much impact, unlike the situation in the United States, Britain, or Australia. More significant in Canada were federal-provincial conflicts that propelled social policy decentralization, soon making the dominant federal role in social housing a politically vulnerable anomaly.

The expanding government role in the early and mid-1970s was enabled by unprecedented prosperity and ample fiscal resources, amid a global resource boom and economic growth rates similar to those of the 1960s. Canada as an oil producer was less affected by the 1973–74 oil crisis and ensuing recession than most peer nations. The 1970s and 1980s program models were dependent on large subsidy flows, reflecting in the housing sphere the transfer-intensive character of Canadian social policy in that period in terms of international norms.

But the expanding state role in housing was also propelled by economic strains in the postwar economic model, including sharply rising inflation, interest rates, and housing prices. By the early 1970s, the real carrying costs of home purchase had doubled in a decade; the first cohort of baby-boomers were flooding into the housing market; and the Canadian postwar private-rental production system was collapsing. With rapid growth, these created enormous pressures of urban change and rental demand that erupted into political life. The housing market was no longer working as well or meeting people's rising expectations. Globally and in Canada, housing and urban issues were one of the main flash-points in youth protests, new activism, and political upheaval. Housing became a mainstream political concern, and the federally led shake-up in social housing policy and the expanding state role were the Trudeau Liberal government's response to these bubbling politics of housing

The model of mixed-income, community-based social housing had little precedent in Canada, the United States, or Britain. It was informed by European models of social housing, it paralleled shifts in US policy at the time, and it responded to urban and neighbourhood agendas in Montreal, Toronto, and other cities. It was part of a broader shift to a "mixed economy of welfare" involving a dual delivery system, partly by government agencies and partly by non-profit community agencies funded by the state.

The essence of the new program model was that CMHC provided mortgage loans (guaranteed private lender mortgages after 1978) for 100 percent of project capital costs. CMHC and the provinces provided operating subsidies to cover amortization and RGI in typically one-quarter to one-half of the units. Social housing production averaged about 19,000 units annually in 1974–85, about 30 percent higher than in 1965–73. In the first half of the period, the old and new program models operated in parallel, with more public housing production than non-profit and co-op production. Then in 1978 the federal government ceased funding new public housing, and non-profit and co-op became almost the sole Canadian approach to social housing. Co-ops were about one-quarter of production in the new programs; provincial and municipal agencies accounted for about one-third; and the largest share was developed by community-based non-profit bodies such as social agencies, service clubs, ethnic associations, and labour unions. Almost all non-profit and co-op housing agencies depended entirely on state funding. Federal expenditures on social housing increased rapidly, a function of high mortgage interest rates and steady production volumes.

The Second Non-profit Decade, 1986–93

At the mid-1980s turning point, management of programs for social housing production was devolved to the provinces, while the federal government retained the lead in framing policy and in providing cost-shared funding. The 1970s federal re-entry into direct program delivery was mostly ended, and a trajectory was set of devolution to the provinces. The pivotal change was a new federal policy framework that emerged at the end of 1985, some fifteen months after the election of the Mulroney Conservative government.

The significance of this turning point was that it clinched the closure of the federally led period of expanding programs, and shifted toward a clear provincial lead in social housing. By partway through this period, provincially managed programs again comprised the majority of Canadian social housing. Without this, the more fundamental devolution of the mid-1990s could not so easily have happened. Policy again made new social housing more low-income-targeted, much of it for people with special needs or disabilities, or who were experiencing homelessness. Social housing moved away from the earlier agenda of comprehensive policy. It was no longer part of an expanding state role that included assisted private rental, land development, and affordable ownership, and it now stood alone as the sole housing sector receiving large direct public funding. Dualism was reinforced, with social housing again highly targeted and increasingly framed in "special needs" terms, and less in terms of mixed-income projects and mixed-tenure urban development. This was a non-market provincial sphere separated from the paramount federal housing policy lead in market housing that operated via tax policy, mortgage insurance, regulation of lending, monetary policy, and macroeconomic management.

The new policy regime was a compromise shaped by three competing forces: neoliberal leanings in the cabinet and federal central agencies; concerns of federal officials about the housing spending trajectory and weak income targeting; and input from provincial and local stakeholders. The new policy was much less neoliberal than expected, and much less so than policy trends in peer nations such as the United States, Britain, France, or Australia. This reflected the tension that characterized the 1984–93 Mulroney Conservative government, between neoliberal voices and "regional brokerage" – the role of public spending in sustaining political support. But as this policy period progressed, and economic and fiscal conditions declined sharply toward the end of it, the balance tilted strongly toward cutbacks.

The housing market swung dramatically in the 1980s and early 1990s, creating a series of strong pressures. Mortgage rates remained in the range of 10 to 13 percent (for five-year terms) through the decade. These and a house price bubble in the latter 1980s put home purchase out of reach for many young middle-income people. With the younger baby-boom cohorts entering the housing market, and a doubling of immigration in 1985–90, rental demand pressures remained intense. There were severe losses of low-cost private rental in the major cities as gentrification accelerated, and rising numbers of homeless people. In Toronto, Vancouver, and other cities, this sustained strong mainstream, middle-class concerns about housing affordability, urban issues, and rental supply. The private-rental production system was almost entirely gone, except in Quebec, and social housing became the main way to build rental housing.

Social housing policy reflected intense debates in 1980s Canada over a larger versus smaller state role, the merits and shortcomings of the market, and targeted versus universal programs. Although market-oriented attitudes on housing and the economy came to the fore, the stakeholder interests of the provinces, the non-profit and co-op housing sector, and municipalities were strong enough to keep the federal government involved in social housing. But incremental devolution created a self-reinforcing spiral of federal marginality, and advocacy was increasingly directed at provincial governments.

Ontario, home to 42 percent of Canadian social housing and since 1949 the strongest social housing partner of the federal government, was governed in 1985–90 by reformist Liberals and in 1990–95 by the social-democratic NDP. These governments responded to the federal pulling-back and to the intense pressures with a large and unprecedented Ontario unilateral social housing program, without federal cost-sharing. This expanded Ontario housing spending seven-fold, stirring up a strong conservative reaction which would affect the politics of social housing nationally at the next turning point.

The 1985–93 program had clear low-income targeting and 60/40 federal/provincial cost-sharing of subsidies to households in "core need" – in effect the lowest 20 to 30 percent of the income spectrum. Unified operating subsidies to each project covered the difference between rent revenues and amortization-and-operating costs. The targeting, funding formula, and provincial delivery brought non-profit housing closer to the public housing model. Provinces could opt to add more funding and deliver a larger program and thereby a more mixed-income one, and the four large provinces did so. The program for co-ops was separated from the main program and delivered federally.

Production volumes were initially maintained at the normalized level of the 1970s and early 1980s, almost 20,000 units annually. As cuts were made the volumes declined, averaging 16,000 units annually across the 1985–93 period. The Ontario unilateral programs averaged an additional 3,000 units annually, keeping total nationwide volumes close to 1970s and 1980s levels. Federal expenditures on social housing subsidy rose only 4 percent in real-dollar terms in the period, as interest rates declined, new unit commitments declined, and provinces assumed a larger share of costs.

Devolution and Retrenchment, 1993–2001

The mid-1990s brought the end of the three-decade prime period of Canadian social housing. The key elements in the policy shift were devolution of virtually all program management to the provinces, the end of funding for new social housing, and the end of social housing as a significant national social policy priority. The changes happened from 1993 to 1995, and were entrenched in new federal-provincial arrangements by the end of the decade.

The pivotal decisions were the ending of funding for new social housing production in 1993 (1995 for Ontario unilateral programs), and decisions in 1995–96 to devolve program management to the provinces, and to the municipal level in Ontario. Federal funding to individual social housing projects and provincial housing agencies was bundled into an annual transfer to each province, initially quite ample but calibrated to phase out over three decades. The change was implemented in devolution agreements, known as Social Housing Agreements, between CMHC and each province and territory.

This change, from one viewpoint sensible administrative rationalization, was the end of a policy era. It ended ongoing funding for non-market housing as an integral part of Canada's housing system. It transferred to the provinces the long-run responsibility for RGI, which was among the half-dozen largest social transfer programs, and phased out explicit housing-related subsidy as an element in such transfers at the federal level. It pulled the federal government back from the political front line in responding to low-income housing needs, and removed CMHC from involvement in strategies to address the emerging issues of aging social housing stock and its adaptation to evolving needs. It meant a doubly large volume of low-income demand to be met at the low end of the rental market, which would soon feed into trends of neighbourhood decline in urban Canada.

The political and economic context was the 1990–93 recession – the worst in sixty years – and its fiscal aftermath. This converged with two other powerful factors: the global triumph of neoliberal ideas which shifted pragmatic middle-of-the-road politics to a more market-oriented place, and a particular Canadian agenda of devolution. The downturn caused a fiscal crisis, with escalating deficits and public debt, and the threat of lower credit ratings and higher interest costs on that debt. The Chrétien-Martin Liberal government elected in 1993 was determined to overcome this, and to restructure and reduce federal fiscal obligations for the long term. In 1995–96, in a sluggish economic recovery, it initiated major unilateral cuts to income-targeted federal programs and to federal-provincial transfers that had been entrenched elements of Canadian social policy and Canadian federalism for two to three decades. After the Quebec referendum in the fall of 1995, in which the separatist vote lost by a hair, devolution of particular program spheres became one strategy to achieve this restructuring while also assuaging Quebec nationalism. Social housing was among the spheres that were devolved – collateral damage from the broader fiscal agenda and the downsizing of the Canadian welfare state.

The housing market context was favourable. The 1990–93 recession had brought a real estate crash, with real prices declining by up to 40 percent in the larger cities and construction of market housing falling by half. This led a developer-landlord sector in distress to wage a virulent campaign against Ontario's social housing, which echoed in federal politics. With inflation now lower, interest rates came rapidly off the high plateau they had been on for over two decades. For home-owners, price and interest rate declines meant great improvement in affordability – back to 1960s levels – and massive net outflow of renters into ownership ensued. Rental housing and housing affordability both evaporated from mainstream middle-class political concerns, for the first time since the 1960s. The housing market was now working well for most people and social housing could no longer ride the coattails of broad support for an active state role.

The change appealed to the provinces in its administrative simplification, recognition of paramountcy, and earmarked federal housing dollars in a time of fiscal pressures. This turning point brought diverging provincial approaches. Ontario took the extreme path of devolving funding responsibility and program management to municipalities. Its agenda was impelled by the populist neoliberalism of the Harris Conservative government elected in 1995, and Ontario's own fiscal crisis. This province, with 42 percent of Canadian social housing, was preoccupied with retrenchment and devolution for seven years, arriving by 2001 at a social housing regime of enormously reduced capacity and an inexorable long-run funding squeeze. Quebec and British Columbia maintained a middling, provincially funded priority for social housing in the face of federal withdrawal, propelled by a social-democratic government in British Columbia and the tripartite politics of social inclusion in Quebec. The other one-third of Canada (by population) mostly experienced stasis and inactive policy for a decade.

Modest Re-engagement in 2002–15

At the turn of the millennium, new program initiatives in affordable housing emerged, amounting to a modest re-engagement in affordable rental by the federal and provincial governments after a decade of inactivity.

The post-2000 initiatives softened but did not reverse the fundamental changes of 1990s retrenchment and devolution. The devolved 1990s institutional arrangements remain. Volumes of production nationwide are far lower than in the thirty-year prime period, and program approaches and volumes vary widely among the provinces. Unlike the prime period, the post-2000 federal and federal-provincial policy frameworks have no operating subsidies, weak low-income targeting, and moderate rather than low rents. Although much of the funding for existing social housing remains in place, there is no policy to expand the non-market housing sector significantly in a growing country, as was the case through 1965–95.

The pivotal decisions were a federal policy framework and multilateral federal-provincial-territorial agreement in late 2001. The result was the Affordable Housing Initiative (AHI), later renamed Investment in Affordable Housing (IAH), implemented with differing elements and different names in each province or territory. The weak federal policy leadership and loose overarching federal-provincial agreement reflect the "collaborative federalism" of the post-devolution era, and the 1999 Social Union Framework Agreement. AHI was one of a set of social policy initiatives arising in this manner through federal-provincial negotiations in 1999–2003.

These programs emerged in a much improved economic and fiscal context. A strong recovery, cutbacks, and lower interest rates put the federal budget into surplus by 1998. The Chrétien-Martin Liberal government tilted back toward centrist politics, with competing voices on how to use the "fiscal dividend," and new spending initiatives to serve social and economic needs or political advantage. The new programs also reflected a renewed concern for urban issues. Cities across the country were seeing rising homelessness and more people living on the margins, in the wake of the profound labour market changes of the 1990s and of reduced social benefits. As the economy recovered, Canada's big cities had rental markets with low vacancy rates, and more tenants with flat real incomes or low incomes facing ongoing increases in market rents.

AHI, never put forward as a long-run program, was sustained for over fifteen years by a series of happy political accidents. Its funding was boosted or extended by "urban agenda" politics, parliamentary deals under the minority Liberal and Conservative governments of 2004–11, the brief international consensus on stimulus spending in the 2008–10 Global Financial Crisis, and a pragmatic approach by the Harper Conservative government to keeping provinces, municipalities and housing advocates assuaged.

AHI and related federal initiatives have averaged somewhat under 4,000 new affordable units annually or 2 percent of national production – about one-fifth the volumes of the thirty-year prime. Shared federal-provincial cost averaged about $400–$450 million annually (out of the total AHI $535 million annually) over 2002–11. But total funding and production in the post-devolution era is much higher than such federal data suggest, and far more divergent by province. The nationwide total in 2002–13 was almost 9,000 units annually (including a 1,200-unit average on reserves) – about 40 percent of the volume that was normalized in the social housing prime period, although much less low-income targeted. This was assisted by special federal funding including the 2006–07 housing trust funds and the housing stimulus in 2009–11. Production declined after 2011 to lower levels.

British Columbia, Quebec, and, for a few years, Alberta had more active policy than other provinces. Their per-capita volumes of new affordable production were over twice as high as the basic nationwide AHI level, and often involved RGI and operating subsidies. These differences arise from a stronger politics of homelessness and of middle-class rental need in British Columbia; ongoing attention to Montreal urban issues and social inclusion in Quebec policy; and enormous growth pressures and fiscal resources in Alberta during the oil sands boom.

BROAD THEMES IN THE POLICY HISTORY

Social Housing Policy and Welfare State Junctures

"The evolution of federal/provincial relations in social housing has broadly paralleled that in the Canadian welfare state as a whole and has been driven by the same underlying political forces."[1] Banting's statement, made in an analysis of the 1970s to mid-1980s history, is borne out across more than six decades. Social housing policy was changed fundamentally by the big welfare state transformations of the 1960s and 1990s, and altered substantially by social policy shifts in the 1970s and 1980s. Social housing programs also echoed various characteristics of broader social policy in successive periods. The early postwar juncture created a basic set of social security programs and with it a residual social housing system. The mid-1960s brought a shift toward a more universalist welfare state, and the ten-fold expansion of social housing activity at that time was an integral part of that policy agenda. The 1970s remodelling reflected an expanding state role generally and in the housing system, and it reflected a new "mixed economy of welfare," with hybrid delivery by the state and state-funded community agencies. The mid-1980s devolution of social housing program management to the provinces, within a federal funding and policy lead, reflected the social policy trends of that period, and so did the tighter targeting and gradual downsizing of those programs. The severe retrenchment of the 1990s, reducing the state share of GDP and devolving many income-targeted programs to the provinces, was part a broader sea change toward smaller, more targeted social programs apart from health and education, and a lesser federal role. In housing as in general, devolution was a means of institutionalizing this reduced state role, and the 1990s curtailment in social housing policy was mostly collateral damage from this broader agenda. Thus trends and turns in the welfare state have consistently been more important than the housing conditions or needs of low-income renters in shaping policy and the scale of activity in social housing.

Other themes in social policy evolution are also reflected in social housing. The dualism characteristic of liberal-welfare regimes is reflected in the separateness of market housing policy and social housing policy, with a partial exception in the 1970s. Incremental devolution of social housing in the late 1970s and 1980s created a self-reinforcing spiral of marginality at the federal level. The declining legitimacy of counter-cyclical spending in orthodox public finance thinking helped undermine social housing policy, and the early 1990s recession was the first in over four decades that did not see augmented federal social housing production as stimulus.

In Canada, the active state role and higher spending that was created in the late postwar period endured and expanded for the better part of two decades after the mid-1970s economic crisis, contrasting with Western Europe and especially our Anglo peer nations. This Canadian "post-postwar" period was influenced by several factors, including less economic turbulence because of net oil self-sufficiency; the way Quebec and other regional politics pulled the political balance away from neoliberalism toward ongoing public spending; the political axis between Toronto and Montreal and the federal government; and in housing a "discourse of rental supply" interacting with middle-class housing concerns. Devolution and retrenchment in the 1990s were all the more abrupt as that "post-postwar" period ended.

Institutional Momentum and Change

Of central importance in the policy history are the institutional arrangements in social housing, and the capacity, practices, and policy momentum they create. The broad political and economic conditions are always most powerful, but the next most important level is institutional. Once CMHC established a significant social housing role, or provincial housing corporations were in place, or co-op and non-profit agencies existed as an interest and a political voice, once annual funding allocations were an entrenched practice and an ongoing strand in federal-provincial relations, then the momentum was large, even if this activity was not important in mainstream politics and even in the face of adverse political and fiscal factors. Social housing as a response to rental affordability and supply issues became normalized, and discourse built up around it. It then took more than minor political or fiscal challenges before political capital would be spent on downsizing or closing the system. It took the severe fiscal crisis of the mid-1990s and the global triumph of neoliberal ideas rippling across Canada to end the social housing era.

Canadian social housing was a system orchestrated by federal policy, and its supposed fragmentation in its heyday is much exaggerated. CMHC was in all periods the main shaper of program models, and federal Cabinets decided on the policy changes it proposed. The three decades of production operated through a series of program regimes which varied in targeting, federal-provincial cost-sharing, subsidy formulas, and delivery roles. But all operated under the NHA, all were shaped by federal decisions on the funding formula and magnitude, and all involved federal-provincial agreements and cost-sharing. All had predominantly low-income targeting (low and moderate in 1979–85), and after the mid-1970s all supported much the same mix of non-profit, co-op, and municipal sponsor/owner corporations. All programs provided financing under the NHA in the form of direct state loans, state-orchestrated financing, or private mortgages resting on the twin pillars of subsidy flow and CMHC guarantees. Ontario in 1987–95 and Quebec and British Columbia after 1996 aligned the design of their unilateral programs with the federal-provincial program of the day.

In the classic telling of Canadian social housing policy history, the great shift occurred in the early 1970s, from public housing to non-profit housing. In the retrospective long view, there are enormous continuities between these program periods, across all three decades of the social housing prime. The issue in the early 1970s juncture was not whether to sustain a substantial social housing sector, as the scale of activity of the 1964–73 public housing programs had become normalized. As the non-profit, community-based delivery gained wide political support, social housing production and its share of overall Canadian housing output was sustained at fairly consistent levels from the mid-1960s to the mid-1990s. The first non-profit decade celebrated in this classic telling was actually a detour from long-run trends in Canadian housing policy, its key features – lesser income targeting, direct federal delivery, and the broadly expanding state role – gone within a decade.

More significant than any differences by period are the underlying politics and the resulting production volumes and housing-system impact, sustained across those thirty years.

Once a program sphere is institutionally entrenched, issues arising within it affect subsequent policy-making. Each turning point in Canadian social housing involved a reaction to the preceeding period. While the mid-1960s turning point was part of a broader political effort to put in place a more ample set of social programs, it also reacted directly against the 1950s program model, its small output, and the dysfunctions of its delivery roles. While the early 1970s turning point was part of a broader turbulence that burst apart the postwar welfare state consensus, it also reacted against the 1964 program model, the rising presence of public housing in middle-class suburbs, the perception of poverty concentration, and the rising subsidy requirements. Although the mid-1980s turning point reversed politically the expanding state role in housing generally and the anomalous federal lead in social housing, it also sought to correct the weak low-income targeting and high subsidies of the 1974–85 program model. And the mid-1990s turning point, although it arose from a broader neoliberal political turn and fiscal crisis, also reacted to political concerns about rising subsidy and intense controversies about Ontario social housing. The decisions at each turning point shaped the issues that arrived at the next juncture and altered the mix of actors that would affect their resolution.

The rightful celebration of community-based groups and initiatives in Canadian social housing should not lose sight of the context for those successes. Community-based housing achieved non-trivial scale in the period when it was orchestrated by systematic state support. About half of Canadian social housing remains in the state sector, including its municipal level.

The vivid debates and the lurching policy recipes over three decades all took place within this overarching regime. The active policy period of the 1960s to 1980s rested on a dialogue among the federal and provincial governments, the municipal level, and the community-based sector, and on a widening expertise in policy and delivery, which were shaped and framed by this institutional context.

The Housing Market and Urban Development

Conditions in the housing market and agendas in urban development were powerful factors in the evolution of Canadian social housing policy. Ideas of "reconstruction" and slum redevelopment propelled the early postwar decisions. The public housing priority in Ontario, the strongest federal partner through the 1950s and 1960s, was intimately connected to that province's strong involvement in managing the urban growth of its big city, and its agenda of nourishing the golden goose of economic growth. Although the federal 1964 changes were propelled by international ideas about social housing and urban renewal as part of a proper welfare state, the invention of the provincial housing corporation arose from these Ontario concerns and entailed a specific aim to integrate public housing with private-sector apartment production, which then comprised up to half of all housing production and was sprinkled across the central city and postwar suburbs. The political controversy which this production regime quickly aroused was a tangled bundle of opposition to high-rise development in general, suburban social change, and public housing in particular.

Urban development concerns and social welfare ideas together propelled the social housing priority at the mid-1960s and early-1970s junctures. There was a strong political concern to ensure sufficient new housing supply in rapidly growing urban Canada. This context made urban and housing issues into national ones, bridging the divide between the local and national scale, between municipal and federal government, and between urban planning and housing policy. Canada's postwar system of housing provision, with far more rental demand per capita than in the United States or Australia, kept rental supply needs on the policy agenda, and social housing as part of that. The realities on the ground led to political claims and pressures that engendered a policy response and a deployment of state resources. In the 1980s and 1990s the strong local-federal political connection weakened, the connection of urban social issues to federal policy faded somewhat, and withdrawal from social housing was one consequence. Rapid urban expansion was continuing but (measuring in percent growth in numbers of households) the growth rate by the 1990s was half of its 1950s-to-1970s levels, and the postwar transformation was complete.

The three decades of active social housing policy, from the mid-1960s to the mid-1990s, were precisely the period during which rental supply and home-buyer affordability for the middle class were consistently on the policy agenda. Price and interest-rate escalation from the mid-1960s to the mid-1970s in Canada's key cities doubled the carrying cost of buying a home, and put that out of reach for lots of people. Global and Canadian interest-rate spikes in the early 1980s put many at risk of mortgage default; this and the real estate bubble of the late 1980s shut many young adults out of ownership. In Montreal, the decline of older rental neighbourhoods seemed to put the well-being of the city at risk. Annual increases in rental demand were huge, creating tight markets and rent increases that affected the baby-boomer offspring of the broad middle class. Canadian cities in the 1980s saw a then-shocking arrival of street homelessness.

While these broader, mainstream concerns did not directly support a priority for social housing, they set the context. They supported a vigorous discourse about housing market issues and housing policy, and a sense that the market was not working well. This propelled an expanding state role from the mid-1960s to the 1980s, in efforts to manage overall supply, take a direct public role in land development, and to subsidize home purchase, new private rental, new social rental, and housing repair. When rental supply was significant on the overall policy agenda, there was political space for an argument that some of it should be social housing. When neighbourhood issues were big political concerns, social housing investment was one means to address these. The 1973–85 period was when political opinion liked social housing most – when it was least a matter of just low-income housing. Social housing rode on the back of these mainstream housing concerns and was one part of the expanded state role that responded to them

These concerns evaporated in the 1990s as house prices crashed and interest rates plunged, leading to an exodus of middle-income households from rental, weak net rental demand, a sidelined landlord-developer sector, and social residualization of rental housing. Rental housing by the 1990s was a problem of "others" outside the political mainstream. This new environment was much less favourable to a state role in housing generally or any political priority for social housing.

In Canada, a shift proceeded decade by decade in rental production, from market dominance to social housing dominance. It was almost entirely a market sector in the first decade (1955–65), and then a market sector at unsustainable levels with a strong top-up of social housing (1965–75). In 1975 to 1985 it was a fairly even mix of private rental, assisted private rental, and social housing; and finally (1985–95), it became a sector with production strongly dominated by social housing. These phases were driven by on-the-ground housing conditions in urban Canada and were shaped in mainstream politics, but this long-run trajectory was not politically sustainable in a liberal-welfare regime.

Ideas and Policy Borrowing

Changing ideas shaped the periods and turning points in Canadian social housing, with strong elements of policy borrowing from the United States, Britain, and Northwestern Europe. The early postwar turning point was informed by ideas of a new state role in social welfare and housing, legitimated by "reconstruction" thinking and carried to Canada by British housing officials who immigrated here. The two large expansionary turning points in Canadian social housing, the mid-1960s and early 1970s, reflected the period of peak welfare state expansion across most affluent Western nations. The mid-1960s turning point in social housing was an integral element of the program of the 1963–68 Pearson Liberal government through which it intended to bring Canadian social policy up to international norms. The early-1970s turning point was propelled by the protests and political upheavals against the established order that shook all liberal democratic societies in the period, with a spirit of creative innovation and suspicion of both the state and capitalism. Policy in the 1970s was shaped by a new systems thinking and a practice of comprehensive policy reviews at the federal and provincial levels. The closing turning point of the mid-1990s reflected not only a fiscal crisis, but also the reverberations in Ottawa of global neoliberal ideas.

Within social housing, borrowed and adapted ideas were important. The 1949–64 period imported the US model, with its successful emphasis on supporting market financing, market production, and home-ownership. But it also imported a version of the US public housing model, with its residual scale and targeting, federal financing, local housing authorities, and types of projects, while the other institutional model, Limited Dividend, came from the United Kingdom. Many of the leading postwar professionals in the field immigrated from those countries. The mid-1960s turning point reflected a new priority shared across most affluent Western nations, of subsidizing large numbers of low-income renters in social housing, a model replacing either break-even working-class housing or rather small low-income-targeted systems. The mixed-income, community-based housing recipe of the 1970s was borrowed from European models which had long interested Canadian advocates and policy-makers. Canada took imported ideas in particular directions, reflecting domestic realities and politics. The idea of a mix of prices and tenures became embedded in planning-and-housing thinking in Canada's large cities. A concern for supply of purpose-built rental housing became entrenched in the context of high rental demand, and of the dramatic rise and collapse of a private-rental development sector on a scale unknown in the United States or Australia. The adoption of European-style mixed-income community housing as the main model for two decades was the product of the particular Canadian politics of housing and a local-federal political axis.

The entrenching of such ideas is part of the way social housing became deeply established during its thirty-year prime. Public agencies were founded across the country with mandates reflecting certain ways of thinking. The provincial and municipal roles established in some degree in the 1950s and more strongly in the 1960s and 1970s became the focus of a public discourse about overall housing needs and mixed housing production, and about attempting to manage this systemically. These normalized ideas defined the bounds of what was pragmatic for a middle-of-the-road government or minister, in ways that were rather different in the thirty-year heyday than in the periods before or since.

In the 1950s and 1960s, social housing – though arousing local opposition – had little connotation of low-income ghettos in broader Canadian political discourse, but by the 1970s attitudes were turning. The advent of the non-profit model in the mid-1970s not only offered a better social model, but also served to sequester the inevitable stigmatization of low-income housing within the pre-1974 public housing sub-sector. This helped foster widespread support for social housing in Canada while its production waned around the world. By the latter 1980s and the 1990s, with more stringent low-income targeting, the stigmatization was starting to attach itself to non-profit housing as well.

Concern over rising subsidy requirements is a recurring theme in the policy history. It was there already in the 1960s as provincial housing corporations started their large development programs. It contributed to the policy shift to the mixed-income non-profit housing model in 1973. It became an enormous concern of federal central agencies in the years that followed, and informed the changes of 1985. It was a large part of why social housing became characterized as a boondoggle by Ontario neoliberals in the 1990s; and in the fiscal crisis of the 1990s it clinched the policy choice of devolution federally. In the low-tax Canada of the early twenty-first century, any favourable attitudes toward social housing face a high fiscal barrier.

Actors and Contingent Events

Although policy change was strongly shaped by the contexts and political currents, change was made by particular actors and propelled by specific events. At the policy junctures in the 1940s and mid-1960s, policy was shaped by a small circle of public servants and activists. Senior public servants of a market-oriented mindset wrote the 1949 NHA, and those of a more welfarist mindset wrote the amendments of 1964. The environment in each case was one of tight connections between local activists and players in the federal government. In the invention of the provincial housing corporation model in 1964, the key cabinet minister was fed ideas by an advisory group with a strong presence of progressive, concerned citizens, and a transformation in program delivery was plotted by CMHC and provincial public servants. This was the era of the "small group of thoughtful, committed citizens"[2] changing at least the policy regime.

By the early-1970s juncture, the range of political voices, claims, and interests had exploded. No longer was it a small circle of experts and advocates, but a large constituency of local activists, tenant organizations, social welfare coalitions, and elected officials at all levels. People from outside the housing policy establishment pushed forward ideas to sympathetic federal public servants and, circumventing the experts, directly to federal cabinet ministers. By the 1980s, the politics of welfare state retrenchment created much different dynamics than the former politics of welfare state expansion. Amid a fractured politics, neoliberal voices from business interests, politicians, and federal central agencies became far more important in shaping policy-making than the many political claims from what came to be seen as special-needs sectors or local interests.

Particular elections were important in policy change, especially those in 1963, 1984, and 1993 federally. These brought to power actors that pushed through agenda-driven policy change, set in place a new set of attitudes and priorities, or chose particular political resolutions. The 1963 election brought to power a new government with a social policy agenda that included social housing. The 1984 election brought a new climate of tension between market rationalism and regional brokerage, which shaped a new compromise in social housing. The 1993 election brought to power a government determined to restructure and reduce long-term federal social spending, and social housing retrenchment and devolution were part of the fallout of this. The politics of minority government boosted support for social housing and this helped boost the priority and propel the turning points of the mid-1960s and early 1970s.

Particular individuals were at times important. The federal policy shift in 1964 rested on the integration of social housing into the social policy thinking of Prime Minister Pearson's social policy advisor, Tom Kent. The provincial housing corporation model might never have been born or thrived without Stanley Randall, Ontario's 1960s minister responsible for social housing, who embraced it and oversaw it through years of peak production despite mounting controversy. Policy change in 1970–73 was propelled by strong individuals including the federal minister for CMHC, Paul Hellyer, and Michael Dennis who co-authored the key policy document and then returned home to Toronto to implement the new program regime.

Three very significant decisions in this policy history were quite contingent on political accidents and could easily have gone another way: the provincial housing corporation model, the direct federal role in the early

1970s, and devolution. Provincial housing corporations dominated the scene for a decade, building projects that were 100 percent low-income. They were central in establishing a scale of activity that transformed the systemic impacts of social housing from trivial to significant. But this model was not at all the leading idea in play in the ferment that led to the 1964 changes, and it had no precedent in the United States, Britain, or Canada. This model was an anomaly chosen by a particular Ontario cabinet minister to serve his own ambitions and to respond to the advocacy.

The federal direct re-engagement in social housing programs in the early 1970s was a detour from long-run trends in Canadian social housing, which include federal-provincial funding partnerships, mostly provincial delivery, fairly tight low-income targeting, and gradually stronger provincial roles. The abrupt direct federal role responded to the particular politics of the time, characterized by community-based protest, public housing controversies, and the federal political imperative of "visibility" in the face of Quebec nationalism. But this anomalous turn of events was central in setting in place a program model that retained political support for social housing production for a further two decades.

And what of 1990s-style devolution? We are not referring here to the long-run trend of greater capacity among provincial governments, and their lead role in delivering programs since the mid-1980s. The issue is the downscaling of federal policy vision and leadership, and its withdrawal from shaping broad priorities, frameworks, and resource flows. Although devolution has been a trend across many Western liberal democracies since the 1980s, and often a vehicle for neoliberal retrenchment, it was not a forgone path for Canadian social housing. The political decisions that led to it were particular. The Ontario decisions that relegated funding for some 40 percent of Canadian social housing to the municipal level were just political convenience; they were a way to meet the promise to get the government "out of the housing business" when other approaches proved too difficult, and social housing became collateral damage in a big reordering of provincial-municipal fiscal relations. At the federal level, devolution was not a constitutional priority for the Chrétien Liberal government: it was simply a device to bring anomalous and recalcitrant social housing into line with the 1990s restructuring of Canadian social policy.

And so as the mid-2010s arrived – although few would question the long-standing and appropriate provincial role in delivering programs and moulding policy to regional needs – there was optimism across the country about renewed federal leadership. Many were hopeful that despite the fiscal hurdles, another turning point would arrive before the end of the decade, that Canadian social housing policy was again being renovated.

Table 8.1
Canadian social housing, 1949–1996: Key features of major programs

Program: (date = when project started)	Public housing 1949–1963	Public housing 1964–1978	Non-profit & co-op 1974–1978	Non-profit & co-op 1979–1985	Federal co-op 1986–1992	Federal-provincial 1986–1993	Provincial unilateral 1987 onwards
Also known as	Federal-Provincial public housing	Provincial housing corporation	s.15 & 15.1 (later s.26 & 27) co-op s.34-18 (later s.61)	s.56.1 (later s.95) (includes "MNP" munic.non-profit)	ILM (Index Linked Mortgage)	"F/P"	Homes Now (Ont), Homes BC, AccèsLogis (Que)
Owner	CMHC+PHC §	PHC §	Non-profit, Co-op, or Municipal (some provincial in Que, Sask, Yukon)	Non-profit, Co-op, or Municipal (some provincial in Que, Sask, Yukon)	Co-op	Non-profit, Co-op, or Municipal (some F/P provincial in some cases)	
Financing (100% of original project cost exc. as noted)	75% CMHC loan (25% provincial) Fixed rate. 50-60-year am.	90% CMHC loan (10% provincial) Fixed rate. 50-60-year am.	10% CMHC grant. 90% CMHC loan. Fixed rate. 50-year am.	Private mortg., CMHC guarantee. 35-year am.	Private mortg., CMHC guarantee. 35-year am. Special formula.	Private mortg., CMHC guarantee. 35-year am.	Varied by province (Private mortgage in Ont. 1987-95, with CMHC guarantee)
Rationale for changed funding model	First funding recipe. Federal gov't required strong provincial cost-sharing	Federal priority. Capital costs were biggest challenge. Fed. fiscal capacity.	Not gov't owned. Projects then could break even at market rent, after 10% grant	Reduce federal capital spending. High interest rates then were biggest challenge	Back-loaded (inflation-based) amortization intended to enhance viability	High capital costs, high percent RGI Break-even well above market rent Unified subsidies to make project viable (may vary from this in AccèsLogis)	
Percent RGI	Varied originally. 100% by 1968.	100%	Usually 25%	Usually 25-40% (40-60% if munic)	Usually 40%	Varied by project; norms were 80% in Ont, 100% in BC, 50% in Que.	

Who paid operating subsidy ‡	75% federal, 25% provincial §	50% federal, 50% provincial §	Mostly RGI subsidy only	Federal subsidy equivalent to 2% mortgage rate + related provincial subsidy §	Federal subsidy tied to special mortgage formula	60% fed. on Core Need units (=most RGI). Rest of subsidy provincial. §	100% provincial §
Funding of RGI subsidy	RGI is part of overall operating subsidy for difference between rents & approved costs	Stacked rent supplement, usually cost-shared 50/50 federal-provincial	Some RGI within 56.1 program; Some stacked rent supp, usually 50/50 F-P	Federal ILM rent supplement		RGI is part of operating subsidy for difference between rents & approved costs	Varied by province (Same as F/P in Ontario 1987–95)
Capital Repairs	No reserve funds. Major repairs in operating budget or special funding.	Capital reserve funds, with annual contributions (rarely adequate for long term).					

"s." = section of National Housing Act. CMHC = Canada Mortgage and Housing Corp. "am." = amortization period. "PHC" = provincial housing corporation. "munic." = municipal. Private mortgage refers to lending institution (bank, insurance co., trust co., etc.). Urban Native program not shown. Some variations exist which are not included in this table.

§ = Provincial subsidy in Ontario became a municipal responsibility in 1998; provincial housing stock in Ontario became owned by municipal housing corporations in 2000.

‡ Original cost-share is shown. Federal subsidy share is declining in many cases in recent years under the devolution agreements (Social Housing Agreements).

Table 8.2
Turning points in Canadian social housing: Summary of the social policy and housing/urban factors

Key turning points →	Late 1940s	Mid-1960s	Early 1970s	Mid-1980s	Mid-1990s	Early 2000s
Trends and events in welfare state (social policy)	**Initial main planks of welfare state** • NEW! Old Age Security, Unemployment Insurance, Family Allowances, Disability benefits	**Large expansion of social programs** • NEW! Medicare, CPP/QPP, federal sharing of provincial social costs, subsidized post-secondary educ. • More programs for low income	**Turbulence and ongoing expansion** • Youth protests, bottom-up initiatives, community-based /third sector delivery of services • Stronger provincial role in social policy & programs	**Incremental devolution** • Federal social spending but with devolved delivery, to meet regional political demands • End of large overall expansion	**Major cutbacks and devolution** • Cuts in income-targeted programs • Offloading federal costs to provinces • Market-oriented ideas dominant	**Modest program expansion, soften the effects of cuts** • Reinstated federal cost-sharing • New tax benefits & spending for low-income people (families, homeless, working poor, etc.)
Urban development & neighbourhood agendas	• "Reconstruction" after World War II, slum redevelopm't • Rapid (sub)urban growth (e.g.Toronto doubling in 15 yrs.) • Too little existing housing to rely on filtering-down of older housing	• Rising affluence, rapid (sub)urban growth →added rental demand *(especially young adults and seniors)* • Rental apartments integral in urban development (1/3 – 1/2 of new housing in most larger cities)	• Preserve older central-city neighbourhoods *(fear of US-style inner-city decline)* • Ongoing high rental demand, need for affordable market-rent units • Concern about affordability (home prices, mortg.rates)	• Urban issues less important in national politis • Ongoing high rental demand, need for affordable market-rent units • Rising concern about rising homelessness	• Urban issues a remote concern in national politics • Declining house prices & interest rates, affordability drops off agenda for mainstream • Strong shift to homeownership, zero net added renters in a decade	• Strong local concerns about homelessness • Strong local concerns about rental supply and affordability

Consequences in Social Housing Policy and Programs					
• Small early social housing program	• Active federal policy priority	• Mixed-income social housing, locally delivered	• Shift to provincial lead in program delivery	• End of social housing production (exc. Que, BC)	• AHI - Affordable Housing Initiative (became IAH - Investment in Affordable Housing)
• Social housing as a concern of municipalities + Ontario government	• New provincial housing corporations	• Rising public role in housing, subsidies to all sectors	• Special-needs social housing	• Devolution to provinces (+municipalities in Ontario)	• Some regeneration initiatives
	• Production expands 10-fold		• More low income targeting		

Table 8.3
Social housing commitments, Canada, 1951–2001

	Public housing	Total non-profit & co-op (estimate)	NHA activity for social housing	Total social housing (best estimate)	Social housing: new construction only (estimate)	Total rental production in Canada	Total housing production in Canada
1951	1,495	54		1,549	1,549	18,565	68,579
1952	732	326		1,058	1,058	24,828	83,246
1953	378	430		808	808	29,881	102,409
1954	1,495	640		2,135	2,135	33,177	113,527
1955	968	27		995	995	35,823	138,276
1956	520	740		1,260	1,260	33,554	127,311
1957	1,202	954		2,156	2,100	36,251	122,340
1958	1,073	1,256		2,329	2,300	56,609	164,632
1959	772	739		1,511	1,400	44,340	141,345
1960	735	692		1,427	1,400	36,838	108,858
1961	910	724		1,634	1,600	46,100	125,577
1962	547	1,140		1,687	1,600	52,859	130,095
1963	989	1,889		2,878	2,800	69,857	148,624
1964	518	1,717		2,235	2,100	85,324	165,658
1965	2,729	1,847		4,576	3,000	77,890	166,565
1966	5,187	1,847		7,034	5,700	51,551	134,474
1967	8,987	1,847		10,834	10,400	74,258	164,123
1968	9,746	1,847		11,593	11,100	103,383	196,878
1969	17,084	1,847		18,931	17,400	110,917	210,415
1970	19,979	3,527	25,098	25,098	24,664	91,898	190,528
1971	21,480	3,280	26,874	26,874	26,530	106,187	233,653
1972	16,484	2,040	20,421	20,421	19,777	103,715	249,914
1973	13,480	2,516	18,683	18,683	18,424	106,451	268,529
1974	12,504	6,568	22,017	22,017	20,696	74,025	222,123
1975	13,468	5,794	22,197	22,197	21,192	70,361	231,456
1976	13,905	9,717	26,511	26,511	24,675	89,324	273,203
1977	7,016	5,700	15,950	15,950	14,209	92,327	245,724
1978	7,897	4,835	15,212	15,212	13,810	77,327	227,667
1979	1,074	17,390	9,966	9,966	7,617	58,387	197,049
1980		19,769	21,008	21,008	13,038	48,329	158,601
1981		19,056	21,972	21,972	16,507	61,609	177,973
1982		20,450	19,160	19,160	15,924	53,162	125,860
1983		20,098	18,272	18,272	14,947	44,124	162,645
1984		17,014	18,254	18,254	15,053	40,000	134,900
1985		17,812	19,649	19,649	17,905	37,000	165,826
1986		16,987		16,987	9,594	41,000	199,785
1987	.	21,100		21,100	20,100	52,000	245,986
1988		19,700		19,700	18,800	38,000	222,562
1989		17,400		17,400	16,500	34,551	215,382
1990		17,100		17,100	16,300	34,494	181,630
1991		24,400		24,400	23,200	33,607	156,197

Table 8.3 (*continued*)

	Public housing	Total non-profit & co-op (estimate)	NHA activity for social housing	Total social housing (best estimate)	Social housing: new construction only (estimate)	Total rental production in Canada	Total housing production in Canada
1992		22,100		22,100	21,100	32,349	168,271
1993		12,200		12,200	11,600	19,566	155,443
1994		4,500		4,500	4,300	12,922	154,057
1995		3,900		3,900	3,700	8,705	110,933
1996		3,112		3,112	2,800	7,170	124,713
1997		2,739		2,739	2,500	7,693	147,040
1998		1,296		1,296	1,200	6,531	137,439
1999		2,542		2,542	2,300	9,280	149,968
2000		3,937		3,937	3,500	10,260	151,653
2001		3,989		3,989	3,600	14,897	162,733

Note: Data omit 340 public housing units and 52 charitable LD units in 1950. Blank cells indicate program not in existence or category not applicable.

Source: CMHC, *Canadian Housing Statistics*, various series & years; CMHC, *Housing in Canada* for early 1950s; CMHC market monitoring reports (title varies) for total rental and other production; provincial unilateral as per Table 8.4 following; related estimates (rounded).

Table 8.4
Social housing commitments: Details 1951–2001

	Non-profit & co-op 1950–78	Section 56.1 & F/P (later s. 95)			RRAP non-profit component	Provincial unilateral		
		Non-profit	Co-op	Total		Ontario	Quebec	BC
1951	54							
1952	326							
1953	430							
1954	640							
1955	27							
1956	740							
1957	954							
1958	1,256							
1959	739							
1960	692							
1961	724							
1962	1,140							
1963	1,889							
1964	1,717							
1965	1,847							
1966	1,847							
1967	1,847							
1968	1,847							
1969	1,847							
1970	3,527							
1971	3,280							
1972	2,040							
1973	2,515							
1974	6,567				2,212			
1975	5,793				1,149			
1976	9,716				2,068			
1977	5,699				5,564			
1978	2,620	1,922	292	2,214	467			
1979	20	15,487	1,883	17,370	7,358			
1980		14,981	4,788	19,769	7,208			
1981		13,496	5,560	19,056	4,039			
1982		13,872	6,578	20,450	7,556			
1983		13,934	6,164	20,098	7,387			
1984		13,137	3,877	17,014	5,628			
1985		13,080	4,732	17,812	1,034			
1986		12,933	4,054	16,987		200		
1987		16,239	4,560	20,799		300		
1988		15,114	3,618	18,732		1,000		
1989		13,679	2,487	16,166		1,200		
1990		11,933	2,253	14,186		2,900		
1991		12,129	2,271	14,400		10,000		
1992		10,735	387	11,122		11,000		150

Table 8.4 (*continued*)

	Non-profit & co-op 1950–78	Section 56.1 & F/P (later s. 95)			RRAP non-profit component	Provincial unilateral		
		Non-profit	Co-op	Total		Ontario	Quebec	BC
1993		6,526	602	7,128		5,100		150
1994		1,348		1,348		3,200		150
1995		1,100		1,100		2,800		150
1996		1,312		1,312		900		454
1997		1,439		1,439				874
1998		550		550			46	1,264
1999		1,050		1,050			592	671
2000		1,250		1,250			1,187	917
2001		1,050		1,050			1,039	1,493

Note: For col 1, a 1964–66 total is attributed equally 1965–1969. Some 1980s provincial unilateral units not tallied. Blank cells indicate program not in existence. 56.1 is s. 95 in 1990s–2000s.

Sources: CMHC, CHS, various series & years; CMHC, *Housing in Canada* for early 1950s; SHQ annual reports; BC Housing completions; provincial data for Ontario unilateral, attributed by year as per GTA project data.

Table 8.5
New affordable rental housing in post-1996 programs

	Ontario (approx.)	Quebec Accès-Logis	Quebec LAQ	BC	Alberta	Other provinces (est.)	On-reserve (s. 95)	Total (approx.)
1996	0	0	0	454	0	200	1,312	2,000
1997	0	0	0	874	0	300	1,439	3,000
1998	0	46	0	1,264	0	100	550	2,000
1999	0	592	0	671	0	300	1,050	3,000
2000	400	1,187	0	917	0	600	1,250	4,000
2001	400	1,039	0	1,493	0	700	1,050	5,000
2002	300	1,312	0	1,890	0	600	1,030	5,000
2003	2,800	2,026	420	1,203	700	1,000	968	9,000
2004	2,000	1,324	1,248	862	700	900	978	8,000
2005	1,500	1,994	1,776	1,474	755	1,100	1,045	10,000
2006	1,800	1,525	2,255	1,523	628	1,100	4,393	13,000
2007	2,000	1,385	1,471	1,514	2,686	900	1,442	11,000
2008	1,000	1,683	894	1,172	2,842	900	945	9,000
2009	1,700	2,046	316	1,475	3,289	1,000	1,117	11,000
2010	1,400	2,163	110	1,685	2,011	1,000	1,054	9,000
2011	1,500	2,206	67	1,863	1,212	800	647	8,000
2012	1,000	1,278	0	911	155	700	603	5,000
2013	1,000	2,796	0	1,399	200	800	546	7,000

Note: Data include assisted private rental (1/3 of Ontario and about 1/2 of Quebec LAQ, unknown but small shares elsewhere). Data are commitments or funding approvals (definitions vary) except BC is completions.

Sources: SHQ annual reports; Alberta data from annual reports; BC Housing data; Ontario: occasional MMAH data and GTA municipal project reports; Other provinces & territories estimated at 20% of combined Ontario + Quebec + BC (i.e. prorated population). Section 95 on-reserve from CMHC, *Canadian Housing Statistics*.

Table 8.6
Social housing and net change in Canadian occupied housing stock, 1961–2001

A. Housing Stock	1961	1966	1971	1976	1981	1986	1991	1996	2001
Social housing	14,000	24,000	77,000	190,000	288,000	390,000	485,000	579,000	592,000
Rental	1,549,000	1,911,000	2,398,000	2,735,000	3,140,000	3,411,000	3,746,000	3,942,000	3,953,000
Owner-occupied	3,006,000	3,270,000	3,637,000	4,431,000	5,142,000	5,581,000	6,272,000	6,878,000	7,610,000
Total	4,555,000	5,181,000	6,035,000	7,166,000	8,282,000	8,992,000	10,018,000	10,820,000	11,563,000

B. Net Change	1961–66	1966–71	1971–76	1976–81	1981–86	1986–91	1991–96	1996–2001	1966–96
Social housing	10,000	53,000	113,000	98,000	102,000	95,000	94,000	13,000	555,000
Rental	362,000	487,000	337,000	405,000	271,000	335,000	196,000	11,000	2,031,000
Owner-occupied	264,000	367,000	794,000	711,000	439,000	691,000	606,000	732,000	3,608,000
Total	626,000	854,000	1,131,000	1,116,000	710,000	1,026,000	802,000	743,000	5,639,000
Social housing % net change in:									
Rental housing	3	11	34	24	38	28	48	**	27
Total housing	2	6	10	9	14	9	12	2	10

Note: Social housing excludes Entrepreneurial and many or most Rent Assistance and On-Reserve (these components of 1995 social portfolio totalled 99,600 units per *Canadian Housing Statistics*, 1996); also excludes various bed-units (congregate). Total social housing in Canada has been estimated at approximately 680,000. All data rounded. Unoccupied units not accounted for in social housing. Data negative or exceeding 100 percent is noted ** . Social housing is a subset of rental. Commitments to 1969, 1979, etc. are deemed to equate to completion by census date 1971, 1981, etc.

Source: Occupied private dwelling counts from census; social housing from *Canadian Housing Statistics* & related sources (see Table 8.3).

List of Abbreviations

AHI	Affordable Housing Initiative – Program 2011–2018 (succeeded by the Investment in Affordable Housing program)
AHOP	Assisted Home Ownership Program
AHP	Affordable Housing Initiative – Program 2002–2011
BC	British Columbia
CAP	Canada Assistance Plan
CCF	Co-operative Commonwealth Federation
CHF	Co-operative Housing Federation of Canada
CHRA	Canadian Housing and Renewal Association
CHS	*Canadian Housing Statistics* (CMHC annual statistical reporting publication)
CHST	Canada Health and Social Transfer
CMA	Census metropolitan area
CMHC	Canada Mortgage and Housing Corporation (Central Mortgage and Housing Corporation until 1978)
CNIT	Core need income threshold (income ceiling at which average market rent in the local housing market equals 30 percent of household income)
CPI	Consumer price index
CUM	Communauté urbaine de Montréal
DHA	Dominion Housing Act
EI	Employment Insurance Program
FCM	Federation of Canadian Municipalities
FPT	Federal-provincial-territorial (referring to legal agreements or ministers' meetings)
GDP	Gross domestic product
GIS	Guaranteed Income Supplement

HLM   *Habitations à loyer modéré* (France); *habitations à loyer modique* (Quebec) – Social housing with moderate regulated rents

IAH   Investment in Affordable Housing (program, 2011–2018)

ILM   Index linked mortgage

IMF   International Monetary Fund

IYSH   International Year of Shelter for the Homeless (UN-designated year, 1987)

LAQ   Logement abordable Québec (program, 2002–2008)

LD   Limited dividend (housing programs)

LSR   Local service realignment – official Ontario term for the fiscal trade of responsibilities between the provincial and municipal governments, implemented in 1997-1998

MBS   Mortgage-backed securities

MNP   Municipal Non-Profit (program or project under the programs of 1974–1995)

MP   Member of Parliament

MPP   Member of Provincial Parliament (Ontario)

MTHA   Metropolitan Toronto Housing Authority

MURB   Multiple Unit Residential Building (Canadian federal tax incentive, 1975–1982)

NATO   North Atlantic Treaty Organization

NDP   New Democratic Party

NEBR   National Bureau of Economic Research (US)

NHA   National Housing Act

NHI   National Homelessness Initiative (1999–2007, succeeded by the Homelessness Partnering Strategy)

NWT   Northwest Territories

OECD   Organization for Economic Co-operation and Development

OHC   Ontario Housing Corporation

OMHM   Office municipal d'habitation de Montréal – Montreal municipal housing corporation

ONPHA   Ontario Non-Profit Housing Association

OPEC   Organization of Petroleum Exporting Countries

PCO   Privy Council Office

PEI   Prince Edward Island

PMO   Prime Minister's Office

PQ   Parti Québécois

PRQC   Programme de revitalisation des quartiers centraux

RGI   Rent-geared-to-income – Housing unit, rent level, and/or
          funding involving subsidized rents calibrated at a ratio to
          each household's income, typically 25–30 percent.
RRAP   Residential Rehabilitation Assistance Program
SCPI   Supporting Communities Partnership Initiative (1999–
          2007)
SHQ   Société d'habitation du Québec
SRO   Single room occupancy building (residential hotel, usually
          low-income)
SSHRC   Social Sciences and Humanities Research Council
SUFA   Social Union Framework Agreement
TREB   Toronto Real Estate Board
WHL   Wartime Housing Limited

List of Persons Interviewed

VINCE BRESCIA. Policy advisor to minister of municipal affairs and housing, 1995–96; other Ontario public service positions; former president & CEO, Federation of Rental-Housing Providers of Ontario; and other positions.

DAN BURNS. Staff of CMHC Task Force on Low Income Housing, 1970–71; manager then director of neighbourhood planning, City of Toronto, 1970s–80s; commissioner of housing, City of Toronto, 1988–91; deputy minister of housing, Ontario, 1992–95; deputy minister of municipal affairs and housing, Ontario, 1995–97; other DM positions, 1997–2002; retired.

SHARON CHISHOLM. Executive director, Canadian Housing and Renewal Association, 1994–2007; University of St Andrew's, Scotland.

DAVID CLUFF. Director of various CMHC divisions: Program Planning and Analysis 1987–96, Assisted Housing 1996–99, Strategic Policy and Planning 1999–2002, Policy and Research 2002–04; retired.

PAUL CONNELLY. Manager, program development / government relations, Ontario Non-Profit Housing Association, 1990s; housing consultant.

TERRY COOKE. Chairman, Regional Municipality of Hamilton-Wentworth, 1994–2000; member, Who Does What Panel, 1996; president & CEO, Hamilton Community Foundation.

DAVID CROMBIE. Mayor, City of Toronto, 1972–78; MP, 1978–88; cabinet minister, 1978 and 1984–88; former president, Waterfront Regeneration Trust; retired.

ART EGGLETON. Mayor, City of Toronto, 1980–91; MP, 1993–2004; cabinet member, 1993–2002 including president of the Treasury Board, 1993–96; senator; and other positions.

CAMERON GRAY. Development officer and deputy supervisor of properties, City of Vancouver, 1986–91, director, Housing Centre, City of

Vancouver, 1991–2007, managing director, social development, City of Vancouver, 2008–09.

SHIRLEY HOY. Director, policy and planning, Metro Toronto Community Services Department, 1980s; assistant deputy minister, housing operations, Ontario Ministry of Housing, 1993–95; commissioner of community services, Metro Toronto, 1996; acting chief administrative officer, Metro Toronto, 1997; commissioner of community and neighbourhood services, City of Toronto, 1998– 2000; CEO, Toronto Lands Corporation; and other positions.

JAMES MCGREGOR. Coordinator, Conseil de développement du logement communautaire, 1976–86; political advisor to Montreal mayor Doré, 1986–89; director for development, Société d'habitation et de développement de Montréal (SHDM), 1989–2001; director, Solidarité 5000 logements, Housing Department, City of Montreal, 2002–07; vice-president for housing development, Société d'habitation du Québec, 2007–11; president, Groupe habitat conseil inc.

DAVID PETERS. Community Housing Branch, Ontario Ministry of Housing, 1974–78; director of policy and programs, Housing Department, City of Toronto, 1989–93; commissioner of housing, City of Toronto, 1994–97; general manager, Ontario Housing Corporation, 1999–2000; director, housing supply, Ontario Ministry of Municipal Affairs and Housing, circa 2001–05; government relations, Ontario Non-Profit Housing Association, 1998 and circa 2006–09; and other positions; retired.

STEVE POMEROY. Housing policy consultant, 1995–present. Previously at CMHC BC Regional office, 1980s; director, CMHC Centre for Future Studies in Living Environments, 1989–94; participant, CMHC and Treasury Board task forces on social housing, early 1990s.

JOYCE POTTER. Staff, Ministry of State for Urban Affairs, 1970s; director of program evaluation, CMHC, 1981–86; executive director, operations review, and then other non-program positions, CMHC, 1987–91; special advisor on social housing, Regional Municipality of Ottawa-Carleton and director of housing, City of Ottawa, 1998–2002; chair of the Ontario Regions Social Housing Group, 1998–2002; and other positions; retired.

SHAYNE RAMSAY. CEO, BC Housing, 2000–present. Previously director of development services, BC Housing; director of housing policy and program development, BC Ministry of Municipal Affairs and Housing; CEO, Homeowner Protection Office, Province of British Columbia.

ALAN REDWAY. Minister responsible for CMHC, 1989–91. MP 1984–93. Previously mayor of East York (Ontario), 1977–82 and member of Metropolitan Toronto Council; retired.

DON RICHMOND. Policy assistant to Ontario premier Robarts, 1963–65 and 1967; deputy commissioner of planning, Municipality of Metropolitan Toronto, 1973–80s; general manager, Metropolitan Toronto Housing Company Limited, 1982–92; Metro Toronto commissioner of community services, 1993–95; executive chairman, Metropolitan Toronto Housing Authority, 1996–97; and other positions; retired.

MARC ROCHON. President, Canada Mortgage and Housing Corporation, 1995–2000; retired. Previously in various other senior federal government positions.

PETER SMITH. General manager, Peel Non-Profit Housing Corporation, 1980s; president, Andrin Homes Limited; chairman, board of directors, Canada Mortgage and Housing Corporation, 1995–2000; and other positions.

KEITH WARD. Co-ordinator/manager of policy and of development planning, Cityhome, 1977–86; director of policy and development, Peel Non-Profit Housing Corporation, 1986–90s; commissioner of housing and property, Regional Municipality of Peel, 1998–2009; president, Ontario Non-Profit Housing Corporation, various dates; president, Housing Services Corporation, various dates; consultant.

QUEBEC HOUSING OFFICIAL (QHO). Person with a career history of senior roles in housing policy in Montreal/Quebec.

SENIOR CO-OP OFFICIAL (SCO). Person with career history of senior roles in co-op housing sector organizations at the local and national levels, interviewed on the basis of no attribution of information or opinions by name.

SENIOR HOUSING OFFICIAL 1 (SHO1). Person with a career in senior policy/management positions at CMHC in the 1970s; and other positions; interviewed on the basis of no attribution of information or opinions by name.

SENIOR HOUSING OFFICIAL 2 (SHO2). Person in senior policy/management positions at CMHC in the 1980s and 1990s; and other positions; retired; interviewed on the basis of no attribution of information or opinions by name.

SENIOR POLITICAL OFFICIAL (SPO). Person with a career history which includes relevant senior political and policy positions at the federal and provincial levels; interviewed on the basis of no attribution of information or opinions by name.

Notes

CHAPTER ONE

1 More strictly, social housing is housing resourced and operated by governments or non-profit agencies on a non-market basis. "Non-market" refers to the rents, which are lower than in the market; the manner of access or "who gets in," with priority given to people with low incomes or other disadvantages; financing of capital costs, arranged by government usually at below-market interest rates or with state guarantees; provision of subsidies; and long-run asset value, which once debt-free becomes a resource to sustain low rents rather than to deploy for maximum return. Publicly assisted private rental and state-assisted home-ownership were of much importance in Canadian and European policy in the 1970s and 1980s, but are not within the scope of this book.

2 Harloe, *The People's Home?*; summary data in Suttor, *Rental Paths from Postwar to Present*.

3 Harloe, *The People's Home?*

4 Gourevitch, *Politics in Hard Times*, 217.

5 Castles, *Comparative Public Policy*; Esping-Anderson, *The Three Worlds of Welfare Capitalism*.

6 Murie, "Dynamics of Social Exclusion," 154.

7 Schwartz, *Housing Policy in the United States*; Suttor, *Rental Paths*.

8 Hulse, "Housing Allowances and Private Renting."

9 Myles, "When Markets Fail"; Castles, *Comparative Public Policy*.

10 On these three points, see respectively O'Connor, "Welfare Expenditure and Policy Orientation"; Myles, "When Markets Fail"; Castles, *Comparative Public Policy*, 135. Civilian consumption refers to public expenditure other than for capital formation, subsidies and transfers, military expenditure, and debt service.

11 Picot and Myles, *Income Inequality and Low Income*, 13–14, 27; Myles, "When Markets Fail"; Gottschalk and Smeeding, "Cross-National Comparisons."

12 See Card and Freeman, *Small Differences That Matter*; Zuberi, *Small Differences That Matter*.

13 See Suttor, "Canadian Social Housing," chapter 6, for an analysis of systemic impacts in the Toronto housing system.

14 Deepening concentrations of poverty in postwar Toronto rental neighbourhoods since the 1980s were largely a function of declining incomes in private renters and among home-owners, not of added social housing; and social housing development in the prime period tended to disperse rather than concentrate poverty. See Suttor, "Canadian Social Housing," chapter 7, for an analysis of this in Greater Toronto; also Suttor, *Rental Housing Dynamics*, for a review of the broader dynamics and concepts.

15 Prior research has defined periods of Canadian social housing policy in varying ways. Humphrey Carver, in *Compassionate Landscape*, described a 1945–55 period of "innocence and authority" led by a trusted government and experts; one of "expanding horizons" in 1955–67, when broader ideas about social needs and urbanization reframed the housing agenda; and "the turbulence" after 1967. John Sewell, in *Houses and Homes*, speaking of housing policy more broadly and drawing on Fallis, defined 1954–63 as a period of "stabilization and growth," 1964–77 as one of "equity and affordability," and 1978 onward as one of "stagflation and restraint"; devolution was yet to arrive. Roberto Leone and Barbara Wake Carroll, in "Decentralisation and Devolution in Canadian Social Housing Policy," adapted Carroll's earlier periodization of Canadian housing policy more broadly and identified six optimistically named periods: "economic development" in 1945–68; "social development" in 1968–78; "financial restraint" in 1978–86; "disentanglement" in 1986–94; "disengagement and privatisation" in 1994–2001; and "reengagement" in 2001 to the present. J. David Hulchanski, in "How Did We Get Here?," described four periods: before 1964, when governments "avoided any significant involvement"; 1964–84 with a "commitment to building a non-market social housing sector as part of a broader social safety net"; 1984–93 with a "decline in the allocation of new federal money"; and post-1994 again "no significant federal involvement" but also devolution and subsequently modest new-supply initiatives. Hulchanski's framing is adopted with modifications here.

16 For critiques, see Smith, "Canadian Housing Policy in the Seventies"; Smith, "Crisis in Rental Housing"; Lithwick, "Decline and Fall of the

Housing Market"; Fallis, "Federal Government and the Metropolitan Housing Problem"; Fallis, "Progressive Housing Policy."

17 Banting, "Social Housing in a Divided State."

18 Bacher, *Keeping to the Marketplace*.

19 Bacher, "Drift within Close Confines, 1955–1992."

20 Fallis, "Housing Finance and Housing Subsidies in Canada"; Fallis, "Federal Government and the Metropolitan Housing Problem"; Fallis, "Social Policy Challenge and Social Housing"; and other publications.

21 Fallis, "Social Policy Challenge and Social Housing"; Fallis, "Progressive Housing Policy in the 21st Century."

22 Hulchanski, "Canada"; Hulchanski, "What Factors Shape Canadian Housing Policy?"; and other publications.

23 Hulchanski, "What Factors Shape Canadian Housing Policy?"

24 Ibid.; Hulchanski and Drover, "Housing Subsidies in a Period of Restraint."

25 Carroll, "Housing Policy in the New Millennium."

26 Carroll and Jones, "Road to Innovation."

27 Carroll, "Post-War Trends in Canadian Housing Policy."

28 Leone and Carroll, "Decentralisation and Devolution."

29 Dennis and Fish, *Programs in Search of a Policy*.

30 Rose, *Canadian Housing Policies*.

31 Central Mortgage and Housing Corporation became Canada Mortgage and Housing Corporation from 1978 onwards.

32 Klodawsky and Spector, "Renovation or Abandonment?"

33 Prince, "Canadian Housing Policy Context"; Prince, "Holes in the Safety Net."

34 Wolfe, "Canadian Housing Policy in the Nineties."

35 Carter, "Current Practices for Procuring Affordable Housing"; Carter, *Perspectives on Canadian Housing Policy*; Carter, "Canadian Housing Policy"; Carter, *Canadian Housing Policy*.

36 Hackworth, "Durability of Roll-out Neoliberalism"; Hackworth, "Political Marginalisation, Misguided Nationalism Systems"; Hackworth and Moriah, "Neoliberalism, Contingency and Urban Policy."

37 See especially Purdy, "From Place of Hope"; Purdy, "By the People, For the People"; Purdy and Kwak, "Introduction."

38 Pomeroy and Falvo, "Pragmatism and Political Expediency."

39 Notable other sources for non-specialist readers or students include Sewell, *Houses and Homes*; Cole, *Under Construction*, on the co-op sector; Oberlander and Fallick, *Housing a Nation*, a 1970s federal insider account; and sources cited in later chapters.

40 Banting, "Social Housing in a Divided State," 121.

41 For example, interwar Canada had far less state pension coverage than the UK, Australia, or most affluent nations. See Esping-Andersen, *Three Worlds of Welfare Capitalism*.

42 Shostack, "Business and Reform."

43 See Harloe, *The People's Home?*, for a selected international comparison; see comparative summary in Suttor, *Rental Paths*.

44 Suttor, *Rental Paths*.

45 See Schwartz, *Housing Policy in the United States*, 125ff, on US public housing production by year.

46 Battle, "Back to the Future"; Myles, "When Markets Fail"; O'Connor, "Welfare Expenditure and Policy Orientation in Canada"; Battle, "Relentless Incrementalism," 191.

47 Banting, *Welfare State and Canadian Federalism*.

48 Mishra, "Collapse of the Welfare State Consensus?," 93ff.

49 Battle, "Relentless Incrementalism."

50 Prince, "Holes in the Safety Net," 839; Battle, "Relentless Incrementalism," 189, 202, 204; Hulchanski, "What Factors Shape Canadian Housing Policy?," 231.

51 Cameron and Simeon, "Intergovernmental Relations in Canada."

52 Battle, "Relentless Incrementalism."

53 See Obinger et al., *Federalism and the Welfare State*.

54 Paul Pierson, "Fragmented Welfare States."

55 Wilensky, *Welfare State and Equality*; Myles and Quadagno, "Political Theories of the Welfare State."

56 Marxist theory shares this functionalist logic, with a different emphasis. In "Political Theories of the Welfare State," Myles and Quadagno characterize it thus: "Welfare state expansion … was driven by the dual, if contradictory, imperatives imposed on the capitalist state to create conditions for capital accumulation, on the one hand, and the social legitimation of this mode of production, on the other."

57 Mishra, "Collapse of the Welfare State Consensus?"; Mishra, *Globalization and the Welfare State*, chapter 6.

58 Myles and Quadagno, "Political Theories of the Welfare State," 41.

59 Canadian GDP per capita in 1900 is estimated at $2,900 (1990 dollars), variously 27 to 35 percent lower than that of the US, UK, Australia, and New Zealand, and virtually the same as central and western Europe if we exclude the high outlier (the UK) and its low outliers (Italy, Spain, and Portugal). Estimates are from Maddison project, historical GDP data series. Canadian GDP per capita rose from about 70 percent of US levels in the interwar years to 85 percent by the 1970s.

60 Five-year periods are used here for convenience. Real GDP per capita in 1990 terms was $2,200 (1889), $4,400 (1913), $5,200 (1928), $3,700 (1934), $7,300 (1950), $14,300 (1975), $22,500 (2000). Data from Maddison Project, historical GDP data series.

61 Jenson, "'Different' but Not 'Exceptional'"; Wolfe, "Canadian State in Comparative Perspective."

62 Ibid.

63 Mendelson, *UK in 2011.*

64 See Korpi, "Power Resources Model"; also Myles and Quadagno, "Political Theories of the Welfare State."

65 Among other sources on migration volumes to and from the US see Kalbach and McVey, *Demographic Bases of Canadian Society.* On the 1965–68 US policy changes see Davies and Winer, "Closing the 49th Parallel."

66 Myles, "When Markets Fail"; Jenson, "'Different' but Not 'Exceptional'"; Jenson, "Representations in Crises."

67 Banting, *Welfare State and Canadian Federalism*; Jenson, "Representations in Crises," 662; also Myles, "When Markets Fail," 130.

68 Stone, "Causal Stories"; Rochefort and Cobb, "Problem Definition"; Fischer, *Reframing Public Policy.*

69 Fischer, *Reframing Public Policy.*

70 Gough, "European Welfare States."

71 Grabb and Curtis, *Regions Apart*, 4–105.

72 Forsey, *Life on the Fringe.*

73 Leonard Marsh had previously worked under William Beveridge: see Bacher, *Keeping to the Marketplace*, 165, among other sources.

74 Lewis, *The Good Fight.*

75 Kent, *A Public Purpose.*

76 Torgerson, "Housing."

77 Harloe, *The People's Home?* Regulatory intervention *sans* social housing emerged at the same time in US Progressive Era politics; see Plunz, *History of Housing.*

78 Harloe, *The People's Home?*

79 Saunders, *Social Theory and the Urban Question*, 299–311.

80 Rutherford, *Saving the Canadian City: The First Phase 1880–1920.*

81 Freeman, *Working-Class New York*; White, *London in the Twentieth Century: A City and Its People*, 355–72.

82 Urban issues and urban social movements are also prominent in Marxist thinking, in the focus on "collective consumption," "the urban question," and urban social movements; see Merrifield, *Metromarxism*; Saunders, *Social Theory and the Urban Question*, 180–246.

83 Doling, *Comparative Housing Policy*; Kemp, "Role and Design of Income-

Related Housing Allowances"; Kemeny, "Corporatism and Housing Regimes."

84 Piketty, *Capital in the Twenty-First Century*.

85 See selected data in Suttor, *Rental Paths*. Ireland and New Zealand were fairly rural then, with primate cities' populations under a quarter million.

86 Harris and Choko, *Evolution of Housing Tenure*.

87 See Ames, *City below the Hill*; Toronto, Committee on Housing Conditions in Toronto, *Report of the Lieutenant-Governor's Committee*.

88 The exception was Montreal, comparable then in size to counterparts in Australia (Sydney, Melbourne), the US (San Francisco, Philadelphia), or Britain (Birmingham, Glasgow). But in Montreal, unlike those cities, English-French politics and the Church trumped labour/left politics.

89 Fallis, "The Metropolitan Housing Problem."

90 See Shostack, "Business and Reform," regarding the Toronto Housing Company, an early, soon-failing municipal housing venture (resuscitated as social housing in the 1970s as the Bain Co-op and Spruce Court Co-op). Also Shawn Micallef, "Affordable Housing That Works," *Toronto Star*, 12 September 2013.

91 Hall and Taylor, "Political Science," 938. On historical institutionalism see also Paul Pierson, "Not Just What, but *When*"; Pierson, "Increasing Returns."

92 Pierson, "Increasing Returns," 259.

93 Hall and Taylor, "Political Science"; Thelen and Steinmo, "Historical Institutionalism in Comparative Politics."

94 See Gough, "European Welfare States"; Esping-Andersen, *Three Worlds of Welfare Capitalism*; Arts and Gelissen, "Three Worlds of Welfare Capitalism."

95 Pierson, "Not Just What, but *When*."

96 See Pierson, "Not Just What, but *When*"; Myles and Quadagno, "Political Theories of the Welfare State," 42, 52; Mishra, *Globalization and the Welfare State*.

97 Thelen and Steinmo, "Historical Institutionalism in Comparative Politics."

98 Hall and Taylor, "Political Science and the Three New Institutionalisms," 942.

99 Hacker, "Privatizing Risk."

100 Mahoney and Thelen, "Theory of Gradual Institutional Change."

101 Hall and Taylor, "Political Science and the Three New Institutionalisms"; Pierson, "New Politics of the Welfare State."

102 For general multi-causal approaches to explaining policy change, cate-

gorizing and integrating multiple "theories of public policy," see Ham
and Hill, *Policy Process in the Modern Capitalist State*; Gough, "European
Welfare States" with specific reference to social policy.

103 Simeon, "Studying Public Policy."

104 Hall and Taylor, "Political Science."

105 This is a fair generalization if Canada is compared in terms of the subnational (states, provinces, länder, etc.) share of GDP, public expenditure,
health and welfare spending, as well as taxation autonomy, borrowing autonomy, public debt, etc. See for example Obinger et al., *Federalism and
the Welfare State*; Darby et al., "Fiscal Federalism and Fiscal Autonomy."

CHAPTER TWO

1 King's main agenda upon election in 1935 was restraint of public
spending; see Bacher, *Keeping to the Marketplace*, 94.

2 Maddison historical GDP series data shows growth from $4,800 in 1939
to $7,400 in 1944 (1990 dollars). The 1939 GDP per capita was just 8
percent below the 1928 peak. GDP per capita dipped somewhat in the
1945–49 demobilization and adjustment period but had recovered by
1951 and rose thereafter.

3 Statistics Canada, *Historical Statistics of Canada*, table H1–18. Even net of
personal income tax which was deliberately increased for the war, tax
revenues rose to from 0.4 to 1.5 billion. Total general expenditures of all
governments in Canada rose from 1.3 to 5.7 billion (fiscal 1939/40–
1945/46): Statistics Canada, *Historical Statistics of Canada*, table H148–
160.

4 Statistics Canada, *Historical Statistics of Canada*, table R1–22. The peak
occurred in 1944, 83 percent above the previous 1929 peak. The latter
had risen only 15 percent above that of the late 1910s.

5 Ibid.

6 Bacher, *Keeping to the Marketplace*, 126.

7 Marsh, *Report on Social Security for Canada*; Guest, *Emergence of Social
Security*, 120ff.

8 For evidence regarding wage compression, see empirical data in Podoluk,
Incomes of Canadians; Piketty, *Capital in the Twenty-First Century*, 271–303.

9 Morton, *Short History of Canada*, 214.

10 Calculated from Dominion Bureau of Statistics, census of Canada:
"greater cities" for 1941 (except unitary Edmonton) and CMAs for 1951.
These ten urban centres were the largest in 1941. Rapid growth also
occurred from 1901 to 1931 in percentage terms, and many post-1951
decades swamped the 1940s absolutely; but the combination of high

relative and absolute growth amid an acute housing shortage made the
1940s distinctive.

11 The housing crisis in urban Canada during wartime and demobilization
is portrayed by Bacher, *Keeping to the Marketplace*, with many specific
details, at 127, 143–57 (passim), 174–5; and by Purdy, "'It was tough on
everybody.'"

12 Bacher, *Keeping to the Marketplace*, 175.

13 Brushett, "Where Will the People Go."

14 Sewell, *Houses and Homes*, 27.

15 Central Mortgage and Housing Corporation, *Housing in Canada*, II-5,
VII-8.

16 See summary in Suttor, *Rental Paths*.

17 Kalbach and McVey, *Demographic Bases of Canadian Society*; also
Simmons and Bourne, *Urban Growth Trends in Canada*, 27.

18 Populations in 1941 and 1961 respectively (millions): Montreal 1.2 rising
to 2.2; Toronto 0.9 rising to 1.9; and Vancouver 0.4 rising to 0.8 (Dominion Bureau of Statistics, census of Canada, various years).

19 Central Mortgage and Housing Corporation, *Housing in Canada* and
Canadian Housing Statistics, various years.

20 Average resale price in current dollars: 1953, $14,424; 1963, $16,517
($14,300 in 1953 dollars). Data from Toronto Real Estate Board [TREB],
Market Watch (various dates); CPI 67.0 and 77.2 from Statistics Canada,
Historical Statistics of Canada, calculations by the author.

21 See general discussion in Suttor, *Rental Paths*. The 47 percent is from
Miron, "Demographic and Economic Factors." The Australian 15 percent
is calculated from census data (1947–1971) in Badcock, "Homeownership and the Illusion of Egalitarianism"; the US 20 percent is calculated
from census data (1950–1970) at http://www.census.gov/housing
/census/data/units/units1970.txt and http://www.census.gov/housing
/census/data/units/units1950.txt.

22 Spurr, *Land and Urban Development*.

23 Fallis, "Housing Finance," 885.

24 Computed from CMHC housing starts and completions data in *Housing
in Canada* and *Canadian Housing Statistics*, various years. See data in Suttor, *Rental Paths*, and detailed Toronto data in Suttor, "Canadian Social
Housing."

25 Bacher, *Keeping to the Marketplace*, 67, 70ff.

26 Ibid., 105–6.

27 Ibid., 10, 22–3, and passim.

28 Thompson with Seager, *Canada 1922–1939*.

29 George, "The Bruce Report"; Toronto, Lieutenant-Governor's Committee

on Housing Conditions in Toronto, *Report of the Lieutenant-Governor's Committee* [Bruce report].

30 See Wade, *Houses for All*.

31 Warwick Eather, "We Only Build Houses: The Commission 1945–60," in Howe, *New Houses for Old*, 69–94.

32 On US advocacy and political struggles, see Radford, *Modern Housing for America*, passim. For Australia, see Howe, *New Houses for Old*, 20–44; Troy, "Evolution of Government Housing Policy."

33 See Hayward, "Reluctant Landlords?"; Howe, *New Houses for Old*, 34; Badcock, "Role of Housing Expenditure"; Spearitt, *Sydney's Century*, 82–4, 94ff. South Australia's centrist government took an active role in economic development, and housing as part of that, and was strongly supported in this by the Labor opposition. Victoria's centrist Country Party government in 1938 was dependent on Labor support.

34 See detailed data in Jones, *Australian Welfare State*; summary in Suttor, "Offset Mirrors." Production ramped up quickly in 1946–49 and averaged 12,400 units annually in 1946–64. See also Dalton, "Housing Policy Retrenchment."

35 Radford, *Modern Housing for America*, 180ff; see also 94–109 on the labour housing movement in Philadelphia.

36 See, for example, Freeman, *Working-Class New York*.

37 Ibid.; also Dennis and Fish, *Programs in Search of a Policy*; Hulchanski, "Canada," 298.

38 John Weaver concurred with Bacher on the first point; Weaver made the second point in argument with Bacher and those who shared his views. Weaver, "Denial of Social Experiment," 76.

39 See Helleiner, "Fixation with Floating"; Poapst, "Financing Post-war Housing."

40 Bacher, *Keeping to the Marketplace*, 24.

41 See Weaver, "Denial of Experiment," 82.

42 See Weaver, "Denial of Experiment"; Dennis and Fish, *Programs in Search of a Policy*, 2–4 and chapter 4 passim.

43 See Wade, "Wartime Housing Limited, 1941–1947," 54.

44 For examples, Bacher, *Keeping to the Marketplace*, 124–5.

45 Rose, *Canadian Housing Policies*, 30.

46 See ibid., 32.

47 Current dollars at past points are equated in this book to 2015 dollars by applying the Consumer Price Index (Canada, all items). This understates the difference over time in expenditures relating to housing development, because these rose notably faster than general inflation for much of the period this book covers.

48 Rose, *Canadian Housing Policies*, 31.

49 Cotton, *Big Daddy*, 58.

50 Metropolitan Toronto, Community Services Department, *Backgrounder*.

51 McMahon, *Metro's Housing Company*, 17–18.

52 Richard Plunz, *History of Housing*.

53 Carver, *Compassionate Landscape*, 89. Not until the 1960s was the separate Canadian Association of Housing and Redevelopment Officials (CAHRO) formed, later to become the Canadian Housing and Renewal Association (CHRA).

54 Carver, *Compassionate Landscape*; Carroll and Jones, "Road to Innovation," 287.

55 For example, Englishmen included Humphrey Carver (1940s activist and then chair of the CMHC advisory group circa 1955–67), H.W. "Bob" Suters (managing director of Ontario's Housing Branch before 1964 and then of OHC in the 1960s), and Phil W. Brown (in senior positions at CMHC in the 1980s and 1990s and at the City of Toronto 2000–12). Scotsmen included Stewart Bates (CMHC president from 1955 to the early 1960s), George Cooke (City of Toronto housing commissioner in the early and mid-1980s), and William Clarkin (City of Toronto housing commissioner in the early 1990s). The German-Jewish Hans Blumenfeld came to Canada after two decades working in Philadelphia; Eli Comay (Metro Toronto planning commissioner and chair of the 1973 Ontario housing task force) was born and educated in Detroit.

56 Until the 1970s, Montreal was Canada's primate city by most measures: population, corporate head offices, financial headquarters, etc.

57 Dennis and Fish, *Programs in Search of a Policy*, 132.

58 Quoted in ibid.

59 Ibid., 127.

60 Bacher, *Keeping to the Marketplace*, 83, 86, 91.

61 See Radford, *Modern Housing for America*, 91–101 on the housing developed under the National Industrial Recovery Act in the mid-1930s; for the 1939–41 production see Marcuse, "United States of America."

62 Bacher, *Keeping to the Marketplace*, 91, cites David Mansur's later characterization of the DHA in these explicit terms.

63 See Hulchanski, "Dominion Housing Act"; Bacher, *Keeping to the Marketplace*, 66. The DHA financed only 3,188 loans in its three years of life, mostly to middle or upper-income home-owners, with no rental except in its 1,700 duplexes. The DHA did initiate the system of joint loans whereby federal capital was blended with private in institutional lender mortgages, thus lowering lender risk, interest rates, and the system

of twenty-year mortgages at 80 percent loan-to-value ratios; these would become the mainstays of postwar Canadian housing policy.

64 Bacher, *Keeping to the Marketplace*, 108.
65 According to Dennis and Fish, *Programs in Search of a Policy*, 127, 19,000 units were built in 1941–45 and 27,000 in 1946–49. Rose, *Canadian Housing Policies*, cites 45,930 units built by WHL and CMHC from 1941 to 1949. Wade, "Wartime Housing Limited," 47, cites just under 26,000 WHL units, of which 8,900 were during the end-of-war housing crisis in 1944–46; the latter count plus other units totalled to 20,159 veterans' units by 1949.
66 Average 6,000 units annually on 1946 population of 12.3 million was about 50 units annually per 1,000 population; average 20,000 units (1970–85) on 1981 population of 24.8 million was about 80.
67 Wade, "Wartime Housing Limited"; Bacher, *Keeping to the Marketplace*, 130.
68 Wade, "Wartime Housing Limited," 44.
69 Ibid., 49.
70 Ibid., 50–1; Bacher, *Keeping to the Marketplace*, 124–5.
71 See Wade, "Wartime Housing Limited," 53–4, on C.D. Howe's preference for market-supporting financing mechanisms and yet his pragmatism on direct state provision.
72 Rose, *Canadian Housing Policies*, 28–9, sees these successive decisions in these terms.
73 Bacher, *Keeping to the Marketplace*, 166.
74 Ibid., 86 (on Nicolls), 130 (on Pigott); Wade, "Wartime Housing Limited," on Pigott.
75 Bacher, *Keeping to the Marketplace*, 138–9.
76 Ibid., 131–2.
77 Ibid., 146–7. The report, by Leslie R. Thomson, was entitled *Preliminary Report on the Housing Situation in Canada and Suggestions for Improvement*.
78 Bacher, *Keeping to the Marketplace*, 169–70.
79 Ibid., 163, 172. There were provisions for LD housing; the inadequacy of LD as a strategy for low-rent housing had been understood since the Edwardian years but (like private-sector affordable rental today) still appealed to the market-minded.
80 See Wade, "Wartime Housing Limited," 54; Bacher, *Keeping to the Marketplace*, 177–9. "Central" in the CMHC name referred not to some Ottawa-centric national government but to this consolidation of the various federal housing functions. The proposals internally included at one point a Ministry of Housing, put forward by the Clerk of the Privy Council (Bacher, 179).

81 Cabinet memorandum on the CMHC bill, October 1945, quoted in Wade "Wartime Housing Limited," 54.

82 Bacher, *Keeping to the Marketplace*, 173.

83 Ibid., 182.

84 Wade, "Wartime Housing Limited," 49.

85 Bacher, *Keeping to the Marketplace*, 182–3.

86 Ibid., 183–5.

87 On provincial positions, see Bacher, "From Study to Reality," 133; Bacher, *Keeping to the Marketplace*, 184. See elsewhere in this chapter for the Ontario approach in 1949–50, which was far more facilitative than in Bacher's account.

88 Carver, *Compassionate Landscape*, 82–5; see also Bacher, *Keeping to the Marketplace*, 10.

89 Carroll and Jones, "Road to Innovation," 287.

90 Mark Byrnes, "A Look Back at Montreal's Contentious, First Attempt at Slum Clearance" Atlantic Citylab blog, October 2013 (http://www.citylab .com/housing/2013/10/look-back-montreals-contentious-first-attempt-slum-clearance/7242); Godbout and Divay, *Quebec*, 35; Bacher, *Keeping to the Marketplace*, 14–15.

91 See Dennis and Fish, *Programs in Search of a Policy*, 133. This shift is strongly underemphasized in Bacher's account in *Keeping to the Marketplace*.

92 Carver, *Compassionate Landscape*, 135ff; Oberlander and Fallick, *Housing a Nation*, 45ff.

93 Bacher, *Keeping to the Marketplace*, 214.

94 Dennis and Fish, *Programs in Search of a Policy*, 134–5, 174; Carver, *Compassionate Landscape*, 142; Oberlander and Fallick, *Housing a Nation*, 48; Bacher, *Keeping to the Marketplace*, 214.

95 Dennis and Fish, *Programs in Search of a Policy*, 26.

96 In the joint loan system, CMHC provided federal funds to private lenders for 25 percent of mortgage capital, which enhanced the volumes of capital available and amounted to an interest rate subsidy and partial capital guarantee. This was the main system in 1949–54 and was revived in 1957–64 as well.

97 See Mishra, "The Collapse of the Welfare State Consensus?," 103–4; Smith, *Postwar Canadian Housing*; summary of lending policy in Suttor, *Rental Paths*, 28; Central Mortgage and Housing Corporation, *Housing in Canada 1946–1970*.

98 A below-market rent consuming a large share of income could enable a seniors project to break even, and was deemed fair. For family housing,

such a rent level did not enable a project to break even and was not considered affordable. See McMahon, *Metro's Housing Company*.

99   See Grieve, "Continuity and Change."

100 On 1949–63 LD, see McMahon, *Metro's Housing Company*; Adamson, *National Housing Measures*.

101 Even before the legislation, Ontario contributed $1,000 per unit to Regent Park North – about $11,000 per unit in 2015 dollars.

102 Banting, "Social Housing in a Divided State," 124, is therefore incorrect in characterizing the pre-1964 regime as having a passive provincial role, at least in regard to Ontario where the majority of activity occurred.

103 "Housing Branch History," RG 44–19–1, Administrative files from the Ontario Housing Corporation central registry, Archives of Ontario.

104 Adamson, *National Housing Measures*. The $500 covered about 8 percent of the $6,000 project development costs for a seniors building in the latter 1950s (McMahon, *Metro's Housing Company*, Appendix F).

105 Godbout and Divay, *Quebec*, 19, 20.

106 Ontario, Housing Branch. "History of Housing Branch." 1962. Archives of Ontario, RG 44–19–1, B284555.

107 McMahon, *Metro's Housing Company*, 57, 69.

108 Adamson, *National Housing Measures*, tables 9 (LD) and 13 (public housing). LD nationwide comprised 6,619 municipal and 5,022 charitable units; 5,569 and 1,407 respectively in Ontario. Some of the LD units were bed-units in Homes for the Aged, etc., but by far the majority were self-contained housing units. The totals include some, but very few, charitable units predating 1950. Alternative data for Ontario appear to be undercounts (e.g. letter from Suters to Speaker of the Provincial Parliament, August 4, 1964, RG 44–1, Ministers' correspondence relating to the Ontario Housing Corporation, file "Ontario Housing Corporation 1964," Archives of Ontario). Rose, *Canadian Housing Policies*, 36–7, cites an earlier, less precise 10,000–15,000 units of social housing nationwide as of 1960, with ambiguous inclusion of LD. There were 5,970 combined public housing and LD units in Toronto (Suttor, *Canadian Social Housing*, from administrative data), of which 5,928 were in Metro and 42 in Oshawa. The LD units developed up to 1964 by the Metropolitan Toronto Housing Company Limited totalled 2,678 (38 percent of Ontario) but Toronto also had some charitable LD units (no tally available).

109 See Rose, *Canadian Housing Policies*; Grieve, "Continuity and Change," 46, cites 746 BC public housing units in 1949–64, but Adamson, *National Housing Measures*, is the authoritative source.

110 See Schwartz, *Housing Policy in the United States*, 153. This refers to public housing, not to later social programs such as subsidized income targeted private rental of the 1960s and 1970s or Low Income Housing Tax Credit units of 1986 onwards.

111 See Marcuse, "United States of America."

112 Australian production in 1950–51 through 1964–65 was 240,764, of which 103,651 were sold to tenants or others. See Jones, *The Australian Welfare State*.

113 See comparative data in Suttor, *Rental Paths* and sources therein.

114 Oberlander and Fallick, *Housing a Nation*, 28ff; Rose, *Canadian Housing Policies*, 29–30.

115 Carver, *Compassionate Landscape*, 112; Oberlander and Fallick, *Housing a Nation*, 44; Bacher, *Keeping to the Marketplace*, 179.

116 Banting, "Social Housing in a Divided State," 122; see also Dennis and Fish, *Programs in Search of a Policy*, 131ff.

117 The 2001–15 programs have involved federal funding equal per capita among the provinces, who readily matched with their own funds, unlike the 1950s when take-up was very uneven among them. The recent programs have included funding for First Nations and the territories unimaginable back then. The recent programs have involved grants for a bit over half of project capital costs, the rest covered by market mortgages or provincial or local capital or land, unlike the 75/25 co-financing of full project costs in the 1950s. The recent programs involve no federal operating subsidy, unlike in the 1950s.

CHAPTER THREE

1 Battle, "Back to the Future"; Myles, "When Markets Fail"; Banting, *The Welfare State*; O'Connor, "Welfare Expenditure and Policy Orientation."

2 The national unemployment rate for men averaged 3.6 percent in 1946 through 1957 but averaged 7.7 percent in 1958 through 1962 (respectively 2.1 and 3.4 percent for women). Statistics Canada, *Historical Statistics of Canada*, Series D223–235.

3 GDP from table 1.4 at http://www.statcan.gc.ca/pub/11–210–x/2010000 /t004–eng.htm; deflated by CPI. Average real growth 5.7 percent (1961–65), 5.0 percent (1966–70), 4.2 percent (1971–75).

4 Jenson, "'Different' but Not 'Exceptional.'"

5 See footnote 67 in chapter 1. The US policy change was approved in 1965 and implemented by 1968.

6 Morton, *A Short History of Canada*, 242.

7 See Fulton, *Remember Expo*.

8 Haddow, *Poverty Reform in Canada*; Banting, "Canada."
9 See Bryden, "Prescience, Prudence and Procrastination," 94–6.
10 Bryden, "Prescience, Prudence and Procrastination," 95–7; Beal, *Pearson Phenomenon*.
11 Sharp, *Which Reminds Me...*, 105; Smith, *Gentle Patriot*, 357.
12 Myles, "When Markets Fail"; O'Connor, "Welfare Expenditure and Policy Orientation"; Banting, *Welfare State and Canadian Federalism*; Battle, "Relentless Incrementalism."
13 McDougall, *John P. Robarts*, 142–3.
14 Ibid., 86. This reaffirmed the placement of the Housing Branch in the former Department of Planning and Development through the 1950s.
15 McDougall, *John P. Robarts*, 94.
16 See a summary the Quiet Revolution and Lesage agenda as it pertained to urban issues in Hamel and Rousseau, "Revisiting Municipal Reforms."
17 Banting, "Social Housing in a Divided State," 117–18.
18 See Miron, "Demographic and Economic Factors."
19 For a summary of postwar Australian housing policy, see Burke et al., "Australia." For the sales of public housing from circa 1955 to 1968, averaging about 10,000 homes annually, see Jones, *Australian Welfare State*. For the comparison to Canada, see Suttor, "Offset Mirrors."
20 For a comparison of the rental sector and rental apartment shares of postwar urban growth in these and other countries, see Suttor, *Rental Paths*.
21 Derkowski, "Toronto Housing Market in the Sixties."
22 Toronto, City Planning Division, *Perspectives on Housing Tenure*, 3.
23 Michelson, *Environmental Choice*.
24 McKellar, "Building Technology," 148; Suttor, *Rental Paths*; Maclelland and Stewart, *Concrete Toronto*.
25 Among many examples, Sewell, "Where the Suburbs Came From."
26 See Suttor, *Rental Housing Dynamics*; Suttor, *Growth Management and Affordable Housing* for detailed analysis of Greater Toronto.
27 Myles and Quadagno, "Political Theories of the Welfare State," 35.
28 Mishra, "Collapse of the Welfare State Consensus?," 84.
29 Don Richmond, interview by the author, September 2010.
30 For an account of the US social welfare programs as a similarly enduring turning point, see Bailey and Danziger, *Legacies of the War on Poverty*.
31 See Lewis, *The Good Fight*; Smith, *Unfinished Journey*.
32 Kent, *Public Purpose*.
33 See Schwartz, *Housing Policy in the United States*, 126; Pacione, *Urban Geography*, 229.
34 See comparative data in Suttor, *Rental Paths*.

35 Harloe, *The People's Home?*; Burke et al., "Australia."
36 Don Richmond, interview by the author, September 2010.
37 Smith, *Gentle Patriot*, 331.
38 Tindal, *Structural Changes in Local Government*, 7ff, 20ff; Ontario, *Design for Development*.
39 McDougall, *John P. Robarts*, 212.
40 Godbout and Divay, *Quebec*, 26, 29 on displacement; 39 on blight and slum clearance as central in the concerns. See also Société d'habitation du Québec, *La Société d'habitation du Québec*, 19.
41 Carver, *Cities in the Suburbs*.
42 Ontario Association of Housing Authorities, *Good Housing for Canadians*, 19ff; Rose, *Canadian Housing Policies*, 75.
43 Rose, *Canadian Housing Policies*, 37.
44 For example, letter from Catholic Bishop Morocco, as chair of the "Ecumenical Committee on Housing," to Randall, RG 44–1, Minister's correspondence relating to the Ontario Housing Corporation, file "Housing – General Correspondence Nov. 1963–1964," Archives of Ontario; letter from the secretary-treasurer of the Ontario Federation of Labour to all MPPs, 24 March 1964, RG 3–26, Premier John P. Robarts general correspondence, file "Premier Robarts – Housing Correspondence Nov.61–Dec.64," Archives of Ontario.
45 Dennis and Fish, *Programs in Search of a Policy*, 144–5; Rose, *Canadian Housing Policies*, 37, 78–9; Carver, 1975, 146; McMahon, *Metro's Housing Company*, 38–41.
46 See also text for statement by Macaulay, Minister of Economics and Development, in the legislature, 3 April 1962; letter from Metro Chairman Allen to Macaulay, 9 November 1962: both RG 44–1, Minister's correspondence relating to the Ontario Housing Corporation, file "Hon Stanley J. Randall," Archives of Ontario.
47 Dennis and Fish, *Programs in Search of a Policy*, 176.
48 McMahon, *Metro's Housing Company*, 51ff.
49 Sharp, *Which Reminds Me*; Gordon, *A Political Memoir*; English, *The Worldly Years*, Volume II; McDougall, *John P. Robarts*; Bothwell, *Lester Pearson*; Pearson, *Mike*, Volume 3; Martin, *Very Public Life*; Robertson, *Memoirs of a Very Civil Servant*.
50 See Bryden, 'A Justifiable Obsession,' chapter 6.
51 "Financing of a New Liberal Government" (March 1962), Box 1, file 21, Correspondence March 1962, Thomas Worrall Kent fonds, Queen's University Archives.
52 Humphrey Carver also comments that the former CMHC director of development become Prime Minister Pearson's private secretary in *Compassionate Landscape*, 135, 180.

53 "Check-List for Sixty Days of Action: Secret Memo to the Prime Minister from Tom Kent" (15 April 1963), Box 2, correspondence April 10–30, 1963, Thomas Worrall Kent fonds, Queen's University Archives.

54 "Towards a Philosophy of Social Security," Box 6, file 2, Thomas Worrall Kent fonds, Queen's University Archives. The prior version was written in 1962 for the Kingston conference.

55 Adamson, *National Housing Measures*.

56 See Rose, *Canadian Housing Policies*, 38–40 for a detailed summary of the 1964 NHA provisions. The old 75/25 cost-sharing provision remained part of the NHA. Certain then poorer provinces more concerned about long-term operating impacts, such as Saskatchewan, continued to use the 1949–64 program model in preference to the new one. Later amendments renumbered the relevant NHA sections to s. 34 (the 1949–64 program model) and s. 44 (the 1965–78 program model), by which they are referred to in the various publications of the 1970s and 1980s.

57 Black, *Public Housing Program*, 6.

58 Memo re. federal funding allocations included in Archives of Ontario, RG 44–1, Minister's correspondence relating to the Ontario Housing Corporation, file "Hon. Stanley J. Randall," Archives of Ontario.

59 "The New Plan for Public Housing in Ontario," RG 44–1, Minister's correspondence relating to the Ontario Housing Corporation, file "Hon Stanley J. Randall"; RG 3–26, Premier John P. Robarts general correspondence – Trade and Development, Department of Housing – Correspondence, file "Housing – Correspondence. Economics and Development Nov.61–Dec.64," Archives of Ontario.

60 The rent certificate program was to involve headleasing sets of apartments within a building, or of full buildings. "Headlease" refers to an arrangement where a public or non-profit housing provider leases a set of apartment units from a private property owner, and then handles the residents' tenancies (selection of tenants, leasing, rent collection, etc.).

61 *Ontario Housing*, April 1962; Ontario Housing Corporation, *Federal-Provincial Conference on Poverty and Opportunity*.

62 Ontario Association of Housing Authorities, *Good Housing for Canadians*.

63 *Globe and Mail*, 28 May 2009, "The Unheralded Passing of an Architectural Force."

64 Ontario Association of Housing Authorities, *Good Housing for Canadians*.

65 *Globe and Mail*, 26 August 1964, "Report Puts Forth New View on Housing."

66 Text of Randall's speech to the Ontario Legislature, 23 April 1964; Nicholson comments at press conference announcing the creation of OHC, 19 August 1964; RG 44–1, Minister's correspondence relating to the Ontario Housing Corporation, Archives of Ontario.

67 "Slashing Away the Red Tape That Strangles Public Housing," *Globe &
    Mail*, 22 August 1964.
68 Memo from Suters to Randall, 19 December 1963, RG 44–1, Minister's
    correspondence relating to the Ontario Housing Corporation, file
    "Housing – General Correspondence Nov 1963–1964," Archives of
    Ontario.
69 Ministry of Municipal Affairs and Housing, *Ontario Housing Corporation:
    1964–1984*, 11 (verbatim written account by Albert Rose).
70 McMahon, *Metro's Housing Company*, 51ff.
71 Letter from Nicholson to Randall, 29 May 1964; letters from Randall to
    Nicholson, 19 May 1964 and 29 June 1964; memo from Suters to Ran-
    dall, 26 June 1964, 5–6; Memo from Suters to Randall, 26 June 1964: all
    RG 44–1, Minister's correspondence relating to the Ontario Housing Cor-
    poration, file "Ontario Housing Corporation 1964," Archives of
    Ontario.
72 Archives of Ontario, letter from Randall to Herb Gray, MP, 21 July 1964;
    letter from Suters to Speaker of the Provincial Parliament, 4 August 1964
    (describing the background to OHC including the process of negotiations
    that year with federal officials): both RG 44–1, Minister's correspondence
    relating to the Ontario Housing Corporation, file "Ontario Housing Cor-
    poration 1964," Archives of Ontario.
73 All quotes in this paragraph are from interview Don Richmond, inter-
    view by the author, September 2010.
74 Various files of the Minister of Economics and Development, RG 44–1,
    Minister's correspondence relating to the Ontario Housing Corporation,
    Archives of Ontario.
75 Archives of Ontario, letter Randall to Robarts, 24 November 1964.
76 Archives of Ontario, file "Minutes of Meetings – Ontario Housing Cor-
    poration."
77 Feldman, *Study of Ontario Housing Corporation*, RG 44–1, Minister's corre-
    spondence relating to the Ontario Housing Corporation, file "Ontario
    Housing Corporation January – March 1966," Archives of Ontario.
78 Don Richmond, interview by the author, September 2010.
79 Memo from Suters to Randall, 15 April 1964, RG 44–1, Minister's corre-
    spondence relating to the Ontario Housing Corporation, file "Ontario
    Housing Corporation 1964," Archives of Ontario. This memo was pre-
    pared the day after the cabinet meeting, as a summary of the discussion
    (there was no system of cabinet submissions until 1971).
80 "Ontario Housing Corporation – Press Conference: Comments by the
    Honourable S. J. Randall," RG 44–1, Minister's correspondence relating to

the Ontario Housing Corporation, file "Ontario Housing Corporation 1964," Archives of Ontario.

81 "Notes on An Act to Incorporate the Ontario Housing Corporation"; "Honourable S. J. Randall, 're Housing' in Estimates: Speech to the Ontario Legislature, Thursday, April 23, 1964": both RG 44–1, Minister's correspondence relating to the Ontario Housing Corporation, file "Housing General Correspondence 1963–1964," Archives of Ontario.

82 *Telegram*, 20 August 1964, "Roberts Unifies All Housing in New Corporation"; *Globe and Mail*, 22 August 1964, "Slashing Away the Red Tape That Strangles Public Housing."

83 "Public Housing: The Way Is Clear," *Toronto Daily Star*, 20 August 1964; "New Era in Housing," *Telegram*, 21 August 1964.

84 Memo from Suters to Randall, RG 44–1, RG 44–1, Minister's correspondence relating to the Ontario Housing Corporation, "Ontario Housing Corporation 1964," Archives of Ontario. Other sources express the same goals.

85 Carroll, "Post-War Trends in Canadian Housing Policy," 68.

86 Godbout and Divay, *Quebec*, 76; Dennis and Fish, *Programs in Search of a Policy*, 153.

87 Dennis and Fish, *Programs in Search of a Policy*, 153–4; Godbout and Divay, *Quebec*, 76.

88 Fish, *British Columbia*, 157–8; Grieve, "Continuity and Change," 49–51.

89 Dennis and Fish, *Programs in Search of a Policy*.

90 Ibid., 159. See also Rose, *Canadian Housing Policies*, passim.

91 Ibid.

92 See Harris, "Flattered but Not Imitated."

93 Dennis and Fish, *Programs in Search of a Policy*, 159; Fish and Pond, *Nova Scotia and New Brunswick*. See also Cogan and Darke, *Canadian Social Housing*, 14.

94 Quotes from Don Richmond, interview by the author, September 2010.

95 Memo from Suters to Randall, 26 June 1964, RG 44–1, Minister's correspondence relating to the Ontario Housing Corporation, file "Housing – General Correspondence Nov 1963 – 1964," Archives of Ontario.

96 RG 44–5, Ontario Housing Corporation board of director's meetings files, Archives of Ontario.

97 RG 44–5, Ontario Housing Corporation board of director's meetings files, Archives of Ontario.

98 Text of address by Randall to the Housing Conference, Royal York Hotel, RG 44–1, Minister's correspondence relating to the Ontario Housing

Corporation, file "Housing Conference Toronto February 10, 1967," Archives of Ontario.

99 Banting, "Social Housing in a Divided State," 125; also Vaillancourt and Ducharme, *Social Housing*, 12.

100 Bacher, *Keeping to the Marketplace*, 18; Rose, *Canadian Housing Policies*, 84.

101 Hamel and Rousseau, "Revisiting Municipal Reforms in Quebec," 143.

102 Godbout and Divay, *Quebec*, 29; 30 on the position of the CNTU (Confederation of National Trade Unions / Confédération des syndicats nationaux).

103 See Legault, *La Ville qu'on a batie*, 103–5.

104 Ibid., 108.

105 Ibid., 103, 128.

106 Ibid., 106–7.

107 Ibid., 176.

108 Ibid., 109, 118, 147.

109 Godbout and Divay, *Quebec*.

110 Bacher, *Keeping to the Marketplace*, 18.

111 Dennis and Fish, *Programs in Search of a Policy*, 159; Rose, *Canadian Housing Policies*, 86.

112 Grieve, "Continuity and Change," 84–5; Rose, *Canadian Housing Policies*, 82.

113 There were some exceptions, notably the 12,000 units of seniors public housing developed by the Metropolitan Toronto Housing Company Limited, where the 10 percent was financed by a loan from the Municipality of Metropolitan Toronto.

114 RG 44–5, Ontario Housing Corporation board of director's meetings files, Archives of Ontario.

115 See Report to Treasury Board re OHC financing arrangements and assumption of capital and operating costs for existing public housing; RG 44–1, Minister's correspondence relating to the Ontario Housing Corporation, file "Ontario Housing Corporation 1965," file "Ontario Housing Corporation 1965," Archives of Ontario.

116 Memo from Suters to Randall, RG 44–1, Minister's correspondence relating to the Ontario Housing Corporation, file "Housing – General Correspondence Nov 1963 – 1964"; file "NHA Amendments"; file "Ontario Housing Corporation 1964," Archives of Ontario.

117 RG 44–5, Ontario Housing Corporation board of director's meetings files, Archives of Ontario; see also OHC, 1965, 13

118 Dennis and Fish, *Programs in Search of a Policy*, 148.

119 Letter from Randall to Metropolitan Toronto Chairman Allen, 10 Sep-

tember 1964; RG 44–1, Minister's correspondence relating to the Ontario Housing Corporation, file "Ontario Housing Corporation 1964," Archives of Ontario.

120 Ontario in 1964 set its grants-in-lieu of taxes based on full market rents rather than on actual below-market rents as had been the case in 1949–63. See letter from Suters to the Secretary of the Cabinet Committee on Assessment Loss, Cabinet Office, 28 September 1964, RG 44–1, Minister's correspondence relating to the Ontario Housing Corporation, file "Housing – General Correspondence Nov 1963 – 1964," Archives of Ontario.

121 "Builder proposals" were essentially "turnkey" contracts with exceedingly loose specifications; the proposals they elicited were usually projects with planning and even construction under way, available for OHC purchase upon completion. A turnkey (a form of design/build contract) involves a speculative builder undertaking the development and carrying most of the associated risk, and then selling it to the long-term owner upon completion – "turning the key" to take possession.

122 RG 44–5, Ontario Housing Corporation board of director's meetings files, Archives of Ontario.

123 OHC reported that CMHC obtained "blanket Orders-in-Council" to facilitate the rapid financing decisions required; see RG 44–5, Ontario Housing Corporation board of director's meetings files, Archives of Ontario.

124 Smith, *Postwar Canadian Housing*.

125 Dennis and Fish, *Programs in Search of a Policy*, 194; see also Rose, *Canadian Housing Policies*, 10.

126 Don Richmond, interview by the author, September 2010.

127 OHC, *Federal-Provincial Conference on Poverty and Opportunity*, 3.

128 Memo from Suters to Randall, 26 June 1964; also memo from executive secretary of the Toronto Metropolitan Home Builders' Association to all members, canvassing suitable properties for OHC, 12 June 1964; both RG 44–1, Minister's correspondence relating to the Ontario Housing Corporation, file "Ontario Housing Corporation 1964," Archives of Ontario; "Why Homebuilders Should Co-operate in the Growing Public Housing Program," *Canadian Builder*, December 1965, 17–19; Letter from the President, Ontario Association of Real Estate Boards, to Randall, 30 April 1964, RG 44–1, Minister's correspondence relating to the Ontario Housing Corporation, file "Ontario Housing Corporation 1964," Archives of Ontario; RG 44–5, Ontario Housing Corporation board of director's meetings files, Archives of Ontario.

129 Press release, Department of Economics and Development, 19 August 1964, RG 44–1, Minister's correspondence relating to the Ontario Housing Corporation, Archives of Ontario; "Slashing Away the Red Tape That Strangles

Public Housing," *Globe & Mail*, 22 August 1964. Accordingly, Dennis and Fish's account of OHC evolving toward its development model to circumvent initially frustrating interministerial approval loops (148) is inaccurate, as is their account of why Ontario preferred section 43 to section 40.

130 OHC, *Federal-Provincial Conference on Poverty and Opportunity*.

131 Letter from Randall to Herb Gray, MP for Windsor West, RG 44–1, Minister's correspondence relating to the Ontario Housing Corporation, file "Ontario Housing Corporation 1964"; see also letter from Randall to Albert Rose, 23 December 1968, RG 3–26, Premier John P. Robarts general correspondence, file "Housing – Correspondence Aug/68–Dec./68, Trade & Development," Archives of Ontario.

132 Sewell, *Houses and Homes*, 47–52; Rose, *Prospects for Rehabilitation of Housing*.

133 McMahon, *Metro's Housing Company*, 57, 69.

134 The assignment of responsibility to the GVRD was partly with the intention of dispersed suburban public housing. See Dennis and Fish, *Programs in Search of a Policy*, 186–7.

135 The Communauté urbaine de l'Outaouais was also created in 1969. For the context in Quebec, see Hamel and Rousseau, "Revisiting Municipal Reforms in Quebec," 144. The final metropolitan government to be created in Canada's urban areas of over half a million population was Hamilton-Wentworth in 1974.

136 See above on Ontario urban policy, and see Hamel and Rousseau, "Revisiting Municipal Reforms in Quebec."

137 In Toronto, Montreal, and Vancouver, circa 2011–14, the share of the region's social housing that was located in outer, mostly post-1970s suburbs was 22 percent, 23 percent, and 35 percent respectively, and very large shares were in postwar suburbs. The majority of this housing was developed in the late 1960s through the 1980s. For detailed Toronto data over time, see Suttor, *Canadian Social Housing*, chapter 7; for Montreal, see CMM, *Offre et besoins en logements sociaux*; for Vancouver, see Metro Vancouver, *Housing Data Book*. The suburbanization of social housing was strongly evident in some mid-sized cities such as Ottawa and Kitchener-Waterloo, but less evident in Quebec City, Winnipeg, and Hamilton.

138 Bacher, *Keeping to the Marketplace*, 12, entirely misses the significance of the metropolitan geographic frame in Canadian social housing of the 1960s and 1970s.

139 The data cited are generalized (details in appendix table to this book) and refer to commitments (final approval for the project to proceed)

rather than completions. Ontario data for 1965–68 include significant acquisitions of new apartment buildings.

140 Vaillancourt et al., *Social Housing – A Key Component*, 14.

141 OHC accounted for 75 percent of 1964–72 public housing units nationwide (38,200 of 52,000): Dennis and Fish, *Programs in Search of a Policy*, 150.

142 CMHC, *Canadian Housing Statistics*, various dates. The related programs include municipal LD in Toronto that was effectively converted to public housing in 1979.

143 See Legault, *La ville qu'on a batie*, 120.

144 In the Minister's and Premier's extensive housing files of the period, the only correspondence at all in opposition to OHC is from the Borough of Scarborough, and from a few displaced market tenants in buildings OHC purchased. The many OHC-related letters received were almost all formal municipal requests for public housing or prompter OHC follow-up; or from persons seeking low-rent housing, or jobs, or putting forward "good ideas" for policy.

145 Senior housing official 1, interview by the author, July 2011.

146 Letter from Randall to Robarts, RG 3–26, Premier John P. Robarts general correspondence Archives of Ontario, file "Housing – Correspondence Jan–June 1970 Trade & Development," Archives of Ontario.

147 Don Richmond, interview by the author, September 2010. The observation about race is also from Richmond.

148 Ibid.

149 Fallis, *Housing Programs and Income Distribution*, 90–2.

150 Ontario Housing Corporation, *Ontario Housing Corporation*, Appendix B.

151 Senior housing official 1, interview by the author, July 2011.

152 Don Richmond, interview by the author, September 2010.

CHAPTER FOUR

1 For a non-US perspective on the 1960s global youth culture and its links to consumerism and mass tertiary education, see Judt, *Postwar*, 348, 394.

2 See Klemek, *Transatlantic Collapse of Urban Renewal*. Klemek, however, does not understand or analyze the extent to which public housing in the US was an element in reformist social policy, and the collapse of priority for social housing a retreat from the welfare state. For a celebration of 1970s Australian "Green Bans" where unions allied with urban activists to freeze urban renewal, see "Green Bans Art Walk: 40 Years of Community and Union Action, 1971–2011" at www.greenbans.net.au. On US president Nixon's moratorium on new housing subsidy commitments in

1973, see Schwartz, *Housing Policy in the United States*. On opposition to public housing in London, UK, see Klemek, *Transatlantic Collapse of Urban Renewal*, and White, *London in the Twentieth Century*, 66–77.

3 Bank of Canada, http://www.bankofcanada.ca/rates/interest-rates/selected-historical-interest-rates, rates for five-year mortgage terms.

4 Ibid. Five-year rates were 20.0 to 21.75 percent in July through October 1981, and 19.5 to 19.75 percent in February through June 1982, but just over 18 percent is the 1981–82 average.

5 McCall and Clarkson, *Trudeau and Our Times*, 113.

6 See Oberlander and Fallick, *Housing a Nation*, 72ff, on poverty and housing discourse; Lithwick's *Urban Canada* is the exemplar of systems thinking in housing in Canada in that period.

7 Banting, "Social Housing in a Divided State," 117.

8 Dan Burns and Don Richmond, interviews by the author, September 2010 and July 2011 respectively, on the limited impact of neoliberal ideas; David Peters, interview by the author, October 2010, on the sympathetic attitudes. See Wilson, "The Ontario Political Culture," on the 1970s Ontario political culture.

9 See Badcock, *Unfairly Structured Cities*.

10 Production data from CMHC details in Suttor, "Canadian Social Housing." In the key Toronto market, comprising one-fifth of Canada's households and growth, rental apartment vacancy rates rose from the 1.0–1.6 range in 1965–1968, to a very modest peak of 3.0–3.6 percent in mid-1971 to mid-1972 – and then were lower for the next three decades.

11 Average prices in current dollars (constant 2015 dollars): 1964, $17,360 ($134,000); 1969, $28,929 ($186,000); 1974 $52,806 ($255,000). Source: Toronto Real Estate Board [TREB], *Market Watch* (various dates). This was a 39 percent increase from 1964 to 1969, 37 percent from 1969 to 1974, and 90 percent across the two periods.

12 Calculations are by the author, from TREB resale data and Bank of Canada historical interest rates (10 percent down payment). Carrying costs on this basis peaked at $3,070 in 1981 and later at $4,240 in 1989. See also Derkowski, "Toronto Housing Market in the Sixties."

13 Real prices declined 15 percent in 1975–79 in Toronto but nominal prices rose 19 percent. The 1980–81 price hike was 51 percent in real terms in Toronto; the subsequent price decline was 24 percent in real terms (TREB data).

14 Spurr, *Land and Urban Development*, 20; McMahon, *Metro's Housing Company*, 73; Clayton Research Associates, *Economic Impact of Federal Tax Legislation*.

15 Ley, *New Middle Class*.

16 Toronto, Housing Department, annual reports 1979, 1980, 1981; Keith Ward and Art Eggleton, interviews by the author, September 2010 and July 2011 respectively. Rose, *Canadian Housing Policies*, 107, notes the loss of low-rent units as part of the reasoning and context of the Comay report's emphasis on mixed-price, mixed-tenure urban development.
17 For example, see Gutstein, "The Developers' TEAM."
18 Bacher, *Keeping to the Marketplace*, 25; Carver, *Compassionate Landscape*, 162; Axworthy, "The Housing Task Force."
19 Donnison, *Government of Housing*; Donnison, *Housing Problems and Policies*; Ontario Welfare Council, *Study of Housing Policies in Ontario*.
20 Oberlander and Fallick, *Housing a Nation*, 78ff, on the urban nation discourse; Senior housing official 1, interview by the author, July 2011, on the fear of a dangerous empty downtown and the spectre of US urban decline; David Crombie, interview by the author, June 2011, on the latter.
21 See Klemek, *Transatlantic Collapse of Urban Renewal*.
22 Toronto, *Core Area Housing Study* (1974); Ontario Welfare Council, *A Study of Housing Policies in Ontario*.
23 For example, on Australia: Paris, "Housing Issues and Policies in Australia"; Burke et al., "Australia"; Troy, *History of European Housing in Australia*. On the US: Downs, *Rental Housing in the 1980s*; Orlebeke, "Evolution of Low Income Housing Policy."
24 On CMHC attitudes see Dennis and Fish, *Programs in Search of a Policy*, 263–8. On comparative demand, see Suttor, *Rental Paths*. Senior co-op official, interview by the author, June 2011, on renters as neighbours and children.
25 Spurr, *Land and Urban Development*; Sewell, *Houses and Homes*, 96ff.
26 Scott and Roweis, *Urban Land Question*.
27 Axworthy, "Housing Task Force," 144.
28 Carver, *Compassionate Landscape*, 190.
29 See Bacher, *Keeping to the Marketplace*, 27–8.
30 David Peters, interview by the author, October 2010.
31 Dan Burns and David Peters, interviews by the author, September and October 2010 respectively.
32 Bacher, *Keeping to the Marketplace*, 26, referring to the Hellyer report; also 226.
33 Rose, *Canadian Housing Policies*, 53.
34 David Crombie, interview by the author, June 2011.
35 This was a point emphasized by several persons interviewed.
36 Rose, *Canadian Housing Policies*, 136. Keith Ward, interview by the author, September 2010, regarding the landlord-developer campaigns.
37 Dennis and Fish, *Programs in Search of a Policy*, 246 (the quote), also 14,

21–2, 137, 226–7, 248; Adamson, *National Housing Measures*, 20; Carver, *Compassionate Landscape*; Senior housing official 1, interview by the author, July 2011.

38 *Ontario Housing*, June 1962, article on the matter by CMHC official Stanley Pickett.

39 Memo from Suters to Randall, 19 December 1963, RG 44–1, Minister's correspondence relating to the Ontario Housing Corporation, Archives of Ontario; Text of Nicholson speech to the Ontario Legislature, 23 April 1964, RG 44–1, Minister's correspondence relating to the Ontario Housing Corporation, Archives of Ontario.

40 *Telegram*, 20 August 1964, "Robarts Unifies All Housing in New Corporation"; Press release, Department of Economics and Development, 19 August 1964, RG 44–1, Minister's correspondence relating to the Ontario Housing Corporation, Archives of Ontario.

41 Rose, *Prospects for Rehabilitation*.

42 Senior co-op official, interview by the author, June 2011.

43 Dennis and Fish, *Programs in Search of a Policy*, 226–7, 230–1, 244–6; David Peters, interview by the author, October 2010. Early charitable LD examples in Toronto included the YWCA's McPhail residence, Forward Nine, Central Neighbourhood House, and the infamous Rochdale College.

44 Dennis and Fish, *Programs in Search of a Policy*, 243.

45 Charney with Carreau and Davidson, *Adequacy and Production of Low Income Housing*.

46 Cole, *Under Construction*, 49ff; Dennis and Fish, *Programs in Search of a Policy*, 253, 258–9.

47 See Schwartz, *Housing Policy in the United States*.

48 Vaillancourt and Ducharme, *Social Housing*. BC was the other large user of charitable LD, at 3,300 units, because it provided a provincial capital grant for one-third of project costs. On the latter see Dennis and Fish, *Programs in Search of a Policy*, 243–4, 258; also Grieve, "Continuity and Change."

49 Legault, *La Ville qu'on a batie*, 139. The data he cites indicate that three-quarters of this spending was municipal funds.

50 Legault, *La Ville qu'on a batie*, 127.

51 On the mixed economy of welfare see Banting, "Social Housing in a Divided State," 128. Dan Burns, interview by the author, September 2010, on CYC and LIP.

52 Carroll and Jones, "Road to Innovation," 287–8.

53 See Rose, *Canadian Housing Policies*, 105–6 and Sewell, *Houses and Homes*, 135.

54 Scarborough Township (borough from 1966 on) was always the biggest locale of opposition (Dan Burns and Don Richmond, interviews by the author, September 2010): it had the largest amount of such development in the 1960s relative to existing housing stock and other development, and the prospect of more social housing on the large 1950s Malvern land assembly. See memo from Suters to Randall, 30 December 1963, on Scarborough Township opposition to the Stableford Farm property, RG 44–1, Minister's correspondence relating to the Ontario Housing Corporation, file "Housing General Correspondence Nov 1963 – 1964," Archives of Ontario. Also Dennis and Fish, *Programs in Search of a Policy*, 190–1.

55 Rose, *Canadian Housing Policies*, 103; Dennis and Fish, *Programs in Search of a Policy*, 191.

56 See Alinsky, *Rules for Radicals*.

57 Sewell, *Up against City Hall*; Bacher, *Keeping to the Marketplace*, 226; Letter from chairman, Public Housing Study, Confederation of Resident and Ratepayer Associations, to Chairman of OHC, 27 May 1970; letter from same to Robarts, 25 June 1970: both RG 3–26, Premier John P. Robarts general correspondence, file "Housing – Correspondence Jan–June 1970, Trade and Development," Archives of Ontario. See also letter from same to Robarts, 15 October 1970, transmitting the CORRA committee's recommendations on the matter, RG 3–26, Premier John P. Robarts general correspondence, file "Housing Correspondence July 70–Feb 71, Trade & Development," Archives of Ontario.

58 The three greatest controversies in Toronto's central-city neighbourhoods were High Park (Quebec/Gothic) and St James Town which were primarily private rental, and Yonge/Eglinton which was almost entirely private rental.

59 On the epic battle of Jacobs against Robert Moses, see Caro, *Power Broker*. Metro's dominant first chairman (1953–62), Frederick Gardiner, had visited Moses to learn.

60 Sewell, *Up against City Hall*.

61 Dennis and Fish, *Programs in Search of a Policy*, 182.

62 Bacher, *Keeping to the Marketplace*, 219.

63 Ibid. on zest for demolition; 223–4 on Hamilton, and on extensive documentation of displacement of residents.

64 Dan Burns, interview by the author, September 2010.

65 In 1971, the 77,000 social housing units (virtually all low income) comprised about 8 percent of the 1 million Canadian renter households with incomes below half of median income.

66 Bacher, *Keeping to the Marketplace*, 228; also Dennis and Fish, *Programs in Search of a Policy*, 182.

67 For Toronto's patterns see Suttor, "Canadian Social Housing," chapter 7. In Montreal and Vancouver the early projects were more centrally located.

68 Clarkson and McCall, *Trudeau and Our Times*, 119.

69 See Axworthy, "The Housing Task Force," on the extensive hearings, briefs received, and dialogue, and the energy created by the opportunity to speak directly to the minister.

70 Canada, Task Force on Housing and Urban Development, *Report of the Federal Task Force* [Hellyer task force.]. See 35–6 on non-profit and co-op housing, 54ff on public housing, 69 on urban redevelopment.

71 Bacher, *Keeping to the Marketplace*, 27; 227 on Hellyer's "atom bomb" language.

72 Rose, *Canadian Housing Policies*, 48.

73 Carver, *Compassionate Landscape*, 186; Senior housing official 1, interview by the author, July 2011; Rose, *Canadian Housing Policies*, 48.

74 Oberlander and Fallick, *Housing a Nation*, 99–100; also Senior housing official 1, interview by the author, July 2011.

75 Lithwick, *Urban Canada: Problems and Prospects*.

76 Letters from Randall to Hellyer, Feb. 6, 1969, March 5, 1969, March 12, 1969, March 20, 1969, February 1969, telegram from Randall to Hellyer, Mar 18, 1969, and related correspondence, RG 44–1, Minister's correspondence relating to the Ontario Housing Corporation, file "Housing – Federal Government Jan – Dec 1969 Trade and Development," Archives of Ontario. Also letters from Randall to Andras, July 22, 1970, Oct. 6, 1970: RG 3–26, Premier John P. Robarts general correspondence, file "Housing – General July–Dec 1970, Trade & Development," Archives of Ontario. See also Dennis and Fish, *Programs in Search of a Policy*, 151. Several of the projects coming forward to CMHC under the Special Initiative were sites on which OHC had been negotiating with the same developer-proponent.

77 The SHQ deal, not on offer to OHC despite its mature capacity, and the slow-downs in CMHC approvals of OHC projects, were resented by Ontario which objected sharply (see Rose, *Canadian Housing Policies*, 70; also 47 on the disruption fruitful of relations). OHC tried to placate CMHC, and staff collaboration continued (Dennis and Fish, *Programs in Search of a Policy*, 196). Randall sent fierce complaining letters to Hellyer and appealing collegial letters to his successor, Andras, about the arbitrary delays of funding and project commitments, the sudden lack of collaboration and the frustrations; see Archives of Ontario, letter Randall to Hellyer, February 1969, and related correspondence, file "Housing –

Federal Government Jan – Dec 1969 Trade and Development." See also
Dennis and Fish, *Programs in Search of a Policy*, 151; letter Randall to
Andras, August – October 1970, AO, file "Housing Correspondence Jan –
June 1970 Trade and Development."

78 Oberlander and Fallick, *Housing a Nation*, 105, 113–15; also See Central
Mortgage and Housing Corporation, *Special $200 Million Low-Cost
Housing Program*. Nationwide, 67 percent of the Special Initiative was
moderate-cost home-ownership (ibid., 17). In Ontario, only 163 units of
it were social housing. See also Cole, *Under Construction*, 54–64, on
projects under this program.

79 Senior housing official 1, interview by the author, July 2011.

80 Bacher, *Keeping to the Marketplace*, 28.

81 Dennis and Fish, *Programs in Search of a Policy*, 9, 173ff, 185, 190.

82 Ibid., 18–19

83 Axworthy, "Housing Task Force."

84 For an illustration of Department of Finance reactions to proposals for
active social state role in housing, and on the Hellyer recommendations,
see Bacher, *Keeping to the Marketplace*, 234.

85 CMHC refused to release the report, appeals were made to the minister, a
copy was leaked to the NDP leader, and then the co-chairs arranged for
its publication in breach of their CMHC contract (Dennis and Fish,
Programs in Search of a Policy, preface and publisher's note; Oberlander
and Fallick, *Housing a Nation*, 120; Rose, *Canadian Housing Policies*, 52;
Dan Burns, interview by the author, September 2010). CMHC had
intended that the report be publicly released as a rationale for the policy
changes; CMHC's objections related to the authors' refusal to take out
footnoted references to and quotes from confidential cabinet documents
(Senior housing official 1, interview by the author, July 2011), and
probably also the relentless impugning of CMHC and federal policy.

86 Senior housing official 1, interview by the author, July 2011.

87 See Rose, *Canadian Housing Policies*, 55–7, for a detailed summary of the
1973 NHA amendments.

88 Banting, "Social Housing in a Divided State," 126–7.

89 Dennis and Fish, *Programs in Search of a Policy*, 216; Senior housing
official 1, interview by the author, July 2011.

90 Letter from President of CMHC to the Managing Director of OHC, May
1968, RG 44–1, Minister's correspondence relating to the Ontario
Housing Corporation, file "Housing – Federal Government Jan – Dec
1969 Trade and Development," Archives of Ontario.

91 Canada, Task Force on CMHC, 1979.

92 See Fallis, "Federal Government and the Metropolitan Housing Problem," 381, on resisting decentralization; Banting, "Social Housing in a Divided State," 128, on visibility.

93 Senior housing official 1, interview by the author, July 2011.

94 Dan Burns and David Crombie, interviews by the author, September 2010 and June 2011 respectively.

95 The main issues for NDP support in the minority parliament were income tax rates, Old Age Security, and Family Allowances (McCall and Clarkson, *Trudeau and Our Times: Volume 2*, 103).

96 David Crombie, interview by the author, June 2011.

97 The exception was PEI, which left things to CMHC by agreement.

98 Ontario, Advisory Task Force on Housing Policy, *Report Advisory Task Force on Housing Policy* [Comay Report]. The task force was chaired by Eli Comay, former Metro Toronto Planning Commissioner, who brought a strong social-welfare outlook, a solid research program, a systems mindset, and a strategic style of close ongoing contact with the premier and minister as the task force proceeded. See "Statement by the Honourable Allan Grossman, Minister of Revenue responsible for Ontario Housing Corporation" at the Regional Tri-level Conference, Trent University, May 1973 (mimeo), expounding the task force's recipe while its work was still underway.

99 James McGregor, interview by the author, April 2015.

100 See also Front d'action populaire en reaménagement urbain, *Le FRAPRU à vingt-cinq ans*.

101 See Legault, *La Ville qu'on a batie*

102 Maioni, "The Castonguay Report."

103 Quebec, Groupe de travail sur l'habitation, *Habiter au Québec*.

104 Ibid., 71–3 on objectives; 111–13 on roles.

105 Ibid., 81–107.

106 The Task Force had studied the mid-1970s Ontario model of support to non-profit groups. See IBI Group, *Les programmes de logement de l'Ontario*.

107 James McGregor, interview by the author, April 2015; see also Société d'habitation du Québec, *La Société d'habitation du Québec*.

108 James McGregor, interview by the author, April 2015. See also Société d'habitation du Québec, "Les coopératives d'habitation au Québec."

109 Vaillancourt and Ducharme, *Social Housing*, table 2; Rose, *Canadian Housing Policies*, 87–9.

110 Cogan and Darke, *Canadian Social Housing*, 319; also Grieve, "Continuity and Change."

111 See Cogan and Darke, *Canadian Social Housing*, 37.

112 Banting, "Social Housing in a Divided State," 128; Rose, *Canadian Housing Policies*, 82.

113 Ibid., 131; also Hulchanski, "What Factors Shape Canadian Housing Policy?," 232.

114 Banting, "Social Housing in a Divided State," 131–2.

115 Existing public housing remained a large part of the social housing system. Certain jurisdictions, notably Saskatchewan and (for seniors public housing) Metro Toronto, continued to build public housing until 1985.

116 Banting, "Social Housing in a Divided State," 149.

117 Canada Mortgage and Housing Corporation, *Section 56.1 Non-Profit and Co-operative Program Evaluation*, 45.

118 Hulchanski and Drover, "Housing Subsidies in a Period of Restraint," 51–70.

119 Federal-Provincial Task Force on the Supply and Price of Residential Land, *Down to Earth*.

120 Smith, "Canadian Housing Policy in the Seventies"; Smith, "Crisis in Rental Housing."

121 Canada, Task Force on Canada Mortgage and Housing Corporation, *Report on the Canada Mortgage and Housing Corporation*.

122 Calculated from *Canadian Housing Statistics* data; see Suttor, "Canadian Social Housing: Policy Evolution and Impacts," 224. Ontario had 41 percent of Canada's social housing completions in 1974–78; non-profit and co-op were 34 percent of new social housing elsewhere.

123 Dennis as General Manager of the City of Toronto Non-profit Housing Corporation, Cityhome, had unusually direct links to Mayor Crombie (Dan Burns, interview by the author, September 2010). Two documents articulating the new policies were Toronto, *Core Area Housing Study* and Toronto, Housing Working Group, *Living Room*, both of which were written and adopted quickly. The vision was of a lived-in downtown and mixed-income city-building with a strong municipal lead, with ambitious targets of 4,000 new mixed-income social housing units annually.

124 See Steele, "Canadian Housing Allowances," 69, 76.

125 Data from Canada Mortgage and Housing Corporation, *Canadian Housing Statistics*, various years; see also slightly different data in Dale Falkenhagen, *History of Canada's Residential Rehabilitation Assistance Program*, 23, 24, 32, 40–1, 46, 125 and passim. CHS data show 34,464 dwelling units and 17,206 rooms, total 51,670 (urban and rural), 1974 through 1985. Falkenhagen (40–1) cited 7 percent of 348,600 RRAP unit

commitments in that period as non-profit or co-op, equating to 24,000; and Falkenhagen (125) cited 8,415 non-profit out of 16,800 total bed-units; this would mean that non-profit/co-op dwelling units were 24,000 minus 8,415 or about 16,000.

126 Data from Canada Mortgage and Housing Corporation, *Canadian Housing Statistics*, various years.

127 Senior housing official 2, interview by the author, April 2011.

128 David Peters, interview by the author, October 2010; various issues of *Ontario Housing*, the newsletter of the Ministry of Housing.

129 For example, Ontario carried out overall needs projections and evaluated the non-profit programs in collaboration with CMHC. See Woods Gordon, *Evaluative Study of Non-Profit and Cooperative Housing in Ontario*.

130 The notion that the 1978 changes disentangled the funding formula in the direction of unilateral federal subsidy (Banting, "Social Housing in a Divided State," 132) is misplaced in the case of Ontario.

131 See also reference to municipal non-profit housing and "traditional public housing" as the main way to meet low-income housing needs, in "Remarks by Claude Bennett at the Ontario Municipal Non-profit Housing Conference," 4 September 1982 (mimeo).

132 Canada Mortgage and Housing Corporation, *A National Direction for Housing Solutions*.

133 Fallis, "Federal Government and the Metropolitan Housing Problem," 382–4.

134 Hulchanski, *Canadian Government Housing Expenditures*; Hulchanski and Drover, "Housing Subsidies in a Period of Restraint"; Fallis, "Social Policy Challenge and Social Housing," 20.

135 Fallis, "Social Policy Challenge and Social Housing," citing CMHC data.

136 Rose, *Canadian Housing Policies*, 136.

137 The first assisted private rental program was LD, providing 95 percent mortgages at about 2 percentage points below market levels, with "ingoing income limits" applying in tenant selection; the majority of private LD, 66,000 units, were built in 1968–75; see Crook, "Supply of Private Rented Housing," 341–2; Dennis and Fish, *Programs in Search of a Policy*, 226, 229–37. Direct assistance was soon provided, with loans and grants for up to one-third of project costs from the Assisted Rental Program (ARP; 1974–79 and 1981, 123,000 units) and the Canada Rental Supply Program (CRSP; 1981–84, 24,000 units). Ontario added its own parallel programs and ran assorted smaller programs until 1990. MURB (Multiple Unit Residential Building) tax incentives for individual investors (1974–79 and 1981, 344,000 units overlapping with ARP and CRSP) assisted a large majority of private rental production in

the period. In affordable home-ownership, the federal Assisted Home
Ownership Program (AHOP) of 1974–78 served about 20,000 added
households annually, based on the program total of 95,000. The latter is
from Hulchanski, "Canada." In the 1981–82 recession and peak of
interest rates, the Canada Mortgage Renewal Plan limited existing
owners' cost increases at renewal and the Canada Home Ownership
Stimulation Plan gave grants to new buyers as economic stimulus. For a
definitive overview of programs, see Toronto, Housing Department,
"Non-Profit Co-operative and Public Housing Programs."

138   See catalogues of programs in Bourne, "Recent Housing Policy Issues in
      Canada"; Lithwick, "Decline and Fall of the Housing Market," 40–1.

139   An interpretation concurred with by certain key informants (David
      Peters and Senior co-op official, interviews by the author, October 2010
      and June 2011 respectively).

140   Tallied from Fallis, "The Federal Government and the Metropolitan
      Housing Problem," table 11.3. Making available a percentage of units
      for rent supplement was a condition of many of the assisted private
      rental programs such as ARP and CRSP; the rent supplement cost was
      paid in separate programs and funding envelopes.

141   Crook, "The Supply of Private Rented Housing in Canada"; Hulchanski
      and Drover, "Housing Subsidies in a Period of Restraint"; Pomeroy et
      al., *Private Rental Policies and Programs*; Toronto City Housing
      Department, "Non-Profit Co-operative and Public Housing Programs";
      Hulchanski, "Canada."

142   Tallied from sources cited above.

143   See data in Hulchanski, "Canada."

144   See Kemp, "Role and Design of Income-Related Housing Allowances."

145   See Steele, "Canadian Housing Allowances"; Finkel et al., *Housing
      Allowance Options for Canada*, 22–6.

146   See data for greater Toronto in Suttor, "Canadian Social Housing," 234.

147   See Cogan and Darke, *Canadian Social Housing*, 26.

148   Cole, *Under Construction*, 82–3.

149   Ibid., 146–7. See also the CHF website at http://www.chfcanada.coop
      and Co-operative Housing Federation of BC website at
      http://www.chf.bc.ca.

150   For example, "Coop housing was initiated with the 1973 NHA
      amendments and became an increasingly common form of social
      housing for the next two decades. The cooperative model differed from
      traditional social housing in that it aimed for local tenant management,
      mixed incomes, and integration with the surrounding community."
      Hackworth, "Durability of Roll-out Neoliberalism," 11.

CHAPTER FIVE

1 Calculated from CANSIM Table 380-0064: 4.1 percent from 1983 Q3 to 1986 Q3.
2 Battle, "Relentless Incrementalism," 185; also Banting ,"Three Feder- alisms Revisited."
3 Prince, "From Health and Welfare to Stealth and Farewell," 161.
4 McCall and Clarkson, *Trudeau and Our Times*, 420.
5 Canada, Royal Commission on the Economic Union and Development Prospects for Canada, *Royal Commission on the Economic Union*.
6 Schwartz, "'Economic Rationalism' in Canberra and Canada."
7 Joyce Potter and Steve Pomeroy, interviews by the author, September and October 2010 respectively.
8 Warne, "Canadian Housing Policy," 18.
9 Fallis, "Federal Government and the Metropolitan Housing Problem," 378; Myles, "When Markets Fail," 131.
10 Prince, "From Health and Welfare to Stealth and Farewell," 156–66, 168, 172ff.
11 Battle and Torjman, *How Finance Re-formed Social Policy*, 3–4; also Battle, "Relentless Incrementalism," 186.
12 Prince, "From Health and Welfare to Stealth and Farewell," 173; Dan Burns, interview by the author, September 2010.
13 See Banting, "Social Housing in a Divided State," 140.
14 Ibid., 142.
15 Ibid., 135; Canada, Task Force on Program Review, Housing Study Team, *Housing Programs in Search of Balance*, 30; Joyce Potter, interview with the author, September 2010, described this being raised in the negotiations.
16 Sauder (UBC) series has 102 percent (nominal dollars) and 77 percent (real dollars) for Toronto 1985–89. Data in Toronto Real Estate Board (TREB), *Market Watch* (various dates), CPI-adjusted by the author, are sim- ilar at 97 percent and 73 percent. Vancouver real-dollar prices, unlike those of Eastern Canada, rebounded in fall 1991 and by 1993 exceeded the 1990 peak.
17 Alan Redway, interview by the author, May 2015.
18 Not until the boom years of the latter 1990s did the ownership rates of the 1956–66 birth cohort match those of people born in the interwar years or in 1946–56.
19 Springer et al., *Profile of the Toronto Homeless Population*.
20 Dan Burns, Senior political official, and Art Eggleton, interviews with the author (September 2010, September 2010, and July 2011 respective- ly); Association of Municipalities of Ontario, *Report on Deinstitutionaliza-*

tion; Ontario, Minister's Advisory Committee on the International Year of Shelter for the Homeless, *More Than Just a Roof*.

21 Flichel, "Housing and Urban Policy," 7, 10–11.

22 Warne, "Canadian Housing Policy," 16.

23 Ibid., 16–17.

24 Hulchanski, "How Did We Get Here?," 184.

25 Canada Mortgage and Housing Corporation, *Section 56.1 Non-Profit and Co-operative Program Evaluation*.

26 e.g. Lithwick, "Decline and Fall of the Housing Market," 55–6; Senior housing official, interview by the author, July 2011.

27 See Banting, "Canada," 143.

28 e.g. Lithwick, "The Decline and Fall of the Housing Market," 46.

29 Ibid., 53.

30 Senior co-op official, interview by the author, June 2011.

31 Prince, "From Health and Welfare to Stealth and Farewell," 173; Dan Burns, interview by the author, September 2010.

32 "Claude Bennett – Ontario's Reluctant Minister of Housing," *Impact* 3 (1): 4 – 9 (interview with Claude Bennett, Ontario Minister of Municipal Affairs and Housing); "Remarks by Claude Bennett at the Ontario Municipal Non-profit Housing Conference," 4 September 1982 (mimeo).

33 Senior housing official 2, interview by the author, April 2011.

34 Alan Redway, interview by the author, May 2015.

35 David Crombie, interview by the author, June 2011.

36 For example, *Globe and Mail*, 7 December 1981 on the crisis in low-income housing.

37 Joyce Potter, interview by the author, September 2010.

38 E.g. Hackworth and Moriah, "Neoliberalism, Contingency and Urban Policy," 514.

39 Fallis, "Social Policy Challenge and Social Housing," 15–16.

40 Single Displaced Persons Project, "Case for Long-term, Supportive Housing"; Single Displaced Persons Project, "From Homelessness to Home"; Fagan, *Fred Victor Mission Story*, chapters 16, 17, 18, 20; Ontario Minister's Advisory Committee, *More Than Just a Roof*, 63–7.

41 Toronto Housing Department, "Annual Housing Targets"; Toronto, *Final Report of the Mayor's Action Task Force on Discharged Psychiatric Patients*; Art Eggleton, interview by the author, July 2011.

42 Alan Etherington & Associates, *Evaluation of 90 Shuter Street, Toronto*.

43 Ontario, Minister's Advisory Committee, *More Than Just a Roof*.

44 Ontario, Ministry of Housing, *Annual Report 1987/1988*, 22.

45 McCracken and Jenness, *Social Housing*.

46 Banting, "Social Housing in a Divided State," 155.

47 See Steele, "Canadian Housing Allowances"; Mishra, "Collapse of the Welfare State Consensus?"; Richards and Watson, *Home Remedies*, 7–30; Hulchanski, *Shelter Allowances and Canadian Housing Policy*.

48 e.g. Lithwick, "Decline and Fall of the Housing Market," 55.

49 The Urban Development Institute of Ontario was very present in the media, advocating allowances as the only form of subsidy; *Globe and Mail*, 14 March 1981, E1; Keith Ward, interview by the author, September 2010. At the national level, the industry position was more balanced, stressing the high subsidy costs of social housing and advocating housing allowances as cost-effective, but not opposing social housing as a part of the policy mix. The latter is as characterized by Senior co-op official and Senior housing official 1, interviews by the author, June 2011 and July 2011 respectively.

50 Senior housing official 1, interview by the author, July 2011.

51 Senior housing official 2, interview by the author, April 2011.

52 Lithwick, "Decline and Fall of the Housing Market," 53.

53 The number of renter households rose from 3,140,000 in 1981 to 3,746,000 in 1991 (Statistics Canada, census), with an average of 60,600 annually, somewhat higher in the second than the first half of the decade.

54 Canada, Task Force on Program Review (1985).

55 Senior co-op official, David Cluff, and Senior housing official 2, interviews by the author (June 2011, July 2011, and April 2011 respectively). See also Banting, "Social Housing in a Divided State."

56 The chair was Jim Shapland, a senior executive with Markborough Properties, a large real estate firm.

57 Joyce Potter, interview by the author, September 2010.

58 Canada, Task Force on Program Review (1985).

59 Canada, Minister Responsible for Canada Mortgage and Housing Corporation, *Consultation Paper on Housing*.

60 Senior co-op official, Senior housing official 1, and Alan Redway, interviews by the author, June 2011, July 2011, and May 2014 respectively.

61 Banting, "Social Housing in a Divided State," 136.

62 Joyce Potter, interview by the author, September 2010.

63 Ibid.; Banting, "Social Housing in a Divided State."

64 James McGregor and Quebec housing official, interviews by the author, April and March 2015 respectively.

65 Cole, *Under Construction*, 179–80.

66 Ibid.

67 Dan Burns, interview by the author, September 2010.

68 These included Ian Scott of the inner cabinet and housing ministers

Alvin Curling (1985–87) and Chaviva Hošek (1987–89). The minister's advisor, Sean Goetz-Gadon, had made his early career in the Metro Toronto tenants' movement.

69 Among many sources, see Altus Group Economic Consulting, *Economic Impacts of Residential Construction*.

70 Dan Burns, interview by the author, September 2010, on the priority reflecting the dual agenda.

71 As the "core need" income ceiling was set with reference to average rents in the local housing market, the price level varied by local area.

72 Pomeroy, "Recent Evolution of Social Housing in Canada"; Banting, "Social Housing in a Divided State," 139; Wolfe, "Canadian Housing Policy in the Nineties," 124.

73 Banting, "Social Housing in a Divided State," 147; Alan Redway, interview by the author, May 2015.

74 Steve Pomeroy and Senior co-op official, interviews by the author, October 2010 and June 2011 respectively.

75 These figures include co-op units.

76 Fallis, "Social Policy Challenge and Social Housing," 20.

77 Senior co-op official and David Cluff, interviews by the author, June 2011 and July 2011 respectively.

CHAPTER SIX

1 For the argument that devolution serves diverse responsiveness to diverse subnational preferences, see Wallace E. Oates, "An Essay on Fiscal Federalism," *Journal of Economic Literature* 37, no. 3 (1999): 1120–49. For the argument on scaling-back of the state, see Schwartz, "Small States in Big Trouble."

2 The 1980–81 recession was more severe in Western Canada. Nationally, the fall in GDP and employment was sharper in 1980–81 than 1990–93 but recovery was much slower in the 1990s. Nationally, pre-recession levels were regained in two years in the 1980s but not for about three years (GDP) to four years (employment) to six years (GDP per capita) in the 1990s. The "area under the curve" of lost GDP or employment-years was similar in each case, but the early 1990s was a bigger crisis nationwide, feeding a fiscal crisis. See Cross, "How Did the 2008–2010 Recession and Recovery Compare with Previous Cycles?" Although some economists and much journalistic coverage count two briefer recessions in the early 1990s (applying the criterion of consecutive quarters of shrinking GDP), it was a single long recession if measured by the four standard NEBR criteria of real GDP, incomes, employment, and production.

3 Battle, "Relentless Incrementalism," 185.
4 Pomeroy, "Canadian Perspective on Housing Policy," 627.
5 See Wolfson and Murphy, *New Views on Inequality Trends*.
6 Fallis, "Social Policy Challenge and Social Housing," 19.
7 Dan Burns, interview by the author, September 2010.
8 Canada, Department of Finance, *Budget Plan* (1996), 32; Bourgon, *Program Review*, 15.
9 Senior political official, Senior co-op official, Art Eggleton, David Cluff, and Marc Rochon, interviews by the author (September 2010, June 2011, July 2011, July 2011, and July 2013, respectively).
10 Art Eggleton, interview by the author, July 2011
11 Senior political official and Marc Rochon, interviews by the author, September 2010 and July 2013 respectively; Bourgon, *Program Review*; Interview: SPO.
12 Canada, Department of Finance, *Budget Plan* (1996), 32ff.
13 Battle, *Relentless Incrementalism*, 224.
14 Battle, *Relentless Incrementalism*.
15 On these fiscal-political dynamics, see Battle and Torjman, *How Finance Re-Formed Social Policy*; Prince, "Holes in the Safety Net"; Battle, *Relentless Incrementalism*, 189, 202, 204; Hulchanski, "What Factors Shape Canadian Housing Policy?," 231; Cameron and Simeon, "Intergovernmental Relations in Canada," 54.
16 Ontario, Ministry of Finance, *1995 Ontario Budget Plan*, 29.
17 Canada, *Shaping Canada's Future Together*; Hulchanski, "What Factors Shape Canadian Housing Policy?," 229.
18 Senior political official and Senior co-op official, interviews by the author, September 2010 and June 2011 respectively.
19 Marc Rochon and Senior co-op official, interviews by the author, July 2013 and June 2011 respectively.
20 David Cluff, interview by the author, July 2011
21 Prince, "From Health and Welfare to Stealth and Farewell," 182.
22 Sauder UBC data series; Toronto Real Estate Board, *Market Watch* (various dates).
23 Bank of Canada, http://www.bankofcanada.ca/rates/interest-rates/selected-historical-interest-rates, rates for five-year mortgage terms.
24 Shirley Hoy and Steve Pomeroy, interviews by the author, September and October 2010 respectively
25 See census data in Canada Mortgage and Housing Corporation, "Households by Type and Tenure, Canada, 1971–2011" at http://www.cmhc-schl.gc.ca/en/hoficlincl/homain/stda/data/data_010.cfm.
26 Klodawsky and Spector, "Renovation or Abandonment?," 265; also 267.

27 Ibid.

28 Ibid., 268.

29 Fallis, "Social Policy Challenge and Social Housing," 36; also 27–8.

30 Canada Mortgage and Housing Corporation, *Evaluation of the Urban Social Housing Programs*, 11.

31 Hackworth, "Durability of Roll-out Neoliberalism," 11–12.

32 Murdie, *Social Housing in Transition*; Murdie, "'Blacks in Near-Ghettos?'"

33 Sharon Chisholm, interview by the author, November 2012.

34 Senior housing official 2, David Cluff, and Sharon Chisholm, interviews by the author, April 2011, July 2011, and November 2012 respectively.

35 Sharon Chisholm, interview by the author, November 2012.

36 Marc Rochon, interview by the author, July 2013.

37 Clayton Research Associates, *Costs of a Shelter Allowance Program*; Clayton Research Associates, *Comparison of the Long-Term Cost*.

38 Dan Burns, interview by the author, September 2010; Ontario, Legislative Assembly, Standing Committee on Public Accounts, *Report on Non-profit Housing*; Ontario, Office of the Provincial Auditor, *Ministry of Housing: Non-profit Housing: June 4, 1992*.

39 Ontario, Legislative Assembly, Standing Committee on Public Accounts, *Report on Issues Concerning Houselink*.

40 For examples of the putative muckraking, see Jack Lakey, "Housing Scandal Heats Up for NDP," *Toronto Star*, 22 June 1994; Jack Lakey, "Audit Questions Spending at Toronto Housing Agency," *Toronto Star*, 20 April 1994. For analyses of the negative media campaign, see Laurie Monsebraaten, "The New 'Gimme Shelter' Debate," *Toronto Star*, 28 April 1994; Thomas Walkom, "Juicy Scandal Masks Attack on Non-profit Housing," *Toronto Star*, 22 June 1994.

41 David Peters, interview by the author, October 2010.

42 Senior housing official 2, interview by the author, April 2011.

43 e.g. Klodawsky and Spector, "Renovation or Abandonment?," 261.

44 Ibid., 271ff

45 Fallis, "Social Policy Challenge and Social Housing," 42–3.

46 Klodawsky and Spector, "Renovation or Abandonment?"

47 Steve Pomeroy, Senior housing official 2, Senior housing official 1, David Cluff, Marc Rochon, interviews by the author (October 2010, April 2011, July 2011, July 2011, and July 2013 respectively).

48 David Cluff, interview by the author, July 2011.

49 Ibid.

50 Steve Pomeroy, interview by the author, October 2010; Canada Mortgage and Housing Corporation, *Summary of the 1994–1998 Corporate Plan*, 3.

51 Carter, "Current Practices."

52 Alan Redway, interview by the author, May 2015.

53 Pomeroy, "Canadian Perspective on Housing Policy," 627–8.

54 CMHC, *Summary of the 1994–1998 Corporate Plan.*

55 Brendan Wood International, *Borrowing Efficiency in Non-profit Housing.*

56 See Falkenhagen, *History of Canada's Residential Rehabilitation Assistance Program.*

57 Ibid., 52, 54, 63, 66, 67. RRAP was extended successively for one- or two-year periods, fiscal 1994–95 to 1997–98. See chapter 7 in this book regarding RRAP from 1998–99 onwards.

58 Carter, "Current Practices."

59 Steve Pomeroy and Senior co-op official, interviews by the author, October 2010 and July 2011 respectively.

60 Canada, Department of Finance, *Budget Plan* (1996); Carter, *Canadian Housing Policy.*

61 Senior co-op official, interview by the author, July 2011.

62 Senior housing official 2, David Cluff, and Sharon Chisholm, interviews by the author, April 2011, July 2011, and November 2012 respectively.

63 Canada, Department of Finance, *Budget Plan*, 112–13.

64 Steve Pomeroy, interview by the author, October 2010.

65 Sharon Chisholm, interview by the author, November 2012.

66 For example, Hulchanski, "What Factors Shape Canadian Housing Policy?," 230.

67 See also Prince, "From Health and Welfare to Stealth and Farewell," 182, corroborated by Cluff (David Cluff, interview by the author, July 2011).

68 Senior co-op official and David Cluff, interviews by the author, June 2011 and July 2011 respectively.

69 Marc Rochon, interview by the author, July 2013.

70 Peter Smith, interview by the author, June 2011.

71 Senior co-op official, Peter Smith, and David Cluff, interviews by the author (June 2011, June 2011, and July 2011 respectively).

72 Quotes from Marc Rochon, interview by the author, July 2013.

73 Peter Smith, interview by the author, June 2011.

74 David Cluff, interview by the author, July 2011.

75 David Cluff and Marc Rochon, interviews by the author, July 2011 and July 2013 respectively.

76 Peter Smith, interview by the author, June 2011.

77 Smith, appointed at the same time as Rochon, was well connected in Liberal circles, was previously head of social housing at Peel Region, and was a major figure in the Ontario social housing sector.

78 Peter Smith, interview by the author, June 2011.

79 Marc Rochon, interview by the author, July 2013.

80 Senior co-op official and Peter Smith, interviews by the author, June 2011.
81 Marc Rochon, interview by the author, July 2013.
82 Canada, Minister of Finance, *Budget Plan* (1995), 43.
83 Co-operative Housing Federation of Canada, *Critique of the Federal/Provincial Social Housing Agreement*; Metropolitan Toronto, Community Services Department, "Implications of C.M.H.C. / Saskatchewan Housing Devolution Agreement."
84 Ibid.
85 Canada, *An Act to Amend the National Housing Act*, S.C. 1999.
86 Metro Toronto Community Services, "Implications of C.M.H.C. / Saskatchewan Housing Devolution Agreement." This paragraph is adapted from Suttor, "Offset Mirrors."
87 The provisions regarding the risk reserve, subsidies at the 1995–96 level, and the automatic right to benefit from any more favourable terms another province subsequently negotiated, were approved by cabinet in advance.
88 David Cluff, interview by the author, July 2011.
89 Pomeroy, *Where's the Money Gone?*
90 Carroll and Jones, "Road to Innovation," 287.
91 Shirley Hoy and David Peters, interviews by the author, September and October 2010 respectively.
92 Sharon Chisholm, interview by the author, November 2012.
93 Klodawsky and Spector, "Renovation or Abandonment?," 274.
94 Marc Rochon, interview by the author, July 2013.
95 Senior co-op official, interview by the author, June 2011.
96 In Ontario this covers half of co-op units (19,500) the other half being in devolved Ontario programs. About 30 percent of the 6,600 RGI units in non-devolved co-op projects in Ontario are funded through the devolved system.
97 David Cluff, interview by the author, July 2011.
98 Ibid.
99 SHAs were was signed by New Brunswick, Newfoundland and NWT in April 1997, Nova Scotia in December 1997, Yukon in August 1998, Manitoba in 1998, and Nunavut in July 1999. See Carter, *Canadian Housing Policy*; Canada Mortgage and Housing Corporation, *Annual Report 2000*.
100 David Cluff and Marc Rochon, interviews by the author, July 2011 and July 2013 respectively.
101 Shayne Ramsay, interview by the author, March 2015. By 2006, BC Housing was aiming to redevelop older public housing, take full own-

ership of pre-1970 sites that were 75 percent CMHC-owned, redeploy that land value to other social housing uses, and reconfigure those funding flows.

102   David Cluff and Marc Rochon, interviews by the author, July 2011 and July 2013 respectively. The quote is from Rochon.

103   See letter from Toronto mayor Barbara Hall to the Honourable Diane Marleau, federal minister responsible for CMHC 1996–97 (16 May 1997, mimeo); City of Toronto, Community Services cluster and Urban Development Services cluster, "Background Notes for Meeting of Mayors of Large Urban Municipalities of Ontario with the Honourable Diane Marleau" (ca May 1997, mimeo); Letter from Metro Chairman Alan Tonks to the Honourable Diane Marleau (4 April 1997); Letter from the Ottawa-Carleton social housing working group to Hon. Alfonso Gagliano, minister responsible for CMHC (1 February 1999, mimeo); resolution adopted by Toronto City Council (3 February 1999) for the upcoming Federation of Canadian Municipalities convention; "'Federal Unilaterals' Fight Devolution," ONPHA Quick Connections 7 (1), January 1999; Letter from Dale Reagan, Managing Director Ontario Region, Co-operative Housing Federation of Canada, to Mayors and Regional Chairs (29 October 1997); also Dan Burns, interview by the author, September 2010.

104   Canada Mortgage and Housing Corporation and Ontario Ministry of Municipal Affairs and Housing, joint news release 17 November 1999, "Canada and Ontario Sign Social Housing Agreement."

105   This was evident in some of the interviews, in which certain key actors did not see devolution in these terms (Senior political official, Peter Smith, and Art Eggleton, interviews by the author (September 2010, June 2011, and July 2011 respectively). Smith concurred that most Liberal MPs did not recognize the significance of the institutional change in the federal role that the devolution agreements and 1997 CMHC mandate change brought about.

106   Social housing also remained a priority in NWT and Nunavut, dependent on large federal funds, and in Manitoba in regard to renovation and repair.

107   Although various forms of devolution have been widespread across the OECD since the 1980s, the international literature on social housing records no other case where funding and program management were devolved primarily to the municipal level. (In the German case, Berlin, Hamburg, and Bremen are länder, not municipalities.)

108   For an analysis of the "Local Service Realignment" policy process and its four phases, see Graham and Phillips, "'Who Does What.'" They

identify first an agenda-setting phase from the 1995 election until mid-1996. Second was the Who Does What (WDW) Panel of May to December 1996, and government decisions late that year. This culminated in January 1997 "Megaweek" announcements. Third and fourth were controversy, counter-proposals, and negotiation which settled the shape of policy by August 1997.

109 Dan Burns, interview by the author, September 2010.

110 Ontario, Ministry of Municipal Affairs and Housing, News release, 30 May 1996, "Panel to Sort Out 'Who Does What.'"

111 Ontario, News release, 11 October 1996, "Panel recommends province pay full social service costs"; Ontario, Who Does What Panel, Letters from David Crombie, WDW chair, to Al Leach, Minister of Municipal Affairs and Housing, including final letter 23 December 1996, together with attached list of letters; Letters from David Crombie and Grant Hopcroft, Chair, WDW Social Services Sub-Panel, to Al Leach, dated 11 October, 4 November, and 20 December, 1996.

112 Graham and Phillips, "'Who Does What,'" 183–6; Ontario, Who Does What Panel (1996); Shirley Hoy, Terry Cooke, and David Crombie, interviews by the author, September 2010, February 2011, and June 2011 respectively.

113 Graham and Phillips, "'Who Does What,'" 194–6; also Sancton, "Amalgamations, Service Realignment, and Property Taxes," 148–9; Ontario, Office of the Premier, news release (1 May 1997), "Who Does What: A New Partnership for Taxpayers."

114 Graham and Phillips, "'Who Does What,'" 187; also Terry Cooke, interview by the author, February 2011.

115 David Peters, interview by the author, October 2010; similar account told by Don Richmond, interview by the author, September 2010.

116 Don Richmond, interview by the author, September 2010.

117 Vince Brescia, interview by the author, June 2011.

118 Dan Burns, interview by the author, September 2010.

119 Private-sector property firms in this first phase were emboldened in the "get out of housing" climate to make various proposals to privatize OHC stock. These came from Ontario firms or consortiums and international ones, e.g. Citibank, *Official Submission*; also Shirley Hoy and Vince Brescia, interviews by the author, September 2010 and June 2011 respectively. A Ministry working group examined such proposals. See also Vakili-Zad, "Privatizing Public Housing in Canada."

120 Ontario Non-Profit Housing Association, "Common Goals, Common Sense: New Directions for Social Housing in Ontario" (Presentation to the Minister of Municipal Affairs and Housing, 27 May 1996). The

essence of the proposal was to equalize debt levels between low-debt, older public housing and high-debt, newer non-profit housing, in a more formulaic, less discretionary subsidy regime and fixed envelope. This would insulate housing agencies from the whims of neoliberal senior governments and cash-strapped municipal ones.

121 David Peters, interview by the author, October 2010.

122 Don Richmond, "In Defense of Public Housing," *Globe and Mail*, 9 February 1996.

123 Don Richmond, "Public Housing: Options for the Future" (Toronto, mimeo, 1995); Richmond, "The Devolution Option" (Toronto, mimeo, 1995); Richmond, "Public Housing in Toronto" (Toronto, mimeo, 1995).

124 Dan Burns, interview by the author, September 2010.

125 Vince Brescia, interview by the author, June 2011.

126 Dan Burns, interview by the author, September 2010.

127 Ontario Non-profit Housing Association, memo to ONPHA Executive Committee, "Devolution of Social Housing Responsibility to Municipalities" (December 11, 2006); notes (mimeo) from Dec 4th ONPHA conference call.

128 David Crombie, interview by the author, June 2011.

129 The four largest urban municipalities were exceptions to this but they were not the dominant voices in municipal sector organizations. Metro Toronto, Peel Region, the City of Toronto, and City of Ottawa each had social housing operations that extended across all main programs, ongoing relationships with CMHC and the Ontario ministry in regard to that, and related policy capacity.

130 Terry Cooke and Vince Brescia, interviews by the author, February and June 2011 respectively.

131 Maloney, "Municipal View of Devolution to Municipalities"; Keith Ward, interview by the author, September 2010.

132 David Peters, interview by the author, October 2010.

133 Terry Cooke, interview by the author, February 2011.

134 Ontario, Advisory Council on Social Housing Reform, *Report of the Advisory Council*.

135 Ontario, Social Housing Committee, *Discussion Paper on Social Housing Reform*.

136 David Peters, Terry Cooke, and Paul Connelly, interviews by the author, October 2010, February 2011, and June 2011 respectively.

137 For example, see Hackworth and Moriah, "Neoliberalism, Contingency and Urban Policy." This is consistent with the views and discourse in the housing and municipal sectors in the decade of existence of the SHRA.

138 Shirley Hoy and Dan Burns, interviews by the author, September 2010.
139 Dan Burns and David Peters, interviews by the author, September and October 2010 respectively.
140 Terry Cooke and Paul Connelly, interviews with the author, February 2011 and June 2011 respectively.
141 David Peters, interview by the author, October 2010.
142 Most Ontario municipalities do not have social housing functions. For the vast majority of Ontario's population, "service manager" is the unitary or upper-tier municipality, while in some cases a mid-sized urban municipality is also the service manager for the adjacent semi-rural county or vice-versa. In Northern Ontario, with scattered municipalities and no county government, District Social Services Administration Boards (DSSABs) were created as "service managers." Over one-third of Ontario social housing is funded and program-administered by the City of Toronto and another one-third by eight mid-sized urban municipalities.
143 Calculated from Sauder School of Business, "Canadian Cities Housing & Real Estate Data."
144 Average annual housing starts in the Vancouver CMA were 17,464 in 1986–90 and 18,289 in 1991–96. Starts net of rental were 15,743 in 1986–90 and 16,766 in 1991–96. By contrast, starts net of rental (the latter being mostly social housing used as stimulus) in the Toronto CMA declined from 29,826 in 1986–90 to 13,666 in 1991–96 (Canada Mortgage and Housing Corporation, housing starts data in CANSIM Table 027–0034); see also Gray and Ramsay, *Common Ground, Shared Purpose*, 6.
145 British Columbia, Ministry of Municipal Affairs and Housing, *British Columbia's Strategy for Affordable Housing* (1996), 16.
146 Cameron Gray, interview by the author, April 2015.
147 Ibid.
148 Gray and Ramsay, *Common Ground, Shared Purpose*, 7; Shayne Ramsay and Cameron Gray, interviews with the author, March and April 2015 respectively; BC, Ministry of Municipal Affairs and Housing, *Strategy for Affordable Housing*, 3; BC Housing, *Annual Report, 1995/96*.
149 British Columbia, Ministry of Municipal Affairs and Housing, *Strategy for Affordable Housing*, 21; BC Housing, *Annual Report 1995/96*.
150 See BC Housing, *Introduction to Homes BC*, regarding program structure.
151 Cameron Gray, interview by the author, April 2015; Gray and Ramsay, *Common Ground, Shared Purpose*.
152 Shayne Ramsay and Cameron Gray, interviews with the author, March and April 2015 respectively.

153 BC Housing, administrative data (post-1993); BC Housing, *Annual Report, 1995/96,* cites 11,464 for 1986 through 1993, which equates to an average of 1,433 over the eight years; this is net of 300 unilateral units in BC's unilateral Homeless/At Risk program in 1992–93. 1,800 is widely cited by key informants as the pre-1994 level but this is approximate. The 1996–2001 data includes SRO purchases, discussed below; for non-profit apartments only, the average for the period was precisely 800 units/year for fiscal 1996–97 through 2000–01 (BC Housing, administrative data).

154 British Columbia, Ministries of Health and Human Resources, news release, "Partnership to Stabilize Downtown Housing and Provide Services for Residents" (24 February 1998), backgrounder; "BC Buys Old Hotels for Housing," *Vancouver Sun,* 24 February 1998.

155 BC, Ministry of Municipal Affairs and Housing, *Strategy for Affordable Housing.*

156 Shayne Ramsay, interview by the author, March 2015; BC Housing, *Annual Report 1995/96,* 4.

157 Vaillancourt, "Third Sector and the Co-Construction of Canadian Public Policy."

158 Wiseman, *In Search of Canadian Political Culture,* 176.

159 Ibid.

160 Ibid.

161 Quebec housing official and James McGregor, interviews by the author, March and April 2015 respectively.

162 Société d'habitation du Québec, *Quebec. L'Habitat au Québec 1996–2001,* 18.

163 Quebec housing official and James McGregor, interviews by the author, March and April 2015 respectively.

164 Calculated from Société d'habitation du Québec, annual reports: commitments from 1998 through 2001 by year were 46, 592, 1,187, and 1,039.

165 This characterization is from Paul Connelly, interview by the author, June 2011.

CHAPTER SEVEN

1 The term "reengagement" is from Leone and Carroll, "Decentralisation and Devolution in Canadian Social Housing Policy," although it is important to understand the modest extent of re-engagement.

2 Mendelson, *UK in 2011.*

3 Battle, "Relentless Incrementalism."
4 Quebec participated fully in the negotiations but was not a signatory to the agreement.
5 Cameron and Simeon, "Intergovernmental Relations in Canada," 56–7, 62, 64.
6 See Layton, *Homelessness*, 190.
7 Canada Mortgage and Housing Corporation, *Canadian Housing Observer*, *2010*, table 8 (census data).
8 See Ontario Non-Profit Housing Association, *Where's Home? 2013*, 16, 20, 57–8; Suttor, *Rental Housing Dynamics*, 22.
9 Layton, *Homelessness*, 111.
10 See Distasio and Kaufman, *Divided Prairie City*.
11 Quebec housing official, interview by the author, March 2015; see also Bohemier and Rouleau, "New Resource to Revitalize," 20–2.
12 See United Way of Greater Toronto and Canadian Council on Social Development, *Poverty by Postal Code*; Suttor, *Growth Management and Affordable Housing*.
13 Layton, *Homelessness*, 111–16.
14 Ibid., 120.
15 The economic analysis underlying that coordinated strategy is reflected in technical studies such as Freedman et al., *Case for Global Fiscal Stimulus*; De Resende et al., *The Power of Many*.
16 Metropolitan Toronto, Housing Stakeholder Panel, *Report*.
17 Ontario, Housing Supply Working Group, *Creating a Positive Climate*.
18 See Jenson, "Mapping Social Inclusion"; Shillington, *Role of Housing*; Canadian Council on Social Development conference (November 2001), "A New Way of Thinking? Towards a Vision of Social Inclusion."
19 See Marsh and Mullins, "Social Exclusion Perspective"; Czasny, *Importance of Housing Systems*; Murie and Musterd, "Social Exclusion and Opportunity Structures."
20 Chisholm, "Housing and Social Inclusion"; Chisholm, *Affordable Housing in Canada's Urban Communities*; Andrew, "Cities and Polarization."
21 Layton, *Homelessness*, 30–1, 110–12; Susan Scott, *Beginning of the End*.
22 Layton, *Homelessness*, 10.
23 Ibid., 11–18.
24 See ibid., 25, 27; Toronto, Mayor's Homelessness Action Task Force, *Taking Responsibility for Homelessness*.
25 Layton, *Homelessness*, 90–2, 118.
26 Toronto Disaster Relief Committee, *Homelessness in Toronto*.

27 Laurie Monsebraaten, "Toronto Disaster Relief Committee Folds after 14 Years of Spotlighting Homeless," *Toronto Star*, 8 June 2012.
28 Layton, *Homelessness*, 131.
29 Ibid., 130; Federation of Canadian Municipalities, *National Housing Policy Options Paper*; also Smith, "Part I," 9.
30 Federation of Canadian Municipalities, *National Affordable Housing Strategy*.
31 Smith, "Lessons from the National Homelessness Initiative," 2.
32 The author was present at two such meetings, as a staff member of the Homelessness Action Task Force.
33 Layton, *Homelessness*, 188.
34 Smith, "Lessons from the National Homelessness Initiative," 2ff; Layton, *Homelessness*, 188.
35 Toronto, *Community Plan for Homelessness*.
36 Canada, Human Resources and Social Development Canada, *National Homelessness Initiative*, 13–17.
37 National Housing and Homelessness Network, "Canada's Nation-Wide Housing Crisis."
38 Federation of Canadian Municipalities, *Quality of Life Infrastructure Program*.
39 Layton, *Homelessness*, 189–90.
40 David Cluff, interview by the author, July 2011.
41 Canada, Department of Finance, *Budget Plan* 2000, 120–1.
42 Canadian Housing and Renewal Association, *Submission to the Standing Committee on Finance*; FCM, *Quality of Life Infrastructure Program*.
43 David Cluff, interview by the author, July 2011.
44 Layton, *Homelessness*, 192–3.
45 Liberal Party of Canada, *Opportunity for All*, 26.
46 Federal-Provincial Territorial Ministers of Housing, *Framework for Bilateral Agreements*.
47 For a summary of the bilateral agreements, see Greg Suttor, ed., "What Progress under Federal-Provincial/Territorial Agreements?," *Canadian Housing* 20, no. 1 (2003): 11–16.
48 Cameron and Simeon, "Intergovernmental Relations in Canada."
49 Federal, Provincial and Territorial Ministers, *Framework for Bilateral Agreements*, 1.
50 The sequence can be most easily followed in the series of CMHC-BC agreements on the BC Housing website: http://www.bchousing.org/aboutus/agreements/CANBC; http://www.bchousing.org/aboutus/agreements/CANBC-social; http://www.bchousing.org/aboutus

/agreements/AIAH. See also CMHC at http://www.cmhc-schl.gc.ca/en/inpr/afhoce/fuafho/index.cfm (as of mid-2015).

51 CMHC data show only $359.75 million "committed or announced" in 2002 through 2004.

52 Pomeroy and Falvo, "Pragmatism and Political Expediency," 188.

53 Ibid.

54 Ibid., 187.

55 Ibid., 190.

56 Ibid.

57 See also Steele, "Canadian Housing Allowances," 66 and passim; Finkel et al., *Housing Allowance Options for Canada*, 22–6.

58 Saskatchewan, Ministry of Social Services, *Housing Strategy for Saskatchewan*; Saskatchewan, Ministry of Social Services, "Guide to the Saskatchewan Employment Supplement."

59 Manitoba, *All Aboard*; Manitoba, Department of Family Services and Consumer Affairs, *Annual Report 2009/10*.

60 See SHS Consulting, *Evaluation of Two Housing Allowance Programs*; Ontario, Ministry of Municipal Affairs and Housing, *Investment in Affordable Housing for Ontario: Program Guidelines*; Ontario, Ministry of Municipal Affairs and Housing, *Investment in Affordable Housing for Ontario: 2014 Extension: Program Guidelines*.

61 Federal-Provincial Territorial Ministers of Housing, *Framework for Bilateral Agreements*.

62 See CMHC at http://www.cmhc.ca/en/inpr/afhoce/fias/fias_015.cfm. Also Leone and Carroll, "Decentralisation and Devolution."

63 See Scott, *Beginning of the End*; also the foundation's reports at www.calgaryhomeless.com.

64 Alberta Housing Task Force, *Housing First*.

65 On Alberta social housing programs in recent years, see also Alberta Ministry of Housing and Urban Affairs, *Annual Report 2010–2011*; Tsenkova and Witwer, "Bridging the Gap"; Snow, *Roof over Our Heads 2008*.

66 Alberta, Secretariat for Action on Homelessness, *Plan for Alberta*.

67 James McGregor, interview by the author, April 2015; Vaillancourt and Ducharme, *Social Housing*, 19.

68 Calculated from annual Accès Logis production data in Société d'habitation du Québec, annual reports, various years.

69 Precise BC housing data averaged 1,377 units annually in 2002 through 2008 and 1,467 in 2009 through 2013 (administrative data, excluding shelter beds).

70 BC Housing, news release (December 2004), "Phase II Affordable Housing Agreement Signed."

71 British Columbia, *Housing Matters BC*.

72 Mike Harris's long-time finance minister, Ernie Eves, succeeded him as premier in April 2002, holding office until he lost the October 2003 election.

73 The province did provide an exemption from provincial sales tax of up to $2,000, later raised to $4,000.

74 See provincial data in Ontario Non-Profit Housing Association, *Where's Home? 2013*, 25.

75 One-third of Ontario AHI units had stacked RGI up to 2005–06. See Ontario, Ministry of Municipal Affairs and Housing, *Projects in Profile*.

76 2002 marks the start of AHI, while 2013 is the most recent complete year of data reported out by the larger provinces at the time of writing.

77 Canada, Department of Finance, *2016 Budget Plan*, 97–100.

CHAPTER EIGHT

1 Banting, "Social Housing in a Divided State," 121.

2 An aphorism widely attributed to US anthropologist and social advocate Margaret Mead. See discussion of origins and attribution at https://en.wikiquote.org/wiki/Margaret_Mead.

Bibliography

This bibliography is in two sections: (1) published sources, including those published by public or non-profit agencies or university-affiliated institutes; (2) government documents and unpublished sources.

PUBLISHED SOURCES

Abrahamson, Peter. "The Welfare Modelling Business." *Social Policy & Administration* 33, no. 4 (1999): 394–415.

Alinsky, Saul D. *Rules for Radicals: A Pragmatic Primer for Realistic Radicals.* New York: Random House / Vintage Books, 1972.

Ames, Herbert Brown. *The City below the Hill: A Sociological Study of a Portion of the City of Montreal, Canada.* First published 1897, reprinted 1972 with an introduction by Paul F.W. Rutherford. Toronto: University of Toronto Press, 1972.

Arts, Wil, and John Gelissen. "Three Worlds of Welfare Capitalism or More? A State-of-the-Art Report." *Journal of European Social Policy* 12, no. 2 (2002): 137–58.

Axworthy, Lloyd. "The Housing Task Force: A Case Study." In *The Structures of Policy-Making in Canada*, edited by G. Bruce Doern and Peter Aucoin, chapter 5. Toronto: Macmillan, 1971.

Bacher, John. "Canadian Housing 'Policy' in Perspective." *Urban History Review* 15, no. 1 (1986): 3–18.

– "From Study to Reality: The Establishment of Public Housing in Halifax, 1930–1953." *Acadiensis* 18, no. 1 (1988): 120–135.

– *Keeping to the Marketplace: The Evolution of Canadian Housing Policy.* Montreal and Kingston: McGill-Queen's University Press, 1993.

Badcock, Blair. "Homeownership and the Illusion of Egalitarianism." In *A History of European Housing in Australia*, edited by Patrick Troy, chapter 15. Oakleigh, Victoria: Cambridge University Press, 2000.

- "The Role of Housing Expenditure in State Development: South Australia, 1936–88." *International Journal of Urban and Regional Research* 13, no. 3 (1989): 438–61.
- *Unfairly Structured Cities*. Oxford: Basil Blackwell, 1984.

Baer, William C., and Christopher B. Williamson. "The Filtering of Households and Housing Units." *Journal of Planning Literature* 3, no. 2 (1998): 127–52.

Bailey, Martha J., and Sheldon Danziger, eds. *Legacies of the War on Poverty*. New York: Russell Sage Foundation, 2013.

Banting, Keith G. "Canada: Nation-Building in a Federal Welfare State." In *Federalism and the Welfare State: New World and European Experiences*, edited by Herbert Obinger, Stephan Leibfried, and Francis G. Castles, chapter 3. Cambridge: Cambridge University Press, 2005.
- "Social Housing in a Divided State." In *Housing the Homeless and Poor: New Partnerships among the Private, Public, and Third Sectors*, edited by George Fallis and Alex Murray, chapter 5. Toronto: University of Toronto Press, 1990.
- "The Three Federalisms Revisited: Social Policy and Intergovernmental Decision-Making." In *Canadian Federalism: Performance, Effectiveness, and Legitimacy*, third edition, edited by Herman Bakvis and Grace Skogstad, chapter 8. Don Mills: Oxford University Press, 2nd edition, 2012.
- *The Welfare State and Canadian Federalism*. Revised edition. Montreal and Kingston: McGill-Queen's University Press, 1987.

Battle, Ken. "Back to the Future: Reforming Social Policy in Canada." In *In Pursuit of the Public Good: Essays in Honour of Allan J. MacEachen*, edited by Tom Kent, 35–64. Montreal and Kingston: McGill-Queen's University Press, 1997.
- "Relentless Incrementalism: Deconstructing and Reconstructing Canadian Income Security Policy." In *The Review of Economic Performance and Social Progress. The Longest Decade: Canada in the 1990s*, edited by Keith Banting, Andrew Sharpe, and France St-Hilaire. Montreal: Institute for Research on Public Policy and Centre for the Study of Living Standards, 2001.

Battle, Ken, and Sherri Torjman. *How Finance Re-formed Social Policy*. Ottawa: Caledon Institute of Social Policy, 1995.

Beal, John Robinson. *The Pearson Phenomenon*. Toronto: Longmans, 1964.

Béland, Daniel, and André Lecours. "Sub-state Nationalism and the Welfare State: Québec and Canadian Federalism." *Nations and Nationalism* 12, no. 1 (2006): 77–96.

Bohemier, Jean-Jacques, and Jean Rouleau. "A New Resource to Revitalize the Hochelaga-Maisonneuve Neighbourhood." *Canadian Housing* 15, no. 1 (1998): 20–2.

Bothwell, Robert. *Lester Pearson: His Life and World.* Toronto: McGraw-Hill
  Ryerson, 1978.
Bourgon, Jocelyne. *Program Review: The Government of Canada's Experience
  Eliminating the Deficit, 1994–1999: A Canadian Case Study.* Waterloo, ON:
  Centre for International Governance Innovation, 2009.
Bourne, Larry S. "Recent Housing Policy Issues in Canada: A Retreat from
  Social Housing?" *Housing Studies* 1, no. 2 (1986): 122–8.
Bradford, Neil. *Why Cities Matter: Policy Research Perspectives for Canada.*
  Discussion paper no. F/23. Ottawa: Canadian Policy Research Networks,
  2002.
Brushett, Kevin. "Where Will the People Go: Toronto's Emergency Housing
  Program and the Limits of Canadian Social Housing Policy, 1944–1957."
  Journal of Urban History 33, no. 3 (2007): 375–99.
Bryden, Penny E. '*A Justifiable Obsession': Conservative Ontario's Relations with
  Ottawa, 1943–1985.* Toronto: University of Toronto Press, 2013.
– "Prescience, Prudence and Procrastination: National Social Policies in the
  Pearson Era." In *Pearson: The Unlikely Gladiator,* edited by Normal Hillmer,
  92–103. Montreal and Kingston: McGill-Queen's University Press, 1999.
Burke, Terry, Peter W. Newton, and Maryann Wulff. "Australia." In *Internation-
  al Handbook of Housing Policies and Practices,* edited by Willem Van Vliet,
  chapter 24. New York and London: Greenwood Press, 1990.
Burstein, Meyer. "Combating the Social Exclusion of At-Risk Groups." Re-
  search paper. Ottawa: Policy Research Initiative, 2005.
Cameron, David, and Richard Simeon. "Intergovernmental Relations in
  Canada: The Emergence of Collaborative Federalism." *Publius: The Journal
  of Federalism* 32, no. 2 (2002): 49–71.
Cameron, David. "The Expansion of the Public Economy: A Comparative
  Analysis." *The American Political Science Review* 72 (1978): 1243–61
Canada Mortgage and Housing Corporation. *Canadian Housing Observer
  2010.* Ottawa: CMHC, 2010.
Canada, Policy Research Initiative. *Housing Policy and Practice in the Context of
  Poverty and Exclusion.* Ottawa: Policy Research Initiative, 2005.
Card, David, and Richard B. Freeman, eds. *Small Differences That Matter:
  Labor Market and Income Maintenance in Canada and the United States.*
  Chicago: University of Chicago Press, 1993.
Cardozo, Andrew. "Lion Taming: Downsizing the Opponents of Downsiz-
  ing." In *How Ottawa Spends 1996–97: Life under the Knife,* edited by Gene
  Swimmer, chapter 10. Ottawa: Carleton University Press, 1996.
Caro, Robert A. *The Power Broker: Robert Moses and the Fall of New York.* New
  York: Vintage, 1975.
Carroll, Barbara Wake. "Administrative Devolution and Accountability: The

Case of the Non-profit Housing Program." *Canadian Public Administration* 32, no. 3 (1989): 345–66.

– "Housing Policy in the New Millennium: The Uncompassionate Land-scape." In *Urban Policy Issues: Canadian Perspectives*, second edition, edited by Edmund P. Fowler and David Siegel, chapter 5. Don Mills: Oxford University Press, 2002.

– "Post-War Trends in Canadian Housing Policy." *Urban History Review/Revue d'histoire urbaine* 18, no. 1 (1989): 64–74.

Carroll, Barbara Wake, and Ruth E. Jones. "The Road to Innovation, Convergence or Inertia: Devolution in Housing Policy in Canada." *Canadian Public Policy* 26, no. 3 (2000): 277–93.

Carter, Tom. *Canadian Housing Policy: Is the Glass Half Empty or Half Full?* Ottawa: Canadian Housing and Renewal Association, 2000.

– "Canadian Housing Policy in Transition: Challenges and Opportunities." Paper for the AHURI conference, Brisbane, 2001.

– "Current Practices for Procuring Affordable Housing: The Canadian Context." *Housing Policy Debate* 8, no. 3 (1997): 593–631.

– *Perspectives on Canadian Housing Policy.* Occasional paper no. 17, Institute of Urban Studies, University of Winnipeg, 1989.

Carver, Humphrey. *Cities in the Suburbs.* Toronto: University of Toronto Press, 1962.

– *Compassionate Landscape.* Toronto: University of Toronto Press, 1975.

Castles, Francis G. "A Race to the Bottom?" In *The Welfare State Reader,* second edition, edited by Christopher Pierson and Francis G. Castles, 226–44. Cambridge: Polity Press, 2006.

– *Comparative Public Policy: Patterns of Post-war Transformation.* Cheltenham, UK: Edward Elgar, 1998.

Chisholm, Sharon. "Housing and Social Inclusion: Asking the Right Questions." Paper presented at the Social Inclusion conference organized by the Canadian Council on Social Development, Ottawa, 2001.

– *Affordable Housing in Canada's Urban Communities: A Literature Review.* Ottawa: Canada Mortgage and Housing Corporation, 2003.

Clarkson, Stephen, and Christina McCall. *Trudeau and Our Times. Volume 1: The Magnificent Obsession.* Toronto: McClelland & Stewart, 1990.

Colderley, Christopher A. "Welfare State Retrenchment and the Nonprofit Sector: The Problems, Policies, and Politics of Canadian Social Housing." *Journal of Policy History* 11, no. 3 (1999): 283–312.

Cole, Leslie. *Under Construction: A History of Co-Operative Housing in Canada.* Ottawa: Borealis Press, 2008.

Collier, Keith. "Clearing the Slums: The Evolution of Public Housing in St

John's, Newfoundland, 1910–1956." MA thesis, Department of History, Memorial University of Newfoundland, 2011.

Cotton, Timothy J. *Big Daddy: Frederick G. Gardiner and the Building of Metropolitan Toronto.* Toronto: University of Toronto Press, 1980.

Crook, Tony. "The Supply of Private Rented Housing in Canada." *Netherlands Journal of Housing and the Built Environment* 13, no. 3 (1998): 327–52.

Cross, Philip. "How Did the 2008–2010 Recession and Recovery Compare with Previous Cycles?" *Canadian Economic Observer* 24, no. 1 (2011). Catalogue no.: 11–010–X, internet edition.

Czasny, Karl, ed. *The Importance of Housing Systems in Safeguarding Social Cohesion in Europe: SOCOHO Final Report.* Brussels: European Commission, 2004.

Dalton, Tony. "Housing Policy Retrenchment: Australia and Canada Compared." *Urban Studies* 46, no. 1 (2009): 63–91.

Darby, Julia, Anton Miscatelli, and Graeme Roy. "Fiscal Federalism and Fiscal Autonomy: Lessons for the UK from Other Industrialised Countries." *Scottish Affairs* 41 (2002): 26–55.

Davies, James B., and Stanley L. Winer. "Closing the 49th Parallel: An Unexplored Episode in Canadian Economic and Political History." *Canadian Public Policy / Analyse de Politiques* 37, no. 3 (2011): 307–41.

Dennis, Michael, and Susan Fish. *Programs in Search of a Policy: Low Income Housing in Canada.* Toronto: Hackert, 1972.

Derkowski, Andrzej. "The Toronto Housing Market in the Sixties." In *Canadian Housing: A Reader*, edited by Kamal S. Sayegh. Mimeo. University of Waterloo, 1972.

Distasio, Jino, and Andrew Kaufman, eds. *Divided Prairie City: Income Inequality Among Winnipeg's Neighbourhoods, 1970–2010.* Institute of Urban Studies, University of Winnipeg, 2015.

Doling, John. *Comparative Housing Policy: Government and Housing in Advanced Industrialized Countries.* London: Macmillan Press, 1997.

Donnison, David V. *The Government of Housing.* Harmondsworth, UK: Penguin, 1967.

Dowler, Robert G. *Housing-Related Tax Expenditures: An Overview and Evaluation.* Major report no. 22, Centre for Urban and Community Studies, University of Toronto, 1983.

Downs, Anthony. *Rental Housing in the 1980s.* Washington, DC: The Brookings Institution, 1983.

Dreier, Peter, and J. David Hulchanski. "The Role of Nonprofit Housing in Canada and the United States: Some Comparisons." *Housing Policy Debate* 4, no. 1 (1993): 43–80.

Edelman, Peter. "The Worst Thing Bill Clinton Has Done." *Atlantic Monthly* 279, no. 3 (1997): 43–9.

English, John. *The Worldly Years: The Life of Lester Pearson. Volume II: 1949–1972.* Toronto: Alfred A. Knopf Canada, 1992.

Esping-Andersen, Gøsta. "The Three Political Economies of the Welfare State." *Canadian Review of Sociology and Anthropology* 26, no. 1 (1989): 11–36.

– *The Three Worlds of Welfare Capitalism.* Cambridge: Polity Press, 1990.

– *Welfare States in Transition.* London: Sage Publications, 1996.

Fagan, Cary. *The Fred Victor Mission Story: From Charity to Social Justice.* Winfield, BC: Wood Lake Books, 1993.

Falkenhagen, Dale. *The History of Canada's Residential Rehabilitation Assistance Program (RRAP).* Ottawa: Canada Mortgage and Housing Corporation, 2001.

Fallis, George. "The Federal Government and the Metropolitan Housing Problem." In *The Changing Canadian Metropolis: A Public Policy Perspective*, edited by Frances Frisken, chapter 11. Toronto: Canadian Urban Institute, 1994.

– "Housing Finance and Housing Subsidies in Canada." *Urban Studies* 27, no. 6 (1990): 877–903.

– *Housing Programs and Income Distribution in Ontario.* Toronto: University of Toronto Press / Ontario Economic Council, 1980.

– "Progressive Housing Policy in the 21st Century: A Contrarian View." *Journal of Sociology & Social Welfare* 37, no. 4 (2010): 173–99.

– "The Social Policy Challenge and Social Housing." In *Home Remedies: Rethinking Canadian Housing Policy*, edited by John Richards and William G. Watson, 7–30. Toronto: C.D. Howe Institute, 1995.

Finkel, Meryl, Carissa Climaco, Jill Khadduri, and Marion Steele. *Housing Allowance Options for Canada: Final Report.* Ottawa: Prepared by Abt Associates Inc. for Canada Mortgage and Housing Corporation, 2006.

Fischer, Frank. *Reframing Public Policy: Discursive Discourse and Deliberative Practices.* Oxford: Oxford University Press, 2003.

Fischler, Raphaël, and Jeanne M. Wolfe. "Regional Restructuring in Montreal: An Historical Analysis." *Canadian Journal of Regional Science / Revue canadienne des sciences regionales* 23, no. 1 (2000): 89–114.

Flichel, Eugene. "Housing and Urban Policy: Current Emphasis and Future Directions." In *Perspectives on Canadian Housing Policy*, edited by Tom Carter. Occasional paper no. 17, Institute of Urban Studies, University of Winnipeg, 1989.

Forsey, Eugene A. *A Life on the Fringe: The Memoirs of Eugene Forsey.* Toronto: Oxford University Press, 1990.

Freeman, Joshua B. *Working-Class New York: Life and Labor Since World War II.* New York: The New Press, 2001.

Frisken, Frances, Larry S. Bourne, Gunter Gad, and Robert A. Murdie. "Governance and Social Sustainability: The Toronto Experience." In *The Social Sustainability of Cities: Diversity and the Management of Change*, edited by Mario Polèse and Richard Stren, chapter 3. Toronto: University of Toronto Press, 2000.

Frisken, Frances. *The Public Metropolis: The Political Dynamics of Urban Expansion in the Toronto Region: 1924–2003.* Toronto: Canadian Scholars Press, 2007.

Fulton, Robert. *Remember Expo: A Pictorial Record.* Toronto: McClelland and Stewart, 1968.

George, Ryan. "The Bruce Report and Social Welfare Leadership in the Politics of Toronto's 'Slums', 1934–1939." *Histoire sociale / Social history* 44, no. 87 (2011): 83–114.

Gillies, James. "Some Financial Aspects of the Canadian Government Housing Program: History and Prospective Developments." *Journal of Finance* 8, no. 1 (1953): 22–33.

Goldberg, Michael A., and Jonathan H. Mark. "The Roles of Government in Housing Policy: A Canadian Perspective and Overview." *Journal of the American Planning Association* 51, no. 1 (1985): 34–42.

Gordon, Walter L. *A Political Memoir.* Toronto: McClelland and Stewart, 1977.

Gottschalk, Peter, and Timothy M. Smeeding. "Cross-National Comparisons of Earnings and Income Inequality." *Journal of Economic Literature* 35, no. 2 (1997): 633–87.

Gough, Ian. "European Welfare States: Explanations and Lessons for Developing Countries." In *Inclusive States: Social Policy and Structural Inequalities*, edited by Anis A. Dani and Arjan de Haan, chapter 2. Washington, DC: World Bank, 2008.

Gourevitch, Peter A. *Politics in Hard Times: Comparative Responses to International Economic Crises.* Ithaca: Cornell University Press, 1986.

Grabb, Edward, and James Curtis. *Regions Apart: The Four Societies of Canada and the United States.* Don Mills: Oxford University Press, 2005.

Graham, Katherine A., and Susan D. Phillips. "'Who Does What' in Ontario: The Process of Provincial-Municipal Disentanglement." *Canadian Public Administration* 41, no. 2 (1998): 175–209.

Gray, Cameron, and Shayne Ramsay. *Common Ground, Shared Purpose: Canadian Case Study – Vancouver.* Paper for the Tri-Country Housing Conference. Ottawa: Canadian Housing and Renewal Association, 2002.

Greg Lampert Economic Consultant. *Cost-Effective Housing Assistance: A Com-*

parison of the Costs of Non-profit Housing Versus Shelter Allowances. Prepared
for the Canadian Federation of Apartment Associations, 1999.

Guest, Dennis. *The Emergence of Social Security in Canada.* Third edition. Vancouver: UBC Press, 2003.

Gutstein, Donald. "The Developers' TEAM: Vancouver's 'Reform' Party in
Power." In *The City Book: The Politics and Planning of Canada's Cities,* edited
by James Lorimer, 107–22. Toronto: James Lorimer & Company, 1976.

Hacker, Jacob S. "Privatizing Risk without Privatizing the Welfare State: The
Hidden Politics of Social Policy Retrenchment in the United States." *American Political Science Review* 98, no. 2 (2004): 243–60.

Hackworth, Jason. "The Durability of Roll-out Neoliberalism under Centre-
Left Governance: The Case of Ontario's Social Housing Sector." *Studies in
Political Economy* 81 (2008): 7–25.

– "Political Marginalisation, Misguided Nationalism and the Destruction of
Canada's Social Housing Systems." In *Where the Other Half Lives: Lower In-
come Housing in a Neoliberal World,* edited by Sarah Glynn, chapter 11.
London: Pluto Press, 2009.

Hackworth, Jason, and Abigail Moriah. "Neoliberalism, Contingency and
Urban Policy: The Case of Social Housing in Ontario." *International Journal of Urban and Regional Research* 30, no. 3 (2006): 510–27.

Haddow, Rodney. "Municipal Social Security in Canada." In *Urban Policy Issues: Canadian Perspectives,* second edition, edited by Edmund P. Fowler
and David Siegel, chapter 6. Don Mills: Oxford University Press, 2002.

– *Poverty Reform in Canada, 1958–1978: State and Class Influences on Policy
Making.* Montreal and Kingston: McGill-Queen's University Press, 1993.

Hall, Peter A. "Conclusion: The Politics of Keynesian Ideas." In *The Political
Power of Economic Ideas: Keynesianism across Nations,* edited by Peter A.
Hall. Princeton: Princeton University Press, 1989.

Hall, Peter A., and Rosemary C.R. Taylor. "Political Science and the Three
New Institutionalisms." *Political Studies* 44 (1996): 936–57.

Ham, Christopher, and Michael Hill. *The Policy Process in the Modern Capitalist State.* Second edition. New York: Harvester Wheatsheaf /Simon and
Schuster, 1993.

Hamel, Pierre, and Jacques Rousseau. "Revisiting Municipal Reforms in Quebec and the New Responsibilities of Local Actors in a Globalizing World."
In *Canada: The State of the Federation 2004: Municipal-Federal-Provincial Relations in Canada,* edited by Robert Young and Christian Leuprecht, chapter 6. Montreal and Kingston: McGill-Queen's University Press, 2006.

Harloe, Michael. *The People's Home? Social Rented Housing in Europe & America.* Oxford: Blackwell, 1995.

Harris, Richard. "Flattered but Not Imitated: Co-operative Self-Help and the

Nova Scotia Housing Commission, 1936–1973." *Acadiensis* 31, no. 1 (2001): 103–28.

– "Housing and Social Policy: An Historical Perspective on Canadian-American Differences – A Comment." *Urban Studies* 36, no. 7 (1999): 1169–75.

Harris, Richard, and Marc H. Choko. *The Evolution of Housing Tenure in Montreal and Toronto since the Mid-nineteenth Century*. Research paper no. 166, University of Toronto, Centre for Urban and Community Studies, 1988.

Hayward, David. "The Reluctant Landlords? A History of Public Housing in Australia." *Urban Policy and Research* 14, no. 1 (1996): 5–35.

Helleiner, Eric. "A Fixation with Floating: The Politics of Canada's Exchange Rate Regime." *Canadian Journal of Political Science / Revue canadienne de science politique* 38, no. 1 (2005): 23–44.

Hill, Michael. *Understanding Social Policy*. Oxford: Blackwell, 2003.

Howe, Renate, ed. *New Houses for Old: Fifty Years of Public Housing in Victoria, 1938–1988*. Melbourne: Victoria Ministry of Housing and Construction, 1988.

Hulchanski, J. David. "Canada." In *International Handbook of Housing Policies and Practices*, edited by Willem Van Vliet, chapter 9. New York and London: Greenwood Press, 1990.

– *Canadian Government Housing Expenditures: A Ten Year Review*. Discussion paper no. 19, School of Urban and Regional Planning, University of British Columbia, 1990.

– "The Dominion Housing Act: Setting the Stage for a Permanent Presence in Canada's Housing Sector." *Urban History Review* 15, no. 1 (1986): 19–40.

– "How Did We Get Here? The Evolution of Canada's 'Exclusionary' Housing System." In *Finding Room: Policy Options for a Canadian Rental Housing Strategy*, edited by J. David Hulchanski and Michael Shapcott, chapter 11. Toronto: CUCS Press, 2004.

– *Shelter Allowances and Canadian Housing Policy: A Review and Evaluation*. Research paper no. 147, Centre for Urban and Community Studies, University of Toronto, 1983.

– *The Three Cities within Toronto: Income Polarization among Toronto's Neighbourhoods, 1970–2005*. Toronto: Cities Centre, University of Toronto, 2010.

– "Trends in the Federal Role in Housing and Urban Affairs in Canada." In *Papers Presented at the Tri-Country Conference on Facing Up to Housing and Urban Issues: 1992*, chapter 3. Washington, DC: Fannie Mae Foundation, 1993.

– "What Factors Shape Canadian Housing Policy? The Intergovernmental Role in Canada's Housing System." In *Canada: The State of the Federation 2004: Municipal-Federal-Provincial Relations in Canada*, edited by Robert Young and Christian Leuprecht, chapter 10. Montreal and Kingston: McGill-Queen's University Press, 2006.

Hulchanski, J. David, and Glenn Drover. "Housing Subsidies in a Period of Restraint: The Canadian Experience." In *Housing Markets and Policies under Fiscal Austerity*, edited by Willem van Vliet, chapter 4. New York: Greenwood Press, 1987.

Hulse, Kath. "Housing Allowances and Private Renting in Liberal Welfare Regimes." *Housing, Theory and Society* 20, no.1 (2003): 28–42.

Hulse, Kath, and Wendy Stone. *Housing, Housing Assistance and Social Cohesion*. Melbourne: Swinburne-Monash Research Centre / Australian Housing and Urban Research Centre, 2006.

Jenson, Jane. "'Different' but Not 'Exceptional': Canada's Permeable Fordism." *Canadian Review of Sociology and Anthropology* 26, no. 1 (1989): 69–94.

– "Mapping Social Inclusion: The State of Canadian Research." Ottawa: Canadian Policy Research Networks, 1998.

– "Representations in Crises: The Roots of Canada's Permeable Fordism." *Canadian Journal of Political Science* 24, no. 3 (1990): 653–83.

Jessop, Bob. *The Future of the Capitalist State*. Cambridge: Polity Press, 2002.

John, Peter. *Analysing Public Policy*. London: Pinter, 1998.

Jones, Michael A. *The Australian Welfare State: Growth, Crisis and Change*. Sydney: Allen and Unwin, 1983.

Judt, Tony. *Postwar: A History of Europe since 1945*. New York: Penguin, 2005.

Kalbach, Warren E., and Wayne W. McVey. *The Demographic Bases of Canadian Society*. Toronto: McGraw-Hill Ryerson, 1979.

Kealey, Gregory S. "The Canadian State's Attempt to Manage Class Conflict, 1900–1948." In *Social Welfare, 1850–1950: Australia, Argentina and Canada Compared*, edited by Desmond C.M. Platt, chapter 7. London: Macmillan Press, 1989.

Kemeny, Jim. "Corporatism and Housing Regimes." *Housing, Theory and Society* 23, no. 1 (2006): 1–18.

– *From Public Housing to the Social Market: Rental Strategies in Comparative Perspective*. London and New York: Routledge, 1995.

– *Housing and Social Theory*. London and New York : Routledge, 1992.

– "'The Really Big Trade-Off' between Home Ownership and Welfare: Castles' Evaluation of the 1980s Thesis, and a Reformulation 25 Years On." *Housing, Theory and Society* 22, no. 2 (2005): 59–75.

Kemeny, Jim, Jan Kersloot, and Philippe Thalnann. "Non-profit Housing Influencing, Leading and Dominating the Unitary Rental Market: Three Case Studies." *Housing Studies* 20, no. 6 (2005): 855–72.

Kemp, Peter. "Income-Related Assistance with Housing Costs: A Cross-National Comparison." *Urban Studies* 27, no. 6 (1990): 795–808.

– "The Role and Design of Income-Related Housing Allowances." *International Social Security Review* 53, no. 3 (2000): 43–57.

Kent, Tom. *A Public Purpose*. Montreal and Kingston: McGill-Queen's University Press, 1988.

– *Social Policy for Canada: Towards a Philosophy of Social Security*. Ottawa: Policy Press, 1962.

Kleinman, Mark. "Housing, Welfare and the State." In *Housing, Welfare and the State in Europe: A Comparative Analysis of Britain, France and Germany*, edited by Mark Kleinman, chapter 1. Cheltenham, UK: Edward Elgar, 1996.

Klemek, Christopher. *The Transatlantic Collapse of Urban Renewal: Postwar Urbanism from New York to Berlin*. Chicago: University of Chicago Press, 2011.

Klodawsky, Fran, and Aron Spector. "Renovation or Abandonment?: Canadian Social Housing at a Crossroads." In *How Ottawa Spends 1997–98: Seeing Red: A Liberal Report Card*, edited by Gene Swimmer, chapter 11. Montreal and Kingston: McGill-Queen's University Press, 1997.

Korpi, Walter. "The Power Resources Model." In *The Welfare State Reader*, second edition, edited by Christopher Pierson and Francis G. Castles, 76–87. Cambridge: Polity Press, 2006.

Lacombe, B. "L'Urbanisation au Québec: Rapport du Groupe de Travail sur l'Urbanisation: A Review." *Canadian Public Policy / Analyse de Politiques* 3, no. 2 (1977): 234–9.

Layton, Jack. *Homelessness: The Making and Unmaking of a Crisis*. Toronto: Penguin Books, 2000.

Legault, Guy. *La Ville qu'on a batie: Trente ans au service d'urbanisme et d l'habitation à Montréal 1956–1986*. Montreal: Liber, 2002.

Leone, Roberto, and Barbara Wake Carroll. "Decentralisation and Devolution in Canadian Social Housing Policy." *Environment and Planning C* 28, no. 3 (2010): 389–404.

Lewis, David. *The Good Fight: Political Memoirs, 1909–1958*. Toronto: Macmillan of Canada, 1981.

Ley, David. *The New Middle Class and the Remaking of the Central City*. Oxford: Oxford University Press, 1996.

Lichtheim, George. *A Short History of Socialism*. London: Weidenfeld and Nicolson, 1970.

Lithwick, Harvey. "The Decline and Fall of the Housing Market." In *How Ottawa Spends 1985: Sharing the Pie*, edited by Allan. M. Maslove, 30–57. Toronto: Methuen, 1985.

– *Urban Canada: Problems and Prospects*. Ottawa: Central Mortgage and Housing Corporation, 1970.

Maclelland, Michael, and Graeme Stewart, eds. *Concrete Toronto: A Guide to Concrete Architecture from the Fifties to the Seventies*. Toronto: Coach House Press, 2007.

Maclennan, Duncan, and Gwilym Pryce. "Global Economic Change, Labour Market Adjustment and the Challenges for European Housing Policies." *Urban Studies* 33, no. 10 (1996): 1849–65.

Mahoney, James, and Kathleen A. Thelen. "A Theory of Gradual Institutional Change." In *Explaining Institutional Change: Ambiguity, Agency, and Power*, edited by James Mahoney and Kathleen A. Thelen, chapter 1. Cambridge: Cambridge University Press, 2010.

Maloney, Roger. "A Municipal View of Devolution to Municipalities." *Canadian Housing* 14, no. 1 (1997): 15–16.

Malpass, Peter. "Housing and the New Welfare State: Wobbly Pillar or Cornerstone?" *Housing Studies* 23, no. 1 (2008): 1–19.

Marcuse, Peter. "United States of America." In *International Handbook of Housing Policies and Practices*, edited by Willem Van Vliet, chapter 10. New York: Greenwood Press, 1990.

Marsh, Alex, and David Mullins. "The Social Exclusion Perspective and Housing Studies: Origins, Applications and Limitations." *Housing Studies* 13, no. 6 (1998): 749–59.

Marsh, Leonard. *Report on Social Security for Canada*. First published 1943, reprinted 1975. Toronto: University of Toronto Press, 1975.

Martin, Paul. *A Very Public Life*. Ottawa: Deneau Publishing, 1983.

McCall, Christina, and Stephen Clarkson. *Trudeau and Our Times: Volume 2: The Heroic Delusion*. Toronto: McClelland & Stewart, 1990.

McDougall, Allan K. *John P. Robarts: His Life and Government*. Toronto: University of Toronto Press, 1986.

McKellar, James. "Building Technology and the Production Process." In *House, Home, and Community: Progress in Housing Canadians, 1945–1986*, edited by John Miron, chapter 2. Montreal and Kingston: McGill-Queen's University Press, 1993.

McMahon, Michael. *Metro's Housing Company: The First 35 Years*. Toronto: University of Toronto Press, 1990.

Mendelson, Michael. *The UK in 2011 Is Not Canada in 1996*. Ottawa: Caledon Institute, 2011.

Merrifield, Andy. *Metromarxism: A Marxist Tale of the City*. New York: Routledge, 2002.

Michelson, William B. *Environmental Choice, Human Behavior, and Residential Satisfaction*. New York: Oxford University Press, 1977.

Miron, John R. "Demographic and Economic Factors in Housing Demand." In *House, Home, and Community: Progress in Housing Canadians, 1945–1986*, edited by John Miron, chapter 2. Montreal and Kingston: McGill-Queen's University Press, 1993.

– "Private Rental Housing: The Canadian Experience." *Urban Studies* 32, no. 3 (1995): 579–604.

– *Renters and their Housing Conditions: From the 1980s into the 1990s.* Ottawa: Canada Mortgage and Housing Corporation, 1998.

Mishra, Ramesh. "The Collapse of the Welfare State Consensus? The Welfare State in the 1980s." In *Housing the Homeless and Poor: New Partnerships Among the Private, Public, and Third Sectors,* edited George Fallis and Alex Murray, chapter 4. Toronto: University of Toronto Press, 1990.

– *Globalization and the Welfare State.* Cheltenham, UK: Edward Elgar, 1999.

Morton, Desmond. *A Short History of Canada.* Edmonton: Hurtig Publishers, 1983.

Murdie, Robert A. "'Blacks in Near-Ghettos?' Black Visible Minority Population in Metropolitan Toronto Housing Authority Public Housing Units." *Housing Studies* 9, no. 4 (1994): 435–56.

– *Social Housing in Transition: The Changing Social Composition of Public Sector Housing in Metropolitan Toronto.* Ottawa: Canada Mortgage and Housing Corporation, 1992.

Murie, Alan. "The Dynamics of Social Exclusion and Neighbourhood Decline: Welfare Regimes, Decommodification, Housing, and Urban Inequality." In *Cities of Europe: Changing Contexts, Local Arrangements, and the Challenge to Urban Cohesion,* edited by Yuri Kazepov, chapter 7. Oxford, UK, and Malden, MA: Blackwell, 2005.

Murie, Alan, and Sako Musterd. "Social Exclusion and Opportunity Structures in European Cities and Neighbourhoods." *Urban Studies* 41, no. 8 (2004): 1441–59.

Musterd, Sako, and Wim Ostendorf. "Social Exclusion, Segregation, and Neighborhood Effects." In *Cities of Europe: Changing Contexts, Local Arrangements, and the Challenge to Urban Cohesion,* edited by Yuri Kazepov, chapter 8. Oxford, UK: Blackwell, 2005.

Myles, John. "Introduction: Understanding Canada: Comparative Political Economy Perspectives." *Canadian Review of Sociology and Anthropology* 26, no. 1 (1989): 1–9.

– "When Markets Fail: Social Welfare in Canada and the United States." In *Welfare States in Transition,* edited by Gøsta Esping-Andersen, chapter 5. London, UK: Sage Publications, 1996.

Myles, John, Garnett Picot, and Ted Wannell. "Does Post-industrialism Matter? The Canadian Experience." In *Changing Classes: Stratification and Mobility in Post-industrial Societies,* edited by Gøsta Esping-Andersen, chapter 7. London, UK, and Newbury Park, CA: Sage Publications, 1993.

Myles, John, and Jill Quadagno. "Political Theories of the Welfare State." *Social Service Review* 76, no. 1 (2002): 34–57.

Oberlander, H. Peter, and Arthur L. Fallick. *Housing a Nation: The Evolution of Canadian Housing Policy.* Centre for Human Settlements, University of British Columbia, 1992.

Obinger, Herbert, Stephan Leibfried, and Francis G. Castles, eds. *Federalism and the Welfare State: New World and European Experiences.* Cambridge: Cambridge University Press, 2005.

O'Connor, Julia S. "Welfare Expenditure and Policy Orientation in Canada in Comparative Perspective." *Canadian Review of Sociology and Anthropology* 26, no. 1 (1989): 127–50.

Orlebeke, Charles J. "The Evolution of Low Income Housing Policy, 1949–1999." *Housing Policy Debate* 11, no. 2 (2000): 489–520

Pacione, Michael. *Urban Geography: A Global Perspective.* Second edition. Oxford: Routledge, 2005.

Paris, Chris. "Housing Issues and Policies in Australia." In *Urban Australia: Planning Issues and Policies*, edited by Stephen Hamnett and Raymond Bunker, 79–107. Melbourne: Nelson Wadsworth, 1987.

Patterson, Jeffrey. *A Review of Canadian Social Housing Policy: A Study.* Ottawa: Canadian Council on Social Development, 1977.

Pearson, Lester B. *Mike: The Memoirs of the Rt. Hon. Lester B. Pearson.* Volume 3. Toronto: University of Toronto Press, 1975.

Picot, Garnett, and John Myles. *Income Inequality and Low Income in Canada: An International Perspective.* Statistics Canada, Analytical Studies Branch, research paper 240, 2005.

Pierson, Paul. "Fragmented Welfare States: Federal Institutions and the Development of Social Policy." *Governance* 8, no. 4 (2005): 449–78.

– "Increasing Returns, Path Dependence, and the Study of Politics." *American Political Science Review* 94, no. 2 (2000): 251–67.

– "The New Politics of the Welfare State." *World Politics* 48, no. 2 (1996): 143–79.

– "Not Just What, but *When:* Timing and Sequence in Political Process." *Studies in American Political Development* 14 (2000): 72–92.

Piketty, Thomas. *Capital in the Twenty-First Century.* Cambridge, MA: Harvard University Press, 2014.

Plunz, Richard. *A History of Housing in New York City.* New York: Columbia University Press, 1990.

Poapst, James V. "Financing Post-war Housing." In *House, Home, and Community: Progress in Housing Canadians, 1945–1986*, edited by John Miron, chapter 6. Montreal and Kingston: McGill-Queen's University Press, 1993.

Podoluk, Jenny R. *Incomes of Canadians.* 1961 census monograph series. Ottawa: Dominion Bureau of Statistics, 1968.

Pomeroy, Steve. "A Canadian Perspective on Housing Policy." *Housing Policy Debate* 6, no. 3 (1995): 619–53.

– "The Recent Evolution of Social Housing in Canada." *Canadian Housing* 6, no. 4 (1989): 6–13.

– *Where's the Money Gone? An Analysis of Declining Government Housing Expenditures.* Ottawa: Canadian Housing and Renewal Association, 2007.

Pomeroy, Steve, and Nick Falvo. "Pragmatism and Political Expediency: Housing Policy under the Harper Regime." In *How Ottawa Spends, 2013–2014: The Harper Government: Mid-Term Blues and Long-Term Plans,* edited by Christopher Stoney and G. Bruce Doern, chapter 14. Montreal and Kingston: McGill-Queen's University Press, 2013.

Pomeroy, Steve, Greg Lampert, and Kathleen Mancer. *Private Rental Policies and Programs: Review of the International Experience.* Ottawa: Canada Mortgage and Housing Corporation, 1998.

Prince, Michael J. "The Canadian Housing Policy Context." *Housing Policy Debate* 6, no. 3 (1995): 721–58.

– "From Health and Welfare to Stealth and Farewell: Federal Social Policy, 1980–2000." In *How Ottawa Spends 1999–2000: Shape Shifting: Canadian Governance Toward the 21st Century,* edited by Leslie A. Pal, chapter 2. Don Mills: Oxford University Press, 1999.

– "Holes in the Safety Net, Leaks in the Roof: Changes in Canadian Welfare Policy and Their Implications for Social Housing Programs." *Housing Policy Debate* 9, no. 4 (1998): 825–48.

Purdy, R. Sean. "By the People, For the People: Tenant Organizing in Toronto's Regent Park Housing Project in the 1960s and 1970s." *Journal of Urban History* 30, no. 4 (2004): 519–48.

– "From Place of Hope to Outcast Space: Territorial Regulation and Tenant Resistance in Regent Park Housing Project, 1949–2001." PhD dissertation, History, Queen's University, 2003.

– "'It was tough on everybody': Low-Income Families and Housing Hardship in Post-World War II Toronto." *Journal of Social History* 37, no. 2 (2003): 457–82.

Purdy, R. Sean, and Nancy H. Kwak. "Introduction: New Perspectives on Public Housing Histories in the Americas." *Journal of Urban History* 33, no. 3 (2007): 357–74.

Radford, Gail. *Modern Housing for America: Policy Struggles in the New Deal Era.* Chicago: University of Chicago Press, 1997.

Rice, James J., and Michael J. Prince. *Changing Politics of Canadian Social Policy.* Toronto: University of Toronto Press, 2000.

Richards, John, and William G. Watson, eds. *Home Remedies: Rethinking Canadian Housing Policy.* Toronto: C.D. Howe Institute, 1995.

Robertson, Gordon. *Memoirs of a Very Civil Servant: Mackenzie King to Pierre Trudeau.* Toronto: University of Toronto Press, 2000.

Rochefort, David A., and Rober W. Cobb. "Problem Definition, Agenda Access, and Policy Choice." *Policy Studies Journal* 21, no. 1 (1993): 56–71.

Rose, Albert. *Canadian Housing Policies 1935–1980.* Toronto: Butterworths, 1980.

– *Governing Metropolitan Toronto: A Social and Political Analysis 1953–1971.* Berkeley and Los Angeles, CA: University of California Press, 1972.

Rutherford, Paul F.W., ed. *Saving the Canadian City: The First Phase 1880–1920.* Toronto and Buffalo: University of Toronto Press, 1974.

Sancton, Andrew. "Amalgamations, Service Realignment, and Property Taxes: Did the Harris Government Have a Plan for Ontario's Municipalities?" *Canadian Journal of Regional Science* 23, no. 1 (2000): 135–56.

Saunders, Peter. *Social Theory and the Urban Question.* London: Routledge / Hutchinson, 1981.

Schwartz, Alex F. *Housing Policy in the United States.* Second edition. New York and London: Routledge / Taylor & Francis, 2010.

Schwartz, Herman. "'Economic Rationalism' in Canberra and Canada: Public Sector Reorganisation, Politics and Power." *Australian Economic History Review* 43, no. 1 (2003): 45–65.

– "Small States in Big Trouble: State Reorganization in Australia, Denmark, New Zealand and Sweden in the 1980s." *World Politics* 46, no. 4 (1994): 527–55.

Scott, Allen J., and Shoukry T. Roweis. *The Urban Land Question.* Department of Urban and Regional Planning, University of Toronto, 1976.

Scott, Susan. *The Beginning of the End: The Story of the Calgary Homeless Foundation and One Community's Drive to End Homelessness.* Calgary: Calgary Homeless Foundation, 2012.

Sewell, John. "Where the Suburbs Came From." In *The Second City Book,* edited by James Lorimer and Evelyn Ross, 10–47. Toronto: James Lorimer & Company, 1977.

– *Houses and Homes.* Toronto: James Lorimer & Company, 1994.

– *Up against City Hall.* Toronto: James Lorimer & Company, 1972.

Sharp, Mitchell. *Which Reminds Me … A Memoir.* Toronto: University of Toronto Press, 1994.

Shillington, Richard. *The Role of Housing in the Social Inclusion/Exclusion of Children: Conceptual Framework and Research Plan.* Ottawa: Canadian Housing and Renewal Association, 2001.

Shostack, Hanna. "Business and Reform: The Lost History of the Toronto Housing Company." *City Magazine* 3, no. 7 (1978): 24–31.

Simeon, Richard. "Studying Public Policy." *Canadian Journal of Political Science* 9, no. 4 (1976): 548–80.

Simmons, James W., and Larry S. Bourne. *Urban Growth Trends in Canada, 1981–1986: A New Geography of Change.* University of Toronto, Centre for Urban and Community Studies, major report no. 25, 1989.

Skaburskis, Andrejs. "Filtering, City Change and the Supply of Low-priced Housing in Canada." *Urban Studies* 43, no. 3 (2006): 533–58.

Skelton, Ian. "Planning under Welfare Pluralism: Social Housing Targets and Allocations in Ontario, Canada." *Geoforum* 28, no. 1 (1997): 79–89.

Smith, Cameron. *Unfinished Journey: The Lewis Family.* Toronto: Summerhill Press, 1989.

Smith, Denis. *Gentle Patriot: A Political Biography of Walter Gordon.* Edmonton: Hurtig Publishers, 1973.

Smith, Lawrence B. "Canadian Housing Policy in the Seventies." *Land Economics* 57, no. 3 (1981): 338–52.

– "The Crisis in Rental Housing: A Canadian Perspective." *Annals of the American Academy of Political and Social Science* 465, no. 1 (1983): 58–75

– *The Postwar Canadian Housing and Residential Mortgage Markets and the Role of Government.* Toronto: University of Toronto Press, 1974.

– "Postwar Canadian Housing Policy in Theory and Practice." *Land Economics* 44, no. 3 (1968): 339–49.

Smith, Nancy. "Challenges of Public Housing in the 1990s: The Case of Ontario, Canada." *Housing Policy Debate* 6, no. 1 (1995): 905–93.

Smith, Ralph. "Part I: Lessons from the National Homelessness Initiative." In *Policy Development and Implementation in Complex Files.* Ottawa: Canada School of Public Service.

Snow, David. *A Roof over Our Heads 2008: Affordable Housing and Homelessness Policy in Canada.* Calgary: Canada West Foundation, 2008.

Somerville, Peter. "Explanations of Social Exclusion: Where Does Housing Fit In?" *Housing Studies* 13, no. 6 (1998): 761–80.

Spearitt, Peter. *Sydney's Century: A History.* Sydney: University of New South Wales Press, 2000.

Spurr, Peter. *Land and Urban Development: A Preliminary Study.* Toronto: James Lorimer and Company, 1976.

Steele, Marion. "Canadian Housing Allowances." In *Housing Allowances in Comparative Perspective,* edited by Peter Kemp, chapter 4. Bristol: Policy Press, 2007.

Stone, Deborah A. "Causal Stories and the Formation of Policy Agendas." *Political Science Quarterly* 104, no. 2 (1989): 281–300.

Suttor, Greg. "Canadian Social Housing: Policy Evolution and Impacts on the Housing System and Urban Space." PhD dissertation, University of Toronto, 2014.

– *Growth Management and Affordable Housing in Greater Toronto.* Ottawa: Canada Mortgage and Housing Corporation, 2007.

– "Offset Mirrors: Institutional Paths in Canadian and Australian Social Housing." *International Journal of Housing Policy* 11, no. 3 (2011): 255–83.

– *Rental Housing Dynamics and Lower-Income Neighbourhoods in Canada.* Research Paper 235, Neighbourhood Change Research Partnership, University of Toronto, 2015.

– *Rental Paths from Postwar to Present: Canada Compared.* Research paper 218. Toronto: University of Toronto Cities Centre, 2009.

Thelen, Kathleen, and Sven Steinmo. "Historical Institutionalism in Comparative Politics." In *Structuring Politics: Historical Institutionalism in Comparative Perspective*, edited by Sven Steinmo, Kathleen Thelen, and Frank Longstreth, chapter 1. Cambridge: Cambridge University Press, 1992.

Thompson, John Herd, with Alan Seager. *Canada 1922–1939: Decades of Discord.* Toronto: McClelland and Stewart, 1985.

Tindal, C.R. *Structural Changes in Local Government: Government for Urban Regions.* Ottawa: Institute of Public Administration of Canada, 1977.

Torgersen, Ulf. "Housing: The Wobbly Pillar under the Welfare State." In *Between State and Market: Housing in the Postindustrial Era*, edited by Bengt Turner, Jim Kemeny, and Lennart J. Lundquist. Stockholm: Almqvist & Wiksell, 1987.

Troy, Patrick N. "The Evolution of Government Housing Policy: The Case of New South Wales 1901–41." *Housing Studies* 7, no. 3 (1992): 216–23.

Tsenkova, Sasha, and Melissa Witwer. "Bridging the Gap: Policy Instruments to Encourage Private Sector Provision of Affordable Rental Housing in Alberta." *Canadian Journal of Urban Research* 20, no. 1 – Supplement (2011): 52–80.

United Way of Greater Toronto and Canadian Council on Social Development. *Poverty by Postal Code: The Geography of Neighbourhood Poverty: City of Toronto, 1981–2001.* Toronto: United Way, 2004.

Vaillancourt, Yves, and Marie-Noëlle Ducharme. *Social Housing – A Key Component of Social Policies in Transformation: The Quebec Experience.* Ottawa: Caledon Institute, 2001.

– "Third Sector and the Co-construction of Canadian Public Policy." In *New Public Governance, the Third Sector, and Co-Production*, edited by Victor

Pestoff, Taco Brandsen, and Bram Verschuere, chapter 5. Abingdon, UK, and New York: Routledge, 2012.

Vakili-Zad, Cyrus. "Privatizing Public Housing in Canada: A Public Policy Agenda." *Journal of Housing and the Built Environment* 11, no. 1 (1996): 47–68.

Van Dyk, Nick. "Financing Social Housing in Canada." *Housing Policy Debate* 6, no. 1 (1995): 815–48.

Wade, Jill. *Houses for All: The Struggle for Social Housing in Vancouver, 1919–50.* Vancouver: UBC Press, 1994.

– "Wartime Housing Limited, 1941–1947: Canadian Housing Policy at the Crossroads." *Urban History Review / Revue d'histoire urbaine* 15, no 1 (1986): 40–59.

Warne, Robert D. "Canadian Housing Policy: A Chronology of the Past." In *Perspectives on Canadian Housing Policy*, edited by Tom Carter. Occasional paper no. 17. Institute of Urban Studies, University of Winnipeg, 1989.

Weaver, John. "The Denial of Social Experiment in Canadian Housing Policy before the Second World War." In *Social Welfare, 1850–1950: Australia, Argentina and Canada Compared*, edited by Desmond C.M. Platt, chapter 4. London: Macmillan Press, 1989.

White, Jerry. *London in the Twentieth Century: A City and Its People.* London: Random House / Vintage, 2001 [2008 edition].

Whitehead, Christine. "The Economics of Social Housing." In *Housing Economics and Public Policy: Essays in Honour of Duncan Maclennan*, edited by Tony O'Sullivan and Kenneth Gibb, 135–52. Oxford: Blackwell, 2003.

Wilensky, Harold L. *The Welfare State and Equality: Structural and Ideological Roots of Public Expenditure.* Berkeley, CA: University of California Press, 1975.

Wilson, A.D. "Canadian Housing Legislation." *Canadian Public Administration* 2, no. 4 (1959): 214–28.

Wilson, John. "The Ontario Political Culture." In *Government and Politics of Ontario*, edited by Donald S. MacDonald, chapter 13. Toronto: Macmillan Company of Canada, 1975.

Wiseman, Nelson. *In Search of Canadian Political Culture.* Vancouver: UBC Press, 2007.

Wolfe, David. "The Canadian State in Comparative Perspective." *Canadian Review of Sociology and Anthropology* 26, no. 1 (1989): 95–126.

Wolfe, Jeanne M. "Canadian Housing Policy in the Nineties." *Housing Studies* 13, no. 1 (1998): 121–33.

Wolfson, Michael C., and Brian B. Murphy. *New Views on Inequality Trends in Canada and the United States.* Ottawa: Statistics Canada, 1998.

Zuberi, Dan. *Small Differences That Matter: Social Policy and the Working Poor in the United States and Canada*. Cornell: ILR Press, 2006.

GOVERNMENT DOCUMENTS AND UNPUBLISHED SOURCES

Adamson, R.T. *National Housing Measures and Their Relation to Work and Opportunity Programs*. Background paper for the 1965 national conference on poverty and opportunity. Ottawa: Central Mortgage and Housing Corporation, 1965.

Alan Etherington & Associates. *Evaluation of 90 Shuter Street, Toronto: Final Report*. Ottawa: Canada Mortgage and Housing Corporation, 1987.

Alberta Housing Task Force. *Housing First, An Investment with a Return in Prosperity*. Edmonton: Alberta Ministry of Municipal Affairs and Housing, 2007.

Alberta, Ministry of Housing and Urban Affairs. *Annual Report 2010–2011*. Edmonton: Government of Alberta, 2011.

Alberta, Secretariat for Action on Homelessness. *A Plan for Alberta: Ending Homelessness in 10 Years*. Edmonton: Government of Alberta, 2008.

Altus Group Economic Consulting. *Economic Impacts of Residential Construction*. Ottawa: Canada Mortgage and Housing Corporation, 2009.

An Act to Amend the National Housing Act and the Canada Mortgage and Housing Corporation Act, Statutes of Canada 1999, c. 27.

Andrew, Caroline. "Cities and Polarization." Paper for the conference on social inclusion, Human Resources and Social Development Canada and the Canadian Council for Social Development, 2003.

Archives of Ontario. Series 44–14. Ontario Housing Corporation correspondence files.

– Series 44–5. Ontario Housing Corporation board of director's meetings files.

– Series RG 3–26, Premier John P. Robarts general correspondence.

– Series RG 44–1. Minister's correspondence relating to the Ontario Housing Corporation.

– Series RG 44–19–1. Administrative files from the Ontario Housing Corporation central registry.

Association of Municipalities of Ontario. *CMSM/DSSAB Requirements for a Successful Devolution Program*. Mimeo. Toronto: AMO, 1999.

– *Report on Deinstitutionalization*. Toronto: AMO, 1986.

Biernacki, C.M. *Housing Stock Trends: A Summary, Canada, Ontario and Toronto*. Centre for Urban and Community Studies, University of Toronto, 1976.

Black, David M. *The Public Housing Program: A Preliminary Analysis*. Ottawa: Central Mortgage and Housing Corporation, 1977.

Brendan Wood International. *Borrowing Efficiency in Non-profit Housing.*
    Prepared for the Ontario Ministry of Housing, 1993.

British Columbia Housing Management Commission. "Introduction to
    Homes BC Development Opportunities" (program booklet). Burnaby, BC,
    1998.

- *Annual Report, 1995/96.* Burnaby, BC, 1996.

British Columbia, Ministry of Municipal Affairs and Housing. *British Colum-
    bia's Strategy for Affordable Housing.* Victoria, BC, 1996.

British Columbia. *Housing Matters BC: A Housing Strategy for British Columbia.*
    Burnaby, BC: BC Housing, 2006.

Byrnes, Mark. "A Look Back at Montreal's Contentious, First Attempt at
    Slum Clearance." *Atlantic Citylab* blog, October 2013. http://www.citylab
    .com/housing/2013/10/look-back-montreals-contentious-first-attempt-
    slum-clearance/7242.

Canada Mortgage and Housing Corporation [Central Mortgage and Hous-
    ing Corporation until 1978]. *Canadian Housing Statistics.* [annual]

Canada Mortgage and Housing Corporation, and Ontario Minister of Mu-
    nicipal Affairs and Housing. "Social Housing Agreement." Ottawa: CMHC,
    1999.

Canada Mortgage and Housing Corporation. 2012. *Annual Report 2000.*
    Ottawa: CMHC, 2000.

- *Evaluation of the Federal Co-operative Housing Programs.* Ottawa: CMHC,
    1990.

- *Evaluation of the Public Housing Program.* Ottawa: CMHC, 1990.

- *Evaluation of the Urban Social Housing Programs.* Ottawa: CMHC, 1999.

- "National AHI Funding Table." http://www.cmhc-schl.gc.ca/en/inpr/afhoce
    /fuafho/ahi/fuafho_004.cfm; "National AIH Funding Table." http://www
    .cmhc-schl.gc.ca/en/inpr/afhoce/fuafho/iah/iah_002.cfm.

- *A National Direction for Housing Solutions.* Ottawa: CMHC, 1985.

- *Savings Matrix.* With accompanying reports "The Housing Need Universe,"
    "Client Selection/Prioritization," "Norm Rents," "Level of Assistance," "The
    Private Market as a Source of Affordable Housing." Ottawa: CMHC, 1994.

- *Section 56.1 Non-Profit and Co-operative Program Evaluation.* Ottawa: CMHC,
    1983.

- *Social Housing Review.* Ottawa: CMHC, 1984

- *Summary of the 1994–1998 Corporate Plan.* Ottawa: CMHC, 1994.

Canada. *Shaping Canada's Future Together: Proposals* Ottawa: Ministry of Sup-
    ply and Services Canada, 1991.

Canada, Department of Finance. "Getting Government Right." Fact Sheet no.
    6, 1995 federal Budget papers Ottawa: Department of Supply and Services,
    1996.

– *Budget Plan* 2000. Ottawa, 2000.
– *Budget Plan.* Ottawa: Department of Supply and Services, 1996.
Canada, Human Resources and Social Development Canada, *National Homelessness Initiative: 1999–2003 Progress Report.* Ottawa: HRSDC, 2004.
Canada, Human Resources Development Canada. *Improving Social Security in Canada: A Discussion Paper.* Ottawa, 1994.
Canada, Minister of Finance. *Budget Plan.* 1995.
Canada, Minister Responsible for Canada Mortgage and Housing Corporation. *Consultation Paper on Housing.* Ottawa: CMHC, 1985.
Canada, Prime Minister's Caucus Task Force on Urban Issues. *Final Report: Prime Minister's Caucus Task Force on Urban Issues.* Ottawa: November 2002.
Canada, Royal Commission on the Economic Union and Development Prospects for Canada. *Royal Commission on the Economic Union and Development Prospects for Canada.* Ottawa: Ministry of Supply and Services Canada, 1985.
Canada, Task Force on Canada Mortgage and Housing Corporation. *Report on the Canada Mortgage and Housing Corporation.* Ottawa, 1979.
Canada, Task Force on Housing and Urban Development. *Report of the Federal Task Force on Housing and Urban Development.* [Hellyer task force.] Ottawa, 1969.
Canada, Task Force on Program Review, Housing Study Team. *Housing Programs in Search of Balance – A Study Team Report to the Task Force on Program Review.* Ottawa, 1985.
Canadian Home Builders' Association. "Housing in Canada: Submission to Minister of Finance for Pre-Budget Consultations." Mimeo. Ottawa: CHBA, 1989.
Canadian Housing and Renewal Association. *Submission to the Standing Committee on Finance: 2000 Pre-Budget Consultations.* Mimeo. Ottawa: CHRA, September 2000.
Central Mortgage and Housing Corporation. *Housing in Canada.* Quarterly, various dates.
– *Housing in Canada, 1946–1970 – A Supplement to the 25th Annual Report of Central Mortgage and Housing Corporation.* Ottawa: CMHC, 1970.
– *A Review of Housing in Canada.* Ottawa: CMHC, 1958.
– *Special $200 Million Low-Cost Housing Program: Interim Report.* Ottawa: CMHC, 1971.
Charney, Melvin, with Serge Carreau and Colin Davidson. *The Adequacy and Production of Low Income Housing.* Background report for the Task Force on Low Income Housing. Ottawa: CMHC, 1971.
Citibank. *Official Submission for the Ministry of Municipal Affairs & Housing:*

Assisted Rental Housing Projects: Asset Monetization Potential. Mimeo. Toronto, 1995.

Clayton Research Associates. *Comparison of the Long-Term Cost of Shelter Allowances and Non-profit Housing.* Prepared for the Fair Rental Policy Organization of Ontario. Toronto, 1993.

– *The Costs of a Shelter Allowance Program in Ontario.* Prepared for the Fair Rental Policy Organization of Ontario. Toronto, 1993.

– *Economic Impact of Federal Tax Legislation on the Rental Housing Market in Canada.* Ottawa: Canadian Federation of Apartment Associations, 1998.

Cogan, Susana, and Debra Darke. *Canadian Social Housing Managed by Provincial and Territorial Housing Corporations: Comparative Characteristics.* Ottawa: Canada Mortgage and Housing Corporation, 1982.

Communauté métropolitaine de Montéal. *Offre et besoins en logements sociaux et abordables dans le Grand Montréal.* Montreal: CMM, Métropolitaines series, no. 3, 2013.

Co-operative Housing Federation of Canada, *Critique of the Federal/Provincial Social Housing Agreement.* Mimeo. Ottawa: CHF, 1997.

De Resende, Carlos, René Lalonde, and Stephen Snudden. *The Power of Many: Assessing the Economic Impact of the Global Fiscal Stimulus.* Discussion paper 2010–1. Ottawa: Bank of Canada, 2010.

Donnison, David V. *Housing Problems and Policies: An Introduction.* Background paper no. 1 for the Canadian Conference on Housing, June 1968. Ottawa: CMHC, 1968.

Ekos Research Associates. *Cost-Effective Housing: A Comparison of Non-Profit and Market Housing.* Prepared for the Canadian Housing and Renewal Association. Ottawa: CHRA, 1997.

Environics Research Group. *Background study no. 23.* Prepared for the Ontario Commission of Inquiry into Residential Tenancies. Toronto, 1985.

Federal, Provincial and Territorial Ministers Responsible for Housing. *A Framework for Bilateral Agreements Aimed at Affordable Housing.* Ottawa: CMHC / Federal, Provincial and Territorial Ministers Responsible for Housing, November 2001.

Federal-Provincial Task Force on the Supply and Price of Residential Land. *Down to Earth – The Report of the Federal/Provincial Task Force on the Supply and Price of Residential Land.* Prepared for the Ministers responsible for housing of Canada, British Columbia, Manitoba, Newfoundland, New Brunswick, NWT, Nova Scotia, Ontario, Prince Edward Island, and Saskatchewan. Ottawa, 1978.

Federal-Provincial-Territorial Ministers of Housing. *What We Heard: Federal/Provincial/Territorial Consultation on Opportunities for Savings and Efficiencies, and a New Social Housing Strategy.* Mimeo. Ottawa, 1995.

Federation of Canadian Municipalities. *A National Affordable Housing Strate-gy*. Ottawa: FCM, 2000.
- *National Housing Policy Options Paper: A Call for Action*. Ottawa: FCM, 1999.
- *Quality of Life Infrastructure Program*. Pre-budget submission, Ottawa: FCM, October 1999.
- *Quality of Life Infrastructure Program: Proposal to Finance Minister Paul Martin*. Ottawa: FCM, August 1999.
Feldman, Lionel D. *A Study of Ontario Housing Corporation – Its Program and Prospects*. Prepared for Ontario Housing Corporation. Toronto: OHC, 1965.
Fish, Susan A. *British Columbia: An Institutional Analysis*. Working Paper No. 6 for the CMHC Task Force on Low-Income Housing. Ottawa: CMHC, 1971.
Fish, Susan A., and Patricia Pond. *Nova Scotia and New Brunswick: An Institutional Analysis*. Working Paper No. 5 for the CMHC Task Force on Low-Income Housing. Ottawa: CMHC, 1971.
Freedman, Charles, Michael Kumhof, Douglas Laxton, and Jaewoo Lee. *The Case for Global Fiscal Stimulus*. IMF, staff position note 09/03; 2009.
Front d'action populaire en reaménagement urbain. *Le FRAPRU à vingt-cinq ans*. Mimeo. Montreal: FRAPRU, 2003.
Godbout, Jacques, and Gérard Divay. *Quebec: An Institutional Analysis*. Working Paper No. 2 for the CMHC Task Force on Low-Income Housing. Ottawa: CMHC, 1971.
Grieve, Beverley J. "Continuity and Change: Provincial Housing Policy in British Columbia 1945–1985." MA thesis, School of Urban and Regional Planning, University of British Columbia, 1985.
IBI Group. *Les programmes de logement de l'Ontario*. Background report for the Quebec Groupe de travail sur l'habitation. Quebec, 1975.
Maddison Project. Historical GDP data. http://www.ggdc.net/maddison /maddison-project/data.htm. Accessed September 2012.
Manitoba. *All Aboard: Manitoba's Poverty Reduction and Social Inclusion Strategy*. Winnipeg: 2012.
Manitoba, Department of Family Services and Consumer Affairs. *Annual Report 2009/10*.
McCracken, Mike, and R.A. Jenness. *Social Housing*. Issue paper 8. Prepared for the Ontario Ministry of Intergovernmental Affairs by Infometrica Ltd, 1994.
Metro Vancouver. *Metro Vancouver Housing Data Book*. Burnaby, BC: Metro Vancouver, 2015.
Metropolitan Toronto, Chief Administrative Officer. "Revised Provincial Transfer of Service Responsibilities Plan." May 5 report to the Financial Priorities Committee of Metro Council, 1997.
Metropolitan Toronto, Community Services Department. *Backgrounder: Gov-*

ernment Role and Public Costs for Housing. Toronto: Municipality of Metropolitan Toronto, 1996.

- "Implications of C.M.H.C./Saskatchewan Housing Devolution Agreement." Report to the Human Services Committee of Metropolitan Toronto Council, April 1997.
- "Implications of Provincial Announcements on the Community Services Department; and Transfer of Responsibilities from the Province of Ontario to Metro." Report to the Corporate Administration Committee of Metro Council, adopted 12–13 February 1997.

Metropolitan Toronto, Planning Department. *Housing in Metropolitan Toronto – Affordable or Not?* Toronto, 1980.

- *Housing Patterns and Prospects in Metro.* Toronto, 1996.

Metropolitan Toronto, Stakeholder Panel. *Report of the Housing Stakeholder Panel.* Toronto, 1997.

National Housing and Homelessness Network. "Canada's Nation-Wide Housing Crisis Demands a Nation-Wide Solution: $2 Billion in New Funding for Social Housing." Mimeo. Toronto, September 2000.

Ontario. *Design for Development.* Toronto: Queen's Printer, 1968.

- "Ecker Announces New Plan for Social and Community Services." News release, 14 January 1997.

Ontario, Advisory Council on Social Housing Reform. *Report of the Advisory Council on Social Housing Reform.* Toronto: Ontario Ministry of Municipal Affairs and Housing, 1997.

Ontario, Advisory Task Force on Housing Policy. *Report: Advisory Task Force on Housing Policy* [Comay Report]. Toronto, 1973.

Ontario, Housing Branch. "History of Housing Branch." 1962. Archives of Ontario, RG 44–19–1, B284555.

Ontario, Housing Supply Working Group. *Creating a Positive Climate for Rental Housing Development through Tax and Mortgage Insurance Reforms: The Second Report of the Housing Supply Working Group.* Toronto: Ministry of Municipal Affairs and Housing, 2002.

Ontario, Legislative Assembly, Standing Committee on Public Accounts. *Report on Non-profit Housing.* Toronto, 1993.

- *Report on Issues concerning Houselink Community Homes Inc and the Supportive Housing Coalition.* Toronto, 1994.

Ontario, Minister's Advisory Committee on the International Year of Shelter for the Homeless. *More Than Just a Roof: Action to End Homelessness in Ontario. Final Report of the Minister's Advisory Committee on the International Year of Shelter for the Homeless.* Toronto: Ministry of Housing, 1988.

Ontario, Ministry of Finance. *1995 Ontario Budget Plan.* Toronto: Queen's Printer, 1995.

Ontario, Ministry of Housing. [annual, 1974–75]. *Annual Report of the Ontario Ministry of Housing.*
- *Annual Report 1987/1988.* Toronto, 1988.
- *Comparing Non-profit Housing and Shelter Allowances: Can Shelter Allowances Replace Non-profit Housing?* Toronto, 1994.
- *Consultation Counts: Taking Action on a Housing Framework for Ontario.* Toronto, 1992.
- *Housing Ontario '74: An Initial Statement of Policies, Programs and Partnerships.* Toronto, 1974.
Ontario, Ministry of Municipal Affairs and Housing. *Assured Housing for Ontario – A Position Paper.* Toronto, 1987.
- *Guide to Social Housing Reform.* Materials accompanying the introduction of the legislative bill for the *Social Housing Reform Act.* Toronto, 2000.
- *Investment in Affordable Housing for Ontario: Program Guidelines.* Toronto, 2011.
- *Investment in Affordable Housing for Ontario: 2014 Extension: Program Guidelines.* Toronto, 2014.
- *Ontario Housing Corporation 1964–1984.* Toronto, 1984.
- *Projects in Profile.* Toronto, 2006.
Ontario, Office of the Provincial Auditor. *Ministry of Housing: Non-profit Housing: June 4, 1992* Toronto, 1992.
Ontario, Social Housing Committee. *Discussion Paper on Social Housing Reform.* Toronto: Ministry of Municipal Affairs and Housing. Toronto, 1998.
Ontario, Who Does What Panel. Letters from David Crombie, WDW chair, to Al Leach, Minister of Municipal Affairs and Housing, including final letter 23 December 1996, together with attached list of letters; Letters from David Crombie and Grant Hopcroft, Chair, WDW Social Services Sub-Panel, to Al Leach, dated 11 October, 4 November, and 20 December 1996.
Ontario Association of Housing Authorities. *Good Housing for Canadians: A Study by the Ontario Association of Housing Authorities.* Toronto: Ontario Department of Trade and Development, 1964.
Ontario Housing Corporation. *Federal-Provincial Conference on Poverty and Opportunity. The Social and Economic Aspects of Public Housing.* Report prepared for the conference. Toronto: OHC, 1965.
- *Ontario Housing Corporation: Policies, Programs and Structure.* Toronto, 1972.
- *Report to the Municipality of Metropolitan Toronto 1970.* Toronto, 1970.
- *Report to the Municipality of Metropolitan Toronto 1971.* Toronto, 1972.
- *Report to the Municipality of Metropolitan Toronto 1972.* Toronto, 1973.
Ontario Non-Profit Housing Association. "Common Goals, Common Sense: New Directions for Social Housing in Ontario." Presentation to the Minister of Municipal Affairs and Housing, 27 May 1996.

– "Ontario Needs Non-profit Housing." Mimeo. Toronto: ONPHA, ca 1993.
– *Where's Home 2013? Looking Back and Looking Forward at the Need for Affordable Housing in Ontario.* Toronto: ONPHA, 2013.
Ontario Welfare Council. *A Study of Housing Policies in Ontario: General Report.* Toronto: Ontario Welfare Council, 1973.
– *Housing in Ontario: A Sourcebook.* Toronto: Ontario Welfare Council, 1973.
Quebec (Province), Groupe de travail sur l'habitation. *Habiter au Québec: Rapport du Groupe de travail sur l'habitation.* Quebec, 1975.
Queen's University Archives. F00903. Thomas Worrall Kent fonds.
Richmond, Don. "The Devolution Option." Mimeo. Toronto, 1995.
– "Public Housing in Toronto." Mimeo. Toronto, 1997.
– "Public Housing: Options for the Future." Mimeo. Toronto, 1995.
Rose, Albert. *Prospects for Rehabilitation of Housing in Central Toronto.* Prepared for the City of Toronto Planning Board and Central Mortgage and Housing Corporation. Toronto, 1966.
Saskatchewan, Ministry of Social Services. "A Guide to the Saskatchewan Employment Supplement and Saskatchewan Rental Housing Supplement." Regina, 2011.
– *The Housing Strategy for Saskatchewan.* Regina, 2011.
Sauder School of Business, University of British Columbia. "Canadian Cities Housing & Real Estate Data." http://www.sauder.ubc.ca/Faculty/Research _Centres/Centre_for_Urban_Economics_and_Real_Estate/Residential _Real_Estate_2. Accessed September 2012.
Selby, Joan Louise. "Urban Rental Housing in Canada, 1900–1985: A Critical Review of Problems and the Response of Government." MA thesis, School of Urban and Regional Planning, University of British Columbia, 1985.
SHS Consulting. *Evaluation of Two Housing Allowance Programs: Rental Opportunity for Ontario Families (ROOF) and Short-term Rent Support Program (STRSP): Final Report.* Prepared for the Ontario Ministry of Municipal Affairs and Housing. Toronto, 2012.
Single Displaced Persons Project. "The Case for Long-Term, Supportive Housing." Mimeo. Toronto, 1983.
– "From Homelessness to Home: A Case for Facilitative Management." Mimeo. Toronto, 1987.
Social Planning Council of Metropolitan Toronto. *Strategies for Implementing a New Housing Agenda for Metropolitan Toronto: A Response to the Federal Government's Consultation Paper on Housing.* Toronto: Social Planning Council, 1985.
Société d'habitation du Québec. Annual Reports (various years).
– *L'Habitat au Québec 1996–2001.* Quebec: SHQ, 2001.

– *La Société d'habitation du Québec: Une histoire en trois mouvements.* Quebec: SHQ, 1992.

Springer, Joseph, James Mars, and Melissa Dennison. *A Profile of the Toronto Homeless Population.* Background report for the Mayor's Homelessness Action Task Force. Toronto, 1998.

Toronto (City). *Community Plan for Homelessness in Toronto.* Toronto: Community and Neighbourhood Services Department, 2000.

– 1984. *Final Report of the Mayor's Action Task Force on Discharged Psychiatric Patients.* [Gerstein report].

– 1974. *Core Area Housing Study.*

Toronto (City), City Planning Division. *Perspectives on Housing Tenure.* Toronto, 2006.

Toronto (City), Housing Department. "Annual Housing Targets." Report to the Neighbourhoods Committee of City Council, 6 June 1984.

– *Building Challenges: Confronting Toronto's Rental Crisis.* 1980 and 1981 combined annual report. Toronto, 1981.

– *Housing Policy Review 1976.*

– *New Directions in Housing 1977.*

– "Non-Profit Co-operative and Public Housing Programs." Appendix 4 to Housing Department report dated 7 Sept 1990, to City Council: "Tenancy Issues in Co-operative, Non-profit & Private Rental Housing Projects."

– *No Vacancy: Will the New Federal Housing Programs Work in Toronto?* 1978 annual report. Toronto, 1979.

– *On Target: Program Review 1977 and Planning Strategy to 1980.* Toronto, 1978.

– *Shifting Foundations: Addressing Shelter Needs and Responsibilities in Toronto.* 1982 annual report. Toronto, 1983.

– *Vanishing Options: The Impending Rental Crisis in Toronto.* 1979 annual report. Toronto, 1980.

Toronto (City), Housing Working Group. *Living Room: An Approach to Home Banking and Land Banking for the City of Toronto.* Toronto, 1973.

Toronto (City), Lieutenant-Governor's Committee on Housing Conditions in Toronto. *Report of the Lieutenant-Governor's Committee on Housing Conditions in Toronto* [Bruce report]. Toronto: Board of Control, 1934.

Toronto (City), Mayor's Homelessness Action Task Force. *Taking Responsibility for Homelessness: An Action Plan for Toronto.* [Golden report] Toronto, January 1999.

Toronto (City), Planning and Development Department. *Confronting the Crisis: A Review of City Housing Policy 1976–1981.* Toronto, 1982.

Toronto (City), Shelter, Housing and Support Division. "Annual Progress Report on Let's Build Affordable Housing Development." Report to Community Services Committee of City Council, 2003.

Toronto Disaster Relief Committee. *Homelessness in Toronto: State of Emergency Declaration: An Urgent Call for Emergency Humanitarian Relief & Prevention Measures.* Mimeo. Toronto, 1998.

Toronto Real Estate Board [TREB]. *Market Watch.* [market data publication, various dates].

Woods Gordon. *Evaluative Study of Non-profit and Cooperative Housing in Ontario.* Prepared for Canada Mortgage and Housing Corporation and the Ontario Ministry of Municipal Affairs and Housing. Toronto, 1981.

Index

Aboriginal peoples, 23, 133; housing programs, 23, 105, 133, 135, 137, 141, 164, 169, 186, 197; "Indian Affairs," 93; migration to cities, 83, 154, 155. *See also* On Reserve housing; Rural and Native Housing Program; Urban Native housing

AccèsLogis, 149–50, 166–7, 196

accessory units. *See* second suites

activists and activism: in 1960s, 56, 67; in late 1960s–70s, 76, 77, 83, 85–6, 89, 90, 91–3, 97, 98, 99, 177, 179; in 1980s–early 1990s, 117, 119, 130, 131; in late 1990s–2000s, 148, 158–9, 166; review, 193–4; wartime and early postwar, 31, 39–40. *See also* advocacy and lobbying on housing

addictions, 118

Advisory Committee (Ontario 1963), 58–60, 88, 193

Advisory Group (CMHC 1955–67), 39, 88

advocacy and lobbying on housing: 1930s–50s, 12, 26, 30–3, 34, 35, 36, 38, 39, 40, 172; 1960s–70s, 14, 45, 55, 56, 59, 61, 66, 77, 84, 91–2, 96,

98, 176, 192, 194, 195; 1980s, 117, 118, 119, 120, 121–2, 181; in 1990s, 134, 135, 137, 141, 150; circa 2000 onward, 159, 161, 162, 166, 168, 185

Affordable Home Ownership Program (AHOP), 108

Affordable Housing Initiative (AHI), 4, 151, 152, 162–6; in Alberta, 166; in British Columbia, 167–8; in Ontario, 168–9; in Quebec 166–7. *See also* housing production; Investment in Affordable Housing

Affordable Housing Program. *See* Affordable Housing Initiative

affordable ownership. *See* home-ownership

Agency for Co-operative Housing, 140

Alberta, 9, 23, 38, 64, 79, 113, 123, 139, 140, 166, 167, 169, 172, 186, 204; Alberta Housing Corporation, 66, 101

Allocation-logement (Quebec), 108

Andras, Robert, 95, 96

architecture and design of social housing, 23, 55, 70, 91–2

Assisted Rental Program (ARP), 108, 244n137
Association of Municipalities of Ontario (AMO), 168
Auditor (Ontario), 132
Australia, 16, 17, 20, 77, 79, 174; housing, 30, 50, 51, 52, 85, 88, 118, 157, 190, 192; social housing 6, 7, 14, 31, 42, 43, 46, 53, 61, 63, 71, 72, 175, 178, 179; welfare state, 13, 27, 181
Axworthy, Lloyd, 97

baby boom generation, 49–50, 78, 82, 85, 88, 106, 114, 130, 179, 191
banks, 40, 50, 69, 98, 128, 129, 157
Barrett, Dave, 67, 101
basement apartments. See second suites
Bates, Stewart, 39–40, 57
Bayers Road (housing project), 41
BC Non-Profit Housing Association, 110
Bennett, Claude, 116
Bennett, R.B. (Richard), 26, 35
Bouchard, Lucien, 148
Bourassa, Robert, 100, 121, 148
Bourque, Pierre, 149
Bradshaw, Claudette, 160
British Columbia, 23; formation of BC Housing, 66; Homes BC and AHI-IAH in 2000s, 151, 167–8, 169, 186; housing allowances, 108, 164–5; policy and attitudes in 1940s–60s, 38, 41, 43, 64, 68; policy and attitudes in 1970s, 67, 72, 80, 101, 104, 179; policy and attitudes in 1980s, 121, 123; policy and attitudes in 1990s, 140, 141, 146–8, 150, 172, 184, 188; sector organizations, 110, 140

Bruce report (Toronto), 30
budgets: federal, 127, 134, 135, 136, 137, 153, 161, 163, 169; housing project capital budgets, 101, 109; Ontario, 98, 142. See also deficits; expenditure on housing
builder proposals, 69–70, 71, 233n121

Calgary, 64, 70, 72, 83, 155; Homeless Foundation, 158, 166
Campbell, Gordon, 168
Canada Assistance Plan (CAP), 14, 47, 127, 175
Canada Health and Social Transfer (CHST), 127, 153
Canada Home Ownership Stimulation Plan, 108
Canada Mortgage and Housing Corporation / Central Mortgage and Housing Corporation (CMHC): Advisory Group and 1960s juncture, 39–40, 57, 176, 194; board of directors and chairman, 37, 38, 40, 137; capacity and expertise, 36, 41, 43–4, 187–8; consultations and FPT meetings, 120, 122, 137; financing market housing, 40, 58, 98, 174; formation of, 9, 37, 172; ministers responsible for, 60, 65, 68, 93, 95, 116, 120, 134–5, 137, 159, 161, 163, 194; policy fostering home-ownership, 38, 40, 129; policy reviews and studies, 12, 54, 57, 59, 84, 85, 86, 88, 92, 96–7, 115–16, 120, 133–4, 136, 178, 194; policy supporting private rental, 30, 157; presidents of, 39–40, 57, 131, 136–7; role in devolution, 134, 137–40, 183; role and mandate change, 120, 123, 137–8,

215n31; role in non-profit and co-operative delivery, 88, 98, 101, 106, 109, 110, 113, 121, 134, 135, 150; role in post-2000 programs, 165–6; role in public housing delivery, 40–1, 64–5, 68, 95, 176; role in retrenchment, 113, 134, 135, 137. *See also* expenditure on housing; housing funding formulas; mortgage financing; mortgage insurance; National Housing Act; urban renewal

Canada Pension Plan (CPP), 14, 47, 49, 55, 175, 198

Canada Rental Supply Program (CRSP), 108, 244n137

Canadian Housing and Renewal Association (CHRA), 161. *See also* social housing sector

Canadian Welfare Council / National Welfare Council, 38, 84

capacity. *See* Canada Mortgage and Housing Corporation; housing funding formulas; institutions; professionals; provincial housing corporations

capital grants to housing. *See* housing funding formulas

capital markets, 16, 135

capitalism. *See* investment; political and economic conditions; welfare state

Carver, Humphrey, 39, 54, 57, 87, 222n55

Castonguay, Claude, 100

causation, in policy change: funnel of causation, 22; review of findings, 186–95; theoretical, 15–18

Centennial (1967), 48

Central Mortgage and Housing Corporation (CMHC). *See* Canada

Mortgage and Housing Corporation

Charlottetown Accord, 15, 113, 128

Chicago school (economics), 112, 156

China, 146, 152, 156

Chrétien, Jean, 127, 134, 153, 156, 160, 161, 163, 183, 185, 186, 195

Churchill Park (housing project), 41

Clark, Joe, 103, 119

Clark, W. Clifford, 31, 32, 36, 37

Clark, W. Harold, 31, 59

Coleman, Rich, 168

collaborative federalism, 15, 151, 162, 185

Comay, Eli, 87, 222n55

Common Sense Revolution (Ontario), 142

community development, 118; community development corporations (CDCS), 89

community opposition to social and rental housing, 32, 56, 61, 68, 69, 71, 74, 91, 93, 193

Community Planning Association of Canada, 33, 39, 59, 84

community-based organizations, 14, 54; in housing, 5, 45, 76, 86, 87–90, 94, 97, 98, 99, 101, 104, 109–10. *See also* non-profit and co-operative housing

condominiums, 75, 80, 82, 91, 123, 129, 157; rental conversion to condo, 82, 147, 155

Conservative party and governments. *See also* red Tories
– Alberta, 76, 101, 166
– Europe, 130
– federal: Bennett, 26, 27, 35; Clark, 87, 103; Diefenbaker, 40, 48; Harper, 12, 154, 156, 161,

163–4, 185; Mulroney, 14, 111, 112, 120, 127, 134, 180–1
- Manitoba, 38, 67, 83
- municipal, 33, 74, 158
- Ontario, 33, 49, 74, 80, 128, 132, 142, 144–5, 168, 184
constitution (Canada), 26, 102, 153; amendments and devolution proposals, 13, 15, 27, 113, 125, 128, 195; federal spending power, 157, 38, 157; housing as provincial sphere, 34, 157. See also Charlottetown Accord; Meech Lake Accord
consultations, 74, 88, 120, 136, 145, 153
consumer-survivor movement, 118
Co-operative Commonwealth Federation (CCF), 18, 27, 39, 48, 52. See also New Democratic Party
co-operative housing, 9, 11, 76, 86, 88, 89, 90, 95, 97, 98, 109–10, 121, 122, 123, 131, 135, 139, 140, 177, 180, 182, 187, 188, 196, 200–2; advocacy and lobbying, 117, 119, 120, 123, 135, 139, 140, 144, 145, 181; Co-operative Housing Federation (CHF), 89, 110, 140; as political face of social or non-profit housing, 110, 131; in Quebec, 67, 80, 83, 99–100, 121. See also nonprofit and co-operative housing; social housing sector
core housing need, 122, 131, 182, 197. See also housing need
Cosgrove, Paul, 116
cost-recovery in housing. See low rental
cost-sharing: in social housing, 30, 38, 61, 100, 104, 106, 111, 120, 124, 140, 162, 163, 164, 168, 182, 188,

196–7; in social programs, 14, 47, 56, 127, 175. See also housing funding formulas; municipal role and attitudes in housing
critical junctures, 5, 8, 10, 22. See also turning points in Canadian social housing policy
critical social science, 12
Crombie, David, 85, 98, 143
cross-subsidy. See housing funding formulas
Crowe, Cathy, 159
Curtis report. See Housing and Community Planning report
cutbacks. See retrenchment

Davis, Bill, 80
decommodification in housing, 19, 43, 119, 157
deconversion of housing, 82
deficits (fiscal), 17, 78, 102, 113, 117, 126, 127, 151, 156, 161, 183
deindustrialization, 8, 17, 77, 100, 155
deinstitutionalization (psychiatric hospitals), 117
demand-side versus supply-side housing programs, 118–19, 120. See also housing allowance programs
demobilization, 25, 29, 31, 172
Dennis and Fish report, 12, 84, 86, 89, 93, 95–7
Dennis, Michael, 96, 104, 194
Department of Finance (Canada), 35, 37, 78, 97, 98, 120, 127, 133, 151
Depression (1930s), 12, 26, 27, 28, 30, 31, 126, 173
deregulation (financial), 32, 69, 78, 130

design. *See* architecture and design of social housing

developers (property firms) and development sector, 19, 40, 50, 69–70, 86, 87, 117, 119, 126, 129, 148, 183, 191

devolution: as enduring mode of neoliberal retrenchment, 15, 125, 138, 151, 184, 186–7; federal events of 1990s, 133–4, 136–41, 161, 172, 180–4, 194, 195; federal to provincial, 9, 10, 11, 12, 15, 198; fiscal, ideological and constitutional impetus in 1990s, 125, 128–9, 133, 139, 142, 144, 150, 183, 193; of program management in 1980s, 14, 111, 121, 124, 180; provincial to municipal (Ontario), 141–6, 160, 195

Diefenbaker, John, 40, 47, 48

Dingwall, David, 137

discourse (in policy-making). *See* ideas

displacement of residents, 4, 67, 92

district social services administration boards (Ontario), 257n142

Dominion Housing Act (DHA), 35

Donnison, David, 84

Doré, Jean, 121, 149

downloading. *See* devolution

Downtown Eastside (Vancouver), 148, 155, 167

Dozois, Paul, 39, 63

Drapeau, Jean, 39, 66, 149

drug use, 118

dualism in housing policy, 11, 34, 180, 187

Duplessis, Maurice, 34, 39

Durham regional municipality, 158

Ebsary Estate (housing project), 41

economic change, as factor in welfare state evolution, 13, 15, 16, 17. *See also* political and economic conditions

economic conditions and cycles, 10, 17, 116, 187; downturns and recessions, 44, 47, 75, 77–8, 79, 80, 95, 157; expansions and booms, 14, 16, 27, 44, 47, 50, 51, 83, 112, 152, 173, 174, 175, 179, 186; Global Financial Crisis, 163, 164; recession in early 1990s, 125–6, 183, 249n2. *See also* Depression; GDP and economic growth; political and economic conditions

economic rationalism, 117, 120. *See also* neoliberalism

economic theory and ideas. *See* Chicago school; Keynesian economics

Economics and Development (Ontario department), 41, 49, 53, 58, 60

Edmonton, 28, 51, 64, 72, 83, 158–9, 166

education policy and expenditure, 47, 49, 79, 142, 143, 152, 153, 175, 187

elections
 – in British Columbia: 1972, 80, 179; 1991, 147; 2001, 167
 – federal: 1935, 26; 1945, 27; 1963, 47, 55, 176, 194; 1972, 97; 1979, 87, 103; 1984, 111, 80, 194; 1993, 127, 194; 1997, 141; 2000, 162; 2006, 163
 – in Manitoba: 1969, 67, 179
 – in Ontario: 1943, 27; 1963, 60; 1967, 53; 1975, 80; 1985 and 1987, 121; 1990, 122; 1995, 132; 2003, 168

– in Quebec: 1966, 63; 1976, 80; 1994, 148

elites, 17, 18, 26, 32, 33, 47, 83, 130

emergency (homeless) shelters, 29, 105, 155

Employment and Unemployment Insurance, 8, 13, 14, 27, 28, 47, 51, 127, 173

employment. *See* labour market

Established Programs Financing (EPF), 79, 102, 127

Europe, 7, 13, 16, 17, 25, 77; influence on Canadian social housing, 53, 55, 87–8, 96, 179, 191–2, 193; social housing and housing policy in, 5, 7, 11, 19, 30, 42, 45–6, 61, 70, 118, 125, 130, 132, 156, 157. *See also* United Kingdom

Eves, Ernie, 168

expenditure on housing: block funding, 95, 102; British Columbia, 140; capital commitments, 58, 98, 102; concerns of Department of Finance and CMHC, 69, 87, 98, 113, 115, 120, 181, 193; levels and trends, 106–8, 123–4, 126, 157, 163, 164, 180, 182; Ontario, 99, 124, 128, 142, 144, 182; reductions, 102, 134, 137, 139; share among provinces, 95, 97; spending on assisted private rental and home-ownership, 108, 178, 244n137

expenditure, public, 14, 112, 152, 181, 185; constraint, 58, 78, 87, 102, 112, 113, 126, 156; social spending, 6–7, 14, 15, 16, 112, 113, 126, 154, 173. *See also* retrenchment; stimulus

expertise. *See* professionals

Expo '67, 48, 66

False Creek (Vancouver neighbourhood), 99, 103

Family Benefits, 28, 173

farms and farmers, 17, 19, 20, 28, 35, 50, 55

federalism: collaborative federalism, 15, 151, 153, 162; decentralization and devolution, 79, 101, 112, 113, 124, 125, 135, 183, 195; federal-provincial and federal-territorial agreements in housing, 102, 121, 123, 153, 162, 165, 185, 188; federal-provincial relations, 11, 12, 15, 17, 56, 79, 94, 120–1, 122, 140, 153, 175, 179, 183; theoretical effects on social policy, 16. *See also* devolution; transfers

federal-municipal relations in housing. *See* provincial-municipal and federal-municipal relations in housing

federal-provincial housing program. *See* housing funding formulas; non-profit and co-operative housing; public housing

federal-provincial relations. *See* federalism

federal-provincial-territorial (FPT) ministers responsible for housing, 120, 136, 140, 153, 162

Federation of Canadian Municipalities (FCM), 159–60, 161, 162

filtering of housing, 44, 54, 59, 115, 116, 155, 198

First Nations. *See* Aboriginal peoples

fiscal conditions: in 1960s–70s , 77, 175, 179; in late 1970s–80s, 14, 17, 78, 87, 110, 112; in 1990s, 15, 116–17, 124, 125, 126–8, 132, 136–7, 150, 181, 183–4; Alberta, 101;

fiscal capacity and resources, 6, 13, 26, 27, 56, 66, 173, 186; fiscal dividend and 2000s, 141, 151–3, 155, 156, 160, 163, 185; municipal and provincial-municipal fiscal aspects, 53, 66, 139, 142–4, 146; provincial in 1990s, 138–9, 184. *See also* deficits; stimulus

Flichel, Eugene, 136

Fonds québécois d'habitation communautaire (FQHC), 149–50

Fontana, Joe, 163

food banks, 5, 155

Fordism, 17, 147

Fort McMurray, 166

Foucault, Michel, 12

France, 14, 20, 47, 51, 52, 79, 130; social housing, 7, 43, 52–3, 87, 178, 181

free enterprise, 27, 32, 173

French-English relations (Canada), 17. *See also* federalism; nationalism; Quebec: separatism

Frost, Leslie, 33, 60

fundraising for housing, 104, 166

Gagliano, Alfonso, 140, 159, 160, 161

Garland, Jack, 60

GDP and economic growth: conditions in 1970s and 1980s, 77, 112, 179; in 1996–2008 expansion, 152; rapid increase, 15, 16, 26, 44, 53, 47, 79, 173, 175. *See also* economic conditions and cycles

gentrification, 80, 82, 84, 114, 181

ghettoization in housing, 5, 45, 55, 70, 92, 93, 115, 131, 193

Global Financial Crisis. *See under* economic conditions and cycles

globalization (post-1970s), 16, 111, 126, 130

Golden, Anne, 158, 159

Gordon, Walter, 48, 53

governance, urban, ii, 6. *See also* municipal councils and councillors

Great Britain. *See* United Kingdom

Guaranteed Income Supplement (GIS), 8, 48, 63, 109

Habitations à loyer modéré (HLM, France), 43

Halifax, 25, 28, 36, 41, 65

Hamilton, 27, 28, 36, 50, 70, 92, 158, 160

Harcourt, Michael, 147

Harper, Stephen, 12, 154, 156, 161, 163–4, 185

Harris, Mike, 142, 168, 184

health policy and expenditure, 7, 13, 15, 19, 79, 112, 133, 142, 143, 145, 152, 153, 187; health/medical insurance, 14, 47, 51, 53, 56, 63, 100, 175, 198. *See also* Canada Health and Social Transfer; mental health and mental illness

Hellyer, Paul, 86, 93–5, 96, 97, 194

historical institutionalism, 21. *See also* critical junctures; institutions; turning points in Canadian social housing policy

home purchase prices and affordability, 80–1, 114, 129, 133, 155, 181, 184, 190, 191. *See also* housing market conditions

Homelessness Partnering Strategy (HPS), 161. *See also* National Homelessness Initiative

homelessness, 28–9, 112, 117–18, 133, 152, 155, 157, 158–9, 161–2, 180, 181, 185, 186, 191, 198; Alberta, Calgary, and Edmonton, 155, 158, 166; British Columbia and

Vancouver, 147–8, 155, 167; as national disaster, 159; Ontario and
Toronto, 114–15, 118, 155, 158,
160; Quebec and Montreal, 118.
See also emergency shelters; National Homelessness Initiative;
supportive and special-needs
housing

home-ownership, 28, 126, 155; mortgage insurance for, 34, 40, 44, 68,
128, 181; policy to support home-
ownership, 30, 31, 37, 50, 65, 67,
75, 77, 85, 95, 99, 105, 107–8, 166,
176, 178, 180, 192, 198, 213n1;
rate (percent of households), 130,
154, 164. *See also* home purchase
prices and affordability

Homes BC (program), 146–8, 167–8,
196

household formation and housing
demand, 49–50, 85, 157. *See also*
rental demand

housing allowance (benefit) programs, 94, 103, 108, 118–19, 132,
144, 164–5

Housing and Community Planning
report (Curtis report), 33, 36–7

housing authorities, 34, 56, 93; Ontario and Toronto, 39, 41–2, 59,
68, 132; other countries, 31, 34,
43, 192. *See also* housing corporations; provincial housing corporations

Housing Branch (Ontario), 41, 42,
59, 60, 61, 68; Community Housing Branch, 99, 106

housing condition: abandonment,
66, 155; quality and disrepair, 5,
30, 39, 66, 83, 155, 187

housing corporations (municipal),
109; Metro Vancouver, 72; Montreal, 66; Toronto, 92, 104. *See also*
provincial housing corporations

housing finance. *See* mortgage financing; mortgage insurance

Housing First programs, 118, 166.
See also supportive housing

housing funding formulas: AHI/IAH,
160, 165–6, 168, 169, 185–6; co-
ops in 1985–93, 123; cross-subsidy
from market units to RGI in social
housing, 104, 117; non-profit and
co-op housing in 1974–8, 76, 99,
103–4, 106, 179–80; non-profit
and co-op housing in 1979–85,
102–4, 106, 179–80; non-profit
housing in 1985–93, 111, 122,
182; overviews and general, 43, 62,
179, 188, 189, 196–7; provincial
unilateral programs, 147, 150,
188; public housing and limited
dividend in 1949–63, 40–1, 64,
172–3; public housing in 1964–
78, 57–8, 61, 65, 68; under Social
Housing Agreements, 126, 138;
US funding model, 56. *See also*
cost-sharing; devolution

housing market conditions: in Depression, 32; in World War II, 29,
37, 45, 173–4; in early postwar
years, 49–50; in the late 1960s and
1970s, 50, 77, 78, 80–3, 179; in the
1980s, 114, 181; in the 1990s, 126,
129–30, 133, 154, 150, 183–4; in
the 2000s, 155, 166, 167; downturns, 80, 95, 129; expansions and
booms, 30, 33, 44, 46, 50, 69, 80–1,
91, 114, 154; general significance
for housing policy, 19, 46, 107–8,
189–91. *See also* home purchase
prices; housing need; rental
demand

housing need, 86, 162, 183; Depression and wartime, 28, 29, 31, 36; low-income housing problem, 5–6, 8, 88, 115; marginalization of low-income needs, 44, 131, 138; metropolitan housing problem, 20; social housing normalized and criticized as the policy response, 74, 75, 116, 117, 132, 178, 193

housing production: comparative social housing production in other countries, 35, 43, 53; data series, 200–4; early postwar years, 29, 33, 41–2, 171, 174; Limited Dividend, 41, 88; non-profit and co-operative, 14, 103–4, 102, 123, 178, 180, 182; overall, 24, 129; post-devolution and AHI/IAH, 141, 146–7, 150, 151, 166, 169, 184, 185, 186; private rental apartments, 30, 50–1, 62, 80–1, 82, 157, 176; public housing, 14, 67, 68–9, 72–3, 91, 101, 177; publicly assisted private rental, 108, 114; social housing in general, 3, 4, 6–7, 15, 45, 135, 177, 188, 191; in World War II, 28, 35

housing rehabilitation. See rehabilitation of housing

housing shortages and backlogs. See housing need

Housing Study Team. See Task Force on Program Review

housing system, 11, 20, 26, 44, 71; managed housing system, 80, 87, 117, 186; social housing as share of broader housing system, 126, 133, 138, 150, 157, 164

Howe, C.D. (Clarence), 25, 36, 37, 39

ideas, as a factor influencing housing policy: World War II and early postwar, 30–4; in 1960s, 51–5; in 1970s, 83–7, 90, 96; in 1980s, 115–17; in 1990s, 130–3; in 2000s, 155–7; as factor in policy-making broadly, 18, 22; review, 191–3. See also neoliberalism

income levels and trends (individuals and households), 27, 28, 47, 50, 80, 82, 126, 154, 195. See also GDP

income mix, in urban space and neighbourhoods, 8, 30, 46, 51, 87, 93, 111; mix in social housing (see income targeting in social housing); significance of rental production for urban social mix, 8, 71

income security. See Canada Pension Plan; Employment and Unemployment Insurance; expenditure; social assistance

income targeting in social housing: in 1970s (more income mix), 4–5, 9, 12; in 1980s (tighter targeting), 14, 111–12, 120, 180, 182, 189; in 1990s (targeting in provincial unilateral programs), 147, 149; extent of targeting or mix, 103, 107, 121, 122, 123, 131, 198–9; low-income targeted public housing, 14, 71, 177, 188, 192, 195; origins of mixed-income model, 87–90, 179, 192; post-devolution and AHI-IAH, 138, 151, 162, 163, 167, 168, 169, 184, 186; targeting versus income mix, 14, 116, 120, 131, 133, 181, 186. See also non-profit and co-operative housing; supportive and special-needs housing; universalism in social programs

income targeting in social programs, 14, 15, 43, 48, 53, 116, 124, 127, 133, 183

Index Linked Mortgage (ILM) program, 123, 196
Indigenous peoples. See Aboriginal peoples
industrialization, as a factor in welfare state evolution, 15, 16
inequality and disparities, 6, 7, 28, 55, 154, 157. See also income levels and trends; income mix; income targeting in social housing
inflation, 77–8, 79, 80, 81, 129, 179, 183; inflation adjustment to 2015 dollars, 221n47; wage and price controls, 79
infrastructure. See urban infrastructure
institutions: devolution as institutional change, 12, 15, 125, 134, 138, 141, 142, 145, 146, 172, 187; historical institutionalism, 21; institutional arrangements and capacity in housing, 8, 36, 43–4, 74, 84, 85, 96, 151, 172, 174–5, 184; institutional change in housing, 86, 90, 99, 125, 150; non-profit and co-op sector capacity, 95, 101, 102, 106, 109, 122; provincial institutional capacity, 46, 57, 63, 68; review of significance in housing, 187–9; theory of institutional change, 21–2. See also Canada Mortgage and Housing Corporation; lending institutions; provincial housing corporations
insurance companies. See lending institutions
interest rates. See mortgage interest rates
international influences on policy. See United Kingdom; United States; welfare state

International Year of Shelter for the Homeless (IYSH), 118
investment and financial market conditions, 78, 82, 107, 152, 164
Investment in Affordable Housing (IAH), 164, 165, 169, 185. See also Affordable Housing Initiative

Jacobs, Jane, 51, 92
Jeanne Mance (housing project), 39, 45
Judicial Committee of the Privy Council, 26

Kent, Tom, 48, 57, 194
Keynesian economics: Canadian "post-postwar," 187; countercyclical stimulus, 156; macroeconomic versus redistributive policy, 51; neoliberal challenge, 78; political-economic era, 15, 17; social contract or compact, 17. See also macroeconomic management; neoliberalism; stimulus
Kilbourn, William, 85
King, William Lyon Mackenzie, 26, 35
Kitchener-Waterloo, 51; Waterloo, 160

labour movements and parties, as factor in welfare state evolution: Australian Labor governments, 31; British Labour governments, 52, 130; Canada and comparative, 13, 15, 17–18, 20, 27, 31, 48; international and general, 6, 16; labour and social housing, 19, 56, 89, 100, 109, 122, 149, 180
land development, public-sector, 77, 94, 98, 99, 103, 107, 111, 176, 178,

180, 191; land banking and land assembly, 33, 53, 58, 66, 67, 100, 103

Lastman, Mel, 158, 159

Layton, Jack: FCM vice-president, 159; NDP leader, 163

Leach, Al, 143–4

Legault, Guy, 90, 100

lending institutions, 35, 50, 75, 105. *See also* banks

Lesage, Jean, 63–4, 66

Liberal party and governments
  – British Columbia, 167
  – federal: Chrétien, 127, 128, 134, 135, 139, 141, 152, 153, 156, 162, 183, 185, 195; King–St Laurent, 26, 27, 28, 30, 32, 35, 40; Martin, 163; Pearson, 18, 47, 48–9, 52, 55, 56–7, 175–6, 192; Trudeau, 78, 79, 84, 93, 94, 97, 98, 103, 112, 179; Trudeau *fils*, 169
  – municipal, 85
  – Ontario, 121–2, 168, 181
  – Quebec, 63, 66, 100, 121, 148

liberal-welfare regimes, 6–7, 53, 96, 116, 187, 191. *See also* welfare state

Lieutenant-Governor's Committee on Housing Conditions in Toronto, 30

Limited Dividend (LD) housing program: origins, 34, 192; in 1950s, 40–1, 42, 43, 68, 174; post-1964, 88, 89, 192; private-sector (entrepreneurial) 41, 244n137

Lithwick, Harvey, 87

lobbying. *See* advocacy and lobbying

local initiatives, 89, 90; in housing, 12

Local Service Realignment (Ontario), 142. *See also* devolution

Logement Abordable Québec (LAQ), 166, 204

Logement populaire (LogiPop), 100

London (England), 18, 19, 34, 85

London (Ontario), 158

Low Income Housing Task Force. *See* Dennis and Fish report

low-income housing problem. *See* housing need

low-income rental demand. *See* rental demand

low-income singles, 117; British Columbia and Vancouver, 148; Ontario and Toronto, 118

low-income targeting. *See* income targeting; income targeting in social housing

low rental, low rent, or full-recovery housing programs (1950s), 42, 61, 71, 174

low-rent market housing, 82, 114

Macaulay, Bob, 58, 60

Macdonald, Donald S., 98, 112

macroeconomic management, 15–16, 27, 78, 156, 173, 181

Mahoney, Steve, 163

Manitoba: creation of Manitoba Housing Corporation, 67; Doer period, 165; housing allowances, 108–9, 165; Pawley period, 121, 155; Roblin period, 38, 43, 64, 66; Schreyer period, 67, 72, 80, 83, 178. *See also* Winnipeg

Mansur, David, 37, 38, 39, 42

manufacturing employment, 25, 26, 38, 37, 54, 77, 83, 126, 173

market rents: below-market rents, 71, 166, 168; vis-à-vis economic rents, 105, 117, 160; in social housing, 61, 76, 88, 123, 147, 149, 178, 198. *See also* rental market

Marsh report. *See* Advisory Committee

Martin, Paul (Jr), 134, 153, 156, 160, 163, 183, 185

Marxist and neo-Marxian research, 12, 85

McKay, Elmer, 134

McKnight, Bill, 116, 120, 123

media. *See* news media

Meech Lake Accord, 15, 113

mental health and mental illness, 118, 148, 165, 168. *See also* supportive and special-needs housing

metropolitan government. *See* municipal restructuring

Metropolitan Toronto, 33, 41, 51, 53, 62, 70, 74, 92, 157, 158. *See also* Toronto

Metropolitan Toronto Housing Authority (MTHA), 39, 42, 59, 68, 131

middle class, 28, 33, 48, 82, 159, 173; housing and neighbourhood concerns, 20, 29, 91, 92, 115, 116, 181, 184, 189, 190; income conditions and trends, 126, 154; lower middle class or income, 30, 35, 144, 174; middle-class renters and home-buying, 51, 75, 85, 114, 147, 155, 181, 184, 186, 187, 191; middle-class suburbs, 33, 38, 40, 72, 177

Ministry of State for Urban Affairs, 95, 102

minority government: Canada in 1960s, 18, 48, 55; Canada in 1970s, 78, 97, 103, 194; Canada in 2000s, 152, 153, 163; Ontario, 80, 121, 178

mixed economy, 33, 94, 124; of welfare, 14, 90, 179, 186

mixed-income housing. *See* income targeting in social housing; market rents

monetary policy, 34, 78, 128, 129, 156–7, 181. *See also* mortgage interest rates

Montreal: 1960s conditions, 48, 50, 51, 54, 70; late 1960s–1970s housing politics and initiatives, 66, 74, 92, 98, 99; 1980s (slower growth and related housing issues), 82, 83, 114, 191; 2000s conditions, 154, 166; Communauté urbaine de Montréal, 72; connections to provincial and federal governments, 90, 98, 100, 148, 149, 150, 179, 186, 187; Doré and MCM, 121, 149; early public housing, 14, 34, 39, 45; formation of housing corporation and department, 66–7; as large growing city, 20, 23, 27, 28, 29; neighbourhood renewal and rehabilitation, 89, 100, 105, 135, 149, 155

mortgage-backed securities (MBS), 135

mortgage financing, 30, 32, 34, 40, 69, 75, 94, 98; CMHC financing of producers, land development and related infrastructure, 30, 33, 57, 98; CMHC and government role in financing market housing, 29, 34, 35, 37, 40, 50, 58, 75, 96, 128, 129, 157, 174, 181, 192; social housing (*see* housing funding formulas). *See also* mortgage insurance; mortgage interest rates; private-sector rental

mortgage insurance, 34, 44, 120, 128, 137, 138, 181; for homeowners, 40, 68, 69; Mortgage Insurance

Fund, 137; for private-rental, 30;
for social housing, 102, 122, 134
mortgage interest deductibility, 50,
103
mortgage interest rates, 21, 50, 69,
77–8, 80, 81–2, 108, 114, 115, 126,
129, 154, 156–7, 179, 183–4, 190,
191, 196; in social housing, 58, 96,
104–5, 106, 107, 123–4, 139, 142,
160, 180, 182, 213n1. *See also*
monetary policy
Moses, Robert, 92
Mulroney, Brian, 14, 103, 111–13,
116, 120, 127, 134, 180–1
Multiple Unit Residential Building
(MURB) tax incentive, 108
municipal councils and councillors,
32, 33, 66, 69, 74, 84, 91, 92, 104,
120, 158, 159, 160. *See also* Montreal; Toronto
municipal politics. *See* urban politics
municipal restructuring, amalgamation, and fragmentation, 8, 53, 66,
71–2, 94, 144, 158
municipal role and attitudes in
housing, 29, 32, 37, 38, 39, 89–90,
91, 96, 101, 139, 141, 158, 159,
160, 165, 168, 176, 188, 193; in
Limited Dividend housing, 40–1,
174; in non-profit and co-operative housing, 102, 106, 109, 119,
120, 122, 147, 148, 149, 180; in
public housing, 40–1, 42–3, 45,
46, 56, 57, 63–5, 66–7, 68–9, 72,
172, 174; subsidies and grants to
social housing, 41, 61, 69. *See also*
devolution; Federation of Canadian Municipalities; provincial-
municipal and federal-municipal
relations

munitions. *See* World War II
Murray, James A., 59; and Murray
report, 54, 55, 59, 61, 87

National Child Benefit, 15, 153, 165
National Homelessness Initiative,
153, 160–1
National Housing Act: in 1938, 35;
1944 amendments, 36, 37; 1949
amendments, 11, 25, 26, 38, 40–1,
172, 193; 1950s amendments, 30,
40, 41; 1964 amendments, 55, 56,
57, 60, 65, 175, 176, 193; 1966
amendments, 69; 1969 amendments, 89; 1973 amendments, 76,
97, 104, 178; 1978 amendments,
102; 1990s amendments, 138;
NHA significance in successive
policy periods, 188
National Housing Administration,
35, 36
national housing strategy, 170
National Welfare Council. *See* Canadian Welfare Council
nationalism (Quebec), 183, 195. *See
also* Parti Québécois; quiet revolution
Native housing programs. *See* Aboriginal peoples: housing programs
neighbourhood decline, 5, 6, 44, 116,
155; emerging post-1990s Canadian trends, 71, 183; Montreal, 54,
66, 83, 155, 190; Toronto, 155; US
patterns as spectre, 84; Winnipeg,
83, 155
neighbourhood opposition to social
and rental housing. *See* community opposition to social and rental
housing
neighbourhood renewal: 1970s poli-

cy change, 76, 88, 94, 178; in Montreal, 66, 67, 89, 99–100, 105, 121,
135, 149–50. *See also* False Creek;
St Lawrence
Neilson, Erik, 120
neo-conservatism. *See* neoliberalism
neoliberalism: compromise with
other political currents in 1980s
Canada, 14, 80, 103, 112–13, 117,
119, 120, 124, 179, 181, 187; convergence with fiscal concerns, 87,
150, 189; in economics field, business schools, and central agencies,
78, 112, 116, 132, 181, 194; Harper, 156; ideas regarding housing,
103, 116; institutional and structural change, 12, 195; international climate in 1990s, 6, 130, 132, 18,
192; as new set of ideas, 78, 87;
Ontario, 128, 142, 184; post-neoliberal policy, 157; prevailing in
1990s, 125–6, 127, 183; among
provincial governments, 139, 148;
shifting of the political centre,
126, 150, 183, 193; structural factors dampening impact in 1980s
Canada, 17; Washington consensus, 130. *See also* stimulus
neo-Marxian. *See* Marxist and neo-
Marxian research
New Brunswick, 65, 66
New Deal: Canada, 26, 35; US, 18,
26, 31, 35
New Democratic Party (NDP), 17–
18, 52; British Columbia, 67, 101,
147, 179; Manitoba, 67, 80, 83,
121, 165, 178; Martin, 153, 163;
Ontario, 80, 121, 122, 128, 132,
181–2; Saskatchewan, 164; support for Pearson and Trudeau programs, 48, 55, 78, 98, 175

New Left, 78
New York, 18, 19, 31, 33, 34, 73, 85,
92
New Zealand, 6, 36
Newfoundland, 39, 41, 64, 65; establishment of housing corporation,
66
news media
– amplifying Toronto issues nationwide, 94, 132, 158, 159
– coverage of housing issues: pre-
1945, 31; in 1960s, 62, 74; in
1968–73 transition, 74, 84, 85, 92,
99; in 1980s, 117; in early 1990s,
131, 132; 1998–2003 period, 158,
159, 162; in 2010s, 5, 155
Niagara regional municipality, 158
Nicholson, John, 60, 65
Nicolls, Frank, 36
NIMBY. *See* community opposition
to social and rental housing
non-market housing. *See* social
housing
non-profit and co-operative housing:
1950s–60s antecedents in charitable LD, 41, 43, 58, 88; 1968–73
transition, 94–5; advocacy role of
sector, 110, 119, 144, 145, 181;
British Columbia, 64, 104, 148; capacity-building, 106, 109; congru-
ence with mixed economy of
welfare, 90, 179; dependency on
state, 133; emergence of sector
and sector organizations, 109–10;
European models, 87, 88; expected
versus actual costs, 90, 97, 106,
193; extent of income targeting,
131, 182; municipal and provincial, 106, 109; non-profit RRAP,
105; Ontario and Toronto, 99, 104,
122; origins of program model,

86–90; provincial support, 99, 101, 102; public and political attitudes, 80, 188, 110, 193; Quebec and Montreal, 100–1, 121, 149; successful model, 5, 45; types of sponsor groups, 109, 180. *See also* cooperative housing; housing funding formulas; housing production
northern Canada, 23, 65, 109, 141, 164
Nova Scotia, 41, 43; housing commission, 64, 65
Nunavut, 164. *See also* northern Canada

oil (petroleum), 17, 77, 78, 79, 152, 179, 187; oil sands, 152, 166, 186
Old Age Security (OAS), 8, 13, 14, 27, 48, 173. *See also* Guaranteed Income Supplement (GIS)
On Reserve housing, 105, 164, 167, 173, 186, 204. *See also* Aboriginal peoples
Ontario Habitat Foundation, 86
Ontario Housing Corporation (OHC): as catalyst and model, 65–6; community opposition, 74, 91, 93, 96; integration agenda, 70; invention of the model, 59–63, 88, 176; production heyday, 68–70, 72; serving diverse constituencies, 75; stock transfer to municipalities at devolution, 145–6. *See also* Metropolitan Toronto Housing Authority
Ontario Non-Profit Housing Association (ONPHA), 110
Ontario housing policy: adverse context in early 1990s, 128, 129, 132; Advisory Committee and invention of OHC, 59–62, 176; assis-

tance to non-profits and co-ops and large Ontario share, 104, 106, 178; Davis, 1970s, 80; escalating expenditure, 107, 124, 128, 193; Frost, 1950s, 33, 38, 174; Comay task force, 99; Community Housing Branch, 99, 106; Harris and devolution to municipalities, 1990s, 139, 141–6, 147, 184, 195; housing allowances 2005–15, 160, 165; Housing Branch and municipal initiatives, 41–2; McGuinty and AHI-IAH, 2000s, 168–9; Ministry of Housing, 99; municipal non-profit, 106, 109; OHC heyday and large share of national activity, 69–71, 73, 95, 97, 177; Ontario as diverging case and neoliberal extreme, 23, 172; opposition to public housing, 74, 91–3; Peterson and unilateral programs, 1980s, 118, 121–2, 123, 182; policy collaboration with CMHC in 1960s, 54, 59, 60, 65, 84; Rae, early 1990s, 122, 135; Robarts, catalytic role in mid-1960s, 23, 49, 58, 73; social housing as economic and urban policy, 53, 63, 176, 190. *See also* Ontario Housing Corporation
Oshawa, 158
Ottawa (urban centre and municipality), 28, 41, 50, 51, 70, 158, 159, 160; Ottawa-Carleton regional municipality, 72
overcrowding in housing, 28
ownership. *See* home-ownership

Paris, 18, 34
Parizeau, Jacques, 148
Parti Québécois (PQ), 79, 80, 100, 121, 148, 178

path dependency, 21. *See also* institutions

Pawley, Howard, 121

Pearson, Lester, 46, 47, 48–9, 55, 56–7, 93, 175–6, 192, 194

Peel regional municipality, 158, 160; Peel Coalition for Shelter, 158

pensions, old age: provincial, 49, 63, 100; as social welfare, 13, 19, 51, 56, 133. *See also* Canada Pension Plan; Guaranteed Income Supplement; Old Age Security

Peterborough, 160

Peterson, David, 122

petroleum. *See* oil

Phillips, Art, 85

Pigott, Joseph, 3

planning (urban). *See* urban development

Planning and Development (Ontario department). *See* economics and development

policy borrowing, 39. *See also* Europe; United Kingdom; United States

policy change, factors in. *See* welfare state

policy innovation, 16, 90. *See also* welfare state

policy studies. *See* causation; historical institutionalism; welfare state

policy-making, 12, 21, 23, 32, 43, 90, 99, 189, 194

political and economic conditions affecting housing policy, 22, 186–7; in 1960s, 47–9; 51–2, 74; in late 1960s and 1970s, 76–80, 84, 85–6, 90; in 1980s, 112–13, 117; in 1990s, 126, 130, 133, 139; in late 1990s and 2000s, 148–9, 151–4, 156, 163; Depression, 26, 30–1;

within summary of periods, 172–85; wartime and early postwar, 26–7, 32–4. *See also* housing market; ideas; Keynesian economics; neoliberalism

political culture, 11, 21. *See also* historical institutionalism; ideas; neoliberalism

political visibility, 98, 113, 195

populism (conservative), 48, 158, 184

postwar economic boom, 17, 26–8, 32, 47, 51, 77, 80, 175. *See also* Keynesian economics

poverty, 7, 20, 78, 115, 154, 155, 157; anti-poverty programs, 51, 52, 89, 149, 165, 175; conferences, 57, 70, 88, 90; neighbourhood-level, 8, 71, 72, 155, 157, 189. *See also* income levels and trends; income mix; income targeting in social housing

press. *See* news media

Prime Minister's Office (PMO), 127, 137, 159

private-sector rental: apartment boom circa 1955–75, 30, 50–1; collapsing viability of production in 1970s onward, 80, 82, 114, 157; community opposition, 92–3; down-market sector and rehabilitation, 5–6, 105, 115, 150; encouraging production circa 2000 onward, 157, 162; financing, 69; integration of public housing with private-rental, 46, 69–71, 177, 190; landlord organizations against social housing, 119, 126, 129, 132, 183; production subsidies and other policy support, 30, 95, 108, 116, 178; significance in urban development and social

mix, 8, 46; small landlords, 34; social housing competing with or
displacing, 42, 116, 119, 191. See
also developers; housing production
Privy Council Office (PCO), 127,
136–7
production of housing. See housing
production
professionals: Aboriginal, 106; from
Britain and United States, 31, 33,
39, 192, 222n55; conserving Ontario expertise at devolution, 146;
federal public service 1930s–50s,
32; in housing, 31–2, 36, 37, 189;
provinces, 46, 63, 67, 99; in relation to advocates, 39, 77, 86, 94,
97, 194; from student housing
movement, 86; WHL and CMHC as
centres of expertise, 36, 37, 41, 44,
96. See also Canadian Housing
and Renewal Association
program evaluations, 115–16, 120
program reviews of social housing:
in 1979, 103; in 1984–5, 113, 120;
in early 1990s, 134; in 1994–5,
127, 135–6
Programme achat rénovation pour
coopératives et OSBL (PARCO), 149
Progressive Conservative. See Conservative party
property tax, 41, 69, 160
province-building, 63, 176. See also
institutions
provincial housing corporations:
creation in other provinces, 63–6;
favouring devolution, 139; invention of the OHC model, 14, 55, 59,
60–3, 175, 194; large funding, capacity, and momentum, 45–6, 57,
74, 171, 188, 195; NHA funding

enabled, 57, 60, 175; tool in urban
growth management and varied
agendas, 72, 75, 100, 101, 177, 190;
urban renewal and opposition,
92–3; use of non-profit programs,
109. See also housing funding formulas; Ontario Housing Corporation; Société d'habitation du
Québec; and name of each province
or territory
provincial housing policy and
programs
– cost-shared provincial housing
programs. See Alberta; British
Columbia; Manitoba; Ontario;
Quebec
– diversity among provinces:
1950s, 41–2; 1960s, 64–5, 72–3;
1970s, 99; 1990s, 141–50; 2000s,
165–9
– unilateral programs: British
Columbia, 147–8; Ontario, 118,
122, 124, 181–2; Quebec, 149–
50
provincial-municipal and federal-
municipal relations in housing:
cost-sharing in social housing, 38,
40, 41, 42, 150; federal-municipal
in 1941–64, 32, 56, 64–5; Ontario
in 1949–64, 41–2; Ontario in
1970s, 104, 109; other provinces,
66–7, 102, 147–9; post–2000, 160,
161, 168; Quebec, 63, 66–7, 105,
148–50. See also British Columbia;
devolution; Manitoba; Montreal;
Ontario; Quebec; Toronto; Vancouver; Winnipeg
public debt, 58, 113, 126, 134, 183;
debt service costs and interest
rates, 78, 126, 151, 152, 183, 185
public expenditure. See expenditure

public housing: early postwar, 25, 39–43; municipal devolution in Ontario, 144–6; municipal non-profit as public housing, 106, 109; public perception and opposition, 5, 32, 45, 55, 74, 90–4, 110, 115, 131, 189; relation to private-rental apartment boom, 69–71; replaced by non-profit and co-op housing, 4–5, 97–101; transformed in mid-1960s, 53, 56–68; as two of several policy periods, 9, 171–7; United States, Britain, and Australia, 19, 31, 34, 35, 43, 53. *See also* expenditure; housing funding formulas; housing production

public policy theory. *See* historical institutionalism; welfare state

public service. *See* professionals

punctuated equilibrium, 22

Quebec. *See also* Montreal; quiet revolution; Société d'habitation du Québec
  - Castonguay report, 100
  - Groupe de travail sur l'habitation (*Habiter au Québec*), 100
  - housing programs and decisions of governments: Bourassa Liberals, 100, 121, 148; Duplessis Union Nationale, 34, 39; Johnson Union Nationale, 63; Lesage Liberals, 63; Lévesque Parti Québécois, 100; Parizeau–Bouchard Parti Québécois, 148–50
  - La Haye report, 66
  - nationalism, 79, 128, 183, 195
  - referendum in 1995, 128, 136–7, 183; effects on federal social

policy and housing policy, 14, 17, 49, 80, 153, 178
  - resource groups, 101
  - separatism, 83, 139, 183

quiet revolution, 49, 63–4; state capacity, 49

racialization, racial groups, and discrimination: in Canada, 5, 75, 130, 154; in US, 8, 52, 72

Randall, Stanley, 60–2, 65, 74, 88, 94, 194

rationalization, administrative, 134, 138, 183

real estate market. *See* housing market

real estate sector. *See* developers

recessions. *See* economic conditions

reconstruction, 6, 18, 33, 34, 86, 189, 192, 198; Advisory Committee on Reconstruction, 27, 37; minister and ministry of, 36, 37, 39. *See also* Housing and Community Planning report

red Tories, 31, 67, 83, 85

redistributive social programs, 11, 47, 53, 156. *See also* welfare state

Redway, Alan, 116, 134

referendum. *See under* Quebec

Regent Park (housing project), 33, 41, 45

regional brokerage, 14, 112–13, 124, 127, 181, 194

regionalism, in theories of the welfare state, 16; Western Canada, 14, 79, 102. *See also* Quebec

regulatory barriers, 133

rehabilitation of housing, 37; British Columbia and Vancouver, 148; Ontario, 58, 69, 88, 99; Quebec and Montreal, 66–7, 89, 99–100,

149–50. *See also* Residential Rehabilitation Assistance Program
(RRAP)
rent control, 29, 34, 36, 82
rent geared to income (RGI): adoption of model in Canada, 42, 61,
71; depth of subsidy and rent scale,
123, 134, 146; eligibility of non-
senior singles, 118, 148; as an in-
kind transfer payment, 8, 23, 138,
175, 183; tenant income trends,
107. *See also* housing allowance
programs; housing funding formulas; income mix; non-profit
and co-operative housing; public
housing; rent supplement
rent subsidies. *See* housing allowance programs; rent geared to
income; rent supplement
rent supplement, 58, 105, 138, 166;
stacked on non-profit and co-op
funding, 101, 104, 106, 131, 165,
168
rental apartment development. *See*
housing production; private-sector rental
Rental Assistance Program (British
Columbia). *See* housing allowance programs
rental demand: conditions in 1970s–
80s, 80, 82, 114, 119, 179, 181, 198;
decline in 1990s–2000s, 21, 130,
133, 154, 191; general and postwar, 24, 49, 66, 85, 88, 130, 190–1,
192, 198; social housing vis-à-vis
low-income rental demand, 8, 24,
42, 44, 46, 66, 71, 92, 115, 151, 164,
174, 177, 183
rental demolition and conversion to
condominium, 82, 82, 92, 147,
155, 165

rental housing (private sector). *See*
private-sector rental
rental housing market. *See* housing
market conditions; housing production; private-sector rental;
rental demand
rental supply, discourse of, 85, 88,
187. *See also* housing production
repair programs and subsidized
housing repair. *See* rehabilitation
of housing
reserves (Aboriginal). *See* Aboriginal
peoples
reserves (financial), 137, 138, 139,
197
Residential Rehabilitation Assistance Program (RRAP), 4, 105, 135,
161, 164, 202
residualization of rental or social
housing, 6–7, 11, 44, 55, 151, 155,
186, 191, 192
resource exports, 20, 152. *See also* oil
resource groups, 101, 109
retrenchment: in 1990s, 124, 125,
134–6, 142; initiatives of 2000s
not reversing it, 15, 151, 172, 184;
political dynamics different from
expansion, 21, 22, 194; in social
policy history, 172, 182–4, 187,
194; in welfare state history and
theory, 10, 11, 12, 16, 17, 22. *See*
also devolution
right to housing, 84
Robarts, John, 49, 53, 58, 60, 61–2, 74
Roblin, Duff, 67, 83
Rochon, Marc, 132, 136–7, 140
Roosevelt, Franklin, 26, 31, 35
Rose, Albert, 12, 39, 56, 59, 60, 86,
87, 88
Rural and Native Housing Program
(RNH), 23, 105

rural-urban migration. *See* farms and farmers

San Francisco, 14, 174
Saskatchewan, 27, 39, 64, 68, 109, 120, 140, 164–5
Saulnier, Lucien, 66, 100
Schreyer, Ed, 67, 83
second suites (accessory units) and basement suites, 5, 29, 114
seniors social housing, 5, 55, 66, 115, 164, 177; limited dividend, 41, 64; specific provinces and municipalities, 33, 41, 64, 67, 68, 75, 104, 167
separatism. *See under* Quebec
service manager (Ontario), 146, 160, 168, 257n142
Sewell, John, 85
Sgro, Judy, 153
Shelter Allowance for Elderly Renters (SAFER). *See* housing allowance programs
shelter allowances. *See* housing allowance
shocks, as factor in policy change, 22. *See also* historical institutionalism
single room occupancy (SRO) housing, British Columbia, 148
slums, 28, 34; social housing as slum redevelopment, 31, 46, 54, 55, 72, 177, 190, 198
Smith, Larry B., 103
Smith, Peter (CMHC chairman), 137
social advocacy organizations: in 1960s onwards, 14, 77, 84–5, 91, 92, 96, 119, 120, 122, 133, 139, 166; early period, 18, 30, 31, 39
social assistance, 127, 128, 143, 145, 148, 165; cutbacks, 142, 167
Social Credit government: Alberta,

64; British Columbia, 41, 64, 67, 101
social economy, 149. *See also* non-profit and co-operative housing; social housing; social housing sector
social housing: broader ramifications of production program frameworks, 23, 189; definition, 3, 213n1; overview and summary of turning points and program periods, 8–10, 172–86; review of themes in policy history, 186–95; systemic significance in Canadian housing and urban system, 7, 205; as twentieth-century legacy, 5, 10, 150, 172. *See also* co-operative housing; housing funding formulas; non-profit and co-operative housing; public housing; social policy
social housing (third) sector: advocacy and government relations, 110, 139–40; attitudes in and about, 87, 97, 116, 117, 120, 131, 150, 178, 193; emergence and components of, 109; residual, 11, 126, 138; sector organizations, 110; state support for, 76, 101, 109, 188
Social Housing Agreements, 134, 137–9, 140–1, 183
social housing expenditure. *See* expenditure on housing; housing funding formulas
social housing production. *See* housing production
social housing reform (Ontario), 144–5
social inclusion and exclusion, 149, 157, 165, 184, 186
social policy, reflected in social housing, 4, 7, 13–15, 186–7; in

1940s, 21, 31–3; in 1960s, 46–9, 57, 63; in 1970s, 78–9, 90, 101–2; in 1980s, 112–13; in 1990s, 127, 130–1; in 2000s, 149, 152–3, 156. *See also* expenditure; transfer payments; welfare state

social service agencies, 109, 117

social spending. *See under* expenditure

Social Union Framework Agreement (SUFA), 153, 161, 162, 185. *See also* federalism

Société d'habitation du Québec (SHQ): AccèsLogis and LAQ, 166–7; block funding, 95; formation of, 63–4; no Social Housing Agreement, 140; program administration in 1980s, 121; public housing production in 1970s, 101; supporting non-profits and co-ops, 100

Special Initiative (1970–71 program), 89, 93, 95

special-needs housing. *See* supportive and special-needs housing

spending power. *See* constitution

spending. *See* expenditure

St John's (Newfoundland), 25, 41

St Laurent, Louis, 34, 40

St Lawrence (Toronto neighbourhood), 99, 103

stagflation, 78, 80, 81, 95

stigmatization of housing, 46, 55, 70–1, 110, 131, 178, 193

stimulus (fiscal/economic): in 1930s, 30, 35; in 1970s, 95; in 1980s, 103–4, 106, 112, 116, 135; in 1990s, 113, 116, 122, 129; in 2009–11, 152, 156, 164; as federal role in housing policy, 34, 40, 157; neo-liberal challenge, 116, 156, 187

structural change. *See* economic change; welfare state

subsidiarity, 125

subsidy to housing. *See* expenditure; housing funding formulas

suburban development, 33, 82; rental production as part of, 51, 54, 62, 72, 91, 93, 177, 198. *See also* income mix; urban development

supply-side versus demand-side housing programs, 118–19, 120. *See also* housing allowances; housing production; social housing

Supporting Communities Partnership Initiative (SCPI). *See* National Homelessness Initiative

supportive and special-needs housing, 118, 148, 161, 165, 166, 167–8, 180. *See also* deinstitutionalization; homelessness; low-income singles

Suters, H.W. (Bob), 60

Sweden, 53, 59

Sydney (Australia), 73, 85, 174

systems thinking, 51, 72, 79, 86–7, 192

Task Force on Housing and Urban Development (Hellyer task force), 74, 93–5, 97

Task Force on Low Income Housing. *See* Dennis and Fish report

Task Force on Program Review (1984–5), 120

tax law affecting housing investment, 30, 34, 82, 108, 128, 157, 163, 181. *See also* mortgage interest deductibility

tenant organizations, 77, 84, 120, 194

territories. *See* northern Canada; Nunavut

Thatcher, Margaret, 132

third sector. See community-based organizations; co-operative housing; non-profit and co-operative housing; social housing sector; social service agencies

Toronto Disaster Relief Committee, 159

Toronto Real Estate Board (TREB), 70

Toronto: 1950s public housing and LD, 25, 33, 41; comparison to other cities, 14, 34, 43, 54, 70, 73, 82, 146, 174; early non-profit and co-op programs, 104, 194; focus of Ontario urban policy, 53, 56, 71–2, 176; gentrification and loss of lower-cost private rental, 82, 114, 155; homelessness, 114, 118, 155, 158, 159; housing advocacy and links to federal government, 12, 31, 39, 56, 59, 93, 96, 98, 159, 187; neighbourhood development, decline, and rehabilitation, 88, 103, 155; OHC public housing, 70, 73, 74, 93; opposition to public housing, 74, 91–2, 94; pre-1945 housing issues and initiatives, 20, 29, 31; prominence of rental issues and production, 30, 50–1, 53, 91, 122, 154, 157, 160, 176, 181; rapid growth, 28, 29, 176; real estate and home price trends, 29, 81, 114, 129; supportive housing, 118, 161; urban reform in 1970s, 85, 104. See also Metropolitan Toronto; news media

trade dependency, 17, 32; free trade with US, 112, 126

transfer payments to individuals, 7, 15, 16, 61, 119, 132, 174; RGI as in-kind transfer payment, 8, 23, 138, 175, 183. See also Canada Pension Plan; Employment Insurance; expenditure on housing; Family Benefits; housing allowances; Old Age Security; pensions; social assistance

transfers, federal-provincial for housing: AHI-IAH, 165–6; block funding for social housing, 95, 102; housing trust funds, 163; Social Housing Agreements, 138–9, 182

transfers, federal-provincial for social programs: CAP, 14, 47; EPF, 79; post-devolution initiatives, 15, 152–3; reductions in 1990s, 15, 113, 127–8, 183; transfer-intensive 1960s–80s social policy, 7, 179. See also Canada Assistance Plan; Canada Health and Social Transfer; Established Programs Financing; health policy

transitional housing. See supportive and special-needs housing

Treasury Board: federal, 87, 98, 113, 134, 138; Ontario, 60

tripartite social policy (Quebec), 148–9, 184

Trudeau, Justin, 169

Trudeau, Pierre, 78, 79, 86, 90, 93; housing and urban policy, 93, 97–8, 101–3

trust companies. See lending institutions

trust funds for housing (2006–07), 163–4, 165, 169, 186

turning points in Canadian social housing policy, 3–5, 8–10, 171–84, 196. See also critical junctures

unemployment, 30, 47, 50, 126, 128

Unemployment Insurance. *See* Employment and Unemployment Insurance
unilateral programs. *See* provincial housing programs
Union Nationale. *See* Quebec
United Kingdom: comparison to Canada, 13, 14, 16, 17, 20, 27, 32, 51, 52, 79, 87, 179, 181, 190; influence on Canadian social housing, 30, 33–4, 53, 132, 191–2; influence on Canadian social policy, 18, 52, 112, 127, 131; JCPC, 26; social housing in, 6, 7, 13, 19, 34, 53, 96, 178; World War II, 25
United States: comparison to Canada, 7, 8, 13, 16, 17, 20, 29, 30, 32, 50, 51, 77, 85, 157, 179; influence on Canadian social housing, 33–4, 56, 59, 70, 72, 84, 164; influence on Canadian social policy, 18, 52, 90, 112, 156; social housing in, 6, 7, 13–14, 31, 35, 43, 45, 46, 53, 55, 59, 88, 89, 96; trade, migration and social connections, 17, 47, 48, 152, 156
universalism in social programs, 14, 15, 47, 111, 133, 149, 175, 181, 186; universal housing allowances, 118
urban agenda or urban development agenda: Canada in 1970s, 46, 93–5; 171–2; Canada circa 2000, 141, 152, 153, 163, 185; Ontario in 1960s, 46, 53, 63
urban crisis and decline (United States), 8, 84
Urban Development Institute (Ontario), 87
urban development: CMHC financing supporting, 58, 174; expanding government role in 1960s–70s, 77, 98, 99, 107, 111, 177, 178, 180; federal task force (1969), 93–5; issues as part of urban governance, 6; postwar Canadian patterns, 30, 46, 51, 54; social housing as an element in, 39, 41, 46, 49, 54, 72, 101, 133, 176, 178; as sphere affecting social housing policy, 20–1, 22, 190–1; as sphere affecting welfare state evolution, 18–21; urban development and growth policy, 53, 63, 86, 100. *See also* housing market; housing production; income mix; reconstruction
urban growth rate, 20, 28, 29, 166, 174. *See also* urban development
urban infrastructure, 57, 153, 161
urban land costs, 20, 82, 85, 103, 123; government contributions of land, 147, 160
Urban Native housing program, 105
urban planning and planners, 50, 51, 54, 69, 91, 92, 101, 109. *See also* urban development
urban policy. *See* urban agenda; urban development
urban politics: focus on services and distribution, 19; housing and homelessness issues in 1990s–2000s, 158–9, 160; opposition to social housing, 32, 91–2; support for social housing, 33, 66, 74; urban reform politics in 1970s, 76, 84–5, 91–2, 98, 104
urban renewal, 39, 42, 46, 54, 65–6, 67, 69; opposition and criticism, 76, 86, 92–3, 94; and social housing in Pearson Liberal agenda, 57, 66, 176, 190
urbanization and urban growth: Al-

berta in 2000s, 166; as factor in welfare state evolution, 13, 15, 19, 173, 189–91; later urbanization in Canada, 20; Ontario in 1960s, 53; postwar international and comparative, 6, 52; wartime and postwar in Canada, 28–9, 49–51

veterans' housing, 35, 37, 38

wages: industrial era and globalization era, 16, 17, 47, 126, 130, 154; trends and levels, 19, 20, 27, 28, 54, 55; wage and price controls, 79. *See also* income levels and trends
Wagner, Robert, 31
war production. *See* World War II
Wartime Housing Limited (WHL), 25, 28, 35–6; winding-down, 37–8, 174
Waterloo regional municipality, 160; Kitchener-Waterloo, 51
welfare state: influence of urbanization, 18–21; main periods in Canada, 13–15; review of impact of social policy periods on social housing, 186–9; theories of, 15–

18. *See also* neoliberalism; social policy; urbanization and urban growth
welfare. *See* social assistance; social welfare; welfare state
Western Canada, 14, 79, 102, 113
Who Does What Panel (Ontario), 142
Wilson, Michael, 112
Windsor (Ontario), 27, 28, 41
Winnipeg, 28, 48, 72, 83, 155; neighbourhood decline, 155; social housing in, 67, 83
working class, 35, 43, 53, 54, 83, 93, 192; in Montreal, 54, 83, 100
World War II: economic and manufacturing growth, 25–7, 28, 29, 35; effects on government role and capacity, 25–7; effects on social policy, 27; urban growth and housing shortages, 28–9

youth culture and protests (1960s), 76, 85–6, 179
Yukon, 109. *See also* northern Canada